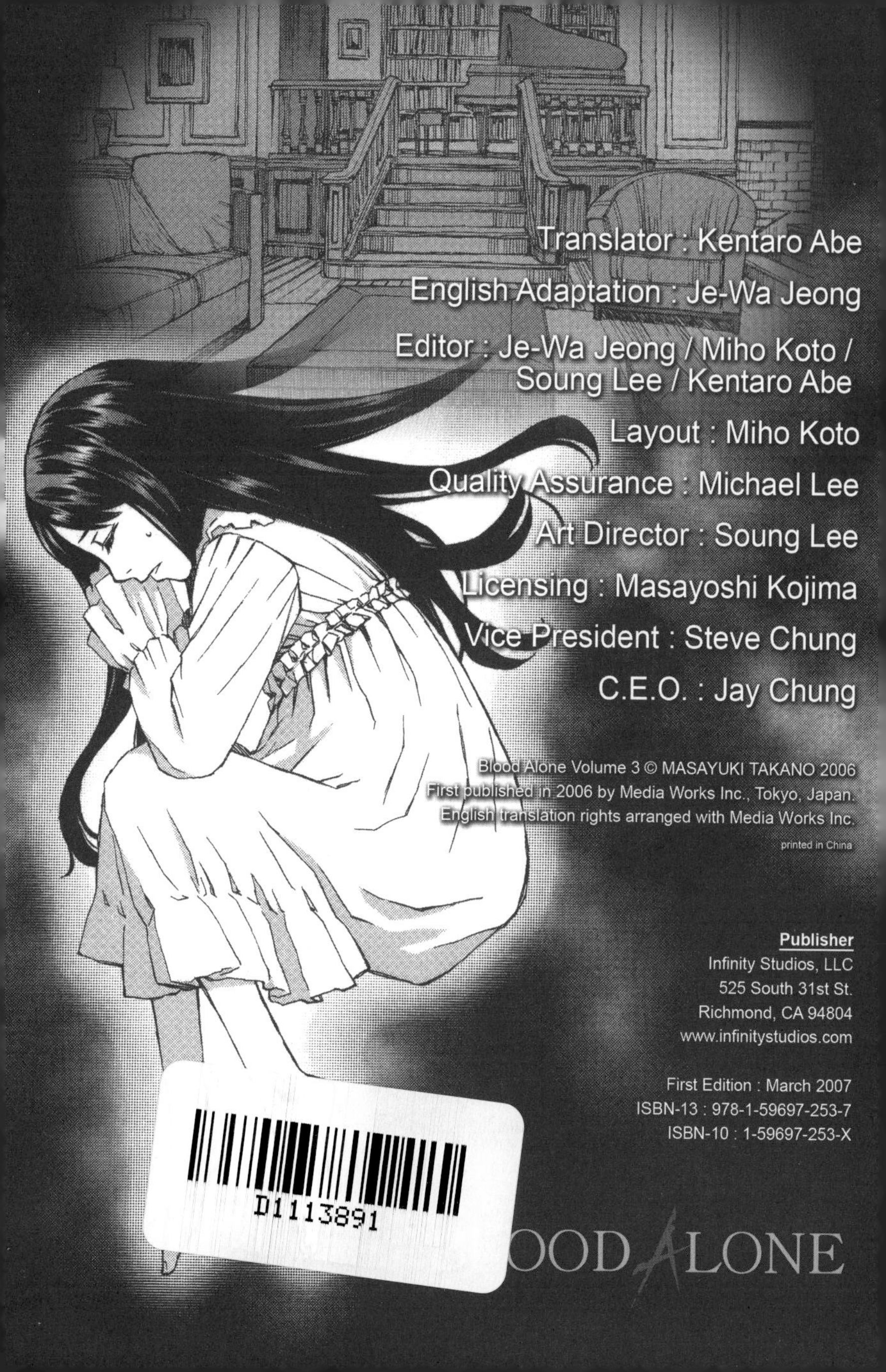

Translator : Kentaro Abe
English Adaptation : Je-Wa Jeong
Editor : Je-Wa Jeong / Miho Koto / Soung Lee / Kentaro Abe
Layout : Miho Koto
Quality Assurance : Michael Lee
Art Director : Soung Lee
Licensing : Masayoshi Kojima
Vice President : Steve Chung
C.E.O. : Jay Chung

printed in China

Publisher
Infinity Studios, LLC
525 South 31st St.
Richmond, CA 94804
www.infinitystudios.com

First Edition : March 2007
ISBN-13 : 978-1-59697-253-7
ISBN-10 : 1-59697-253-X

OOD ALONE

The Characters

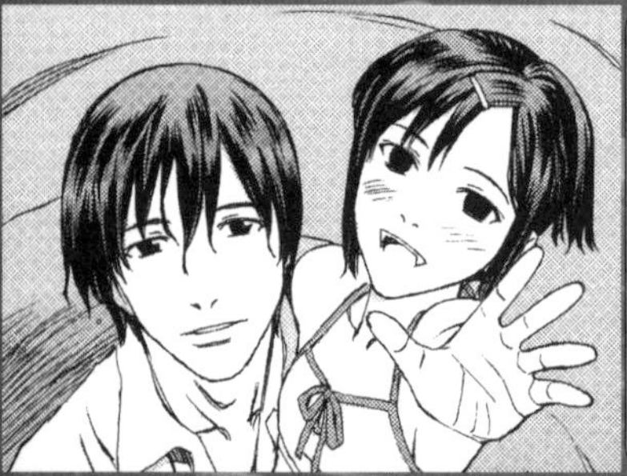

Kuroe Kurose

A young man who makes a living as a novelist and works as a P.I. & man-for-hire on the side. Thanks to the special abilities his eyes have gained, he can see past any tricks by anyone with supernatural powers. He is a bit naïve to the feelings of women around him, and he currently lives with Misaki as her guardian.

Misaki Minato

Little is known about her past except for the fact that her father was a famous musician. Both she and her father were targeted by vampires, and Misaki has been turned as a result. However, the vampire side of her still lays dormant, so she acts no differently than any other girl her age.

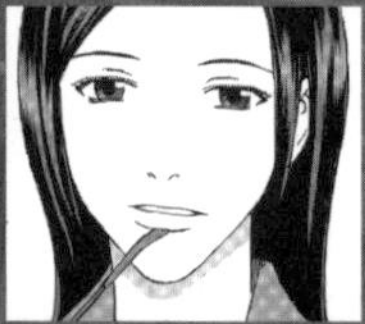

Sayaka Sainome

She is the daughter of a rich doctor, and currently works as the chief of the forensics department with the police. She's known Kuroe since their days as students, and she occasionally calls upon Kuroe for his special abilities. She possibly has feelings for Kuroe, and she also apparently has a special ability.

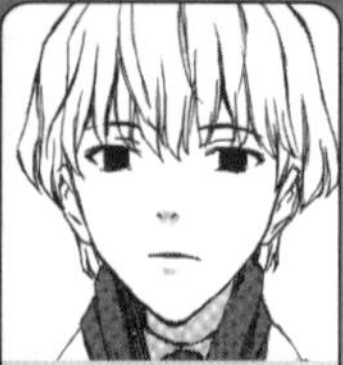

Higure

Despite his looks and the way he acts, he is one of the most powerful vampires left in the world. He is a friend of Misaki, and as an elder vampire, he is also in a sense her mentor.

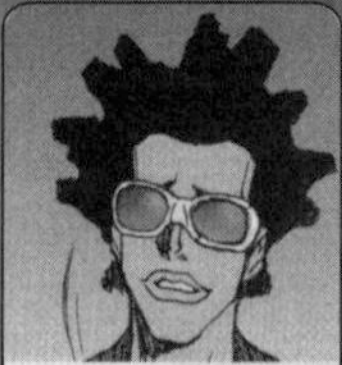

Sly

A vampire who is in the business of selling information as well as working as a man for hire. He apparently has a good working relationship with Kuroe and hates vampires for turning him into one.

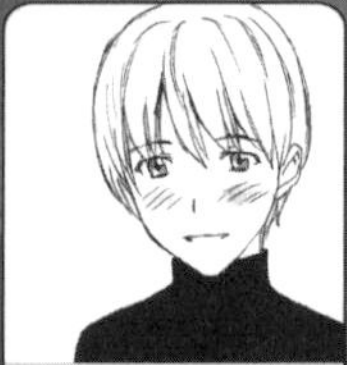

Maria

A renfield who was previously under the influence of a secret order of vampire assassins, she is now under Higure's protection. She is also Misaki's only female friend of the same age.

The story so far...

Upon seeing his sister taken from him by a vampire, Kuroe's life mission was to find his sister and get revenge on the vampire who shattered his life. With the power he gained through an injury to his eyes, he traveled to Europe where a famous vampire hunter trained him to become one of the humans most feared by vampires.

Currently, he lives in Japan with a young girl named Misaki who had the unfortunate fate of being turned. While he thinks of her more as a daughter or as a younger sister, she sees things very differently.

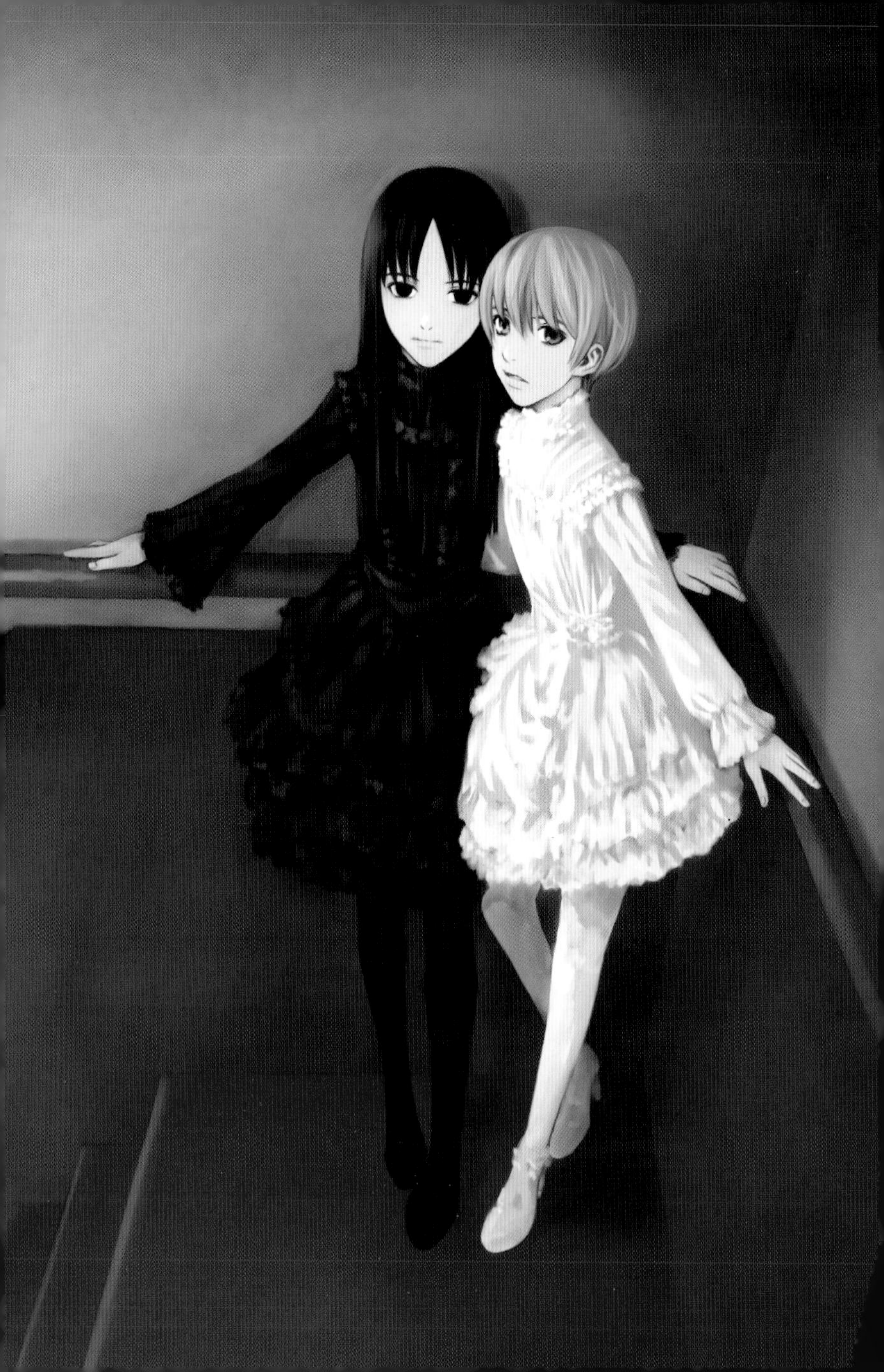

BLOOD ALONE ❸

Episode 15
CHERRY BLOSSOM   5
桜 – Sakura

Episode 16
MY FIRST MEMORY   28
ふたりの思い出 – A Memory Belonging to Just the Two of Them

Episode 17
MIDNIGHT SWIM   64
星空のクロール – Swimming Amongst the Stars

Episode 18
MIDNIGHT CRUISE   94
素顔の彼女 – Her True Face

Episode 19
HOME ALONE   140
あなたのいない部屋 – The Room Without You There

Contents

Episode 15

CHERRY BLOSSOM

桜 – Sakura

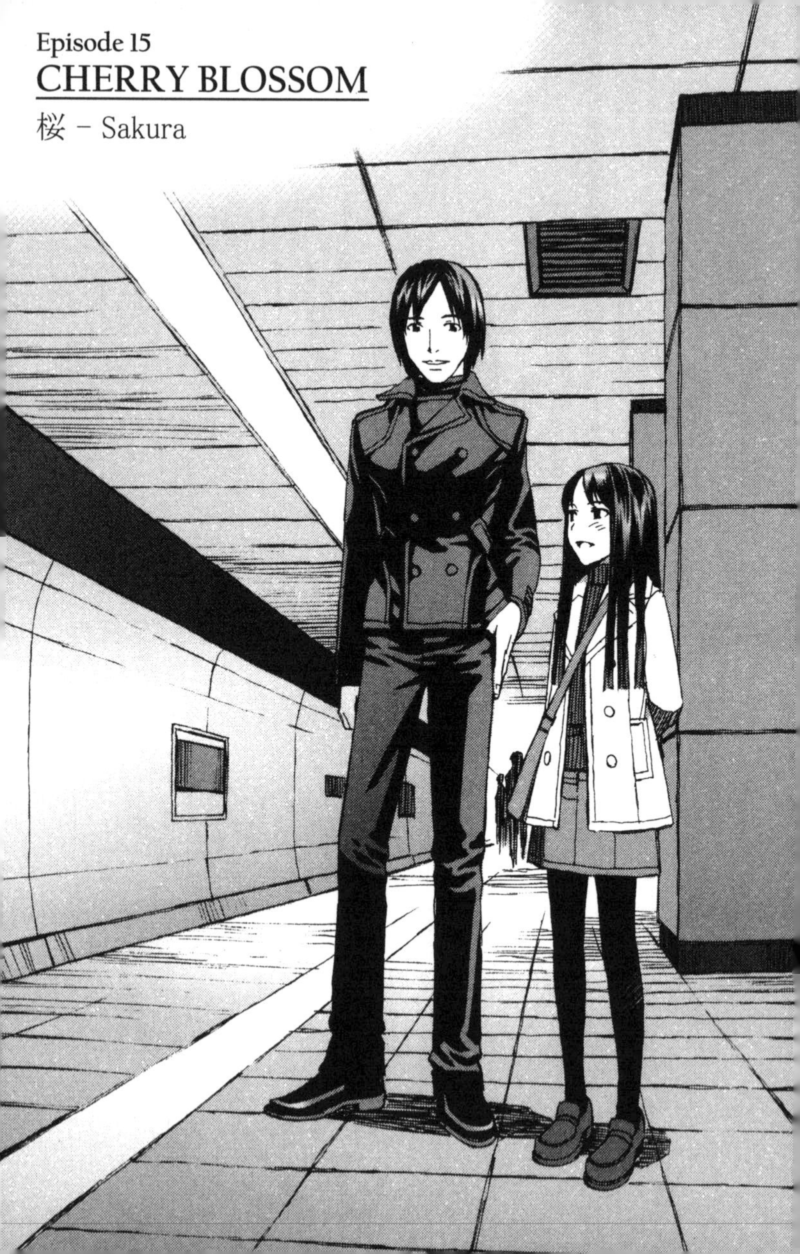

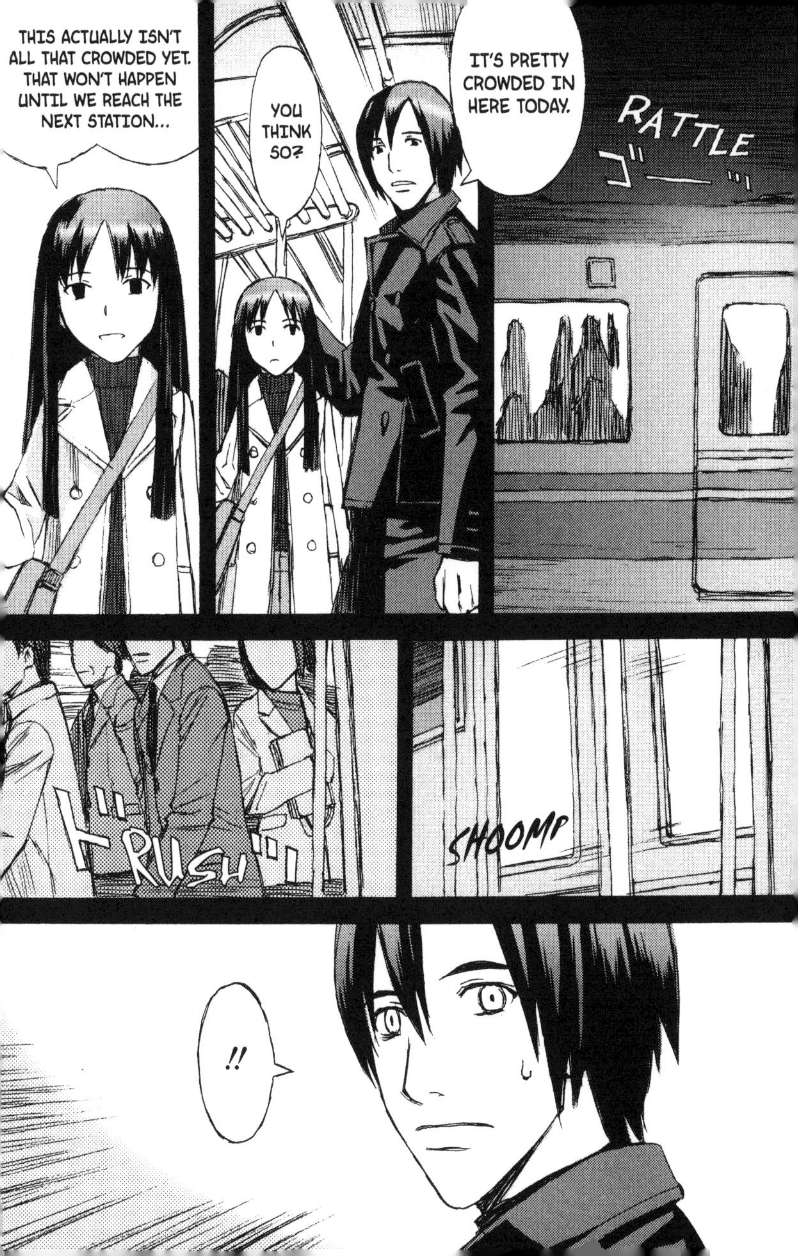
RATTLE
ゴーーッ
IT'S PRETTY CROWDED IN HERE TODAY.
YOU THINK SO?
THIS ACTUALLY ISN'T ALL THAT CROWDED YET. THAT WON'T HAPPEN UNTIL WE REACH THE NEXT STATION...
SHOOMP
RUSH
!!

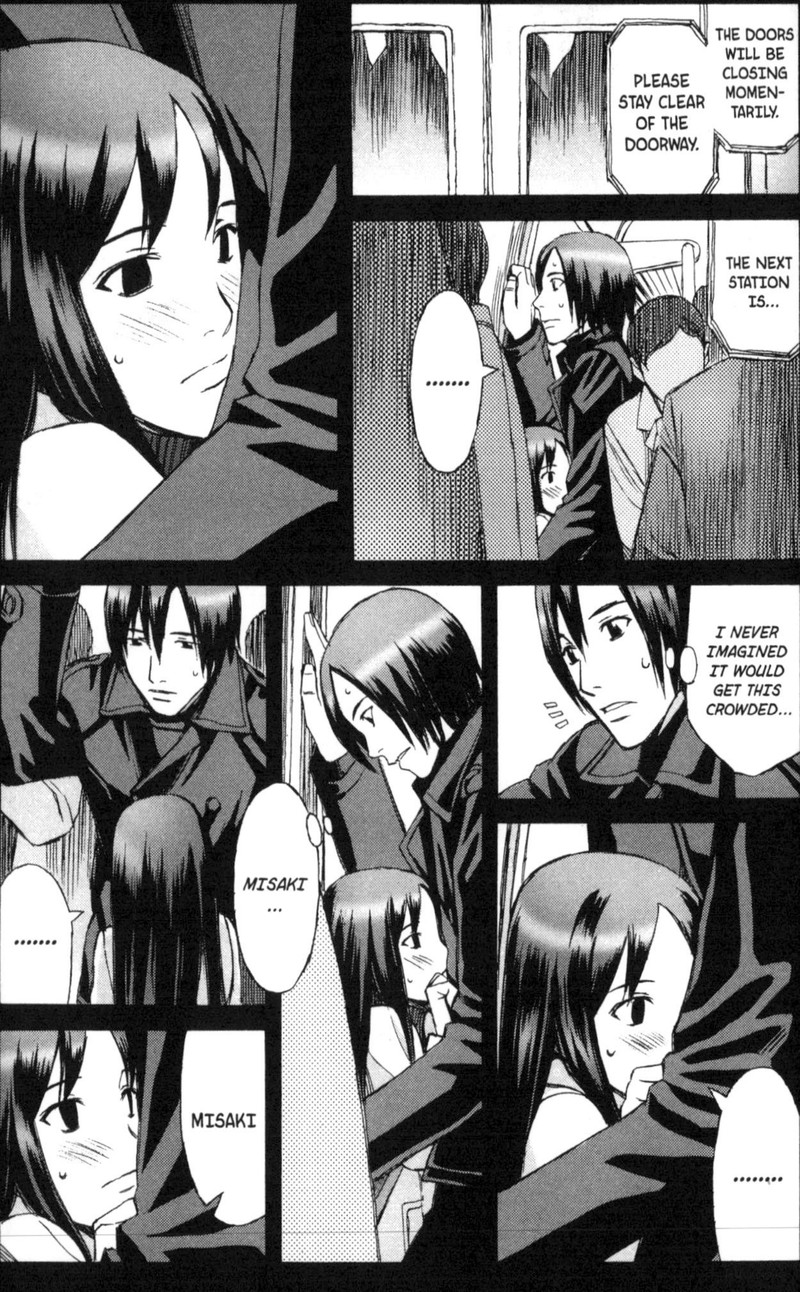
THE DOORS WILL BE CLOSING MOMEN-TARILY.
PLEASE STAY CLEAR OF THE DOORWAY.
THE NEXT STATION IS...
....
I NEVER IMAGINED IT WOULD GET THIS CROWDED...
....
MISAKI ...
....
MISAKI

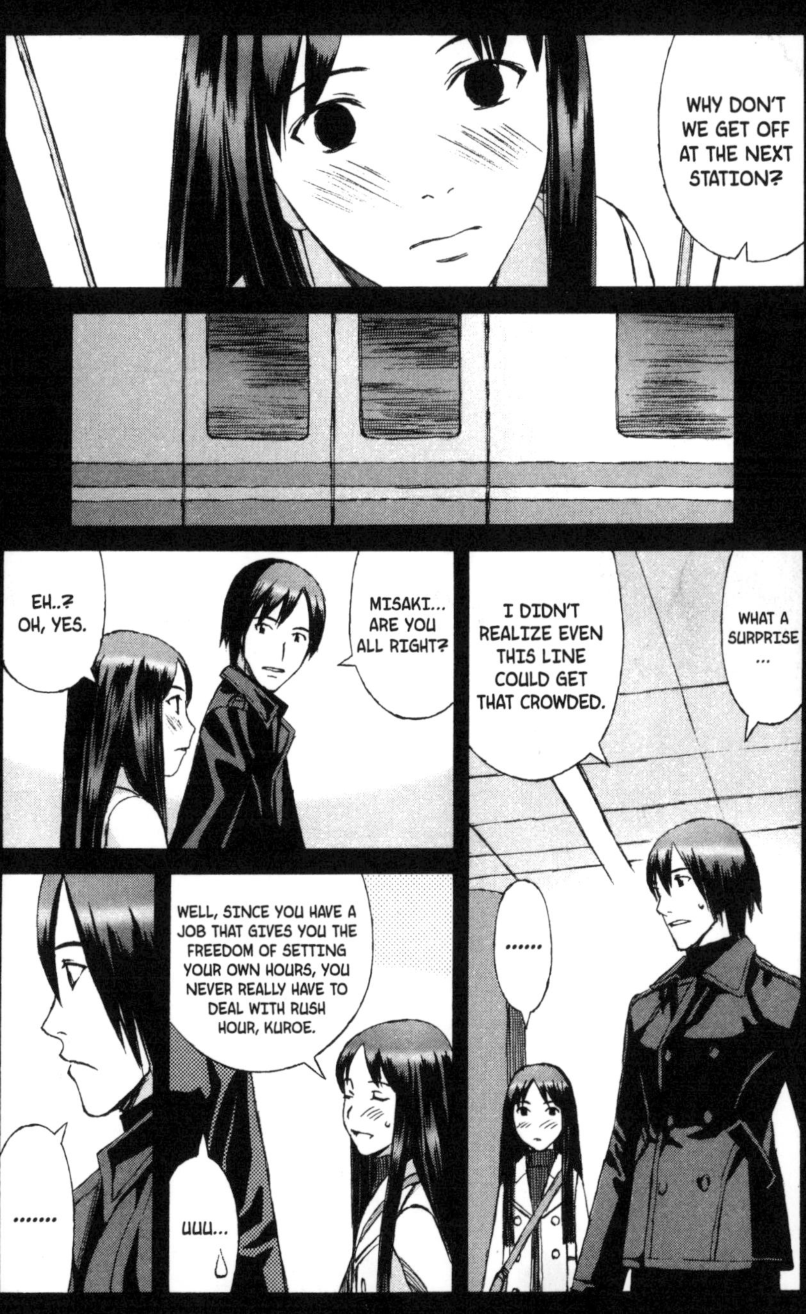
WHY DON'T WE GET OFF AT THE NEXT STATION?
WHAT A SURPRISE ...
I DIDN'T REALIZE EVEN THIS LINE COULD GET THAT CROWDED.
......
MISAKI... ARE YOU ALL RIGHT?
EH..? OH, YES.
WELL, SINCE YOU HAVE A JOB THAT GIVES YOU THE FREEDOM OF SETTING YOUR OWN HOURS, YOU NEVER REALLY HAVE TO DEAL WITH RUSH HOUR, KUROE.
UUU...
....

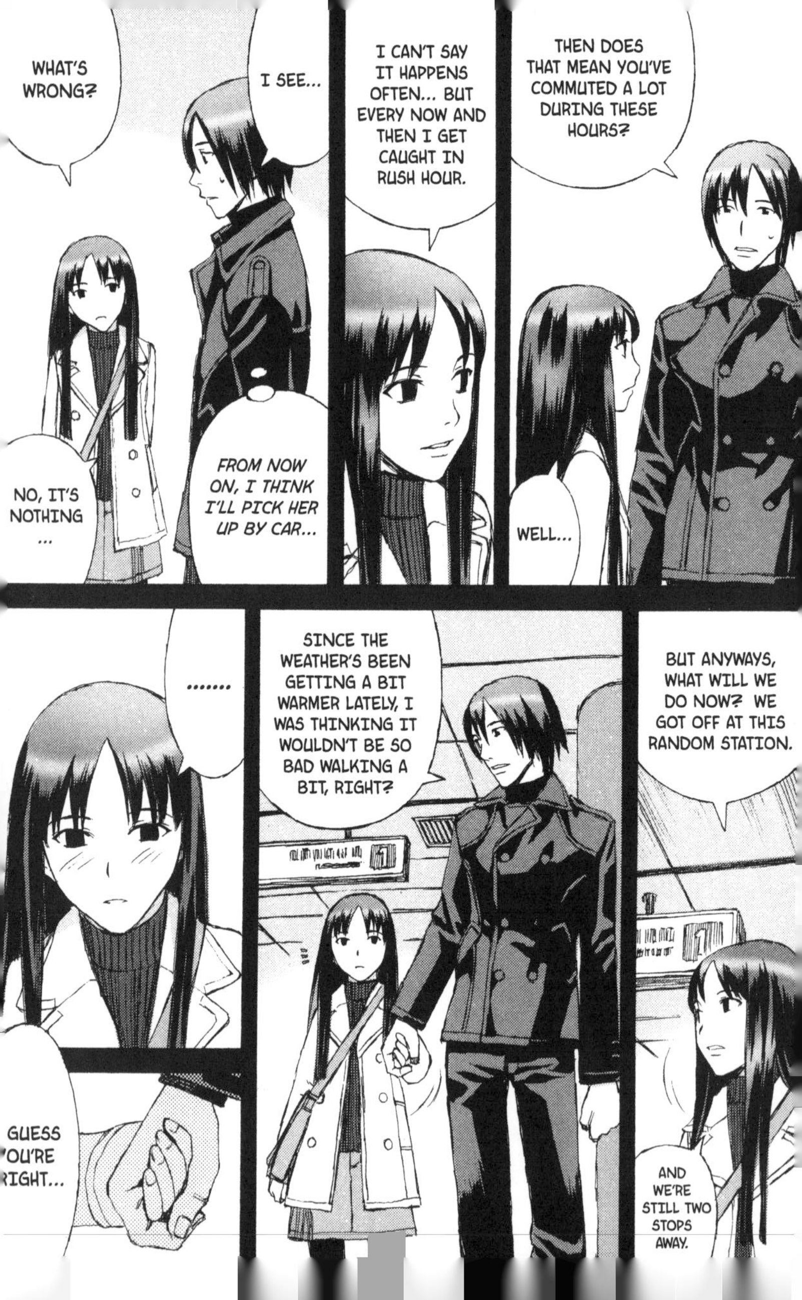
THEN DOES THAT MEAN YOU'VE COMMUTED A LOT DURING THESE HOURS?
WELL...
I CAN'T SAY IT HAPPENS OFTEN... BUT EVERY NOW AND THEN I GET CAUGHT IN RUSH HOUR.
I SEE...
WHAT'S WRONG?
FROM NOW ON, I THINK I'LL PICK HER UP BY CAR...
NO, IT'S NOTHING ...
BUT ANYWAYS, WHAT WILL WE DO NOW? WE GOT OFF AT THIS RANDOM STATION.
AND WE'RE STILL TWO STOPS AWAY.
SINCE THE WEATHER'S BEEN GETTING A BIT WARMER LATELY, I WAS THINKING IT WOULDN'T BE SO BAD WALKING A BIT, RIGHT?
....
GUESS YOU'RE RIGHT...

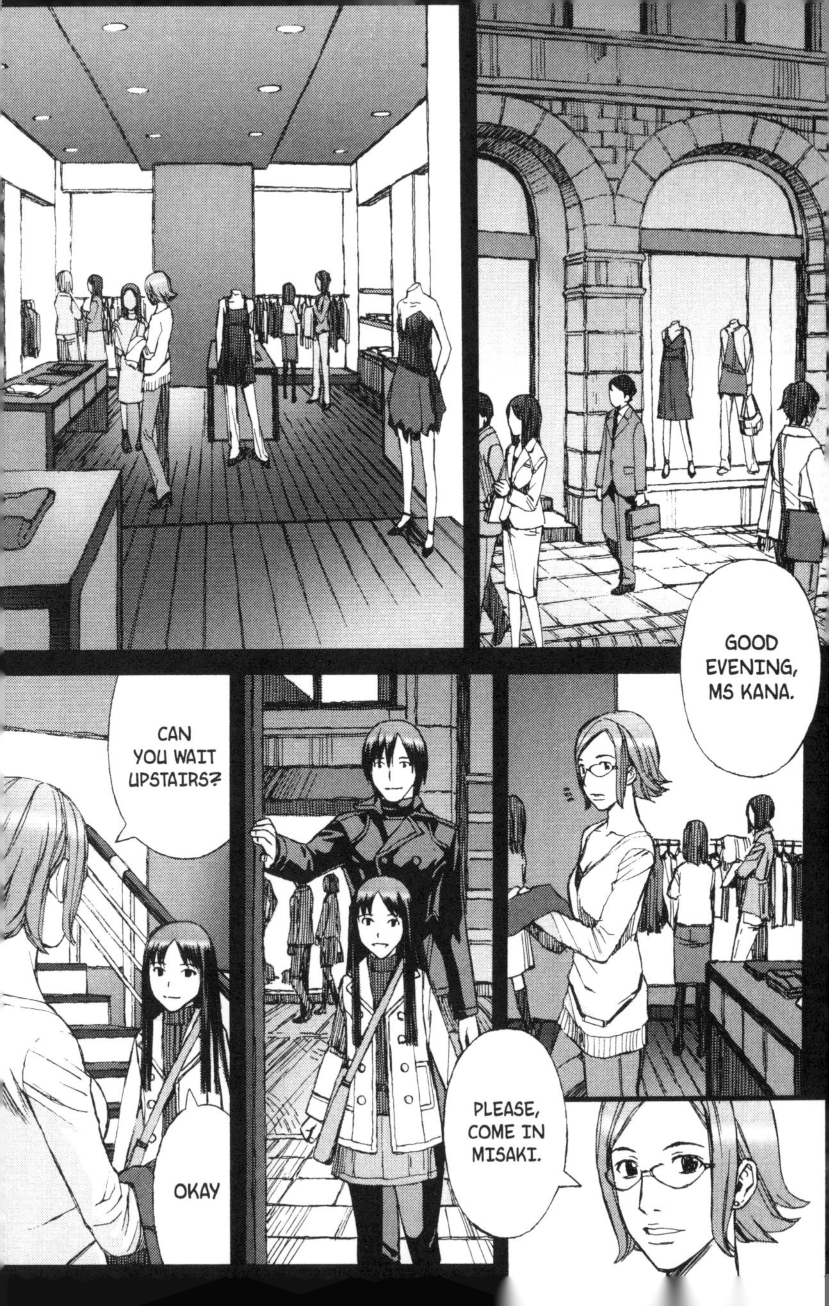
GOOD EVENING, MS KANA.
PLEASE, COME IN MISAKI.
CAN YOU WAIT UPSTAIRS?
OKAY

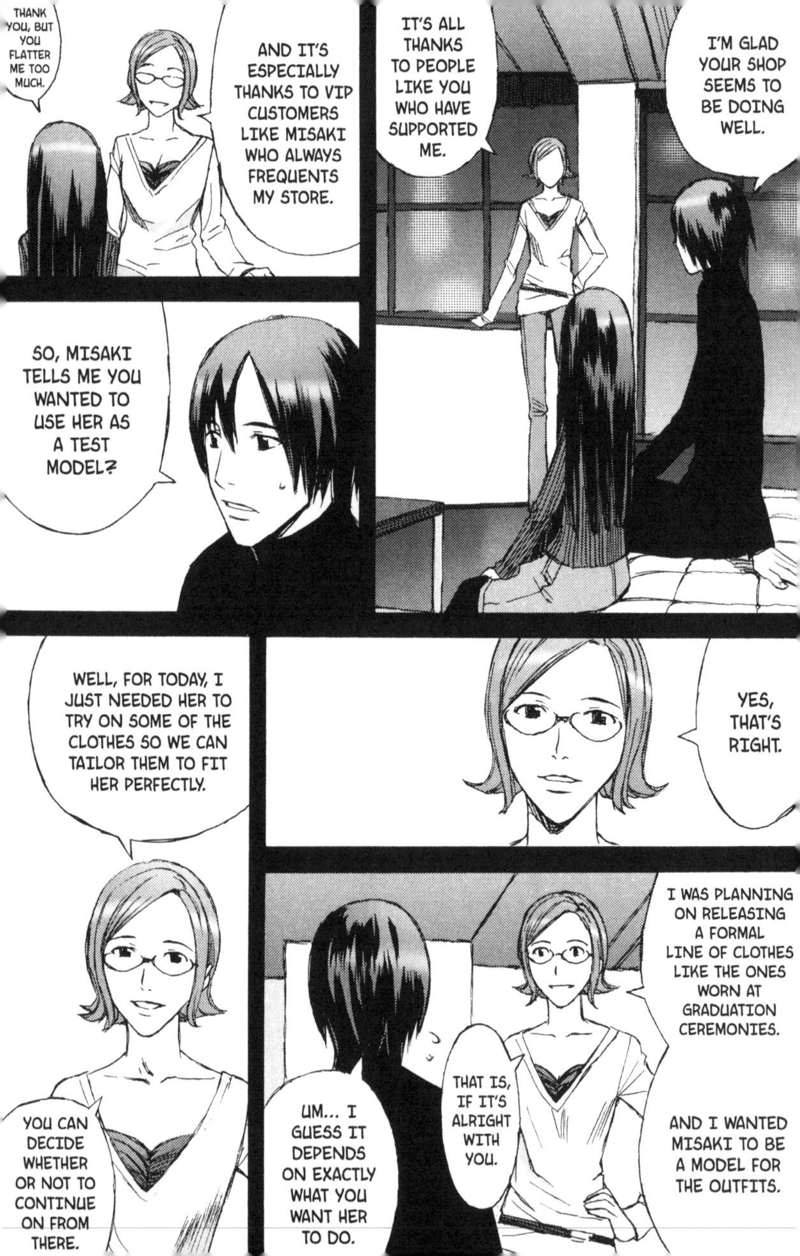
I'M GLAD YOUR SHOP SEEMS TO BE DOING WELL.
IT'S ALL THANKS TO PEOPLE LIKE YOU WHO HAVE SUPPORTED ME.
AND IT'S ESPECIALLY THANKS TO VIP CUSTOMERS LIKE MISAKI WHO ALWAYS FREQUENTS MY STORE.
THANK YOU, BUT YOU FLATTER ME TOO MUCH.
SO, MISAKI TELLS ME YOU WANTED TO USE HER AS A TEST MODEL?
YES, THAT'S RIGHT.
I WAS PLANNING ON RELEASING A FORMAL LINE OF CLOTHES LIKE THE ONES WORN AT GRADUATION CEREMONIES.
AND I WANTED MISAKI TO BE A MODEL FOR THE OUTFITS.
THAT IS, IF IT'S ALRIGHT WITH YOU.
UM... I GUESS IT DEPENDS ON EXACTLY WHAT YOU WANT HER TO DO.
WELL, FOR TODAY, I JUST NEEDED HER TO TRY ON SOME OF THE CLOTHES SO WE CAN TAILOR THEM TO FIT HER PERFECTLY.
YOU CAN DECIDE WHETHER OR NOT TO CONTINUE ON FROM THERE.

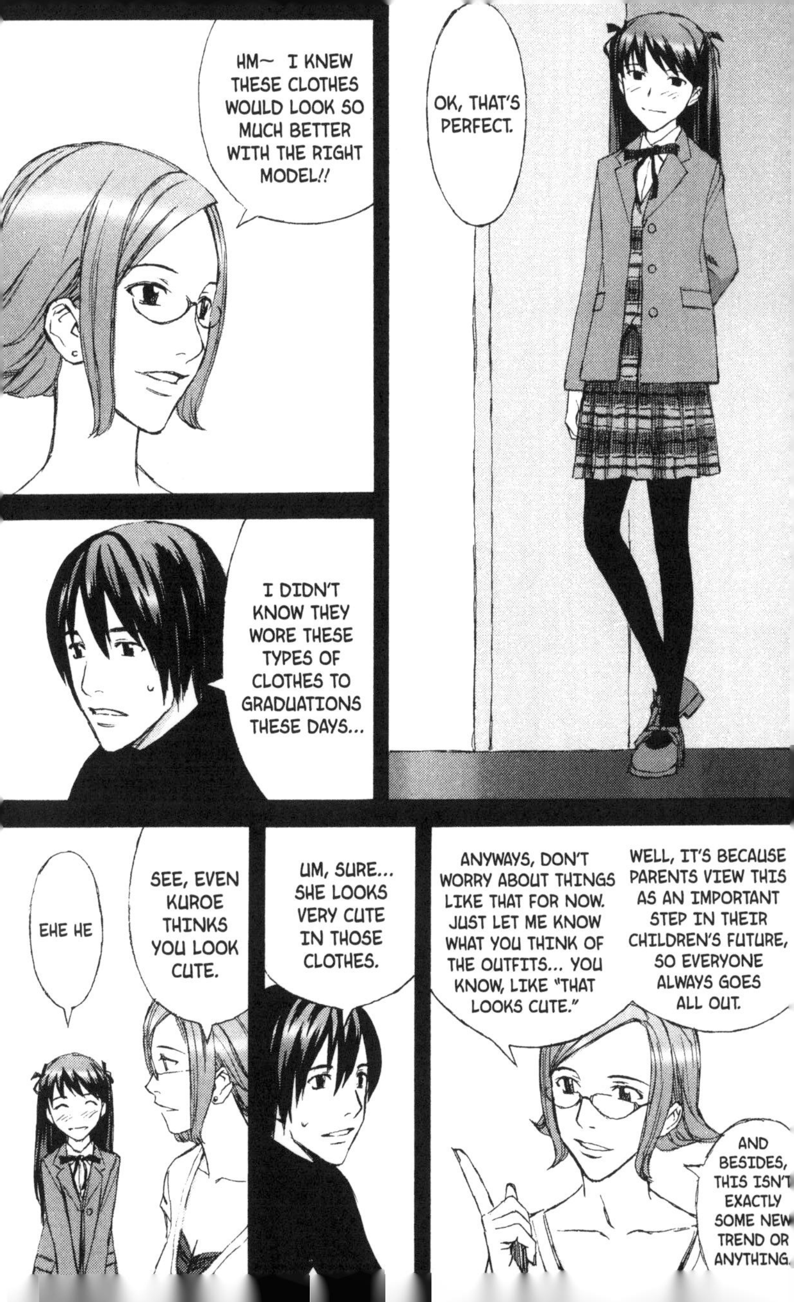

OK, THAT'S PERFECT.
HM~ I KNEW THESE CLOTHES WOULD LOOK SO MUCH BETTER WITH THE RIGHT MODEL!!
I DIDN'T KNOW THEY WORE THESE TYPES OF CLOTHES TO GRADUATIONS THESE DAYS...
WELL, IT'S BECAUSE PARENTS VIEW THIS AS AN IMPORTANT STEP IN THEIR CHILDREN'S FUTURE, SO EVERYONE ALWAYS GOES ALL OUT.
ANYWAYS, DON'T WORRY ABOUT THINGS LIKE THAT FOR NOW. JUST LET ME KNOW WHAT YOU THINK OF THE OUTFITS... YOU KNOW, LIKE "THAT LOOKS CUTE."
AND BESIDES, THIS ISN'T EXACTLY SOME NEW TREND OR ANYTHING.
UM, SURE... SHE LOOKS VERY CUTE IN THOSE CLOTHES.
SEE, EVEN KUROE THINKS YOU LOOK CUTE.
EHE HE

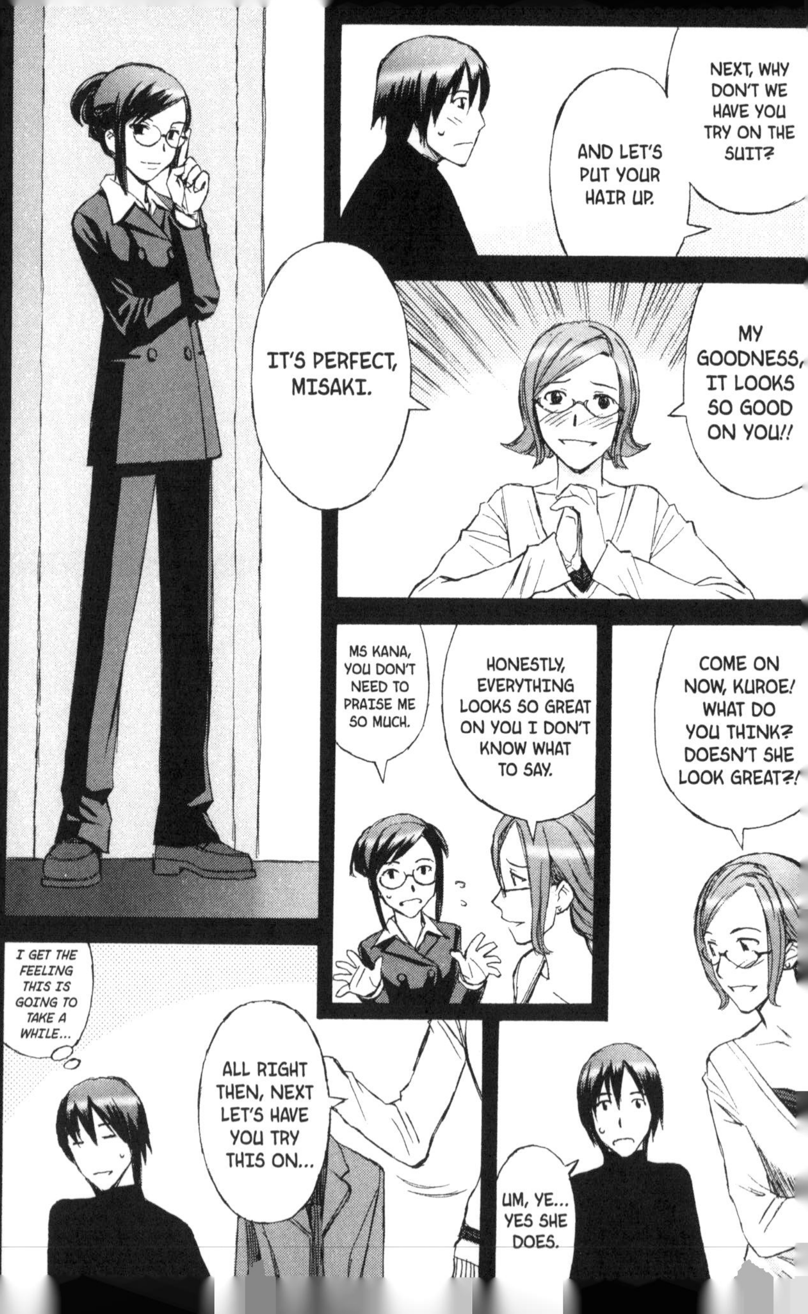
NEXT, WHY DON'T WE HAVE YOU TRY ON THE SUIT?
AND LET'S PUT YOUR HAIR UP.
MY GOODNESS, IT LOOKS SO GOOD ON YOU!!
IT'S PERFECT, MISAKI.
COME ON NOW, KUROE! WHAT DO YOU THINK? DOESN'T SHE LOOK GREAT?!
HONESTLY, EVERYTHING LOOKS SO GREAT ON YOU I DON'T KNOW WHAT TO SAY.
MS KANA, YOU DON'T NEED TO PRAISE ME SO MUCH.
UM, YE... YES SHE DOES.
ALL RIGHT THEN, NEXT LET'S HAVE YOU TRY THIS ON...
I GET THE FEELING THIS IS GOING TO TAKE A WHILE...

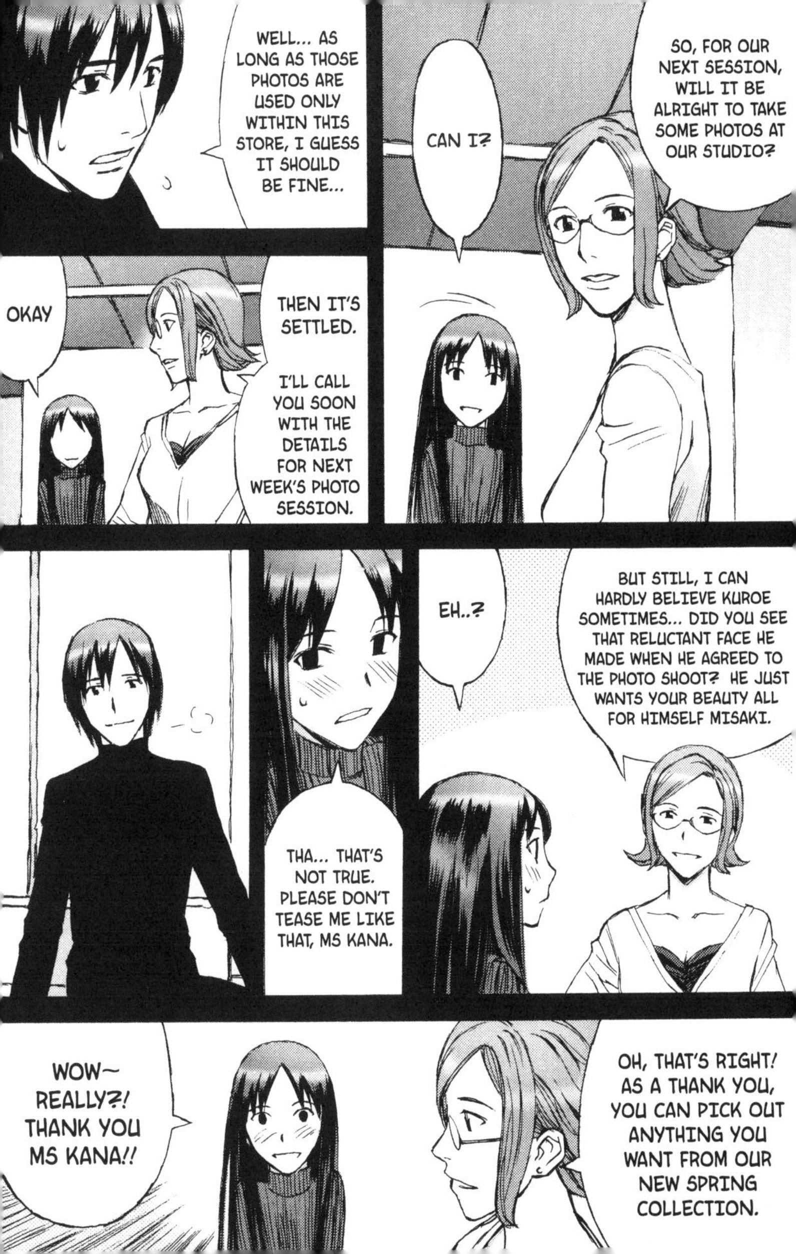
SO, FOR OUR NEXT SESSION, WILL IT BE ALRIGHT TO TAKE SOME PHOTOS AT OUR STUDIO?
CAN I?
WELL... AS LONG AS THOSE PHOTOS ARE USED ONLY WITHIN THIS STORE, I GUESS IT SHOULD BE FINE...
THEN IT'S SETTLED.
I'LL CALL YOU SOON WITH THE DETAILS FOR NEXT WEEK'S PHOTO SESSION.
OKAY
BUT STILL, I CAN HARDLY BELIEVE KUROE SOMETIMES... DID YOU SEE THAT RELUCTANT FACE HE MADE WHEN HE AGREED TO THE PHOTO SHOOT? HE JUST WANTS YOUR BEAUTY ALL FOR HIMSELF MISAKI.
EH..?
THA... THAT'S NOT TRUE. PLEASE DON'T TEASE ME LIKE THAT, MS KANA.
OH, THAT'S RIGHT! AS A THANK YOU, YOU CAN PICK OUT ANYTHING YOU WANT FROM OUR NEW SPRING COLLECTION.
WOW~ REALLY?! THANK YOU MS KANA!!

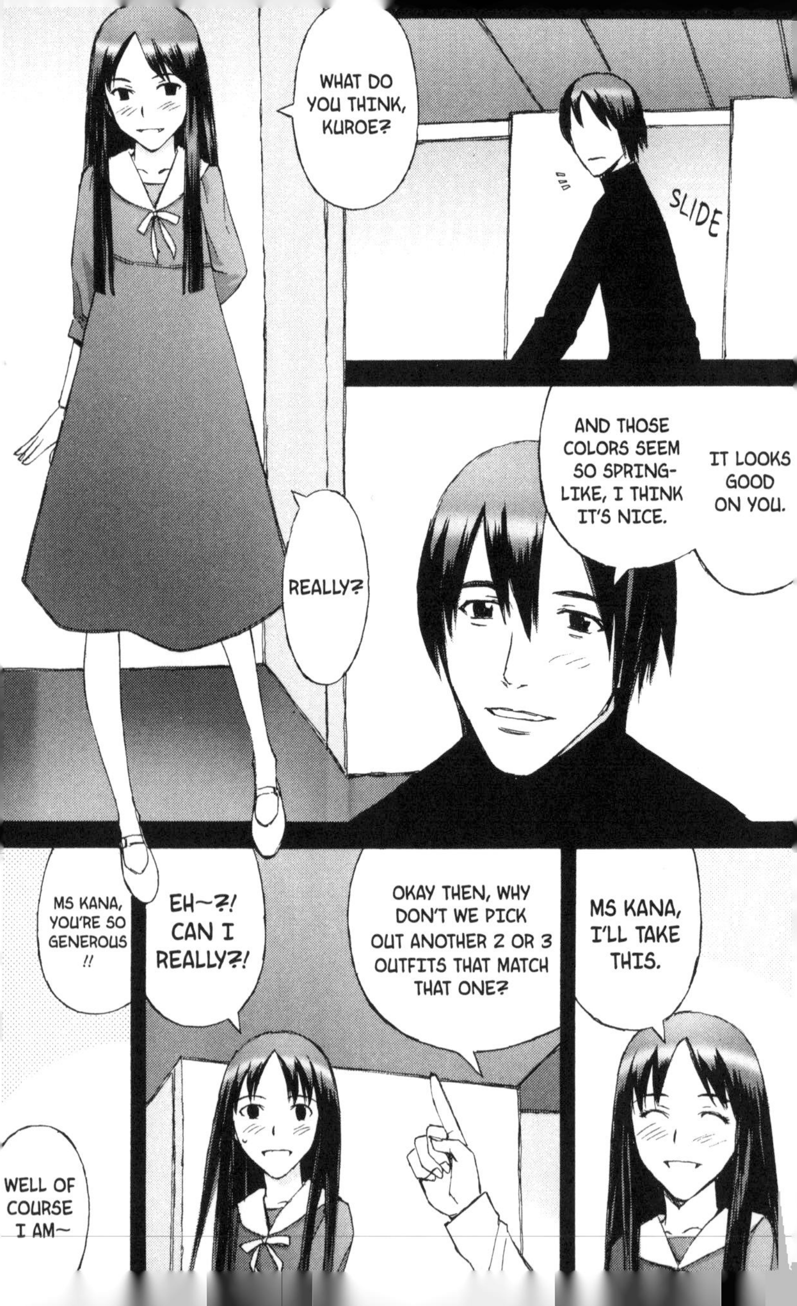
SLIDE
IT LOOKS GOOD ON YOU.
AND THOSE COLORS SEEM SO SPRING-LIKE, I THINK IT'S NICE.
WHAT DO YOU THINK, KUROE?
REALLY?
MS KANA, I'LL TAKE THIS.
OKAY THEN, WHY DON'T WE PICK OUT ANOTHER 2 OR 3 OUTFITS THAT MATCH THAT ONE?
EH~?! CAN I REALLY?!
MS KANA, YOU'RE SO GENEROUS !!
WELL OF COURSE I AM~

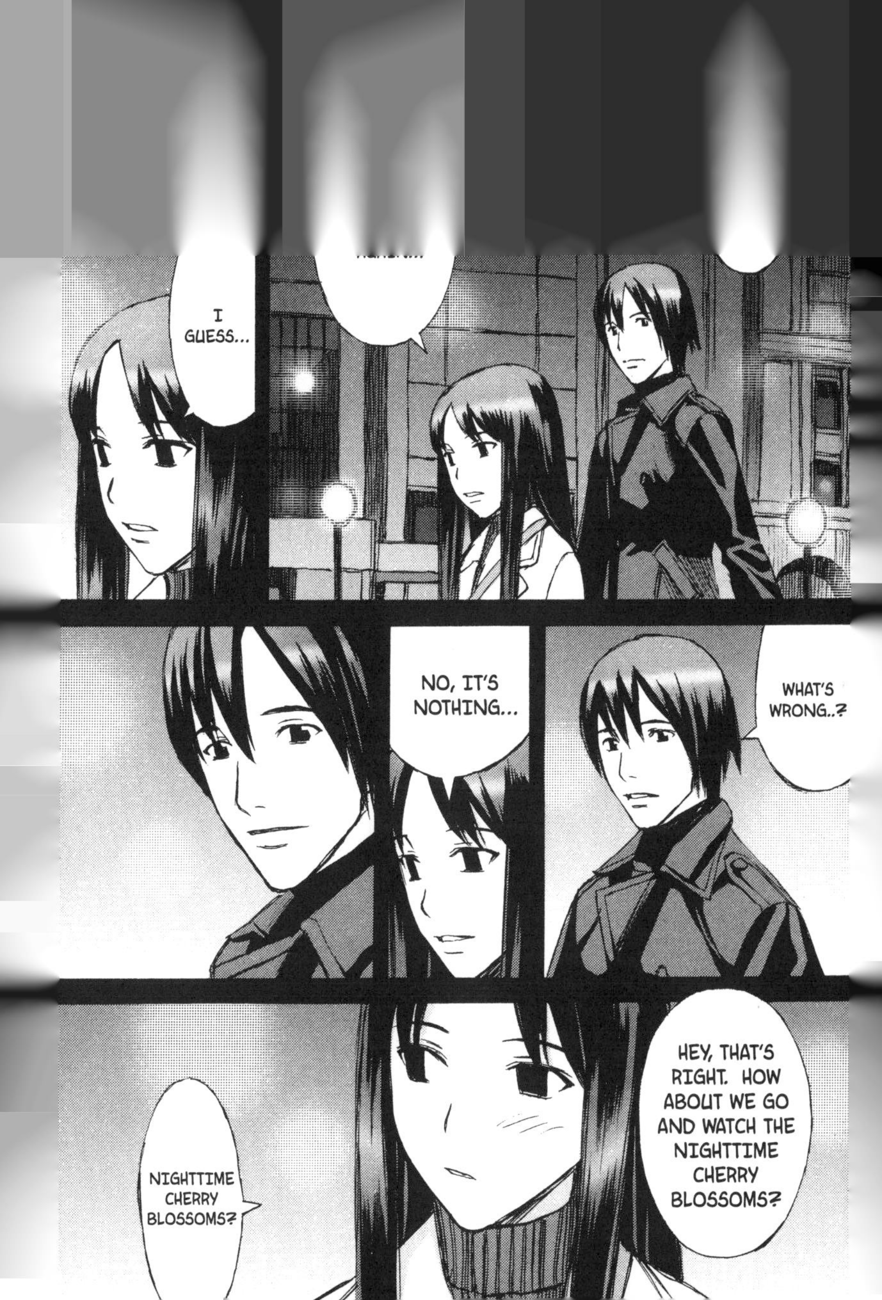
I GUESS...
WHAT'S WRONG..?
NO, IT'S NOTHING...
HEY, THAT'S RIGHT. HOW ABOUT WE GO AND WATCH THE NIGHTTIME CHERRY BLOSSOMS?
NIGHTTIME CHERRY BLOSSOMS?

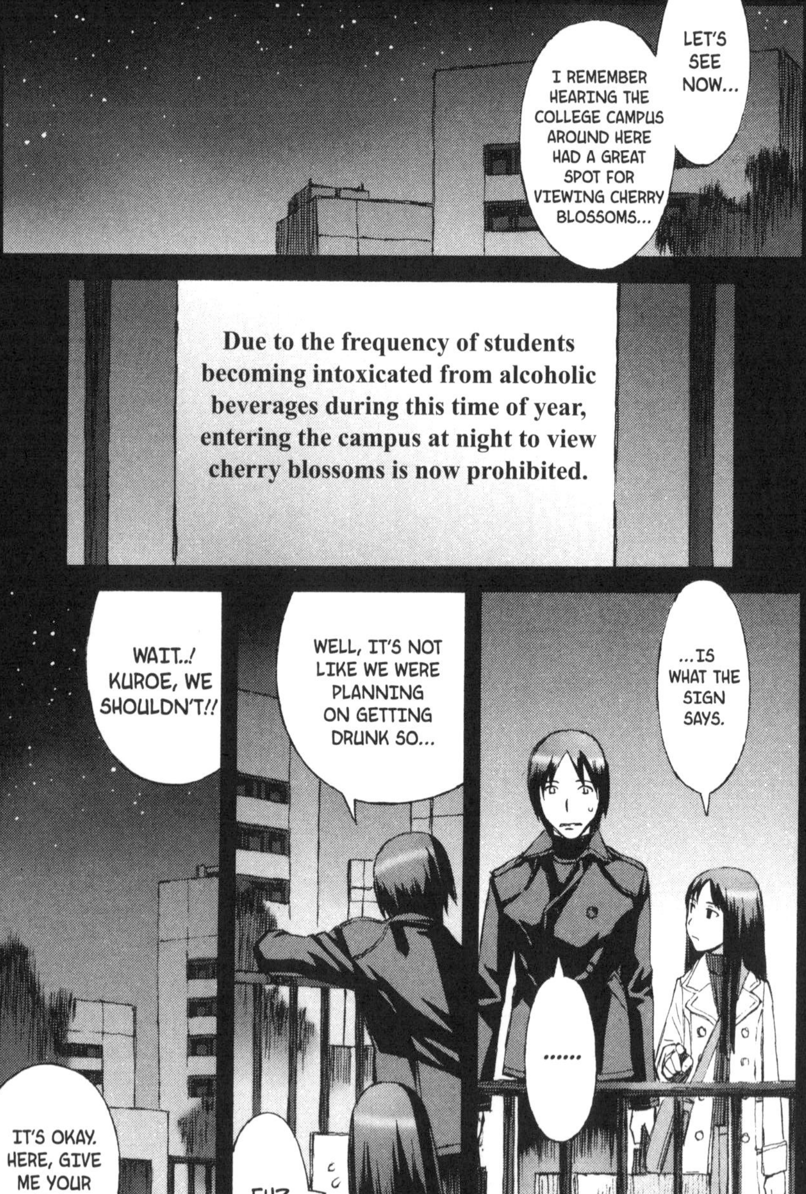
LET'S SEE NOW...
I REMEMBER HEARING THE COLLEGE CAMPUS AROUND HERE HAD A GREAT SPOT FOR VIEWING CHERRY BLOSSOMS...
Due to the frequency of students becoming intoxicated from alcoholic beverages during this time of year, entering the campus at night to view cherry blossoms is now prohibited.
...IS WHAT THE SIGN SAYS.
......
WELL, IT'S NOT LIKE WE WERE PLANNING ON GETTING DRUNK SO...
EH?
WAIT..! KUROE, WE SHOULDN'T!!
IT'S OKAY. HERE, GIVE ME YOUR HAND...

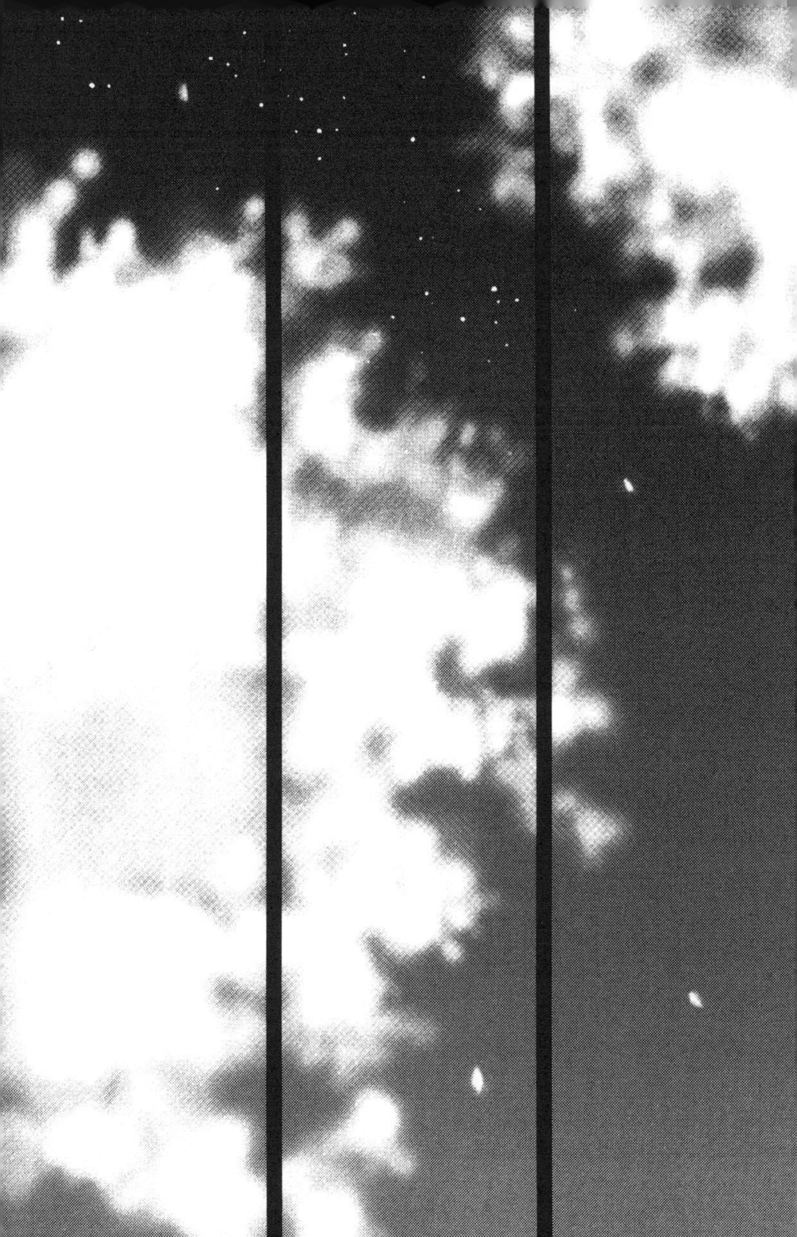

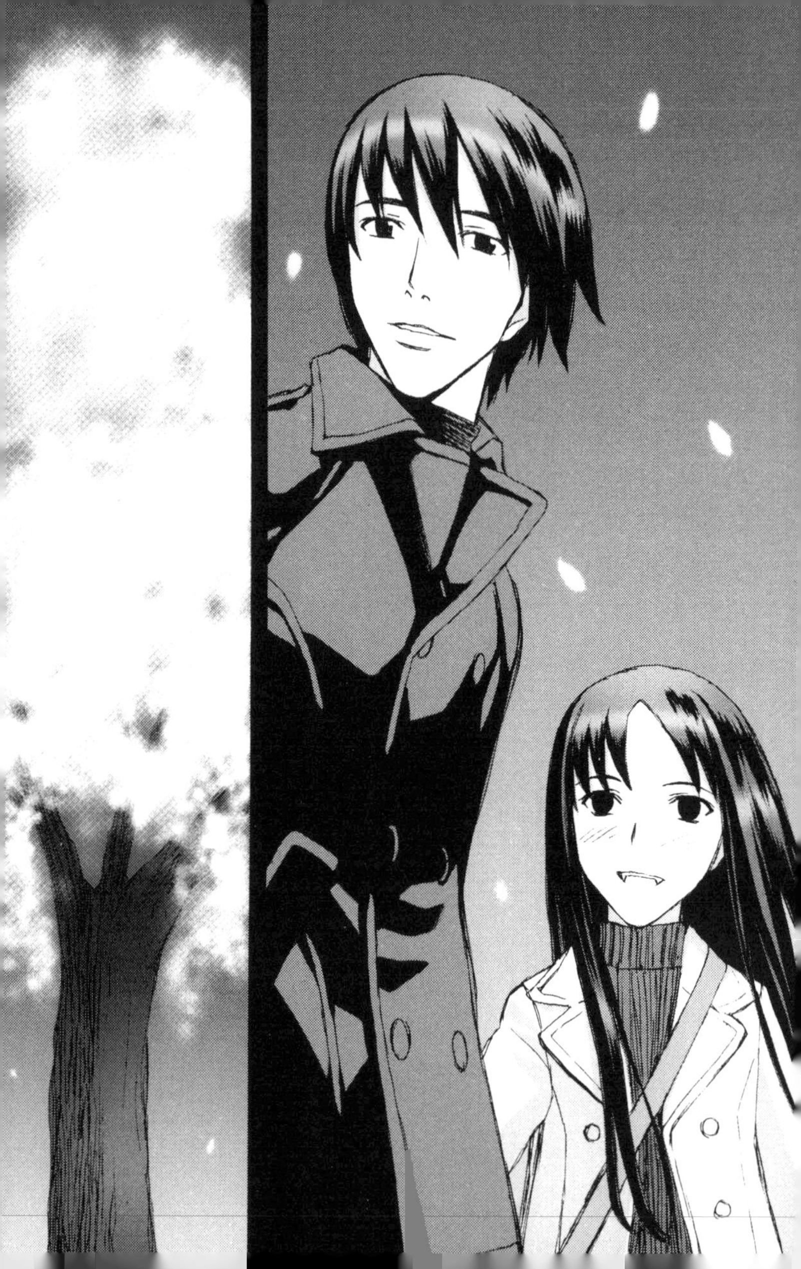

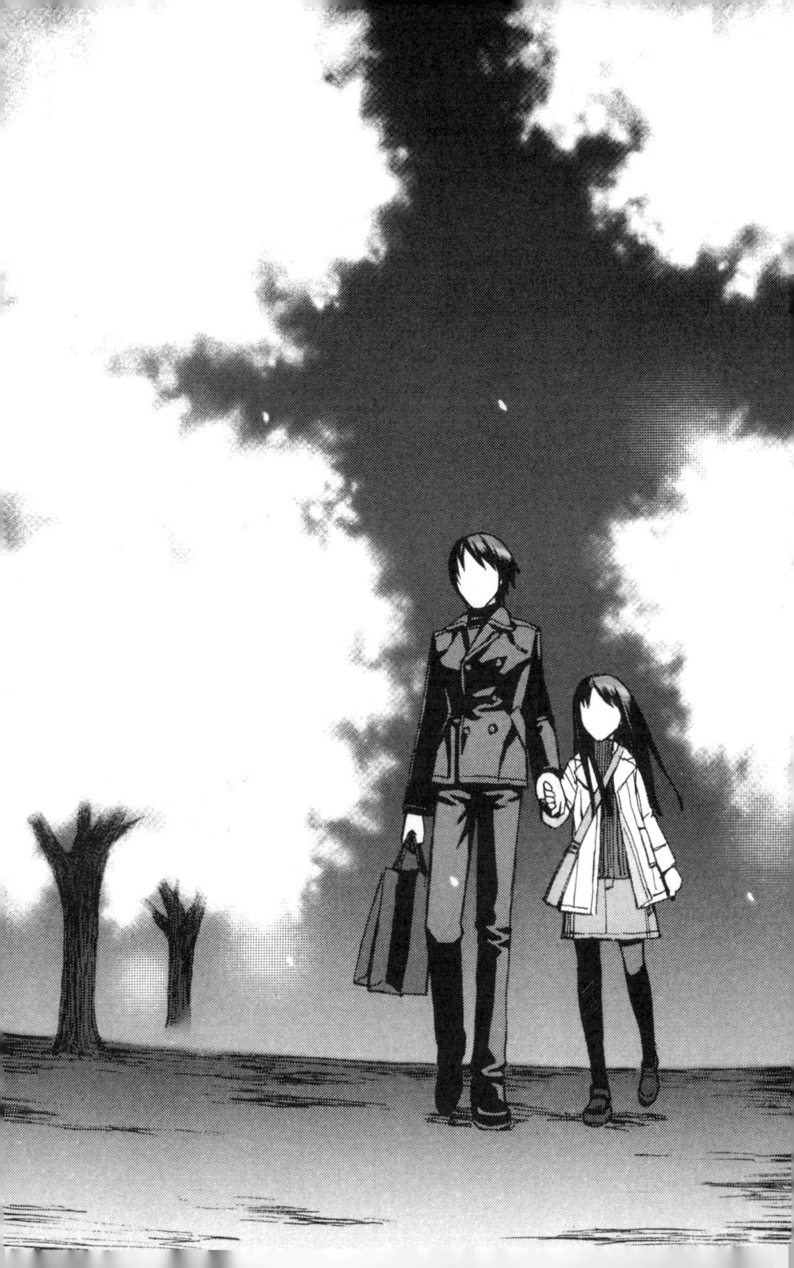

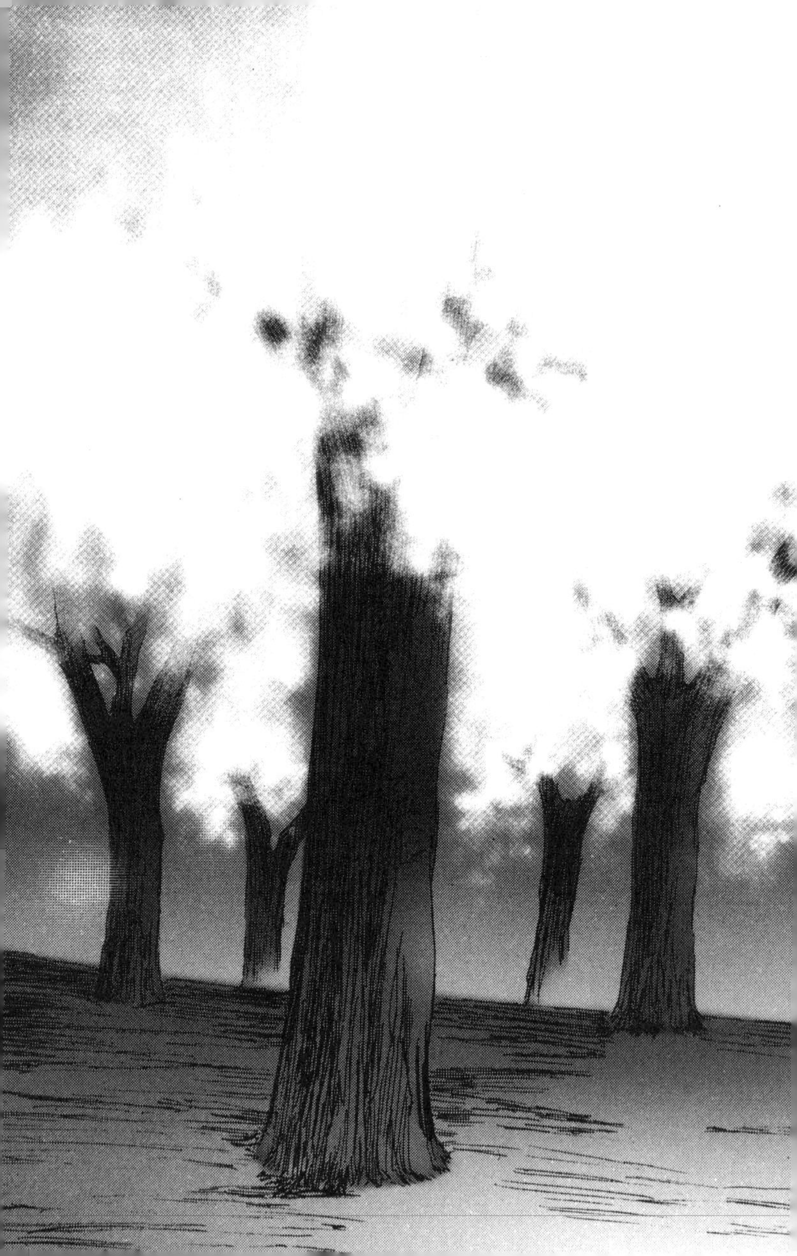

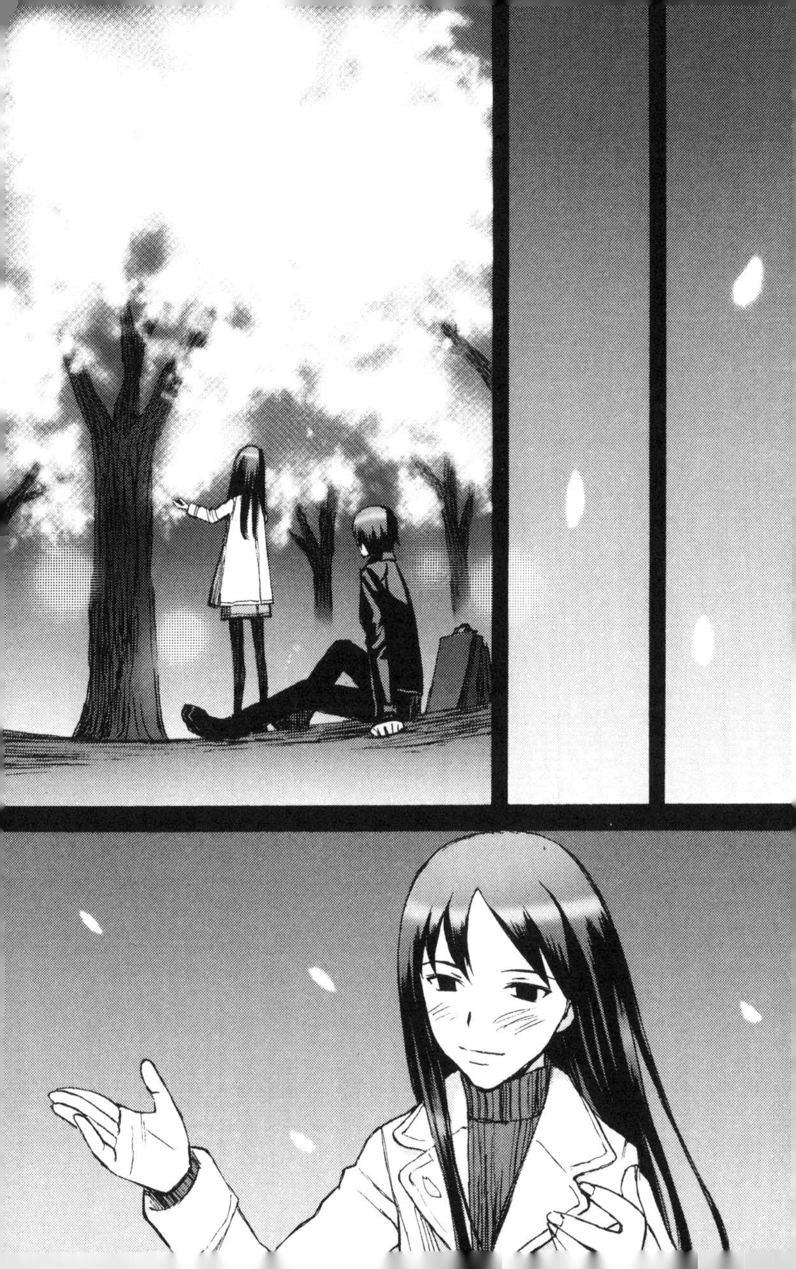

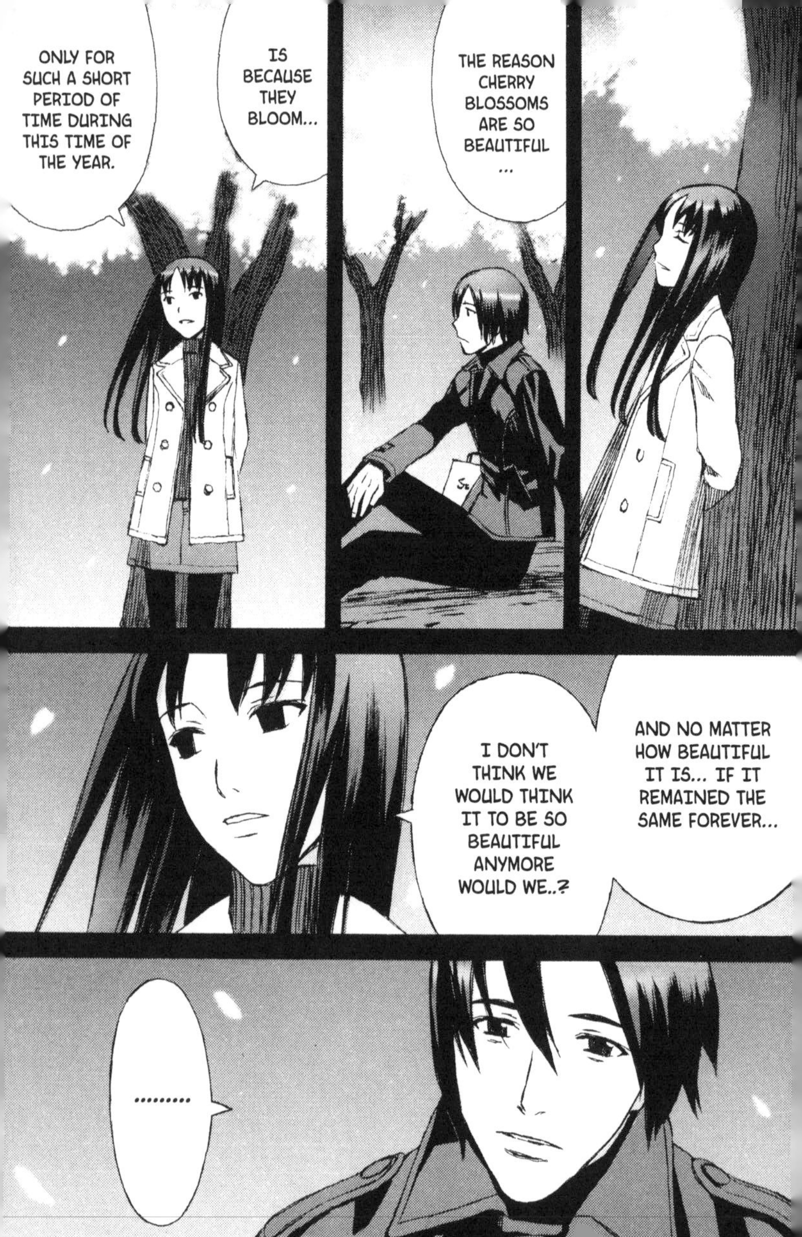
THE REASON CHERRY BLOSSOMS ARE SO BEAUTIFUL ...
IS BECAUSE THEY BLOOM...
ONLY FOR SUCH A SHORT PERIOD OF TIME DURING THIS TIME OF THE YEAR.
AND NO MATTER HOW BEAUTIFUL IT IS... IF IT REMAINED THE SAME FOREVER...
I DON'T THINK WE WOULD THINK IT TO BE SO BEAUTIFUL ANYMORE WOULD WE..?
....

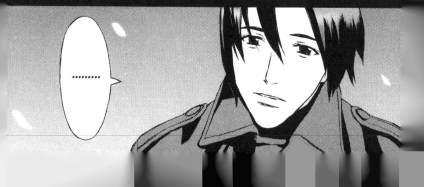

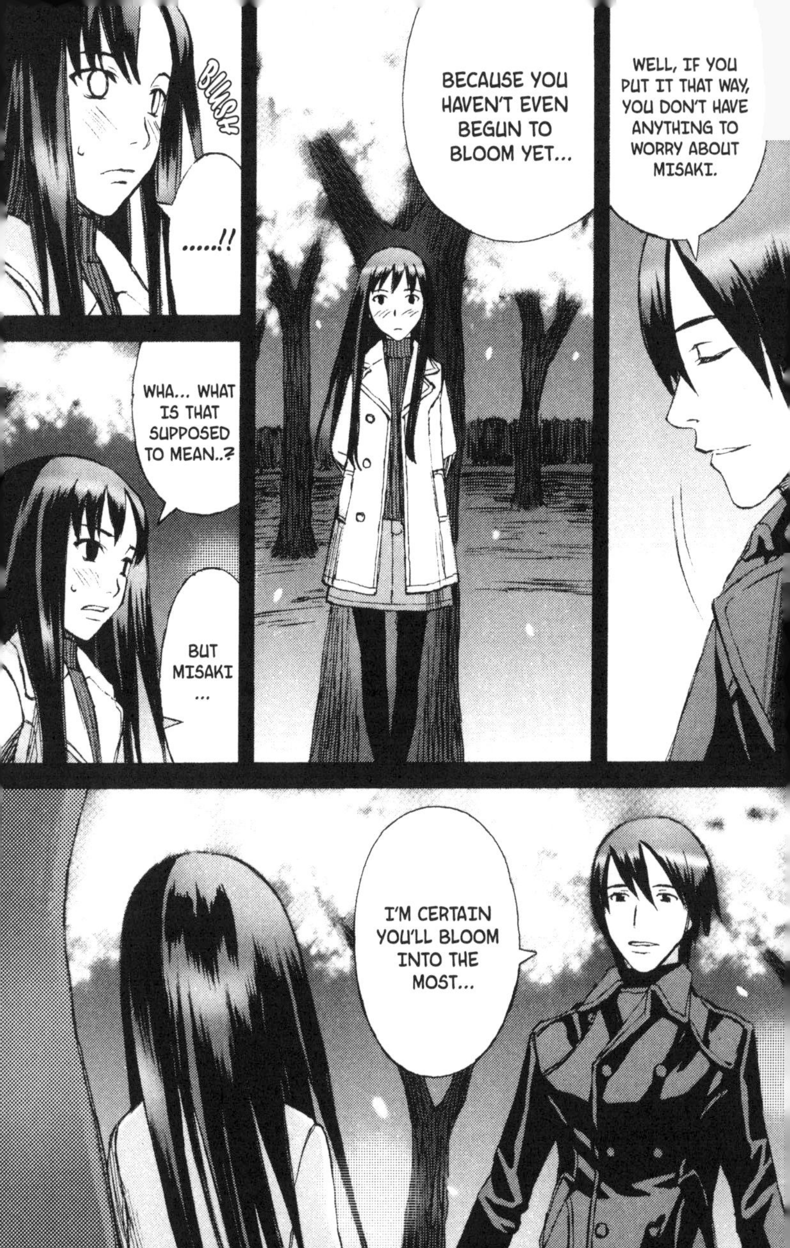
WELL, IF YOU PUT IT THAT WAY, YOU DON'T HAVE ANYTHING TO WORRY ABOUT MISAKI.
BECAUSE YOU HAVEN'T EVEN BEGUN TO BLOOM YET...
BLUSH
.....!!
WHA... WHAT IS THAT SUPPOSED TO MEAN..!?
BUT MISAKI ...
I'M CERTAIN YOU'LL BLOOM INTO THE MOST...

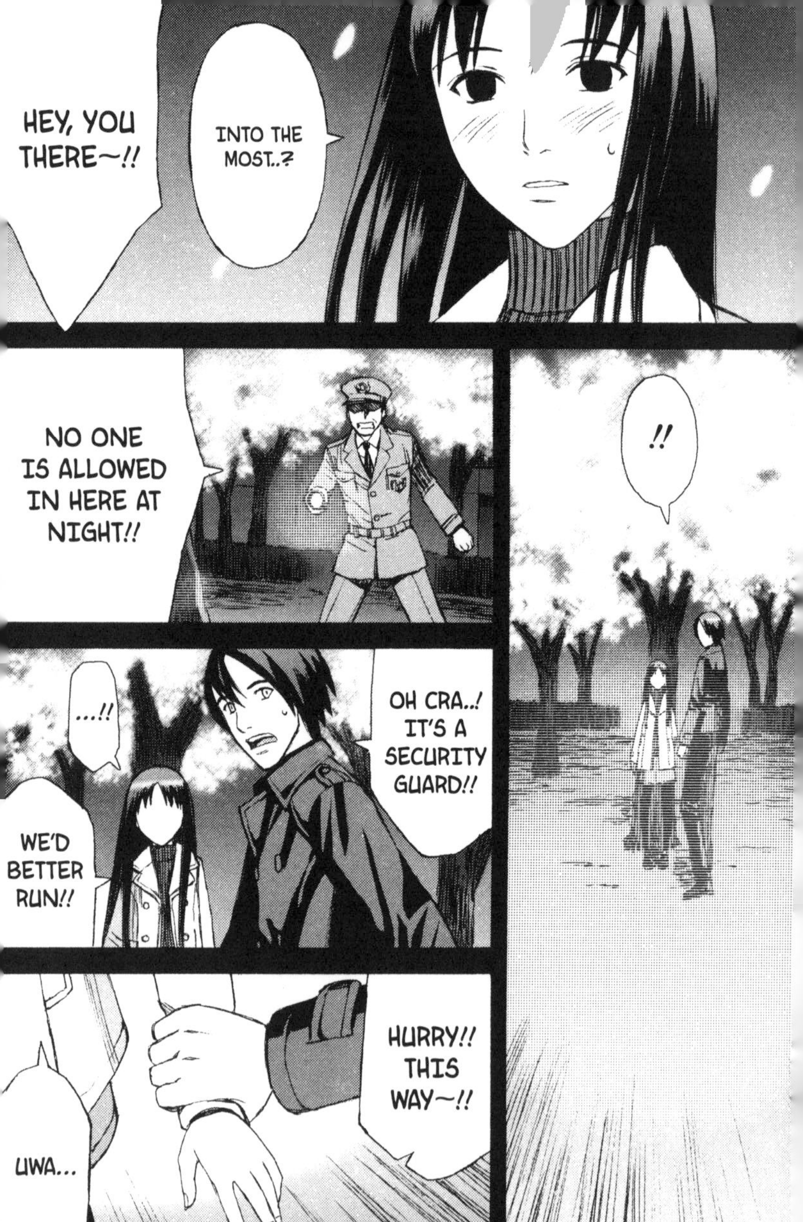
INTO THE MOST..?
HEY, YOU THERE~!!
!!
NO ONE IS ALLOWED IN HERE AT NIGHT!!
OH CRA..! IT'S A SECURITY GUARD!!
...!!
WE'D BETTER RUN!!
HURRY!! THIS WAY~!!
UWA...

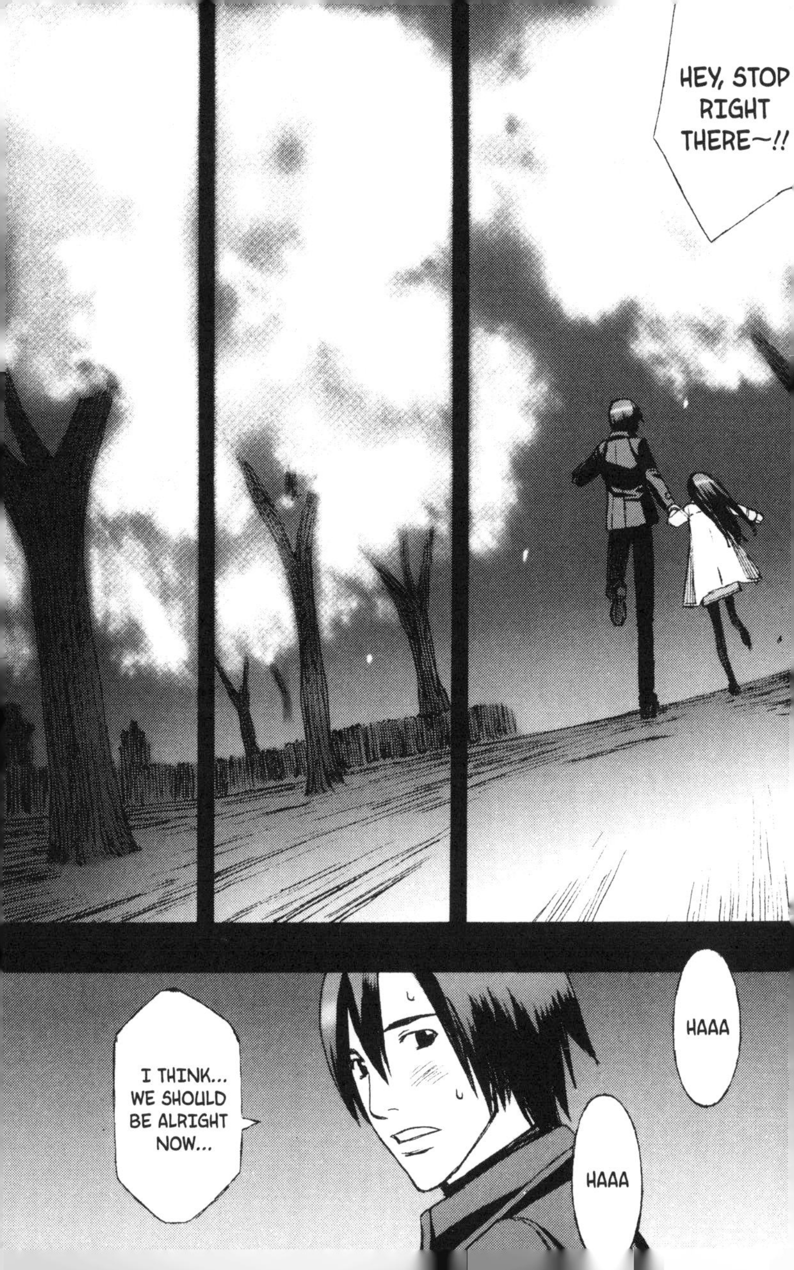
HEY, STOP RIGHT THERE~!!
HAAA
HAAA
I THINK... WE SHOULD BE ALRIGHT NOW...

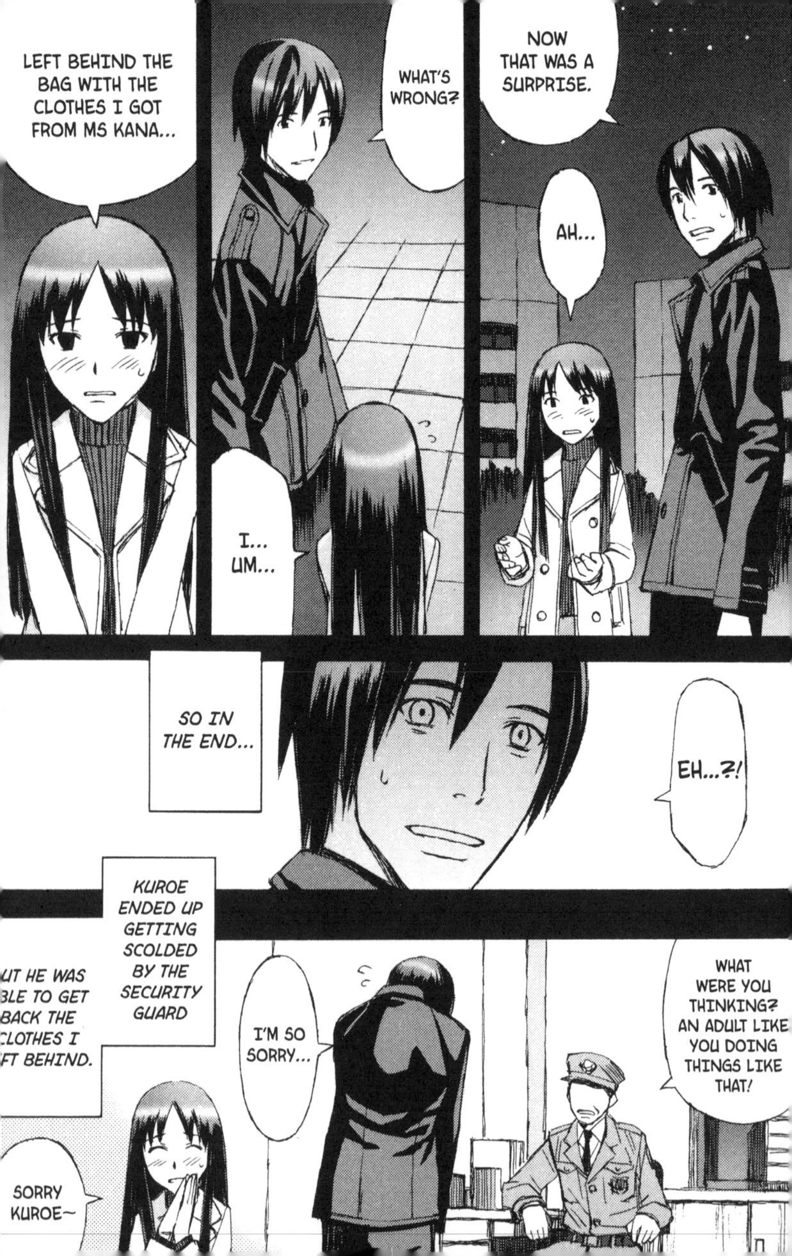
NOW THAT WAS A SURPRISE.
AH...
WHAT'S WRONG?
I... UM...
LEFT BEHIND THE BAG WITH THE CLOTHES I GOT FROM MS KANA...
EH...?!
SO IN THE END...
WHAT WERE YOU THINKING? AN ADULT LIKE YOU DOING THINGS LIKE THAT!
I'M SO SORRY...
KUROE ENDED UP GETTING SCOLDED BY THE SECURITY GUARD
UT HE WAS BLE TO GET BACK THE CLOTHES I FT BEHIND.
SORRY KUROE~

Episode 16
MY FIRST MEMORY
ふたりの思い出 - A Memory Belonging to Just the Two of Them

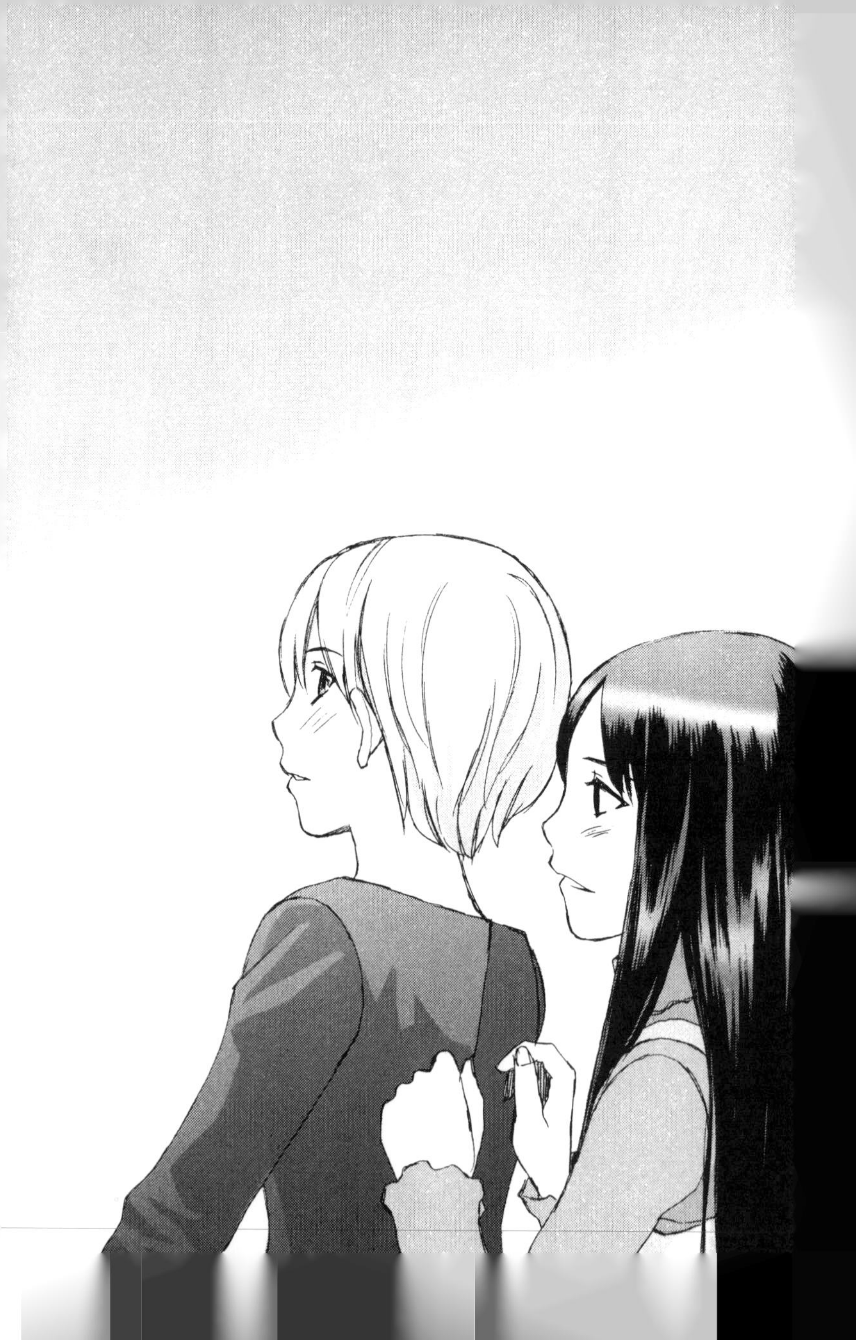

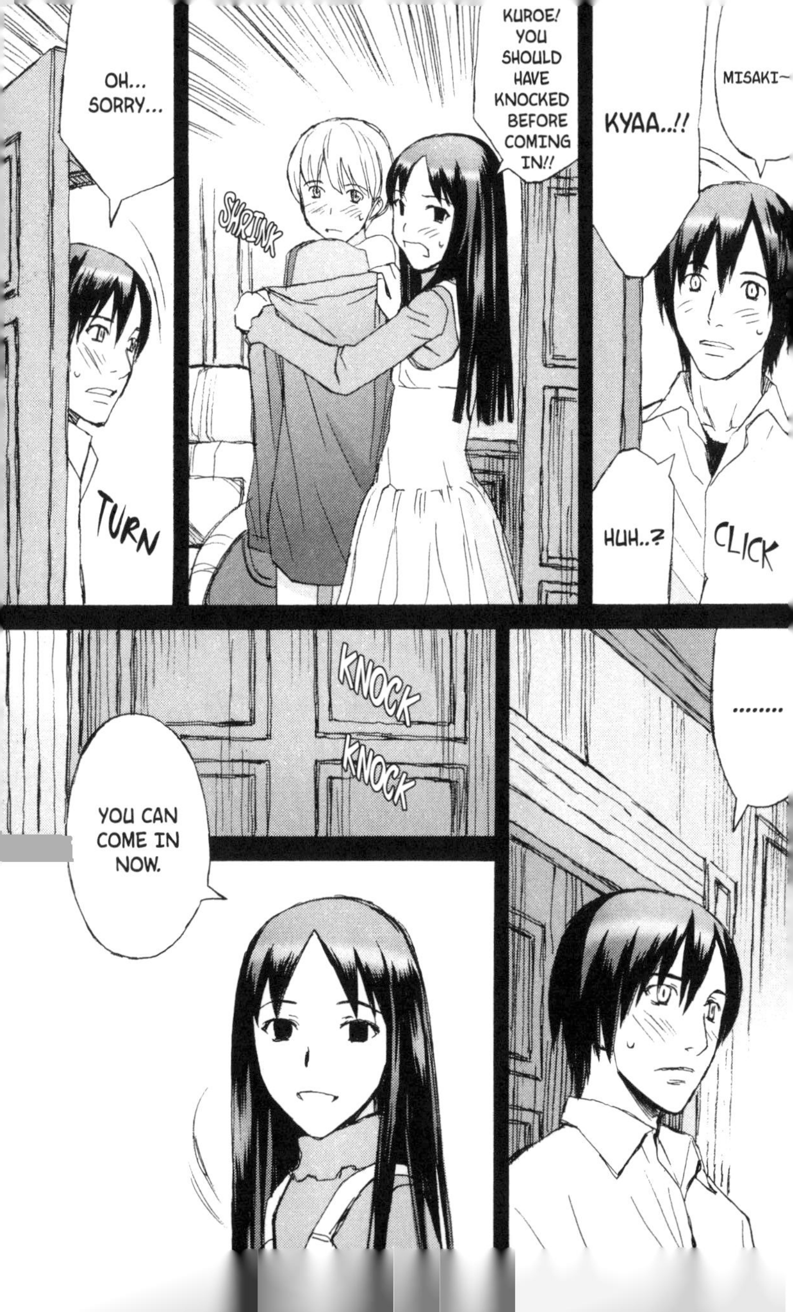
MISAKI~
KYAA..!!
CLICK
HUH..?
KUROE! YOU SHOULD HAVE KNOCKED BEFORE COMING IN!!
SHRINK
OH... SORRY...
TURN
....
KNOCK
KNOCK
YOU CAN COME IN NOW.

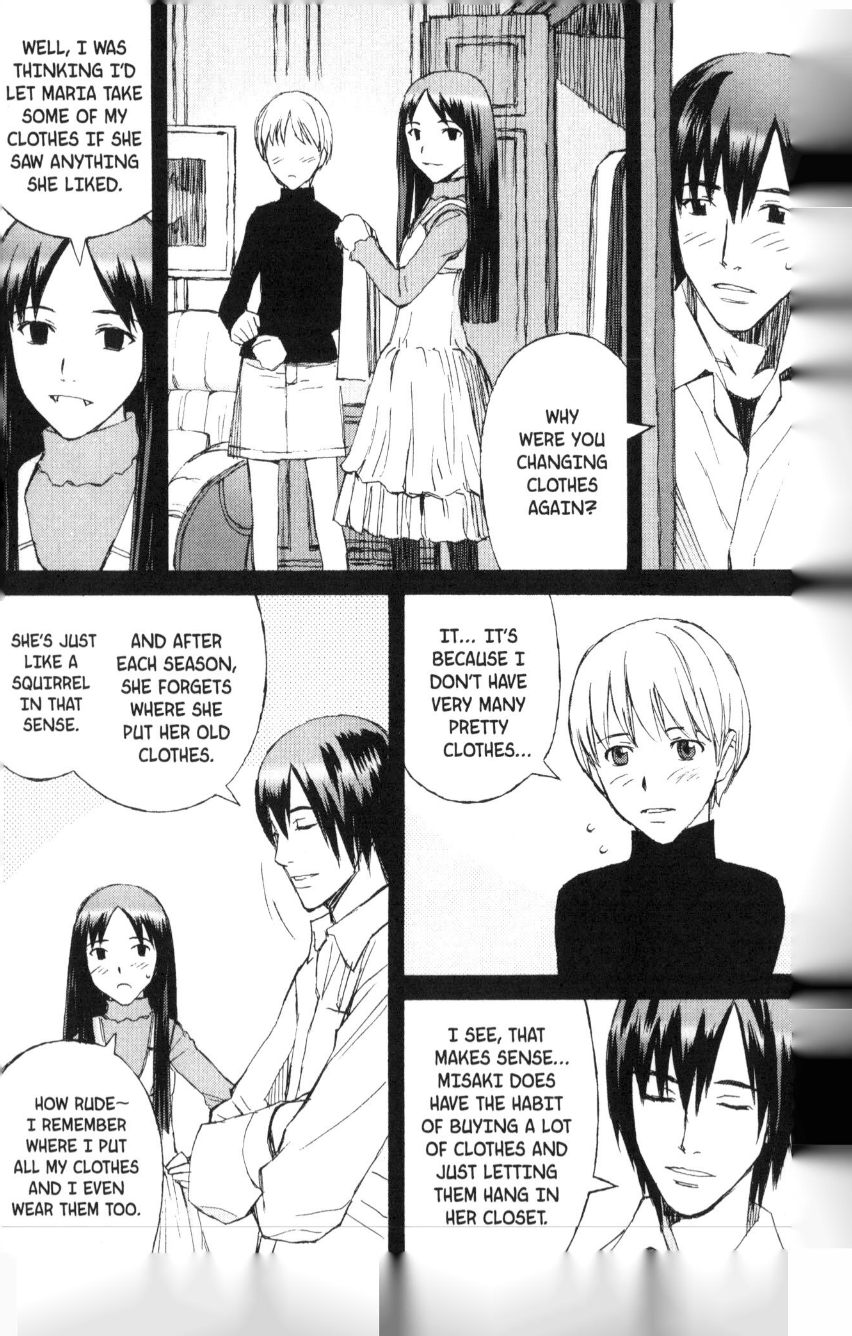
WHY WERE YOU CHANGING CLOTHES AGAIN?
WELL, I WAS THINKING I'D LET MARIA TAKE SOME OF MY CLOTHES IF SHE SAW ANYTHING SHE LIKED.
IT... IT'S BECAUSE I DON'T HAVE VERY MANY PRETTY CLOTHES...
I SEE, THAT MAKES SENSE... MISAKI DOES HAVE THE HABIT OF BUYING A LOT OF CLOTHES AND JUST LETTING THEM HANG IN HER CLOSET.
AND AFTER EACH SEASON, SHE FORGETS WHERE SHE PUT HER OLD CLOTHES.
SHE'S JUST LIKE A SQUIRREL IN THAT SENSE.
HOW RUDE~ I REMEMBER WHERE I PUT ALL MY CLOTHES AND I EVEN WEAR THEM TOO.

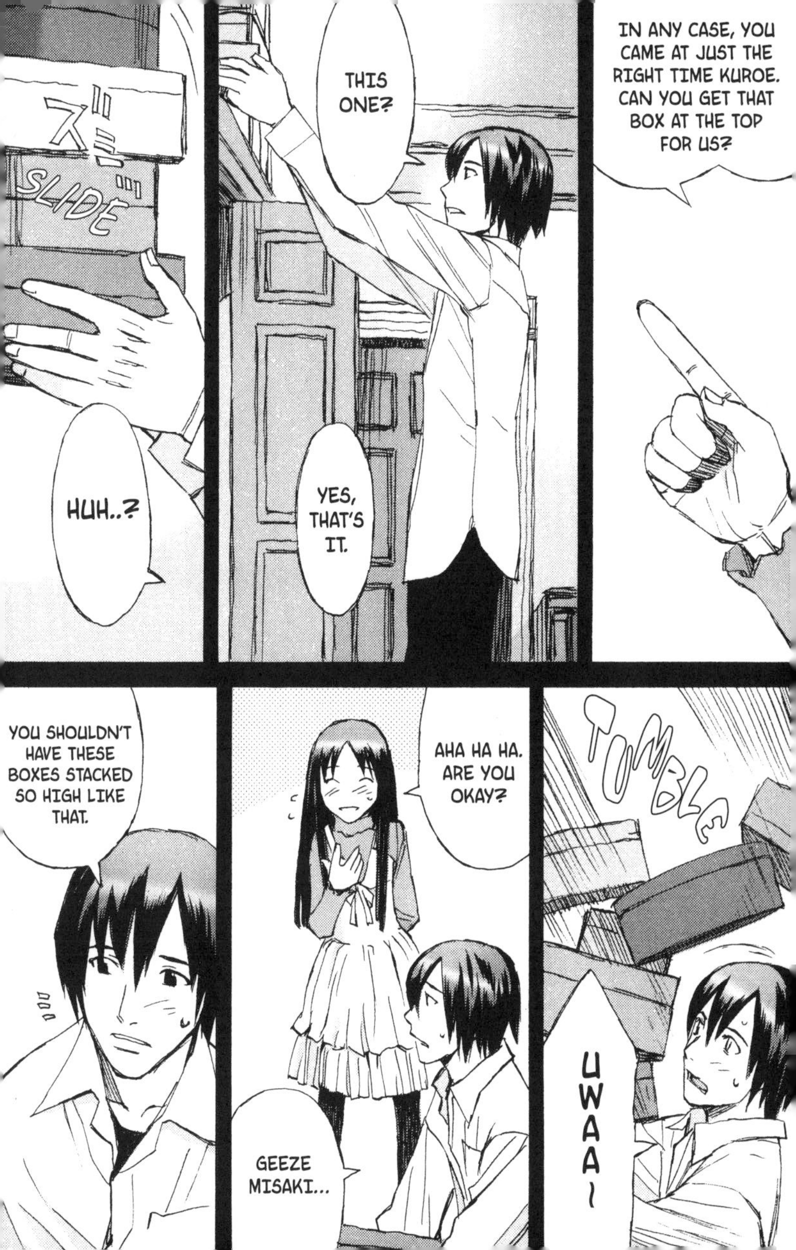
IN ANY CASE, YOU CAME AT JUST THE RIGHT TIME KUROE. CAN YOU GET THAT BOX AT THE TOP FOR US?
THIS ONE?
YES, THAT'S IT.
SLIDE
HUH..?
TUMBLE
UWAA~
AHA HA HA. ARE YOU OKAY?
GEEZE MISAKI...
YOU SHOULDN'T HAVE THESE BOXES STACKED SO HIGH LIKE THAT.

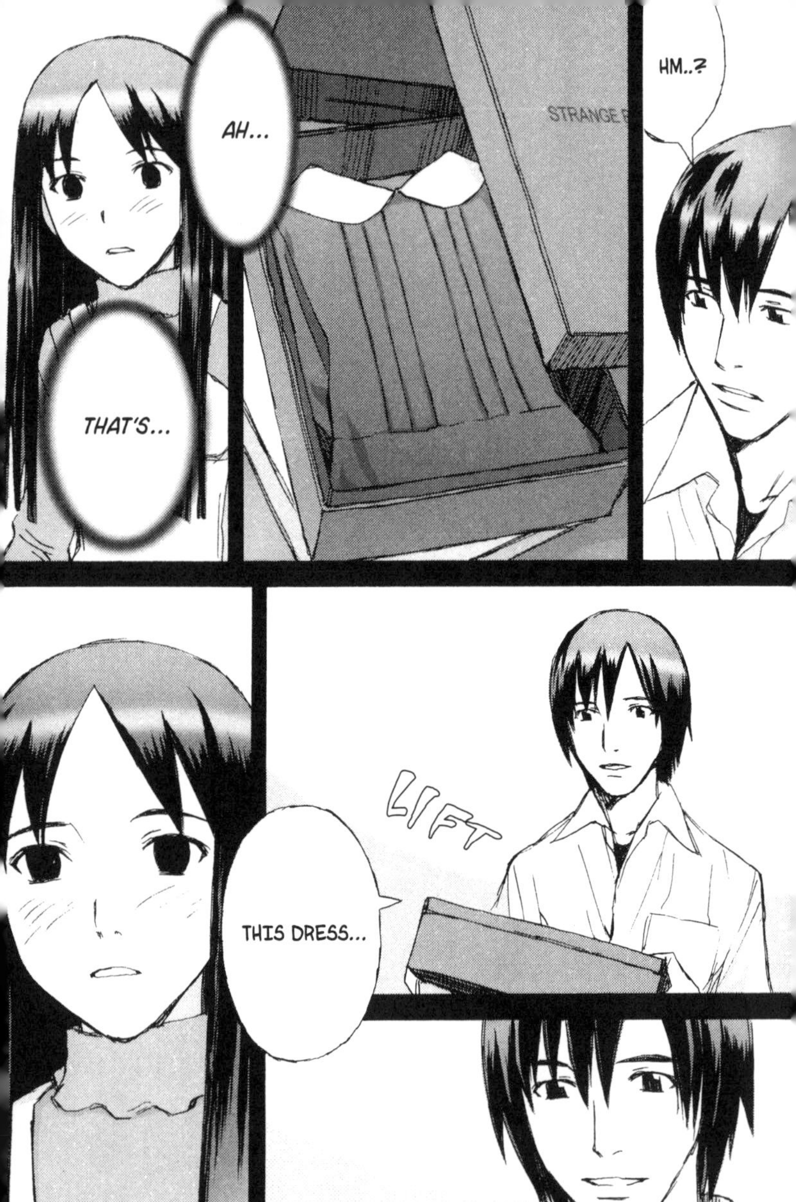
HM..?
STRANGE F
AH...
THAT'S...
LIFT
THIS DRESS...

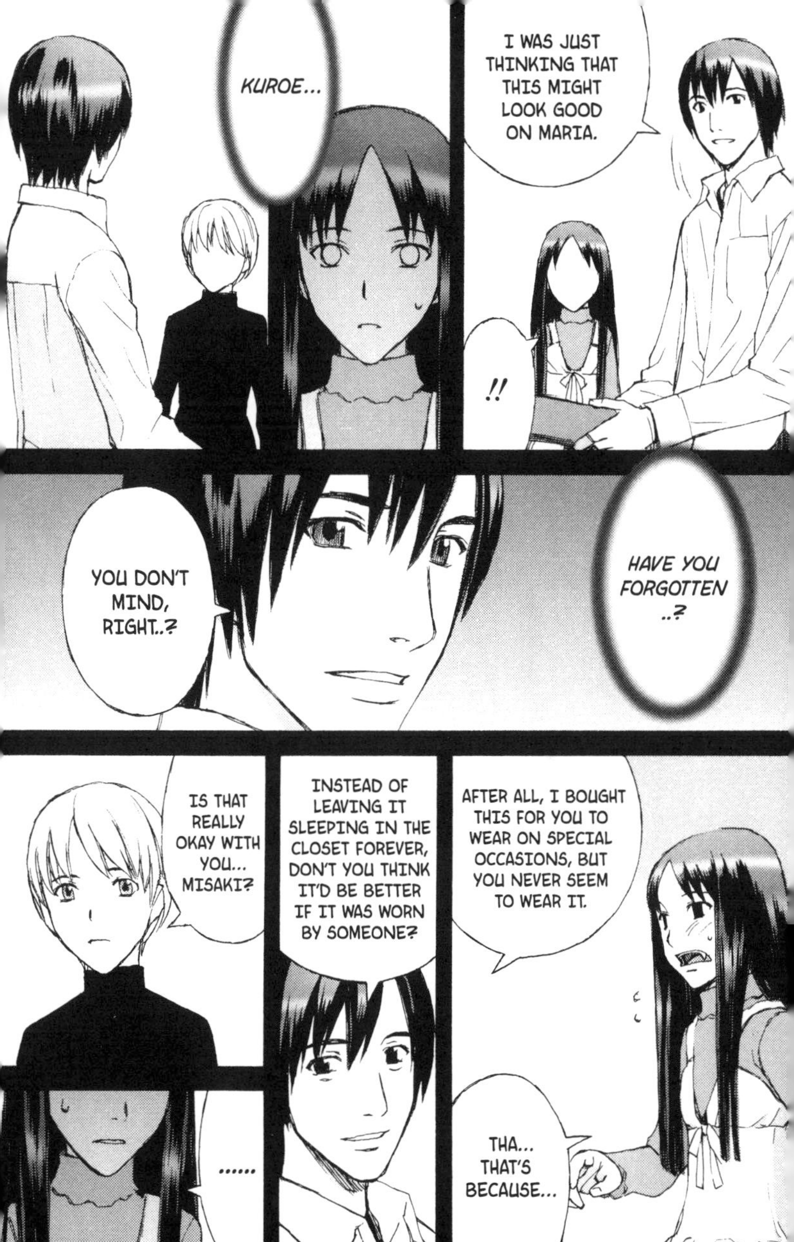
I WAS JUST THINKING THAT THIS MIGHT LOOK GOOD ON MARIA.
!!
KUROE...
HAVE YOU FORGOTTEN ..?
YOU DON'T MIND, RIGHT..?
AFTER ALL, I BOUGHT THIS FOR YOU TO WEAR ON SPECIAL OCCASIONS, BUT YOU NEVER SEEM TO WEAR IT.
THA... THAT'S BECAUSE...
INSTEAD OF LEAVING IT SLEEPING IN THE CLOSET FOREVER, DON'T YOU THINK IT'D BE BETTER IF IT WAS WORN BY SOMEONE?
IS THAT REALLY OKAY WITH YOU... MISAKI?
......

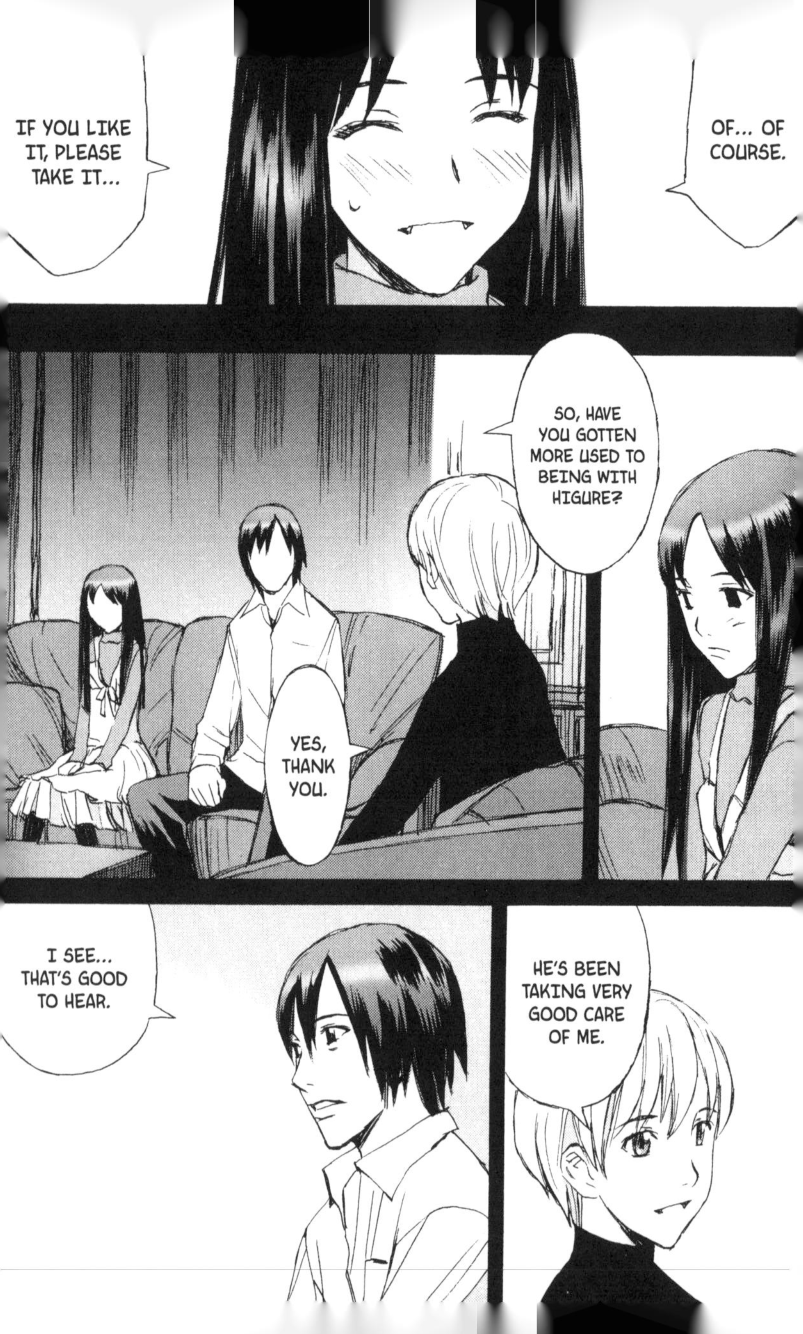
OF... OF COURSE.
IF YOU LIKE IT, PLEASE TAKE IT...
SO, HAVE YOU GOTTEN MORE USED TO BEING WITH HIGURE?
YES, THANK YOU.
HE'S BEEN TAKING VERY GOOD CARE OF ME.
I SEE... THAT'S GOOD TO HEAR.

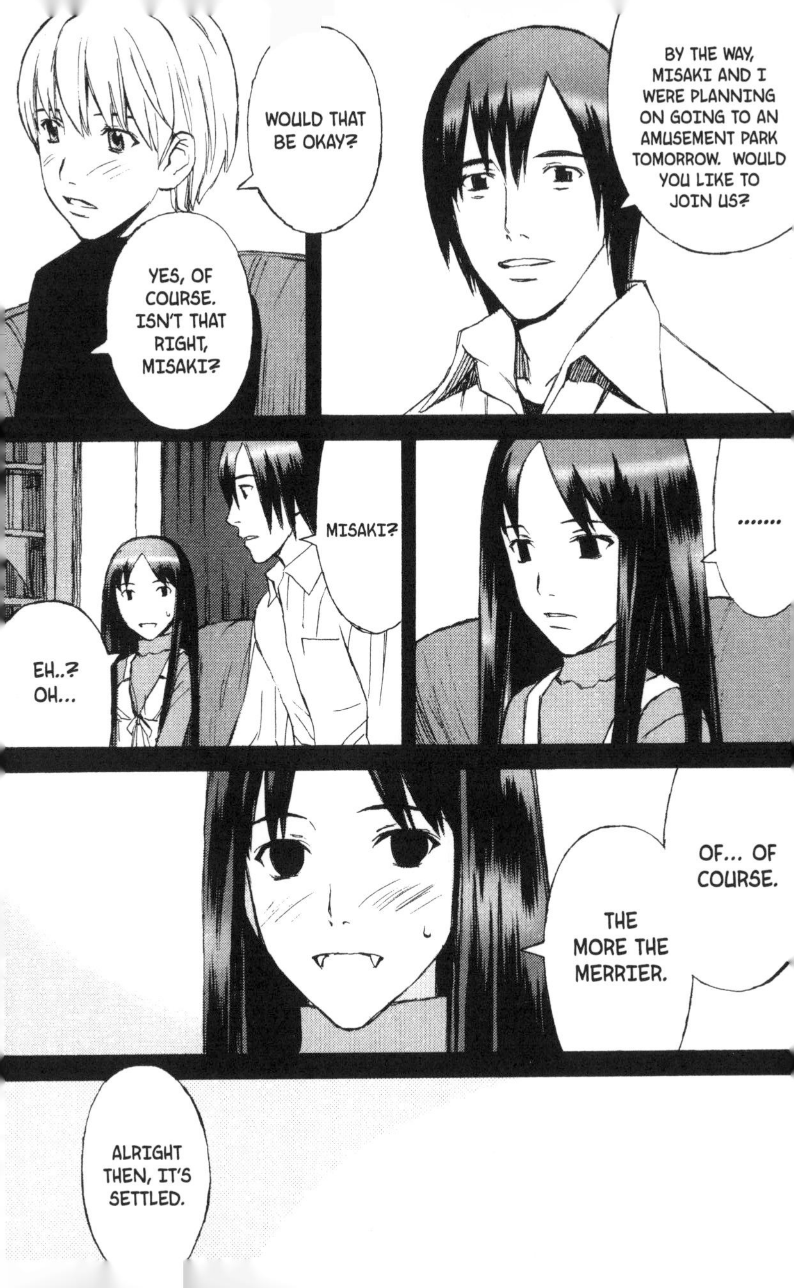
BY THE WAY, MISAKI AND I WERE PLANNING ON GOING TO AN AMUSEMENT PARK TOMORROW. WOULD YOU LIKE TO JOIN US?
WOULD THAT BE OKAY?
YES, OF COURSE. ISN'T THAT RIGHT, MISAKI?
....
MISAKI?
EH..? OH...
OF... OF COURSE.
THE MORE THE MERRIER.
ALRIGHT THEN, IT'S SETTLED.

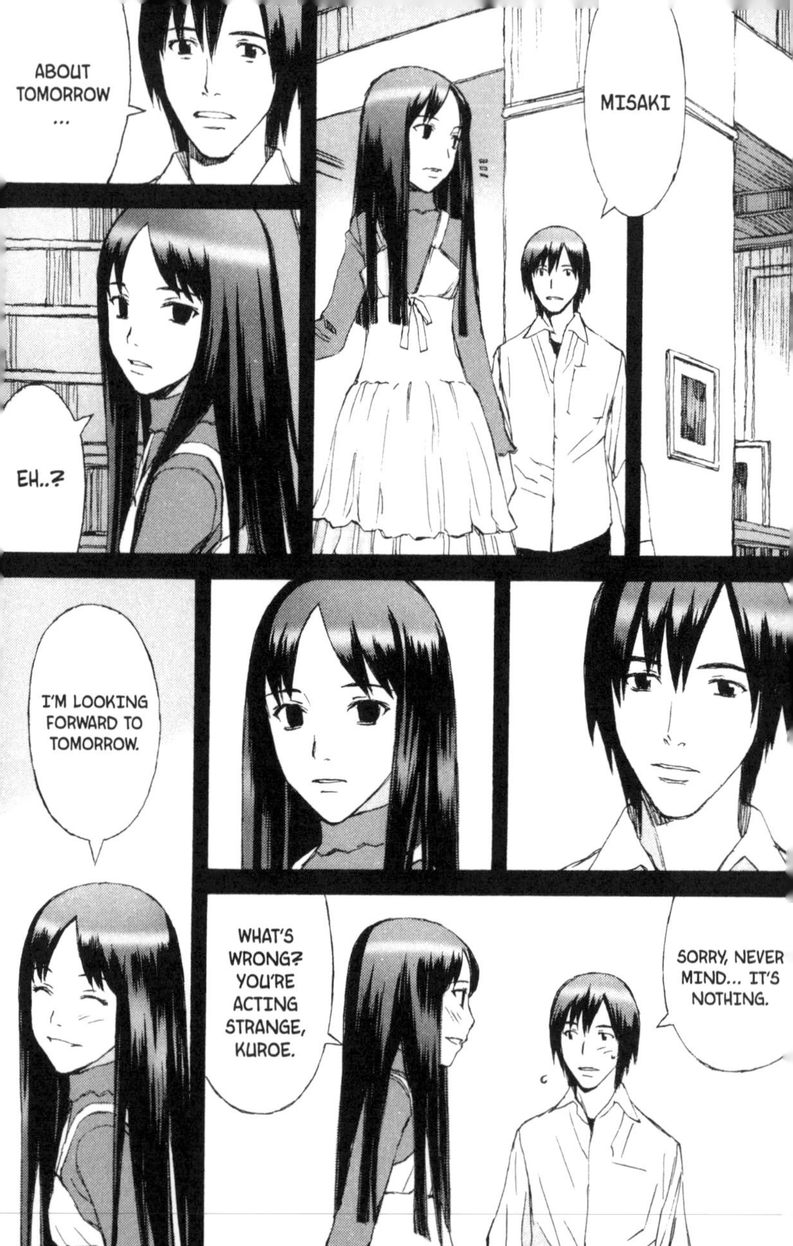
MISAKI
ABOUT TOMORROW ...
EH..?
SORRY, NEVER MIND... IT'S NOTHING.
WHAT'S WRONG? YOU'RE ACTING STRANGE, KUROE.
I'M LOOKING FORWARD TO TOMORROW.

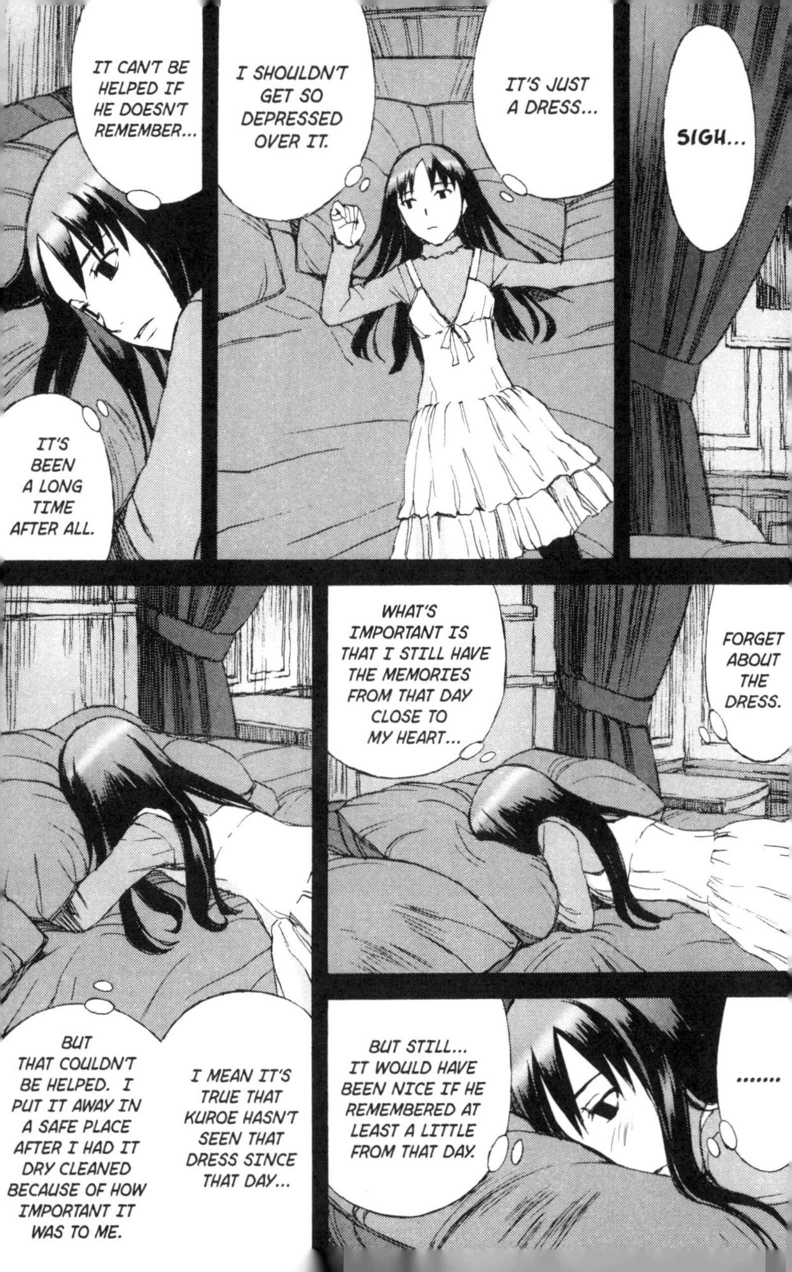
SIGH...
IT'S JUST A DRESS...
I SHOULDN'T GET SO DEPRESSED OVER IT.
IT CAN'T BE HELPED IF HE DOESN'T REMEMBER...
IT'S BEEN A LONG TIME AFTER ALL.
FORGET ABOUT THE DRESS.
WHAT'S IMPORTANT IS THAT I STILL HAVE THE MEMORIES FROM THAT DAY CLOSE TO MY HEART...
....
BUT STILL... IT WOULD HAVE BEEN NICE IF HE REMEMBERED AT LEAST A LITTLE FROM THAT DAY.
I MEAN IT'S TRUE THAT KUROE HASN'T SEEN THAT DRESS SINCE THAT DAY...
BUT THAT COULDN'T BE HELPED. I PUT IT AWAY IN A SAFE PLACE AFTER I HAD IT DRY CLEANED BECAUSE OF HOW IMPORTANT IT WAS TO ME.

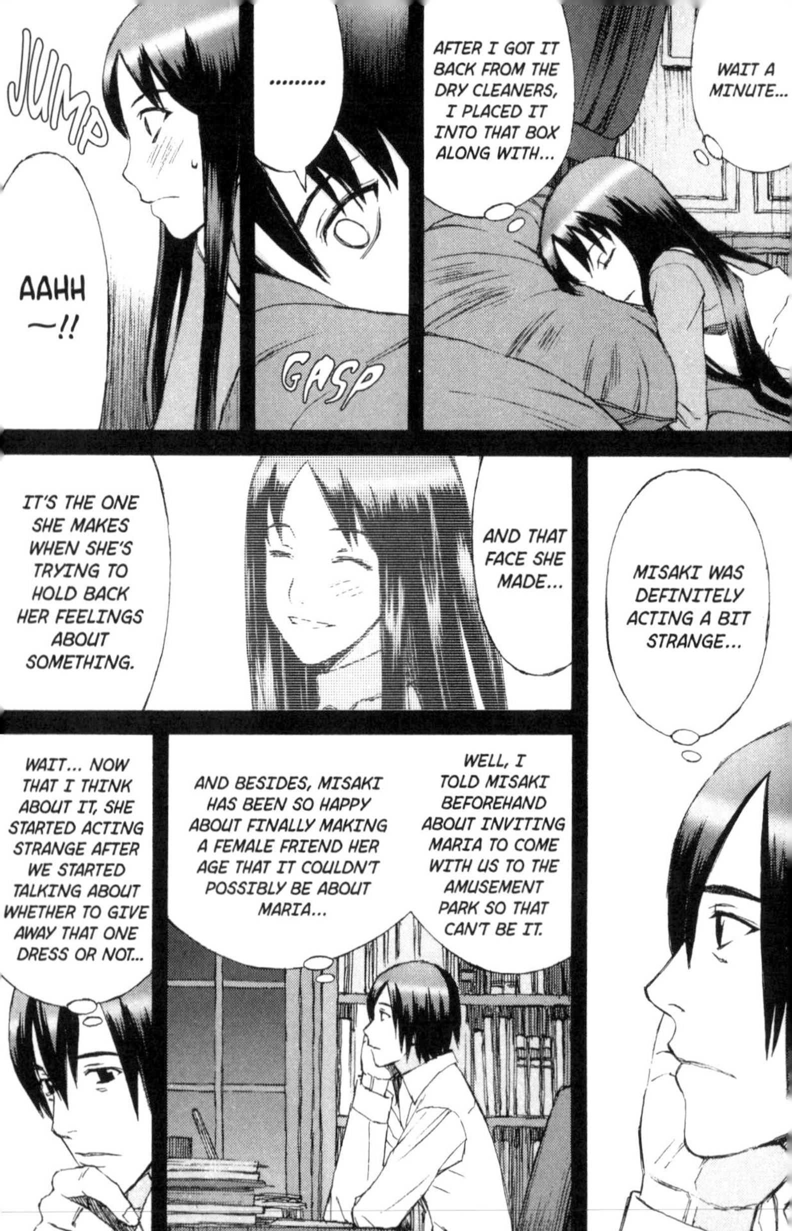
WAIT A MINUTE...
AFTER I GOT IT BACK FROM THE DRY CLEANERS, I PLACED IT INTO THAT BOX ALONG WITH...
....
GASP
JUMP
AAHH ~!!
MISAKI WAS DEFINITELY ACTING A BIT STRANGE...
AND THAT FACE SHE MADE...
IT'S THE ONE SHE MAKES WHEN SHE'S TRYING TO HOLD BACK HER FEELINGS ABOUT SOMETHING.
WELL, I TOLD MISAKI BEFOREHAND ABOUT INVITING MARIA TO COME WITH US TO THE AMUSEMENT PARK SO THAT CAN'T BE IT.
AND BESIDES, MISAKI HAS BEEN SO HAPPY ABOUT FINALLY MAKING A FEMALE FRIEND HER AGE THAT IT COULDN'T POSSIBLY BE ABOUT MARIA...
WAIT... NOW THAT I THINK ABOUT IT, SHE STARTED ACTING STRANGE AFTER WE STARTED TALKING ABOUT WHETHER TO GIVE AWAY THAT ONE DRESS OR NOT...

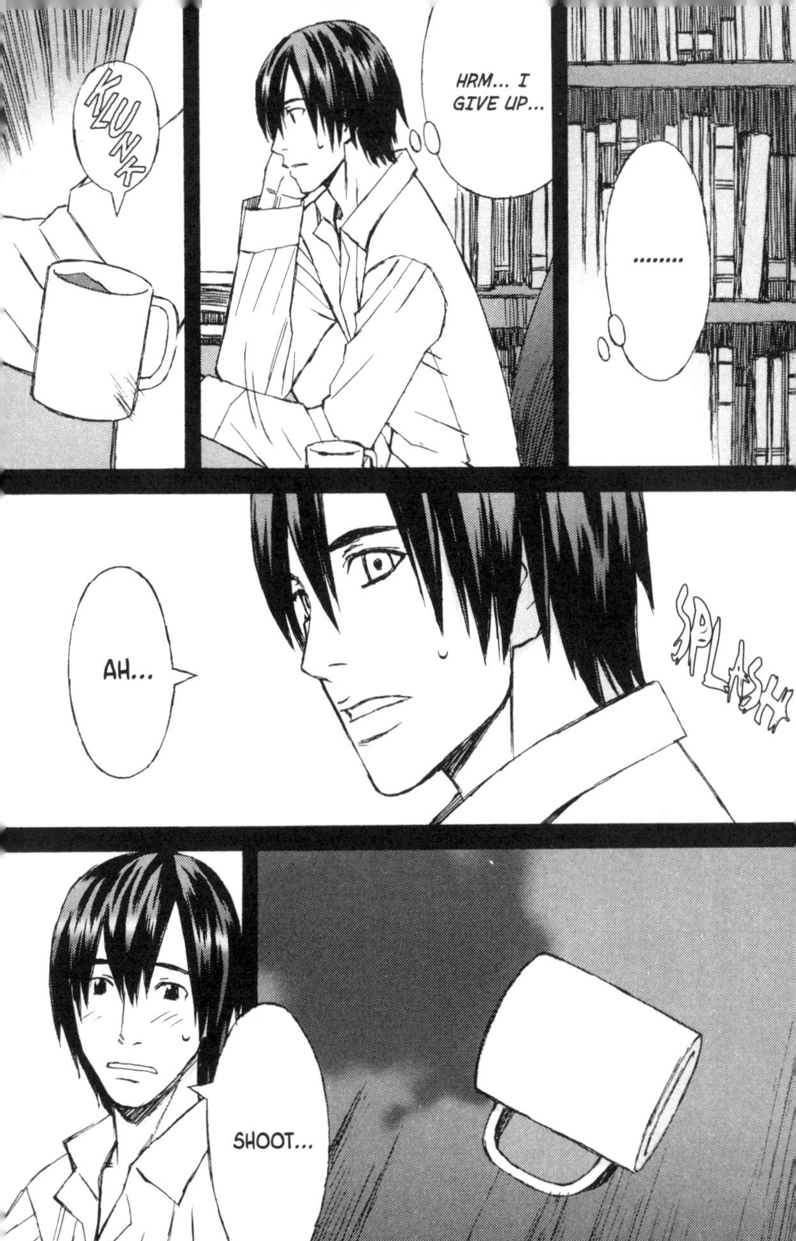
....
HRM... I GIVE UP...
KLUNK
SPLASH
AH...
SHOOT...

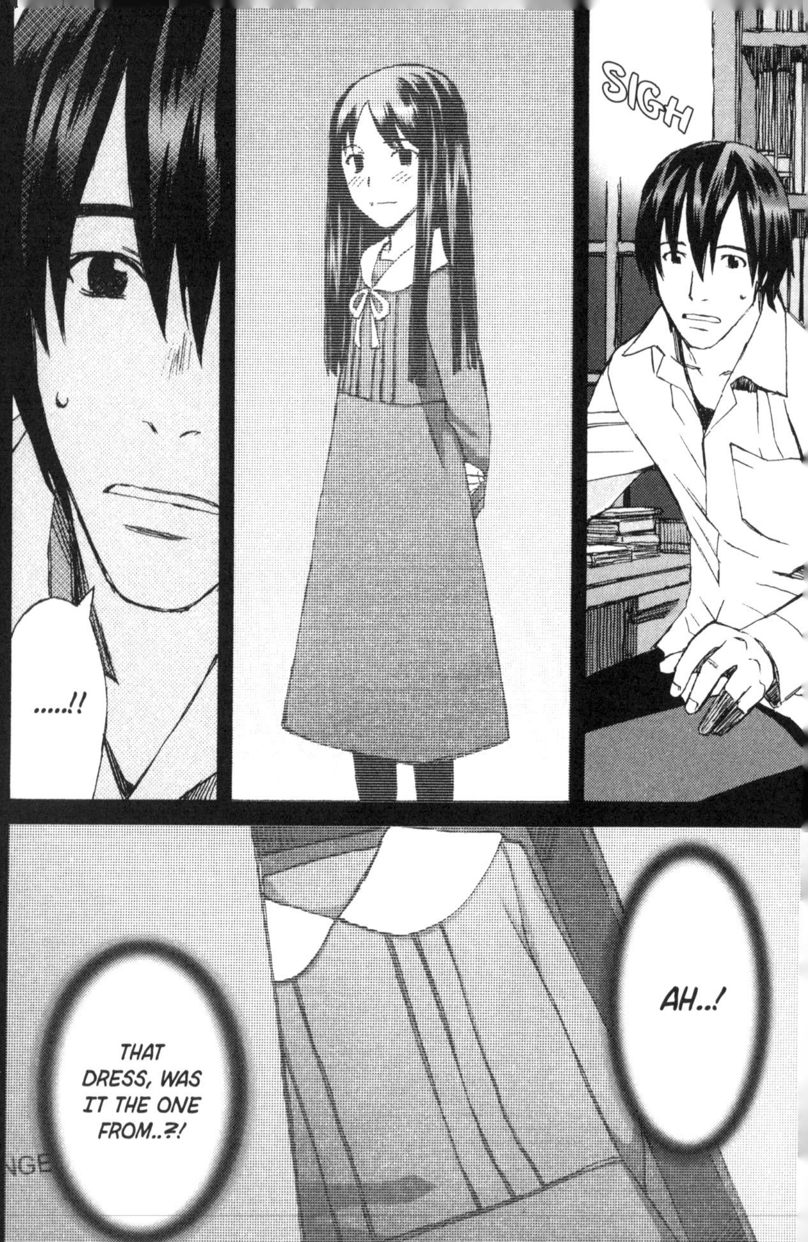
SIGH
......!!
AH..!
THAT DRESS, WAS IT THE ONE FROM..?!

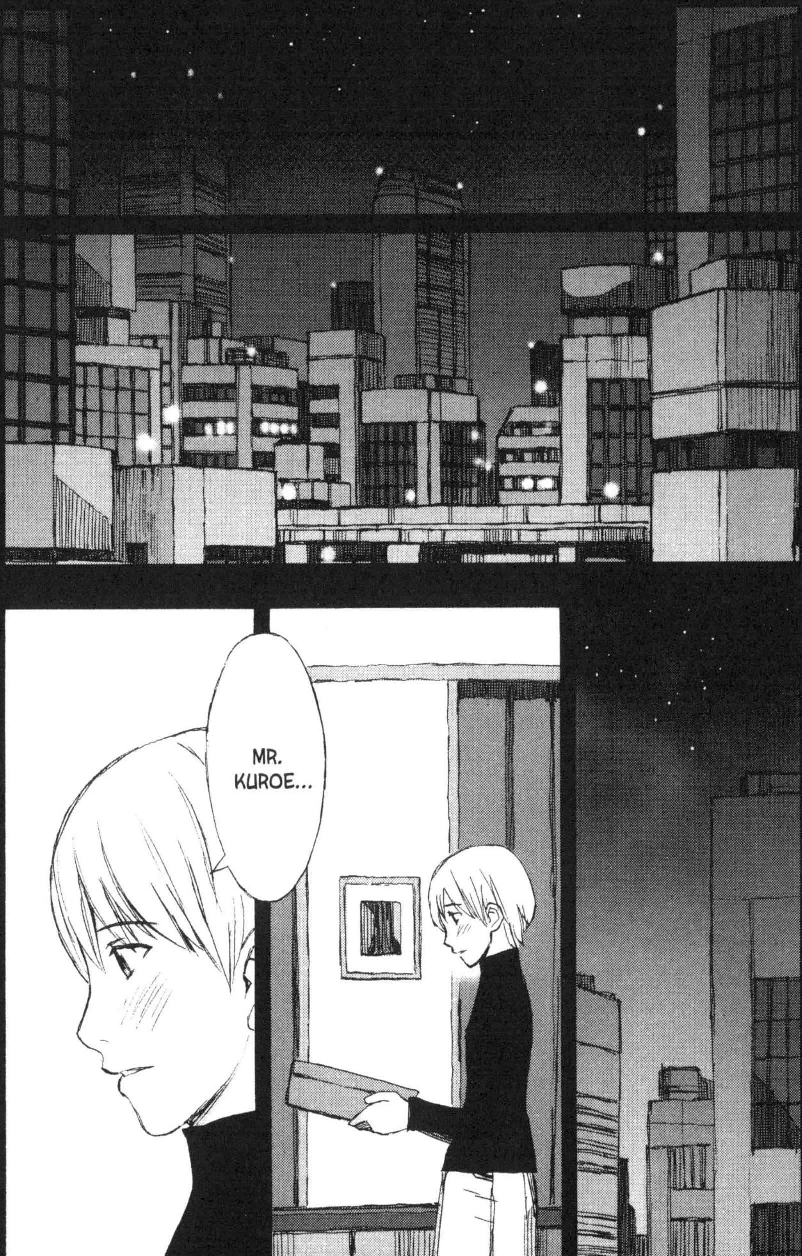
MR. KUROE...

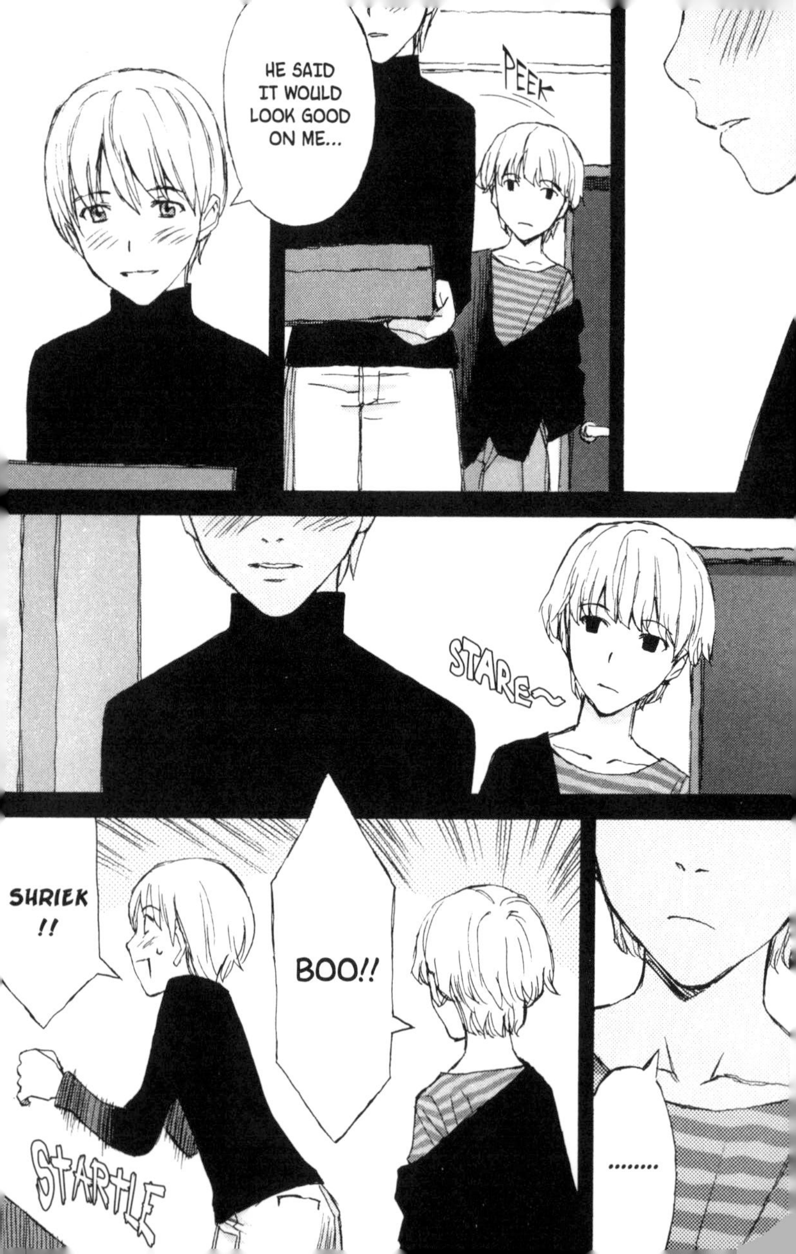

PEEK
HE SAID IT WOULD LOOK GOOD ON ME...
STARE~
....
BOO!!
SHRIEK !!
STARTLE

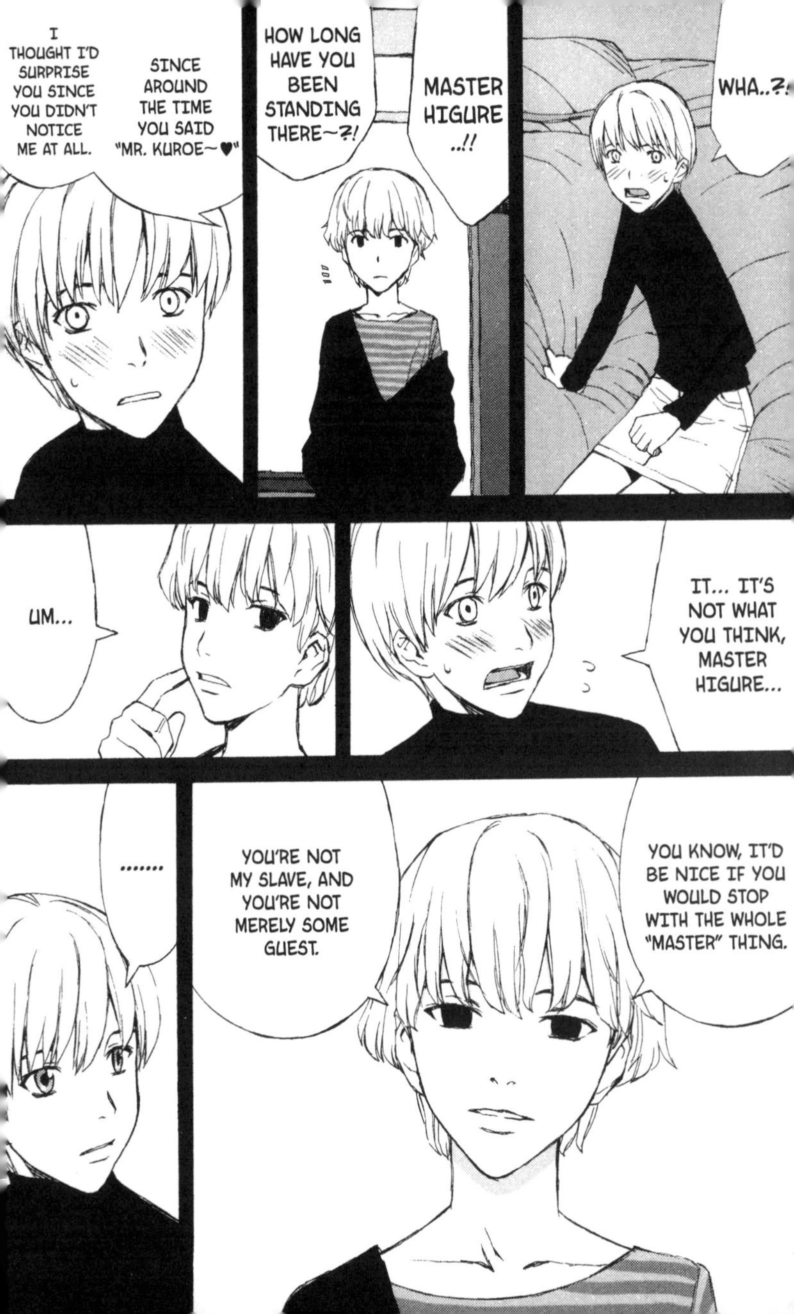
WHA..?!
MASTER HIGURE ..!!
HOW LONG HAVE YOU BEEN STANDING THERE~?!
SINCE AROUND THE TIME YOU SAID "MR. KUROE~♥"
I THOUGHT I'D SURPRISE YOU SINCE YOU DIDN'T NOTICE ME AT ALL.
IT... IT'S NOT WHAT YOU THINK, MASTER HIGURE...
UM...
YOU KNOW, IT'D BE NICE IF YOU WOULD STOP WITH THE WHOLE "MASTER" THING.
YOU'RE NOT MY SLAVE, AND YOU'RE NOT MERELY SOME GUEST.
....

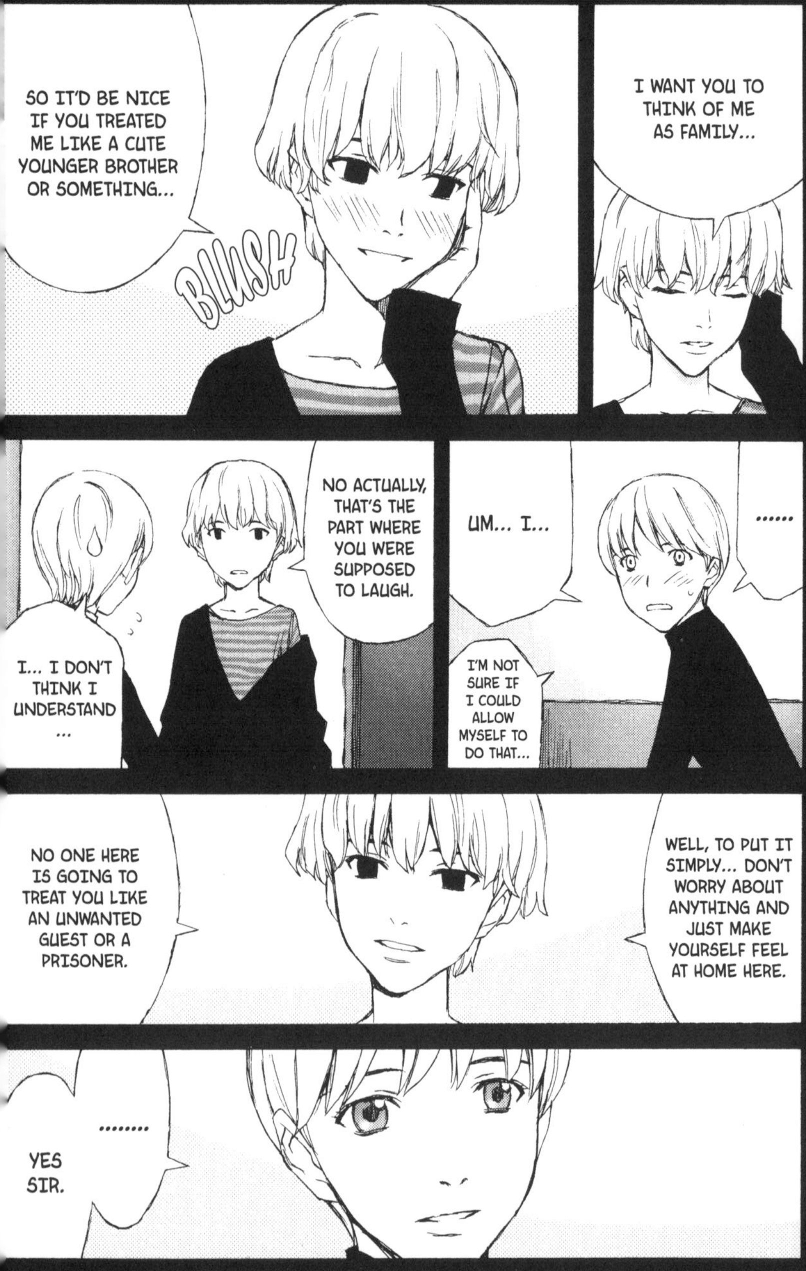
I WANT YOU TO THINK OF ME AS FAMILY...
SO IT'D BE NICE IF YOU TREATED ME LIKE A CUTE YOUNGER BROTHER OR SOMETHING...
BLUSH
......
UM... I...
I'M NOT SURE IF I COULD ALLOW MYSELF TO DO THAT...
NO ACTUALLY, THAT'S THE PART WHERE YOU WERE SUPPOSED TO LAUGH.
I... I DON'T THINK I UNDERSTAND ...
WELL, TO PUT IT SIMPLY... DON'T WORRY ABOUT ANYTHING AND JUST MAKE YOURSELF FEEL AT HOME HERE.
NO ONE HERE IS GOING TO TREAT YOU LIKE AN UNWANTED GUEST OR A PRISONER.
....
YES SIR.

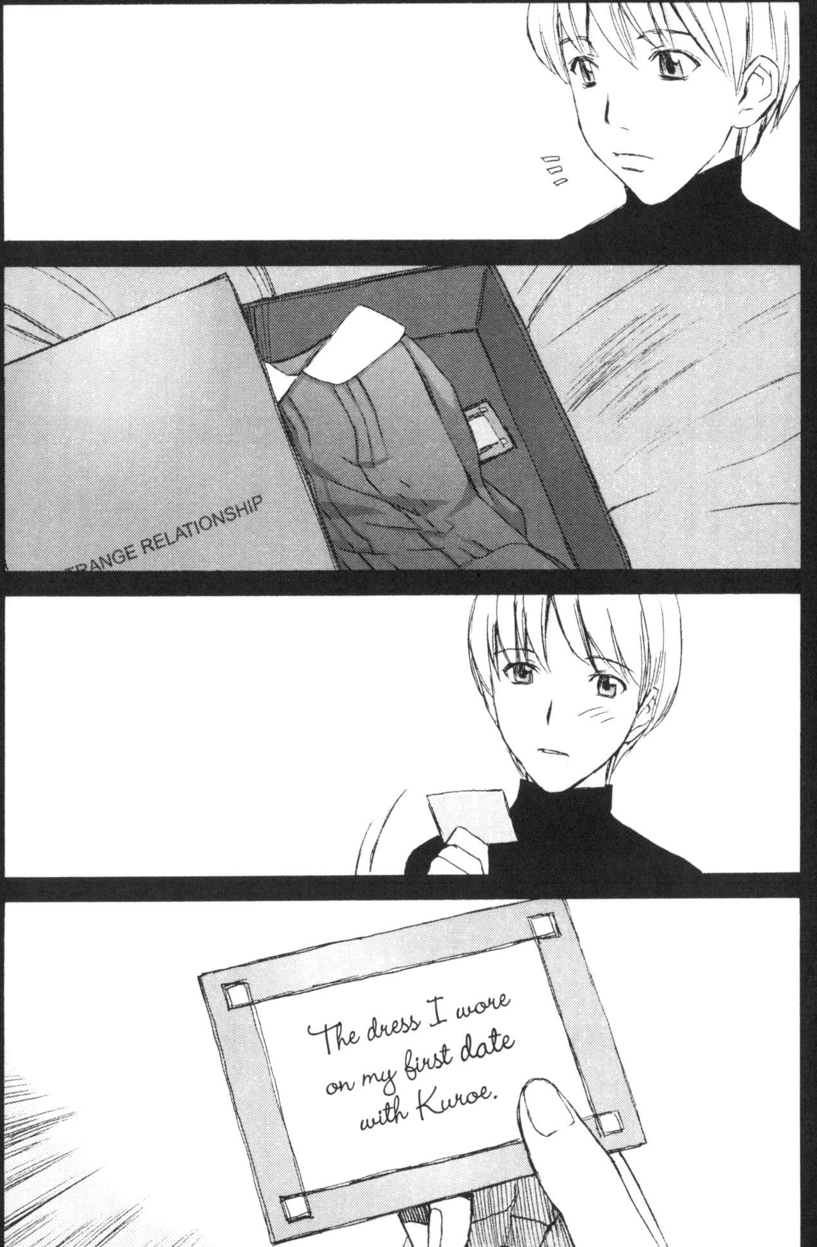

...RANGE RELATIONSHIP
The dress I wore on my first date with Kuroe.

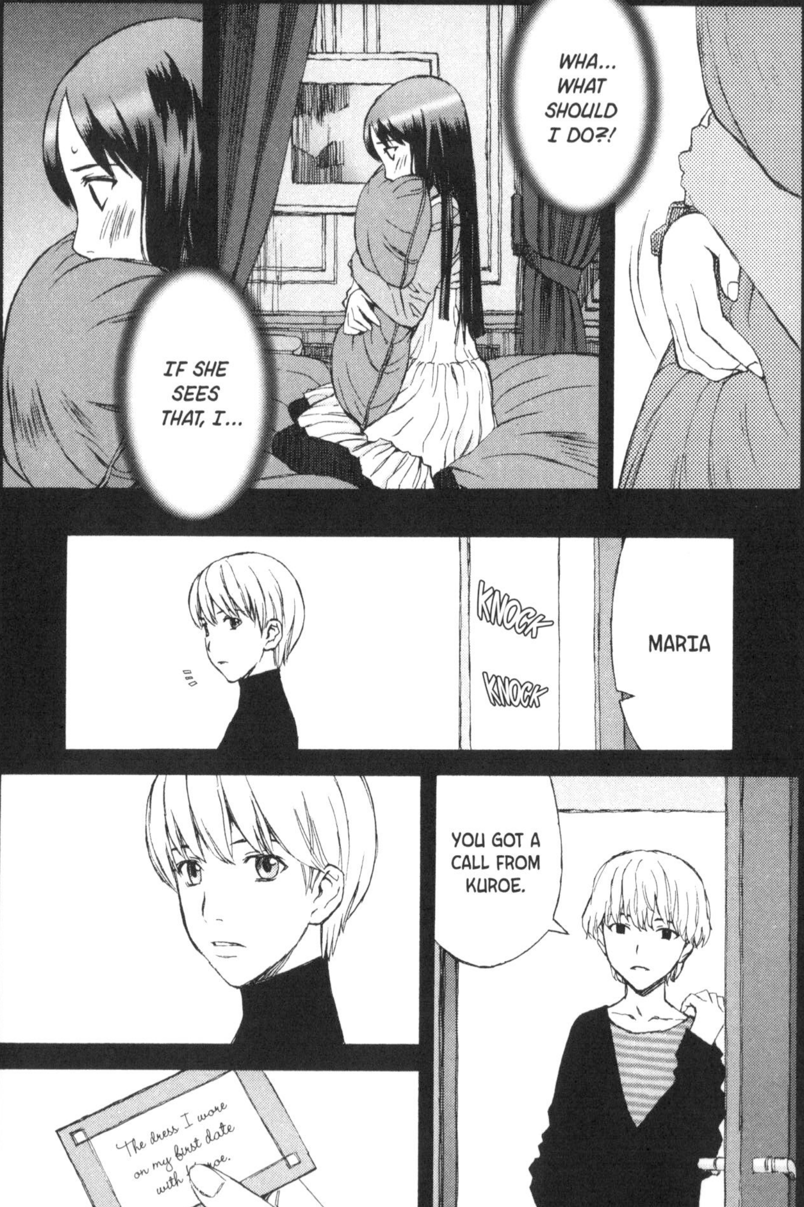
WHA... WHAT SHOULD I DO?!
IF SHE SEES THAT, I...
MARIA
KNOCK
KNOCK
YOU GOT A CALL FROM KUROE.
The dress I wore on my first date with

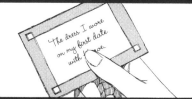

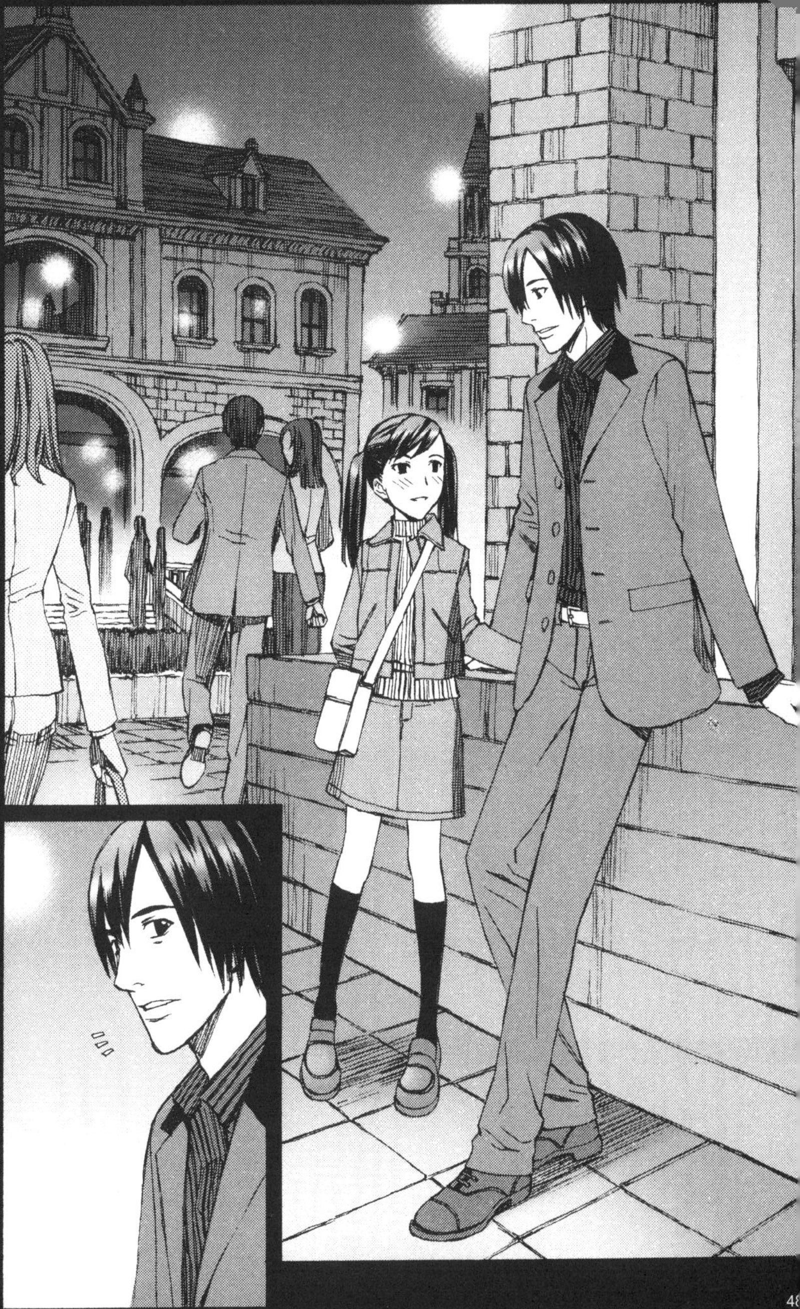

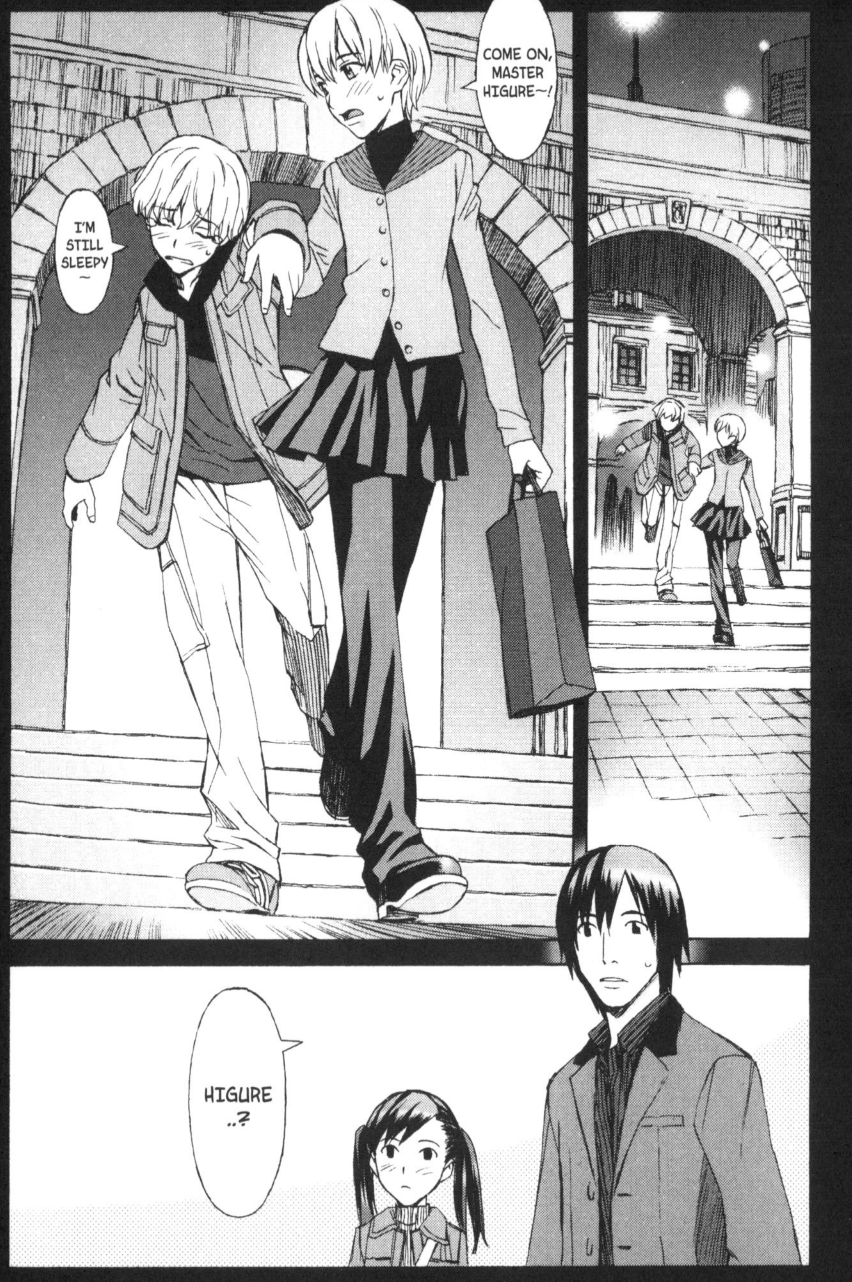
COME ON, MASTER HIGURE~!
I'M STILL SLEEPY ~
HIGURE ..?

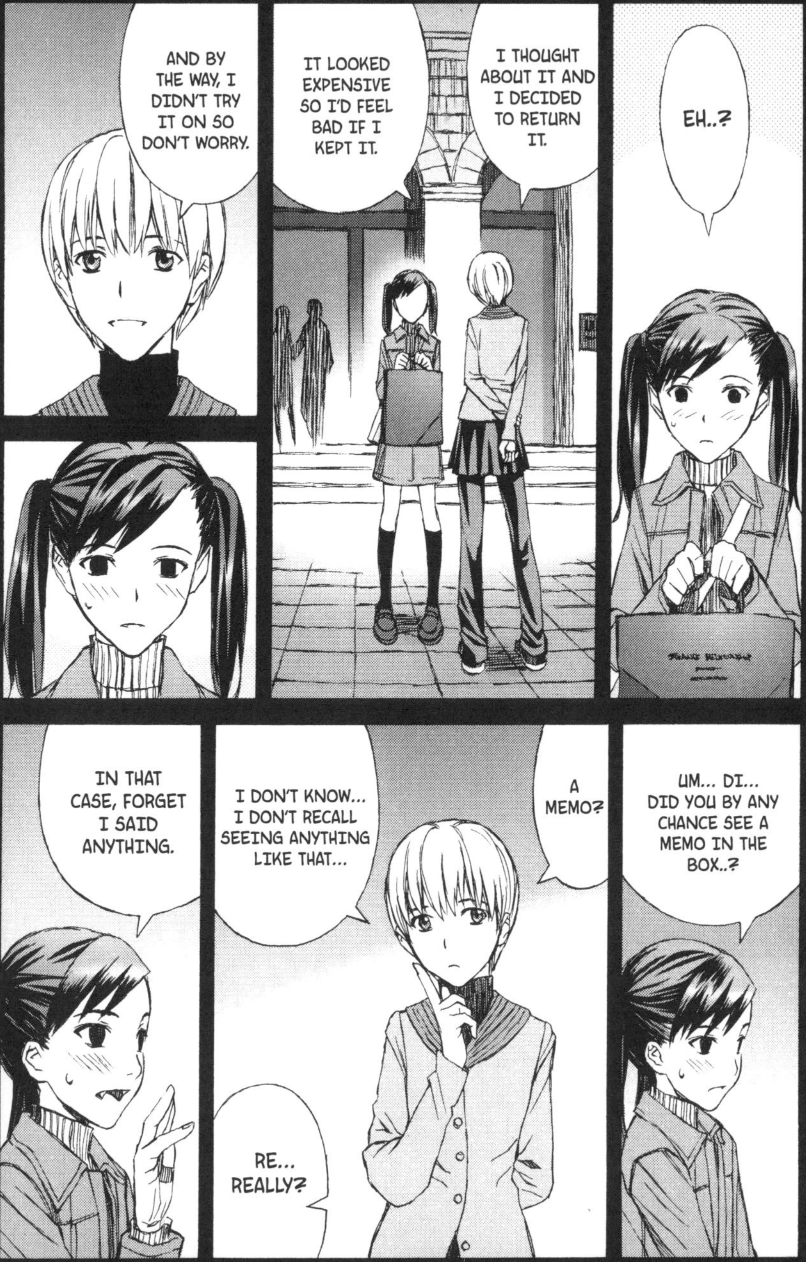
EH..?
I THOUGHT ABOUT IT AND I DECIDED TO RETURN IT.
IT LOOKED EXPENSIVE SO I'D FEEL BAD IF I KEPT IT.
AND BY THE WAY, I DIDN'T TRY IT ON SO DON'T WORRY.
UM... DI... DID YOU BY ANY CHANCE SEE A MEMO IN THE BOX..?
A MEMO?
I DON'T KNOW... I DON'T RECALL SEEING ANYTHING LIKE THAT...
RE... REALLY?
IN THAT CASE, FORGET I SAID ANYTHING.

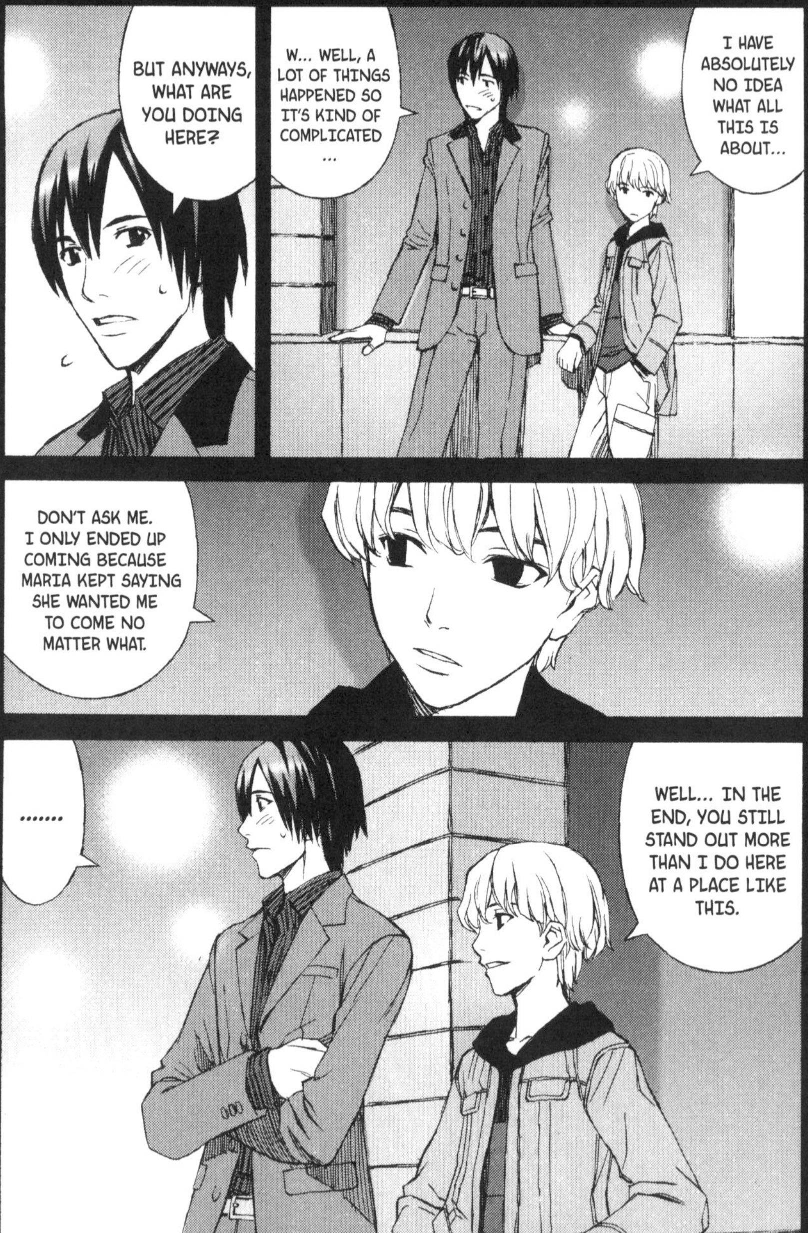
I HAVE ABSOLUTELY NO IDEA WHAT ALL THIS IS ABOUT...
W... WELL, A LOT OF THINGS HAPPENED SO IT'S KIND OF COMPLICATED ...
BUT ANYWAYS, WHAT ARE YOU DOING HERE?
DON'T ASK ME. I ONLY ENDED UP COMING BECAUSE MARIA KEPT SAYING SHE WANTED ME TO COME NO MATTER WHAT.
WELL... IN THE END, YOU STILL STAND OUT MORE THAN I DO HERE AT A PLACE LIKE THIS.
....

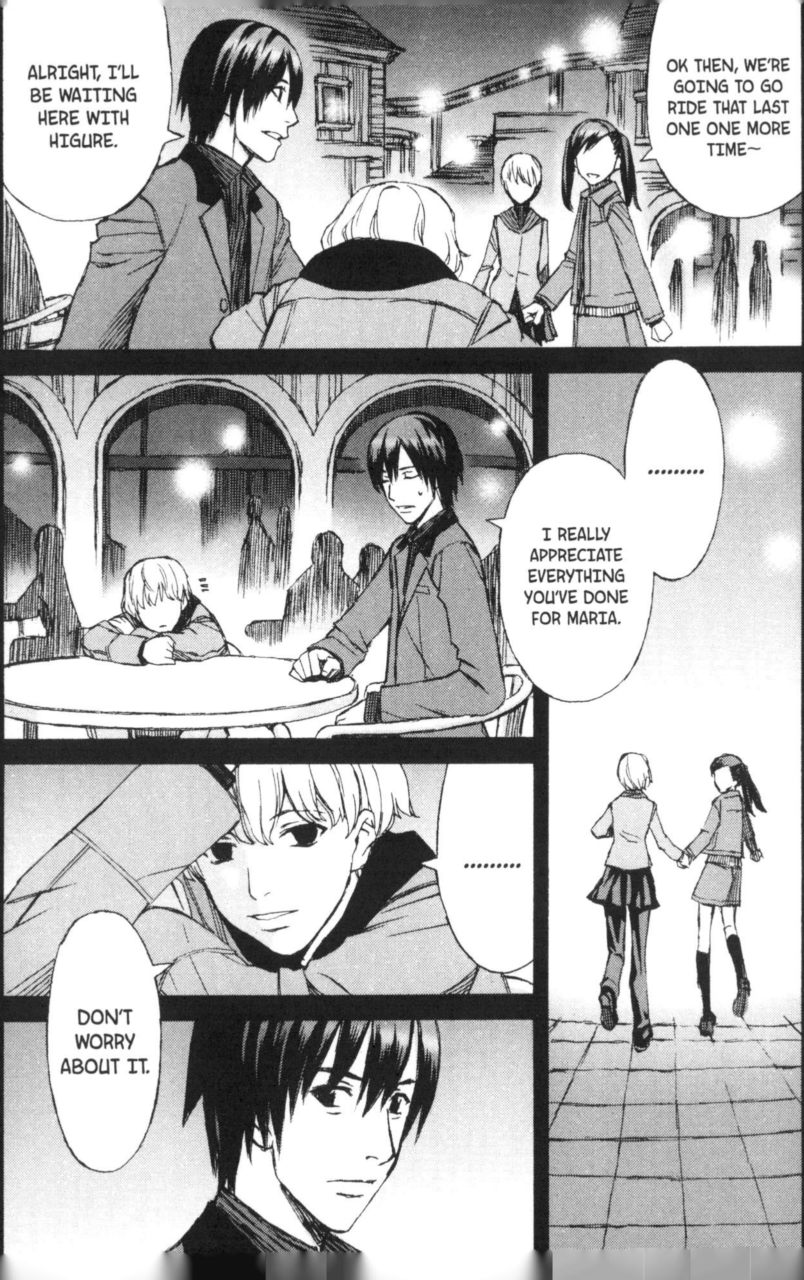
OK THEN, WE'RE GOING TO GO RIDE THAT LAST ONE ONE MORE TIME~
ALRIGHT, I'LL BE WAITING HERE WITH HIGURE.
....
I REALLY APPRECIATE EVERYTHING YOU'VE DONE FOR MARIA.
....
DON'T WORRY ABOUT IT.

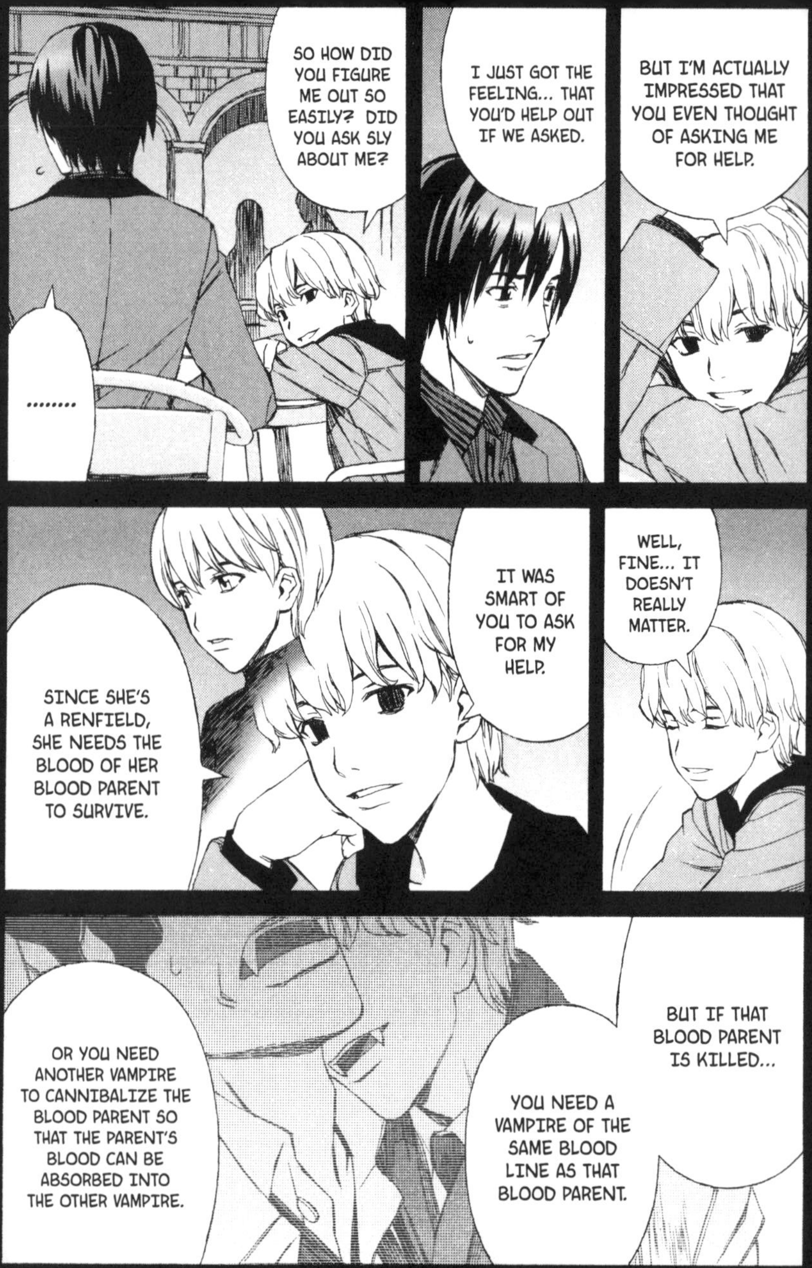
BUT I'M ACTUALLY IMPRESSED THAT YOU EVEN THOUGHT OF ASKING ME FOR HELP.
I JUST GOT THE FEELING... THAT YOU'D HELP OUT IF WE ASKED.
SO HOW DID YOU FIGURE ME OUT SO EASILY? DID YOU ASK SLY ABOUT ME?
....
WELL, FINE... IT DOESN'T REALLY MATTER.
IT WAS SMART OF YOU TO ASK FOR MY HELP.
SINCE SHE'S A RENFIELD, SHE NEEDS THE BLOOD OF HER BLOOD PARENT TO SURVIVE.
BUT IF THAT BLOOD PARENT IS KILLED...
YOU NEED A VAMPIRE OF THE SAME BLOOD LINE AS THAT BLOOD PARENT.
OR YOU NEED ANOTHER VAMPIRE TO CANNIBALIZE THE BLOOD PARENT SO THAT THE PARENT'S BLOOD CAN BE ABSORBED INTO THE OTHER VAMPIRE.

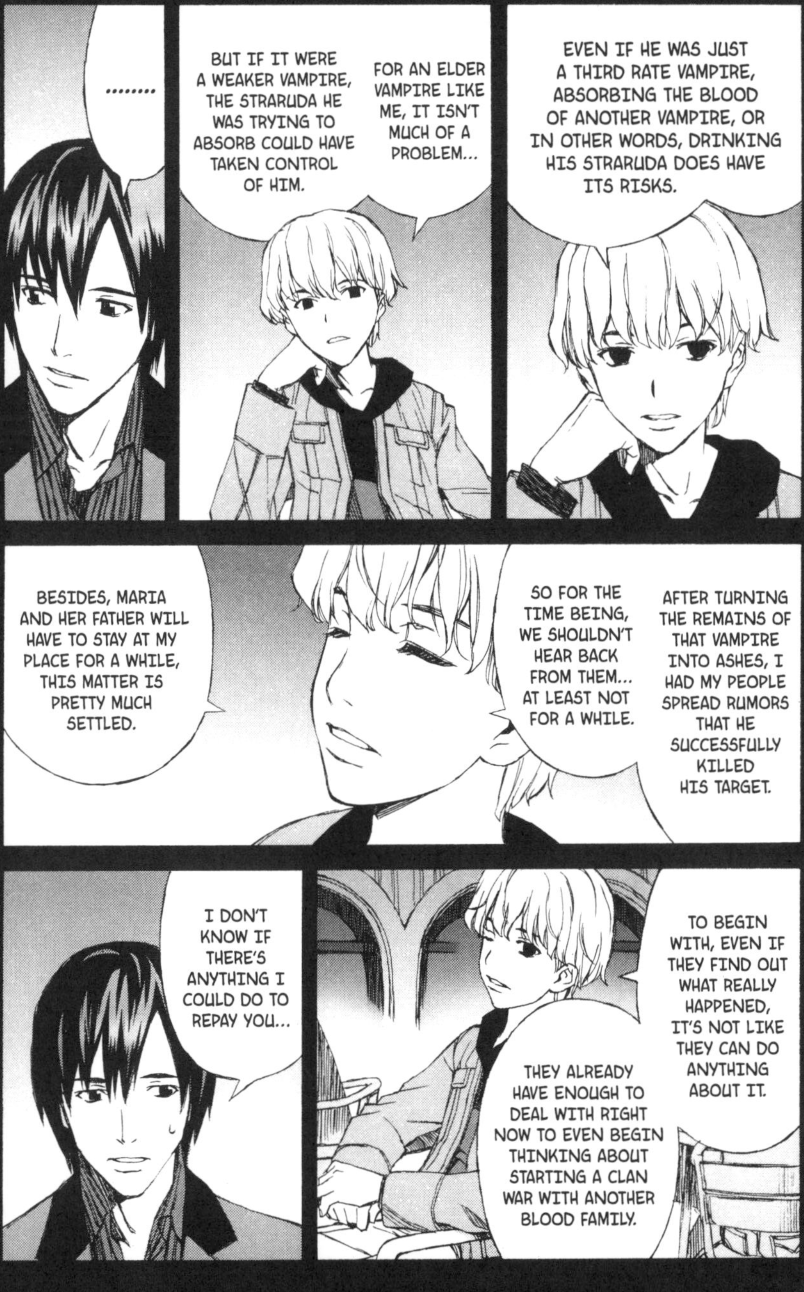
EVEN IF HE WAS JUST A THIRD RATE VAMPIRE, ABSORBING THE BLOOD OF ANOTHER VAMPIRE, OR IN OTHER WORDS, DRINKING HIS STRARUDA DOES HAVE ITS RISKS.
FOR AN ELDER VAMPIRE LIKE ME, IT ISN'T MUCH OF A PROBLEM...
BUT IF IT WERE A WEAKER VAMPIRE, THE STRARUDA HE WAS TRYING TO ABSORB COULD HAVE TAKEN CONTROL OF HIM.
....
AFTER TURNING THE REMAINS OF THAT VAMPIRE INTO ASHES, I HAD MY PEOPLE SPREAD RUMORS THAT HE SUCCESSFULLY KILLED HIS TARGET.
SO FOR THE TIME BEING, WE SHOULDN'T HEAR BACK FROM THEM... AT LEAST NOT FOR A WHILE.
BESIDES, MARIA AND HER FATHER WILL HAVE TO STAY AT MY PLACE FOR A WHILE, THIS MATTER IS PRETTY MUCH SETTLED.
TO BEGIN WITH, EVEN IF THEY FIND OUT WHAT REALLY HAPPENED, IT'S NOT LIKE THEY CAN DO ANYTHING ABOUT IT.
THEY ALREADY HAVE ENOUGH TO DEAL WITH RIGHT NOW TO EVEN BEGIN THINKING ABOUT STARTING A CLAN WAR WITH ANOTHER BLOOD FAMILY.
I DON'T KNOW IF THERE'S ANYTHING I COULD DO TO REPAY YOU...

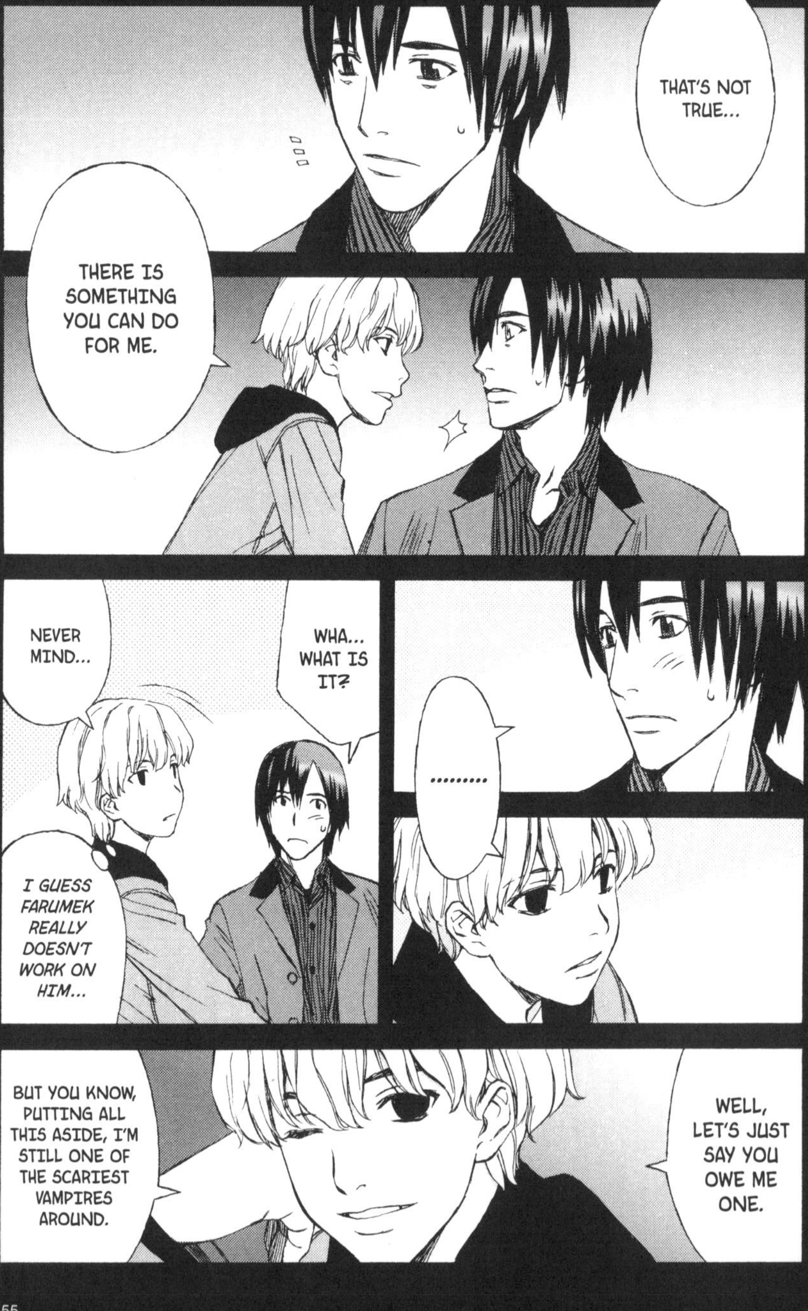
THAT'S NOT TRUE...
THERE IS SOMETHING YOU CAN DO FOR ME.
....
WHA... WHAT IS IT?
NEVER MIND...
I GUESS FARUMEK REALLY DOESN'T WORK ON HIM...
WELL, LET'S JUST SAY YOU OWE ME ONE.
BUT YOU KNOW, PUTTING ALL THIS ASIDE, I'M STILL ONE OF THE SCARIEST VAMPIRES AROUND.

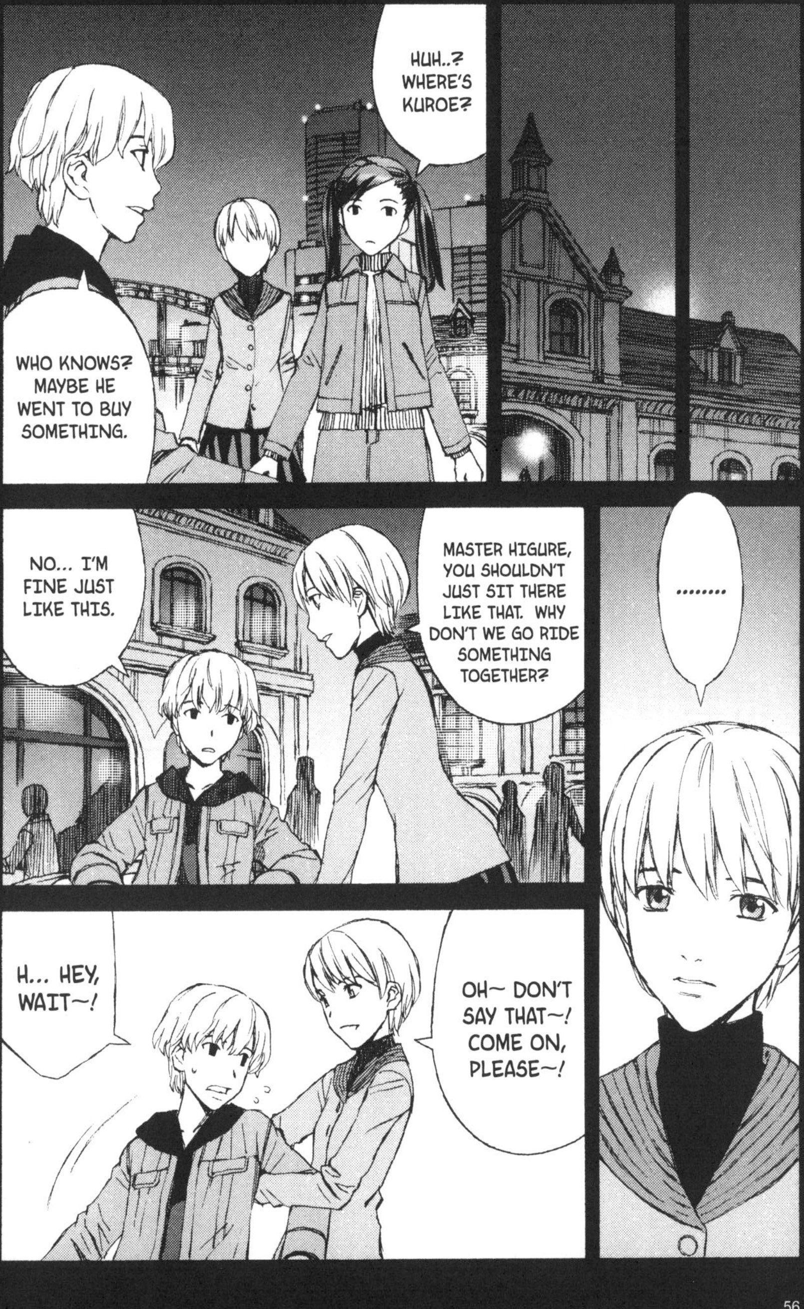
HUH..? WHERE'S KUROE?
WHO KNOWS? MAYBE HE WENT TO BUY SOMETHING.
MASTER HIGURE, YOU SHOULDN'T JUST SIT THERE LIKE THAT. WHY DON'T WE GO RIDE SOMETHING TOGETHER?
NO... I'M FINE JUST LIKE THIS.
OH~ DON'T SAY THAT~! COME ON, PLEASE~!
H... HEY, WAIT~!
....

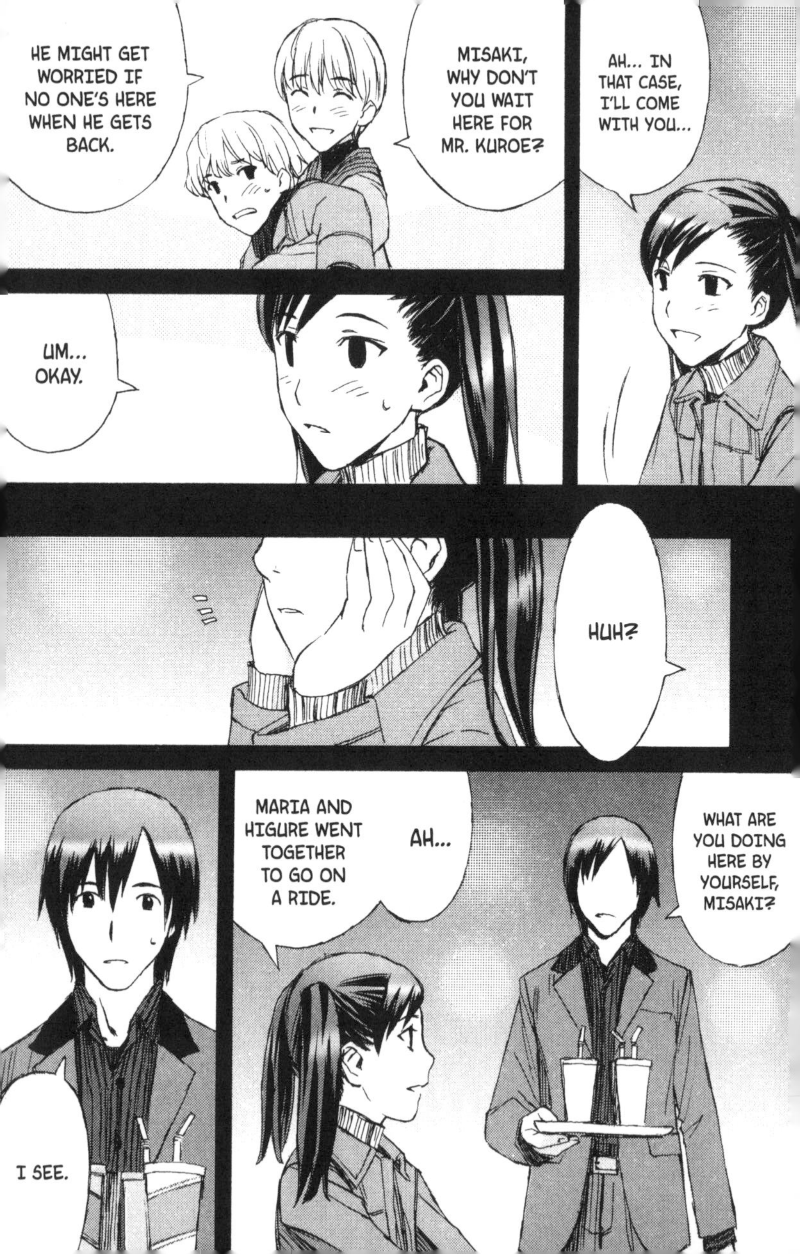
AH... IN THAT CASE, I'LL COME WITH YOU...
MISAKI, WHY DON'T YOU WAIT HERE FOR MR. KUROE?
HE MIGHT GET WORRIED IF NO ONE'S HERE WHEN HE GETS BACK.
UM... OKAY.
HUH?
WHAT ARE YOU DOING HERE BY YOURSELF, MISAKI?
AH...
MARIA AND HIGURE WENT TOGETHER TO GO ON A RIDE.
I SEE.

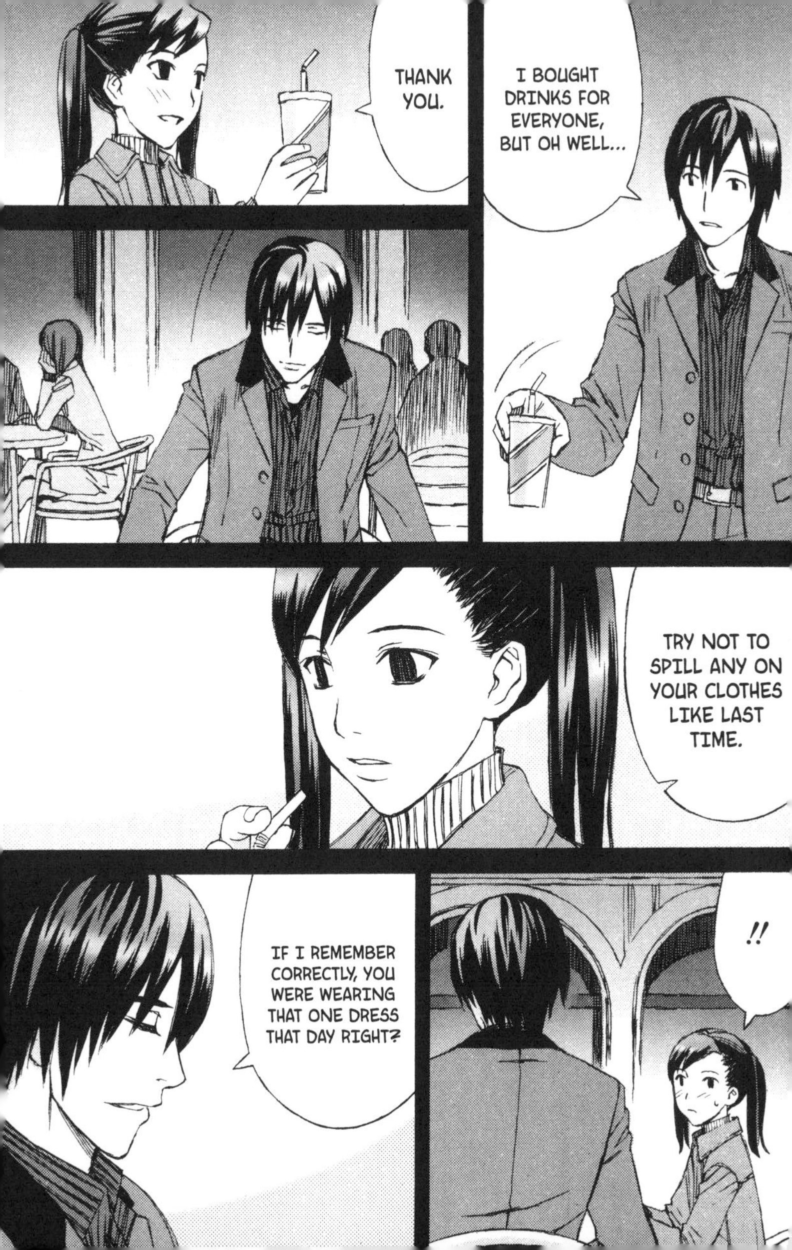
I BOUGHT DRINKS FOR EVERYONE, BUT OH WELL...
THANK YOU.
TRY NOT TO SPILL ANY ON YOUR CLOTHES LIKE LAST TIME.
!!
IF I REMEMBER CORRECTLY, YOU WERE WEARING THAT ONE DRESS THAT DAY RIGHT?

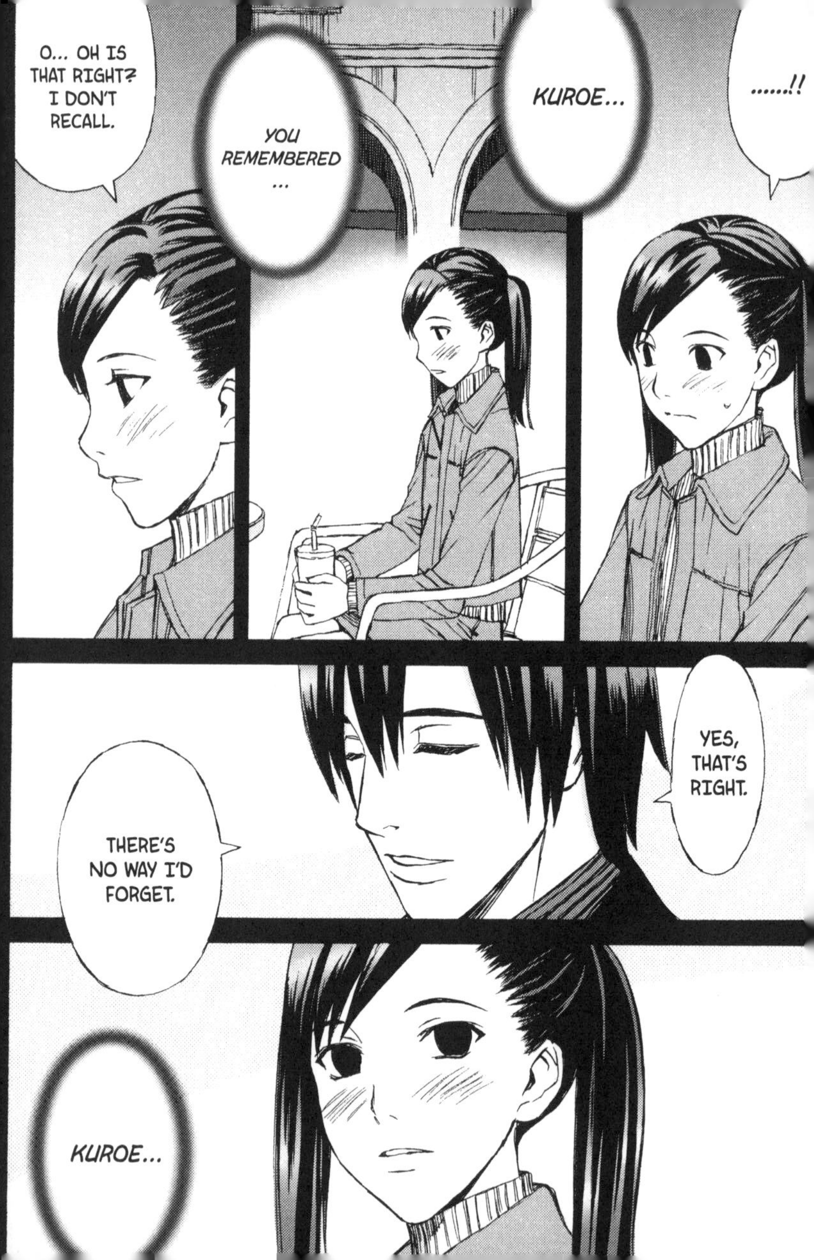
......!!
KUROE...
YOU REMEMBERED ...
O... OH IS THAT RIGHT? I DON'T RECALL.
YES, THAT'S RIGHT.
THERE'S NO WAY I'D FORGET.
KUROE...

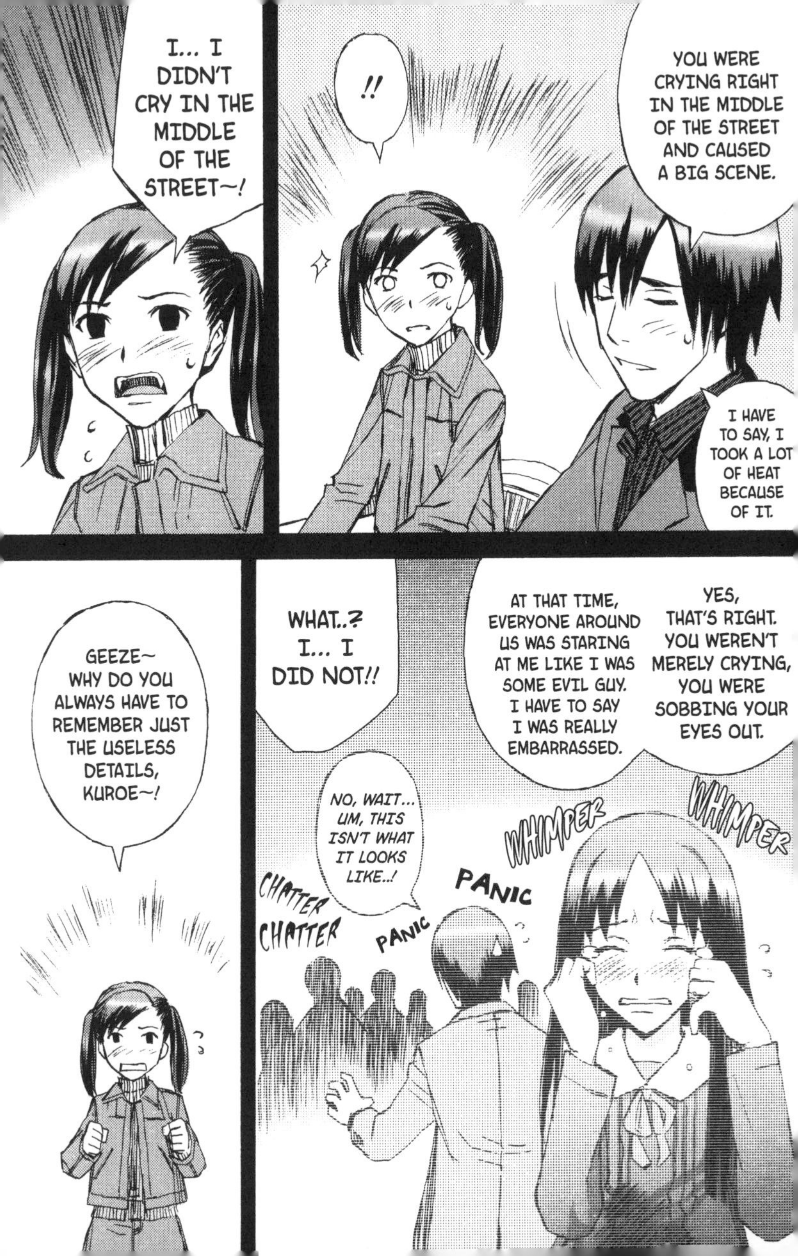
YOU WERE CRYING RIGHT IN THE MIDDLE OF THE STREET AND CAUSED A BIG SCENE.
!!
I HAVE TO SAY, I TOOK A LOT OF HEAT BECAUSE OF IT.
I... I DIDN'T CRY IN THE MIDDLE OF THE STREET~!
YES, THAT'S RIGHT. YOU WEREN'T MERELY CRYING, YOU WERE SOBBING YOUR EYES OUT.
AT THAT TIME, EVERYONE AROUND US WAS STARING AT ME LIKE I WAS SOME EVIL GUY. I HAVE TO SAY I WAS REALLY EMBARRASSED.
WHAT..?
I... I DID NOT!!
WHIMPER
WHIMPER
PANIC
PANIC
NO, WAIT... UM, THIS ISN'T WHAT IT LOOKS LIKE..!
CHATTER
CHATTER
GEEZE~ WHY DO YOU ALWAYS HAVE TO REMEMBER JUST THE USELESS DETAILS, KUROE~!

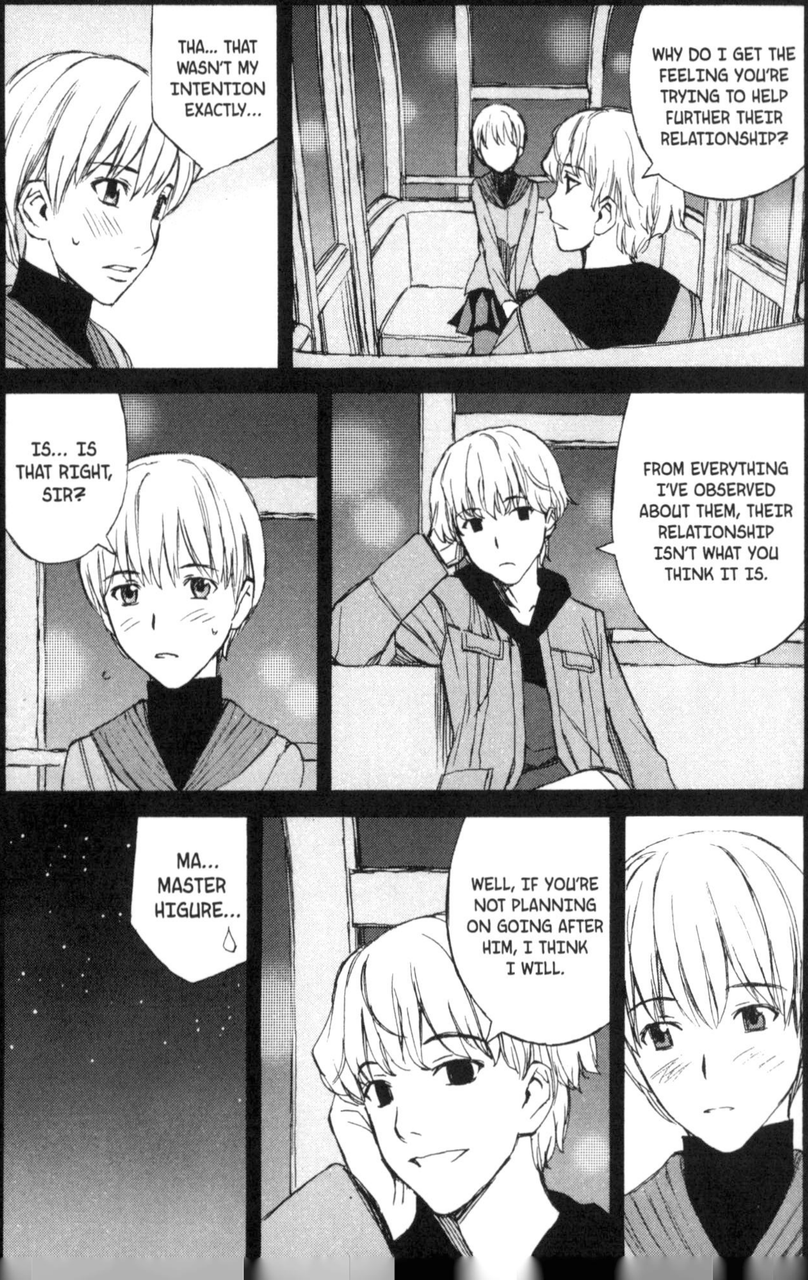
WHY DO I GET THE FEELING YOU'RE TRYING TO HELP FURTHER THEIR RELATIONSHIP?
THA... THAT WASN'T MY INTENTION EXACTLY...
FROM EVERYTHING I'VE OBSERVED ABOUT THEM, THEIR RELATIONSHIP ISN'T WHAT YOU THINK IT IS.
IS... IS THAT RIGHT, SIR?
WELL, IF YOU'RE NOT PLANNING ON GOING AFTER HIM, I THINK I WILL.
MA... MASTER HIGURE...

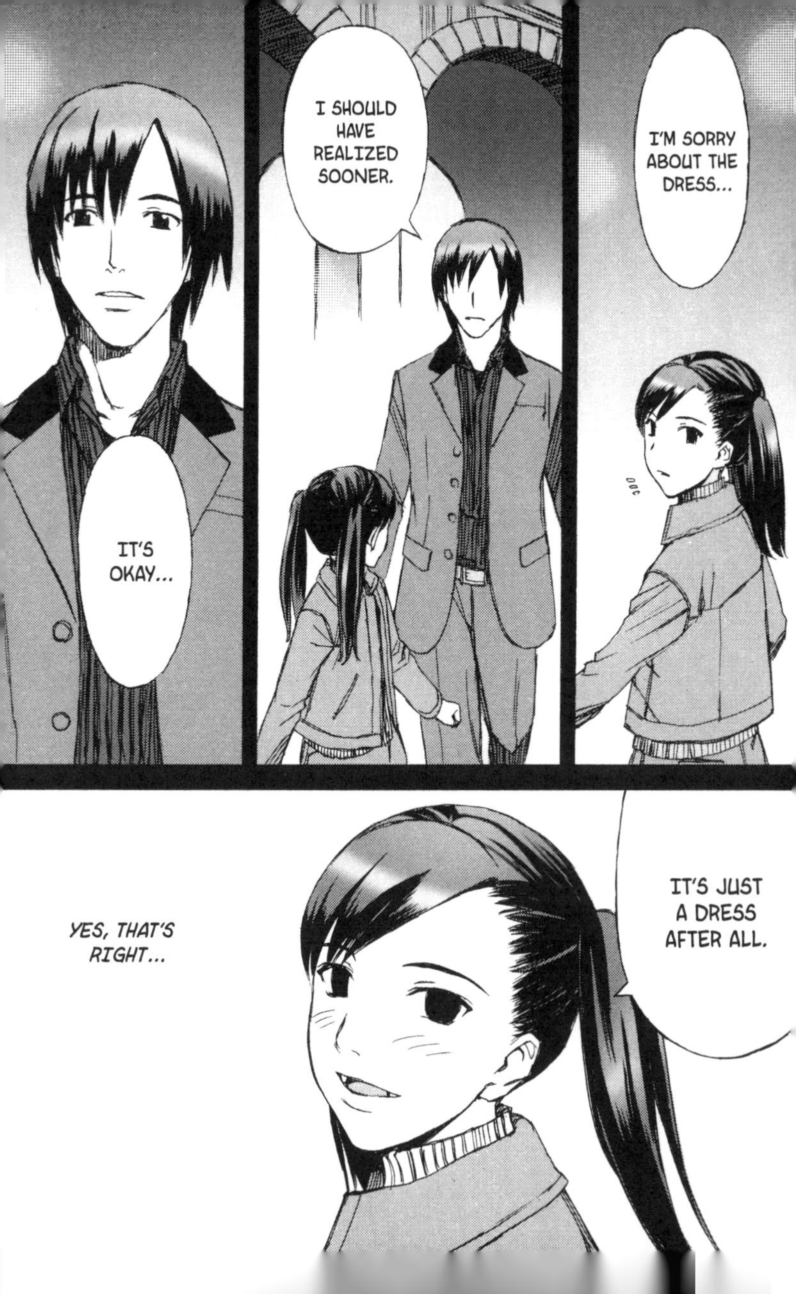
I'M SORRY ABOUT THE DRESS...
I SHOULD HAVE REALIZED SOONER.
IT'S OKAY...
IT'S JUST A DRESS AFTER ALL.
YES, THAT'S RIGHT...

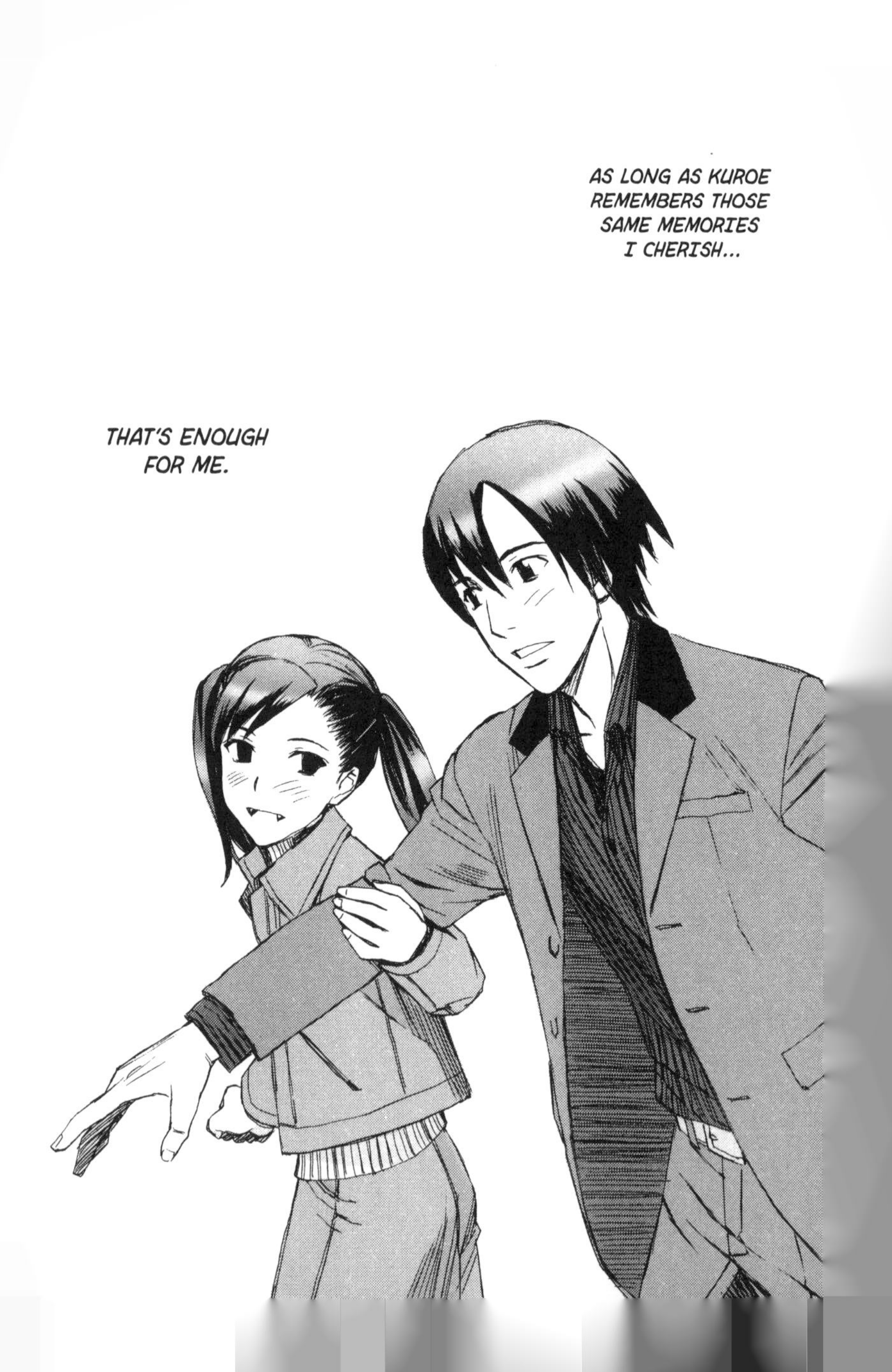
AS LONG AS KUROE REMEMBERS THOSE SAME MEMORIES I CHERISH...
THAT'S ENOUGH FOR ME.

Episode 17
MIDNIGHT SWIM

星空のクロール – Swimming Amongst the Stars

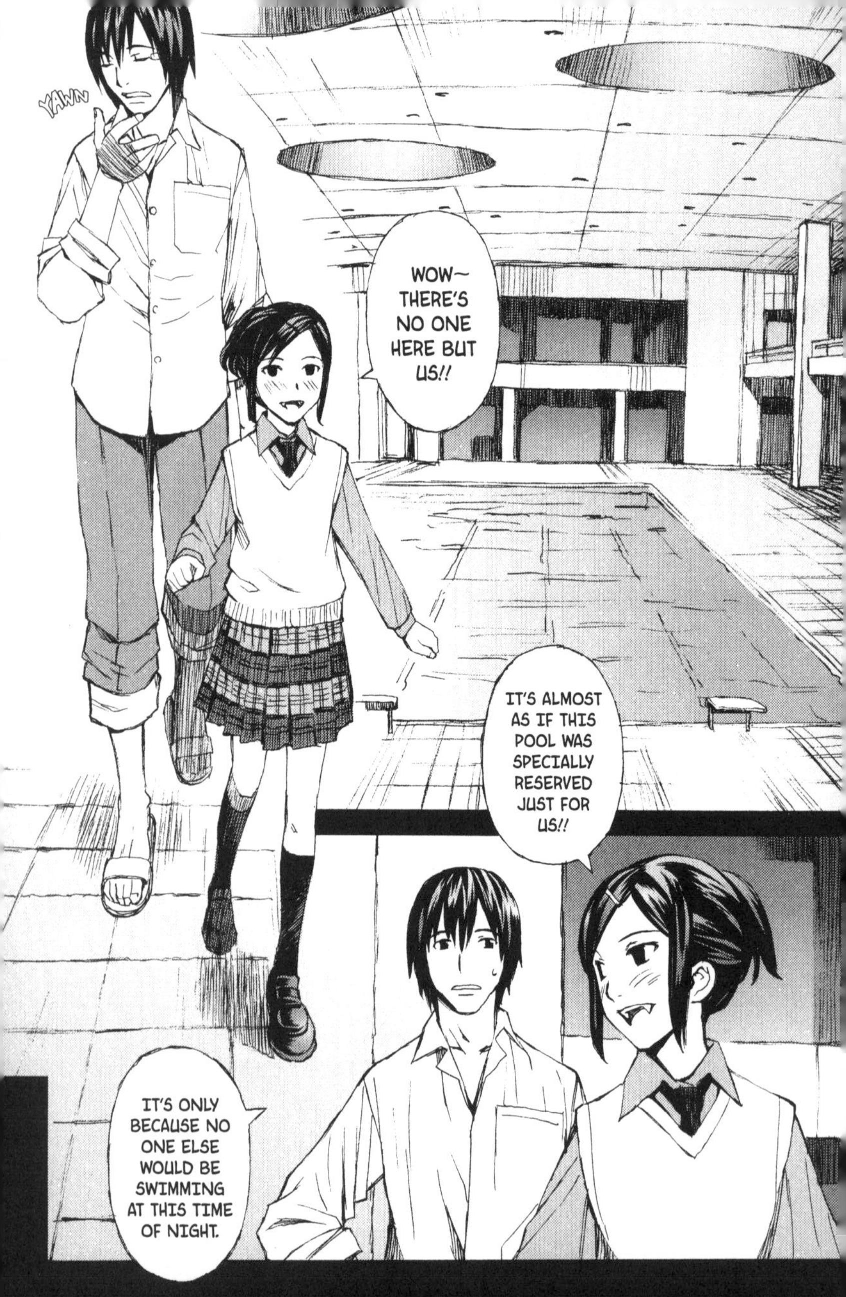
WOW~ THERE'S NO ONE HERE BUT US!!
YAWN
IT'S ALMOST AS IF THIS POOL WAS SPECIALLY RESERVED JUST FOR US!!
IT'S ONLY BECAUSE NO ONE ELSE WOULD BE SWIMMING AT THIS TIME OF NIGHT.

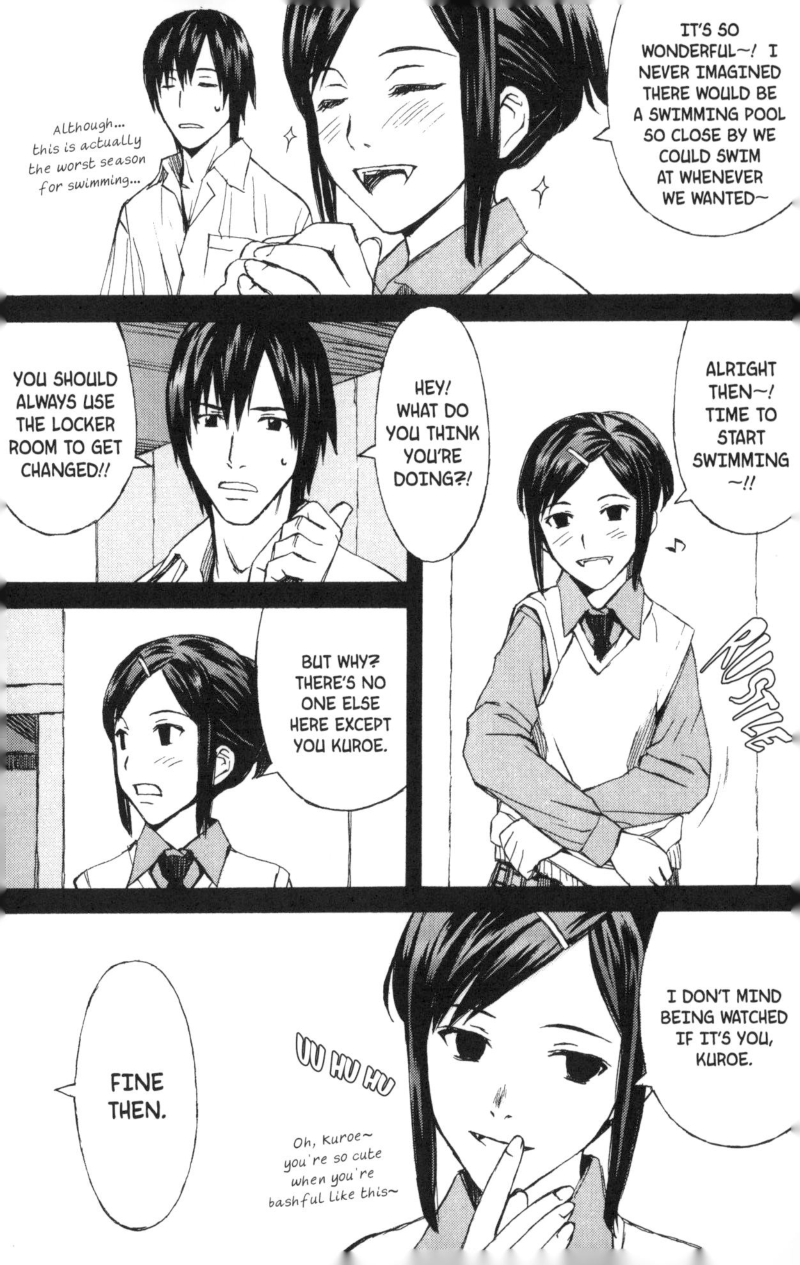
IT'S SO WONDERFUL~! I NEVER IMAGINED THERE WOULD BE A SWIMMING POOL SO CLOSE BY WE COULD SWIM AT WHENEVER WE WANTED~
Although... this is actually the worst season for swimming...
ALRIGHT THEN~! TIME TO START SWIMMING ~!!
RUSTLE
HEY! WHAT DO YOU THINK YOU'RE DOING?!
YOU SHOULD ALWAYS USE THE LOCKER ROOM TO GET CHANGED!!
BUT WHY? THERE'S NO ONE ELSE HERE EXCEPT YOU KUROE.
I DON'T MIND BEING WATCHED IF IT'S YOU, KUROE.
UU HU HU
Oh, Kuroe~ you're so cute when you're bashful like this~
FINE THEN.

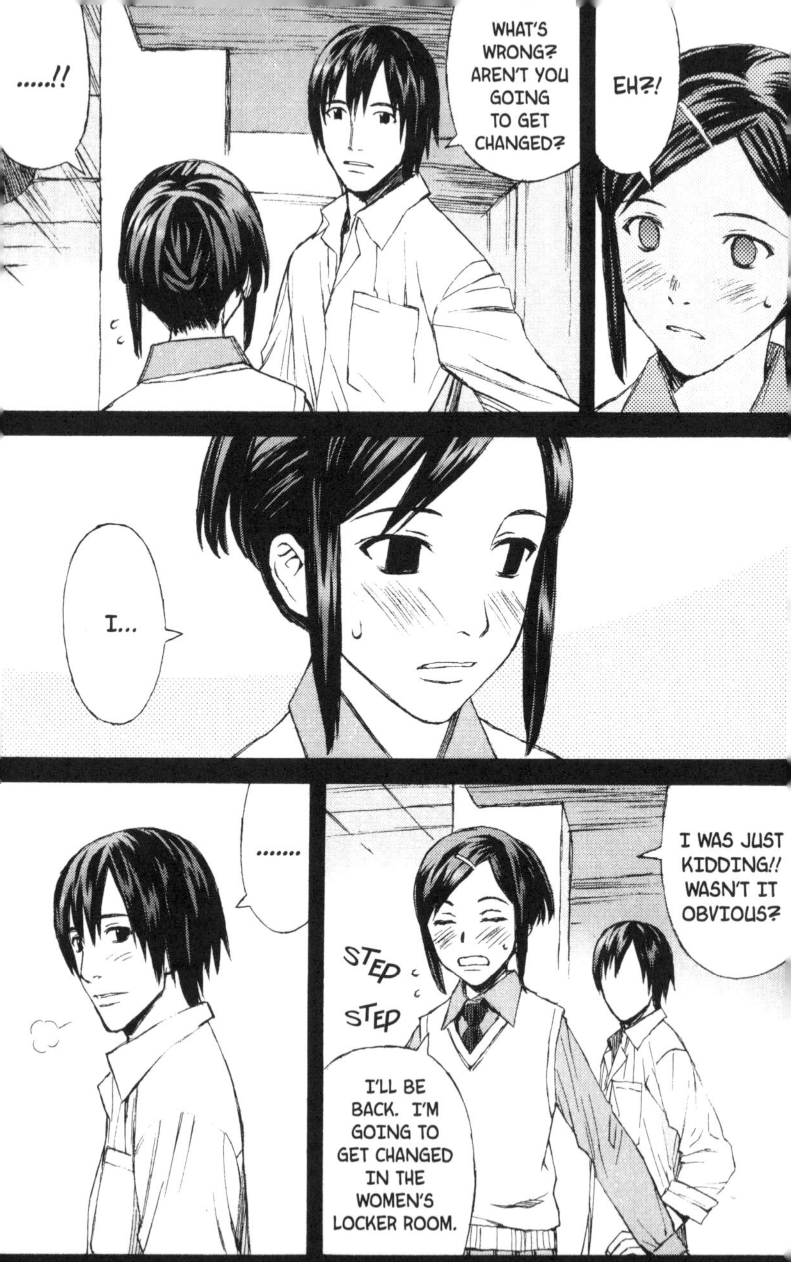
EH?!
WHAT'S WRONG? AREN'T YOU GOING TO GET CHANGED?
......!!
I...
I WAS JUST KIDDING!! WASN'T IT OBVIOUS?
STEP
STEP
I'LL BE BACK. I'M GOING TO GET CHANGED IN THE WOMEN'S LOCKER ROOM.
....

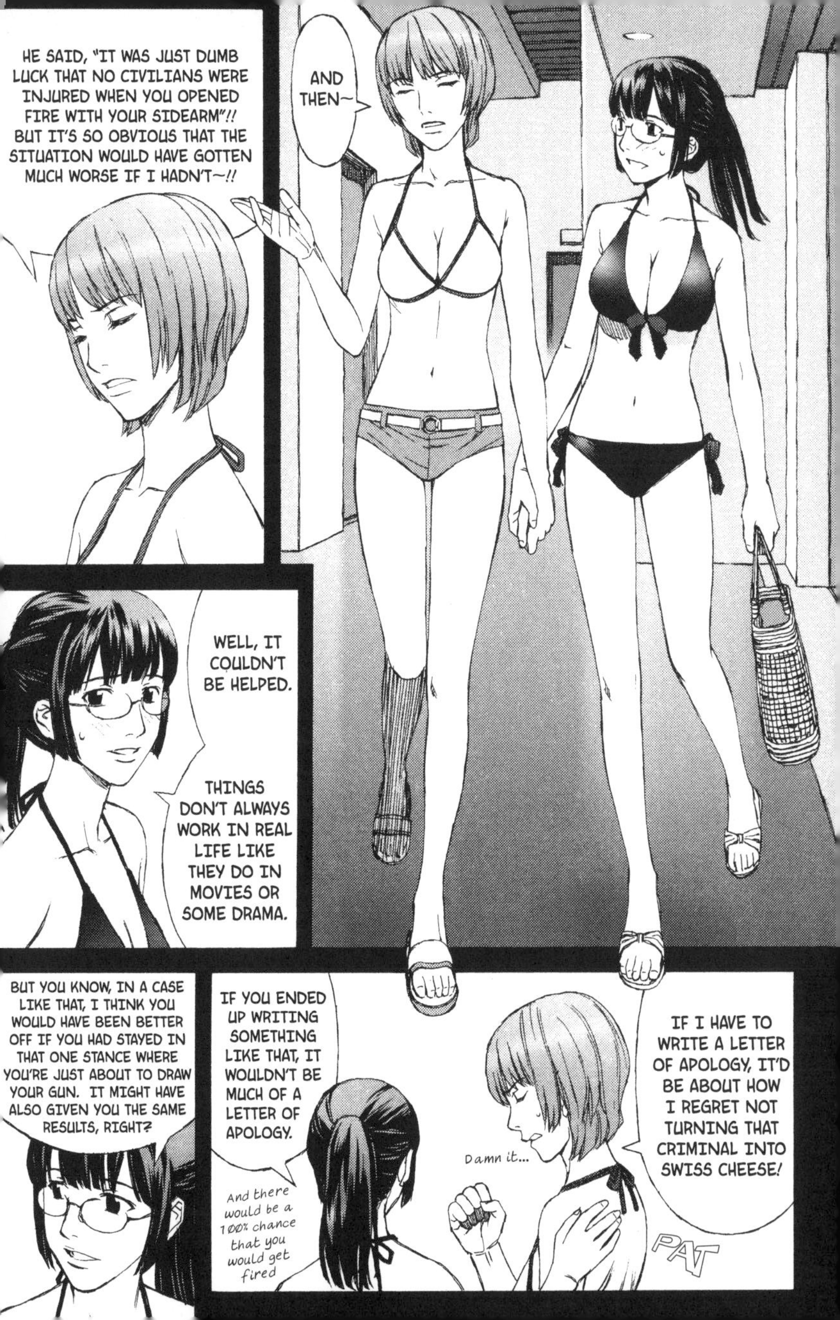
AND THEN~
HE SAID, "IT WAS JUST DUMB LUCK THAT NO CIVILIANS WERE INJURED WHEN YOU OPENED FIRE WITH YOUR SIDEARM"!! BUT IT'S SO OBVIOUS THAT THE SITUATION WOULD HAVE GOTTEN MUCH WORSE IF I HADN'T~!!
WELL, IT COULDN'T BE HELPED.
THINGS DON'T ALWAYS WORK IN REAL LIFE LIKE THEY DO IN MOVIES OR SOME DRAMA.
IF I HAVE TO WRITE A LETTER OF APOLOGY, IT'D BE ABOUT HOW I REGRET NOT TURNING THAT CRIMINAL INTO SWISS CHEESE!
Damn it...
PAT
IF YOU ENDED UP WRITING SOMETHING LIKE THAT, IT WOULDN'T BE MUCH OF A LETTER OF APOLOGY.
And there would be a 100% chance that you would get fired
BUT YOU KNOW, IN A CASE LIKE THAT, I THINK YOU WOULD HAVE BEEN BETTER OFF IF YOU HAD STAYED IN THAT ONE STANCE WHERE YOU'RE JUST ABOUT TO DRAW YOUR GUN. IT MIGHT HAVE ALSO GIVEN YOU THE SAME RESULTS, RIGHT?

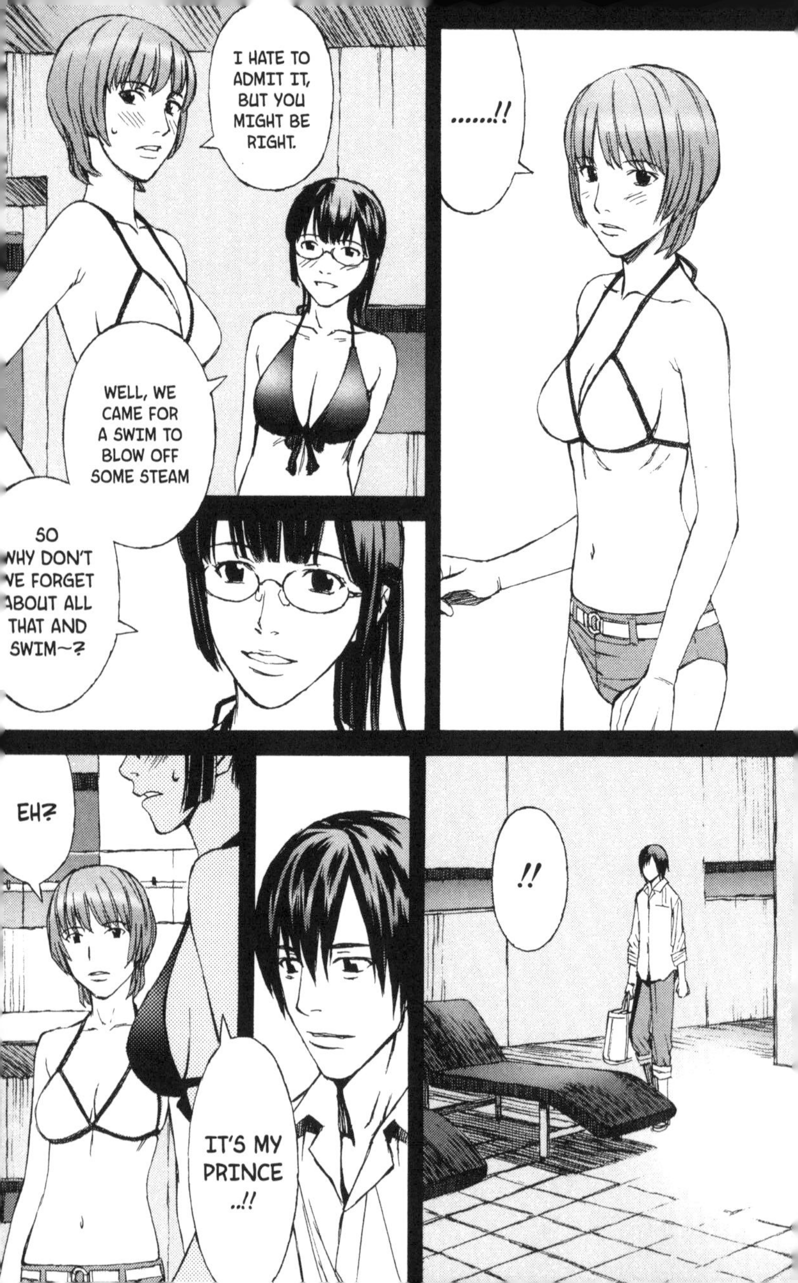
......!!
I HATE TO ADMIT IT, BUT YOU MIGHT BE RIGHT.
WELL, WE CAME FOR A SWIM TO BLOW OFF SOME STEAM
SO WHY DON'T WE FORGET ABOUT ALL THAT AND SWIM~?
!!
IT'S MY PRINCE ..!!
EH?

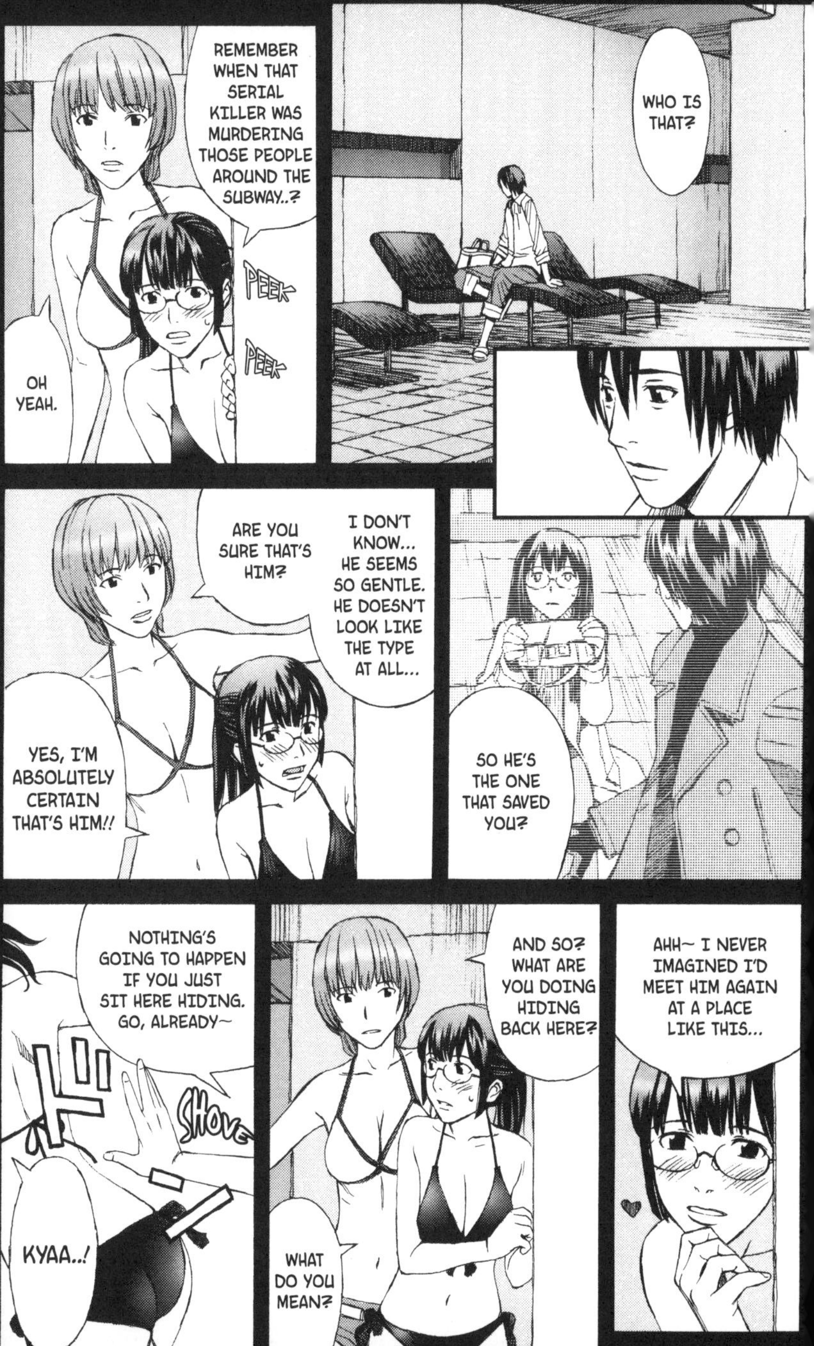
WHO IS THAT?
REMEMBER WHEN THAT SERIAL KILLER WAS MURDERING THOSE PEOPLE AROUND THE SUBWAY..?
PEEK
PEEK
OH YEAH.
SO HE'S THE ONE THAT SAVED YOU?
I DON'T KNOW... HE SEEMS SO GENTLE. HE DOESN'T LOOK LIKE THE TYPE AT ALL...
ARE YOU SURE THAT'S HIM?
YES, I'M ABSOLUTELY CERTAIN THAT'S HIM!!
AHH~ I NEVER IMAGINED I'D MEET HIM AGAIN AT A PLACE LIKE THIS...
AND SO? WHAT ARE YOU DOING HIDING BACK HERE?
WHAT DO YOU MEAN?
NOTHING'S GOING TO HAPPEN IF YOU JUST SIT HERE HIDING. GO, ALREADY~
SHOVE
KYAA..!

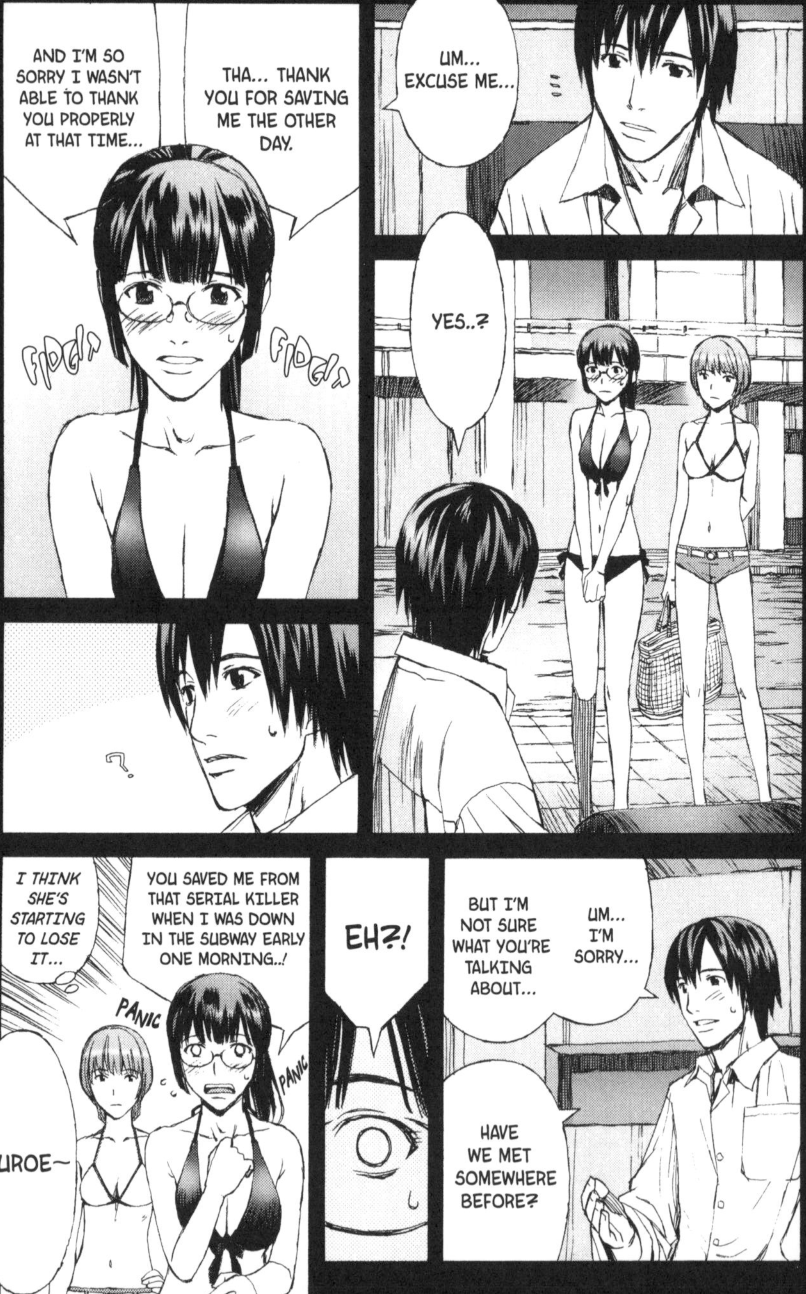
UM... EXCUSE ME...
YES..?
THA... THANK YOU FOR SAVING ME THE OTHER DAY.
AND I'M SO SORRY I WASN'T ABLE TO THANK YOU PROPERLY AT THAT TIME...
FIDGIT
FIDGIT
?
UM... I'M SORRY...
BUT I'M NOT SURE WHAT YOU'RE TALKING ABOUT...
HAVE WE MET SOMEWHERE BEFORE?
EH?!
YOU SAVED ME FROM THAT SERIAL KILLER WHEN I WAS DOWN IN THE SUBWAY EARLY ONE MORNING..!
PANIC
PANIC
I THINK SHE'S STARTING TO LOSE IT...
KUROE~

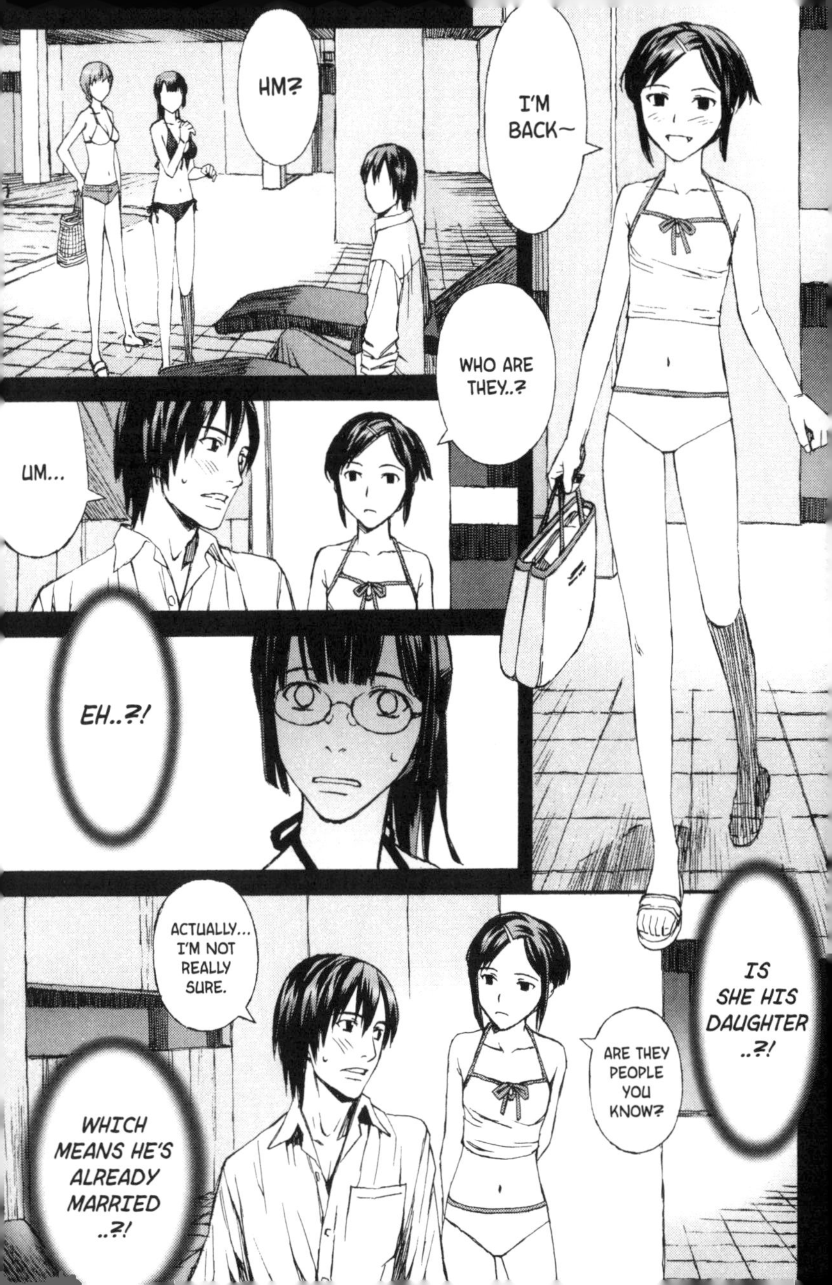
I'M BACK~
HM?
WHO ARE THEY..?
UM...
EH..?!
IS SHE HIS DAUGHTER ..?!
ARE THEY PEOPLE YOU KNOW?
ACTUALLY... I'M NOT REALLY SURE.
WHICH MEANS HE'S ALREADY MARRIED ..?!

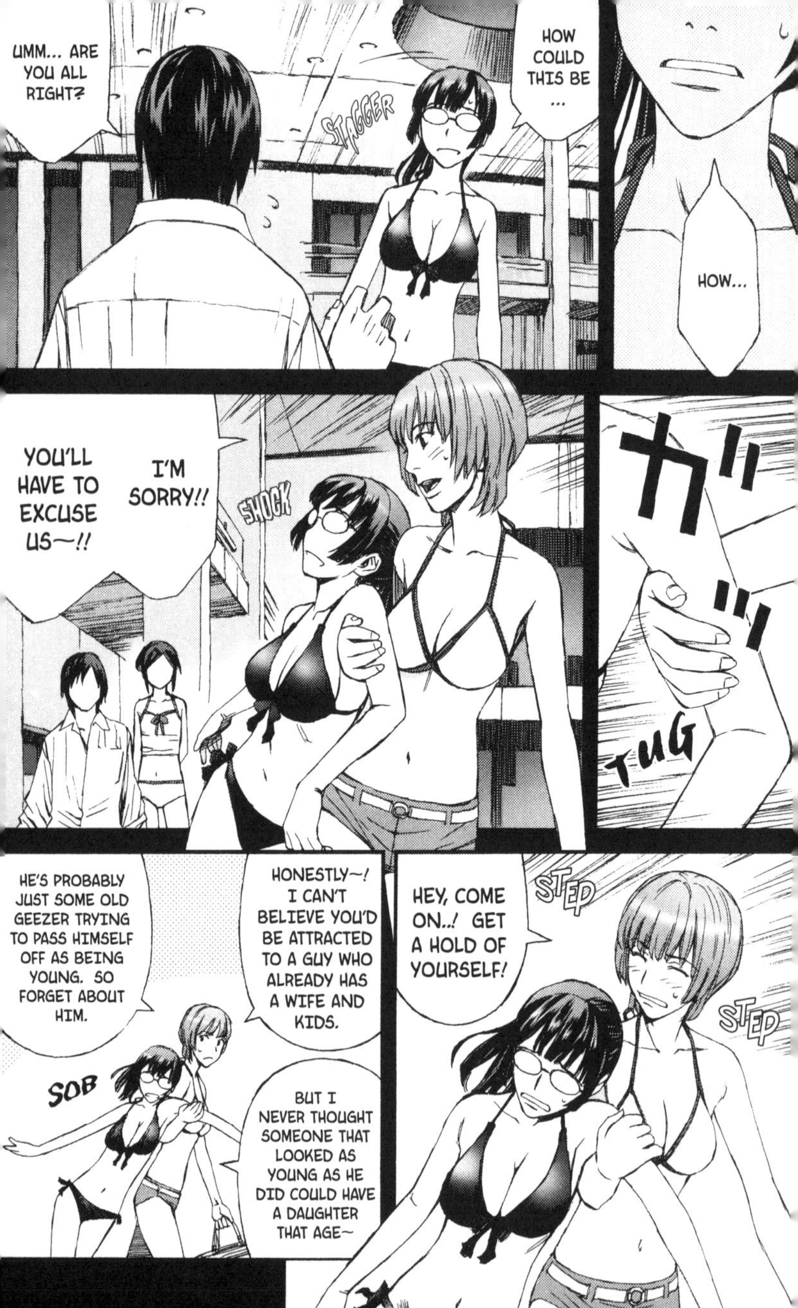
HOW...
HOW COULD THIS BE ...
UMM... ARE YOU ALL RIGHT?
STAGGER
ガッ
TUG
I'M SORRY!!
YOU'LL HAVE TO EXCUSE US~!!
SHOCK
STEP
HEY, COME ON..! GET A HOLD OF YOURSELF!
STEP
HONESTLY~! I CAN'T BELIEVE YOU'D BE ATTRACTED TO A GUY WHO ALREADY HAS A WIFE AND KIDS.
HE'S PROBABLY JUST SOME OLD GEEZER TRYING TO PASS HIMSELF OFF AS BEING YOUNG. SO FORGET ABOUT HIM.
BUT I NEVER THOUGHT SOMEONE THAT LOOKED AS YOUNG AS HE DID COULD HAVE A DAUGHTER THAT AGE~
SOB

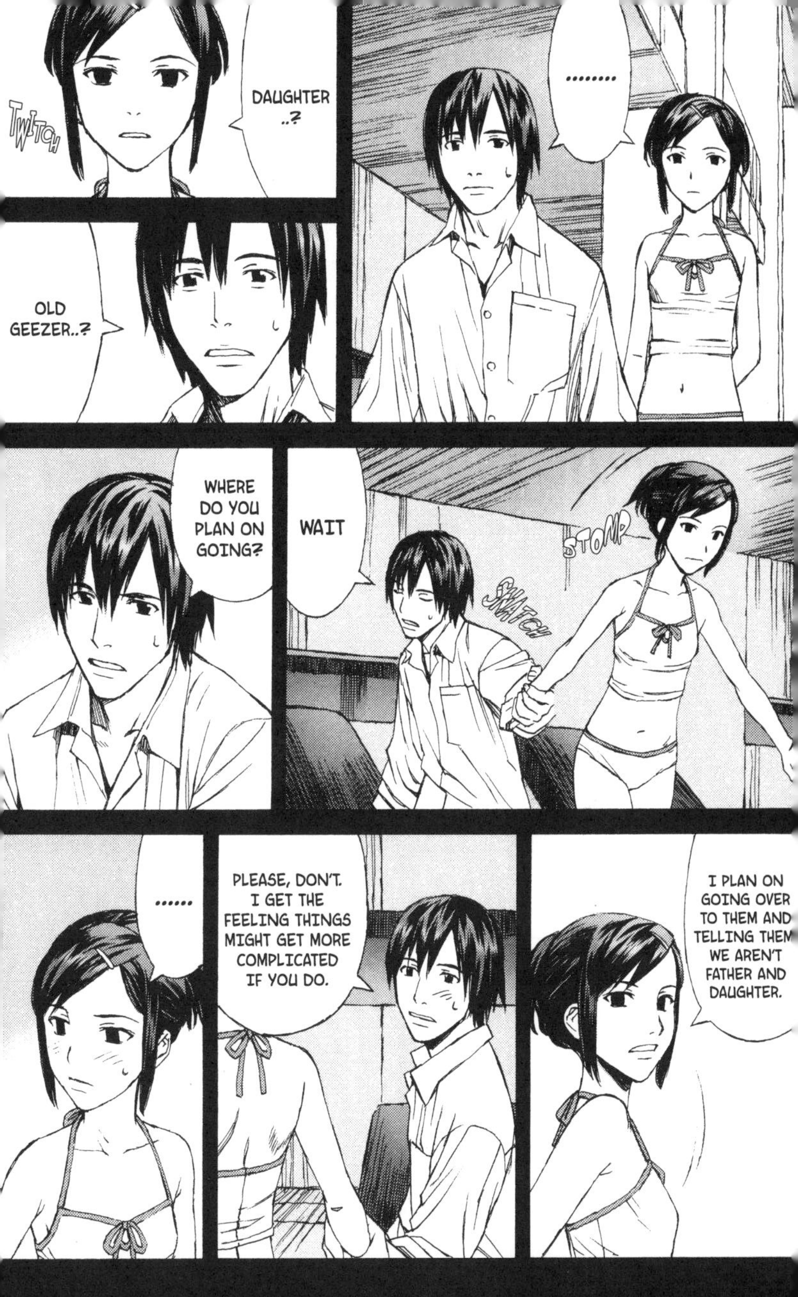
....
TWITCH
DAUGHTER ..?
OLD GEEZER..?
STOMP
SNATCH
WAIT
WHERE DO YOU PLAN ON GOING?
I PLAN ON GOING OVER TO THEM AND TELLING THEM WE AREN'T FATHER AND DAUGHTER.
PLEASE, DON'T. I GET THE FEELING THINGS MIGHT GET MORE COMPLICATED IF YOU DO.
......

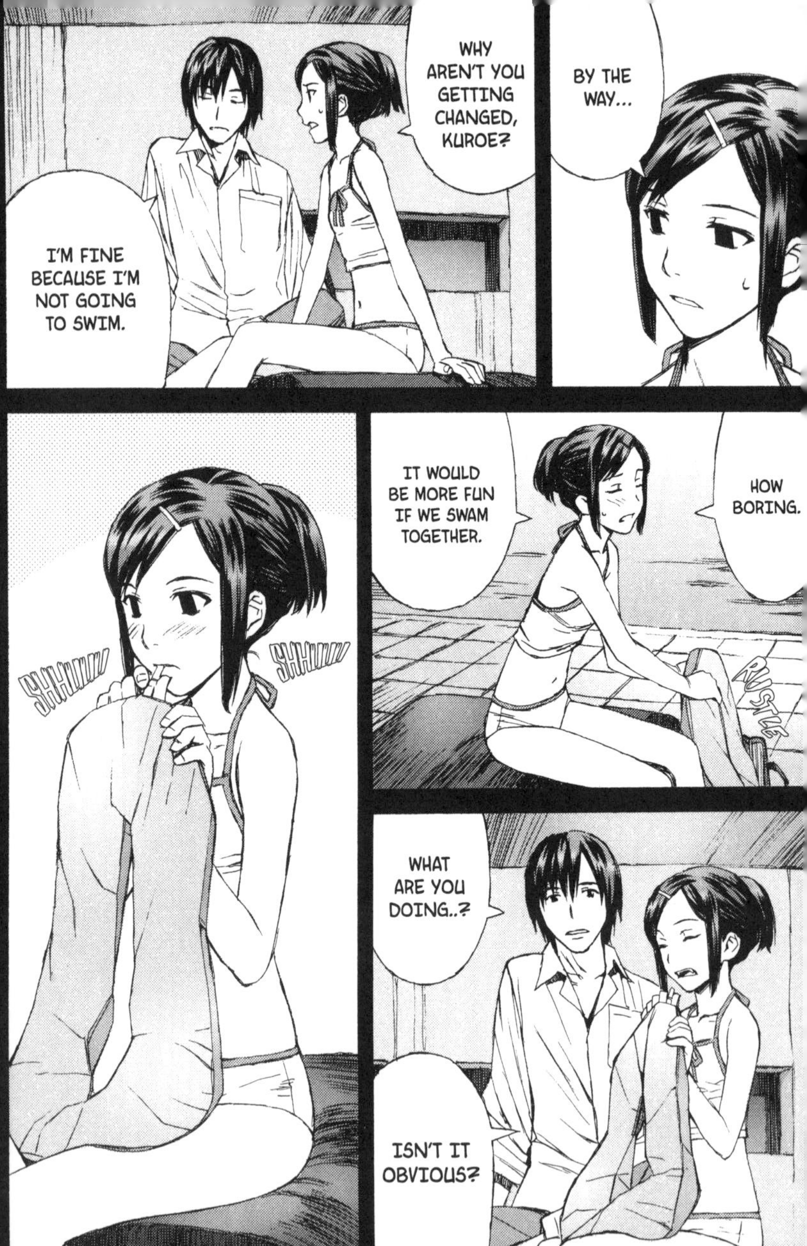
BY THE WAY...
WHY AREN'T YOU GETTING CHANGED, KUROE?
I'M FINE BECAUSE I'M NOT GOING TO SWIM.
HOW BORING.
IT WOULD BE MORE FUN IF WE SWAM TOGETHER.
RUSTLE
WHAT ARE YOU DOING..?
ISN'T IT OBVIOUS?
SHHUUUU
SHHUUUU

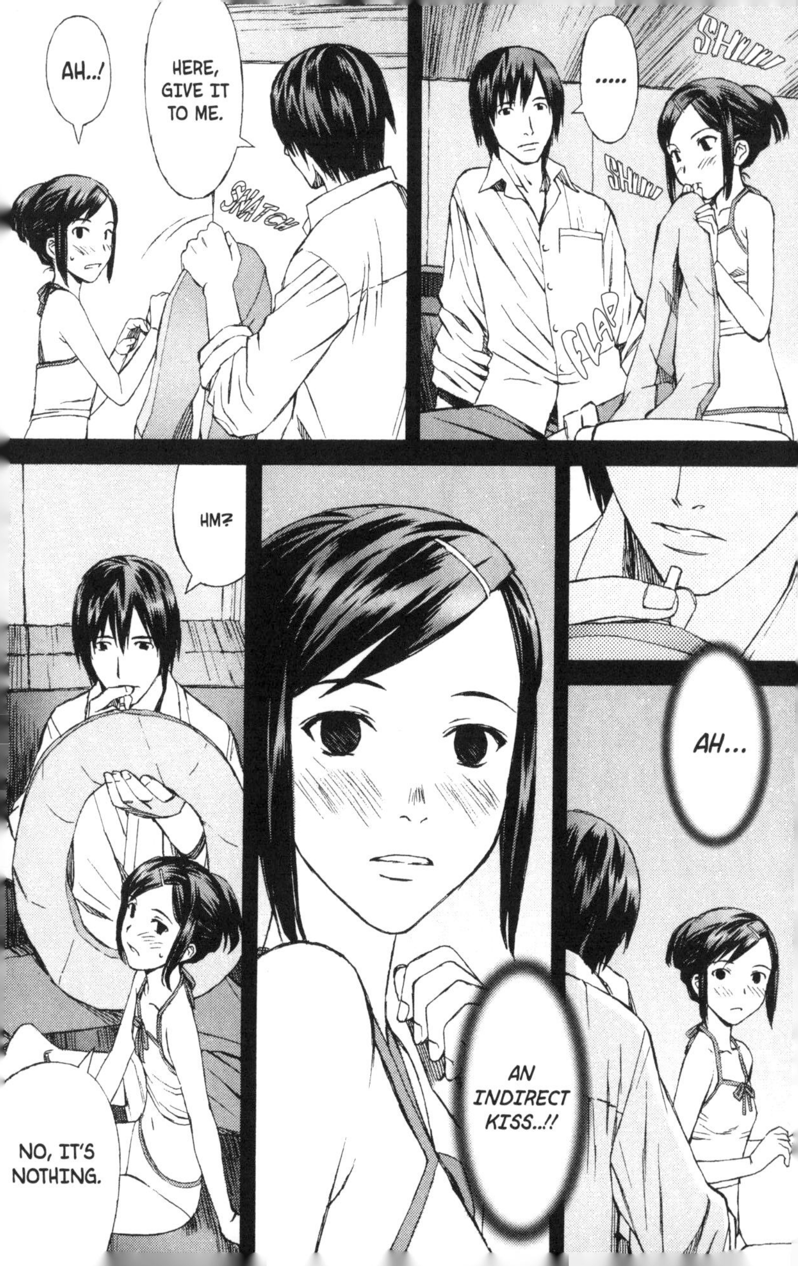
.....
SHUW
SHUW
FLAP
HERE, GIVE IT TO ME.
AH..!
SNATCH
AH...
AN INDIRECT KISS..!!
HM?
NO, IT'S NOTHING.

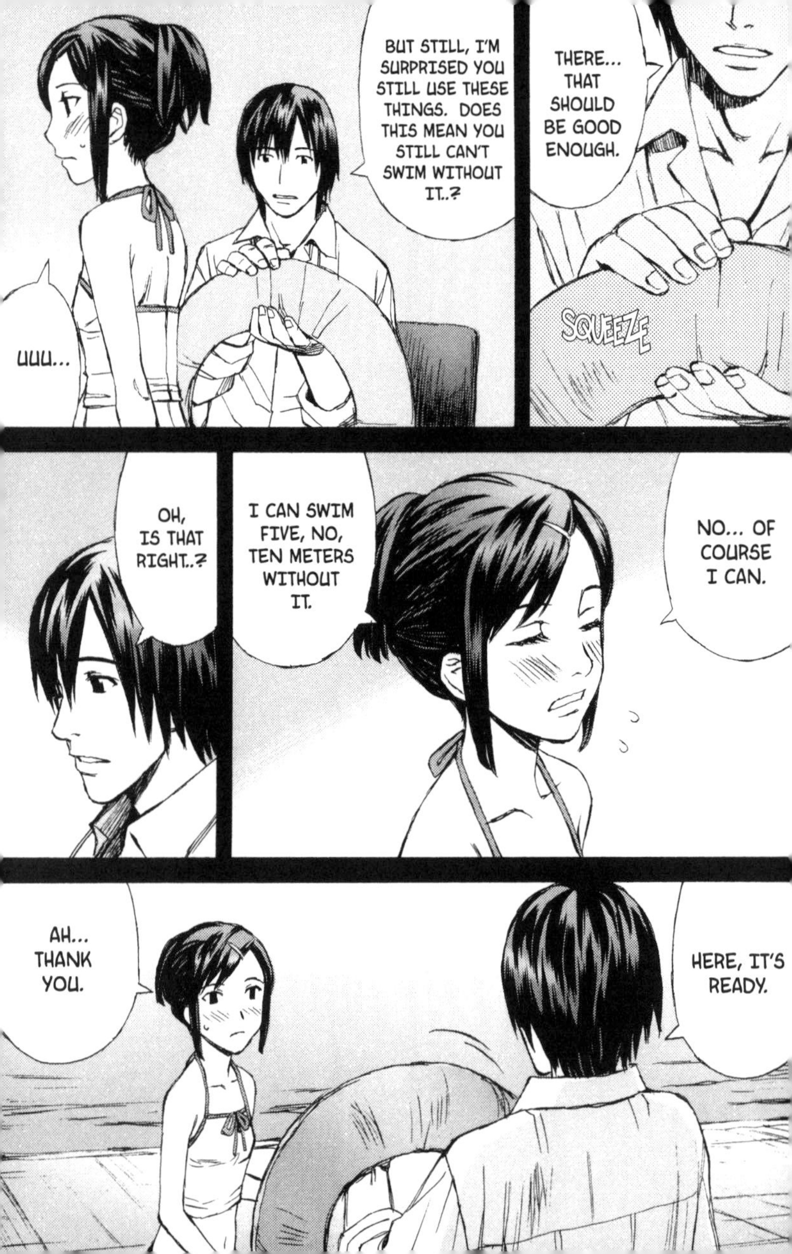
THERE... THAT SHOULD BE GOOD ENOUGH.
SQUEEZE
BUT STILL, I'M SURPRISED YOU STILL USE THESE THINGS. DOES THIS MEAN YOU STILL CAN'T SWIM WITHOUT IT..?
UUU...
NO... OF COURSE I CAN.
I CAN SWIM FIVE, NO, TEN METERS WITHOUT IT.
OH, IS THAT RIGHT..?
HERE, IT'S READY.
AH... THANK YOU.

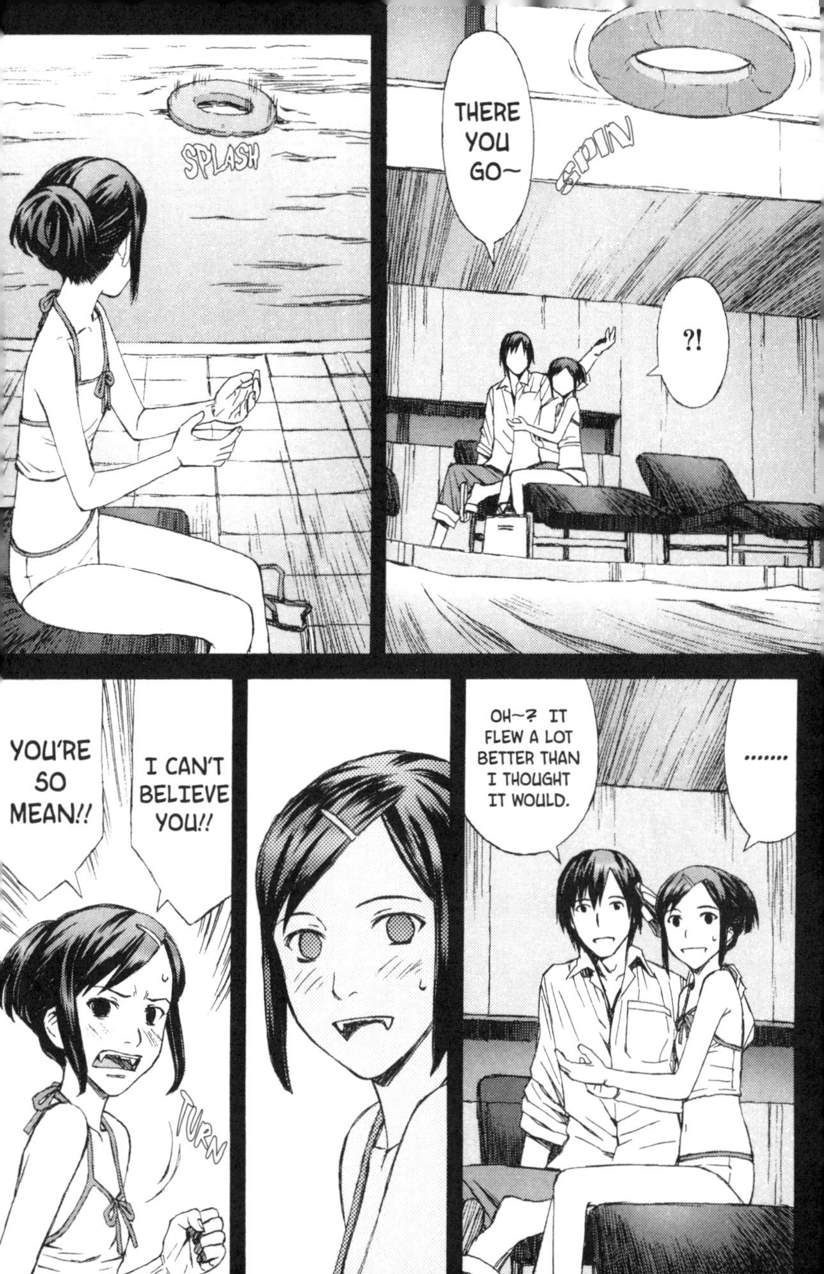
THERE YOU GO~
SPIN
?!
SPLASH
....
OH~? IT FLEW A LOT BETTER THAN I THOUGHT IT WOULD.
I CAN'T BELIEVE YOU!!
YOU'RE SO MEAN!!
TURN

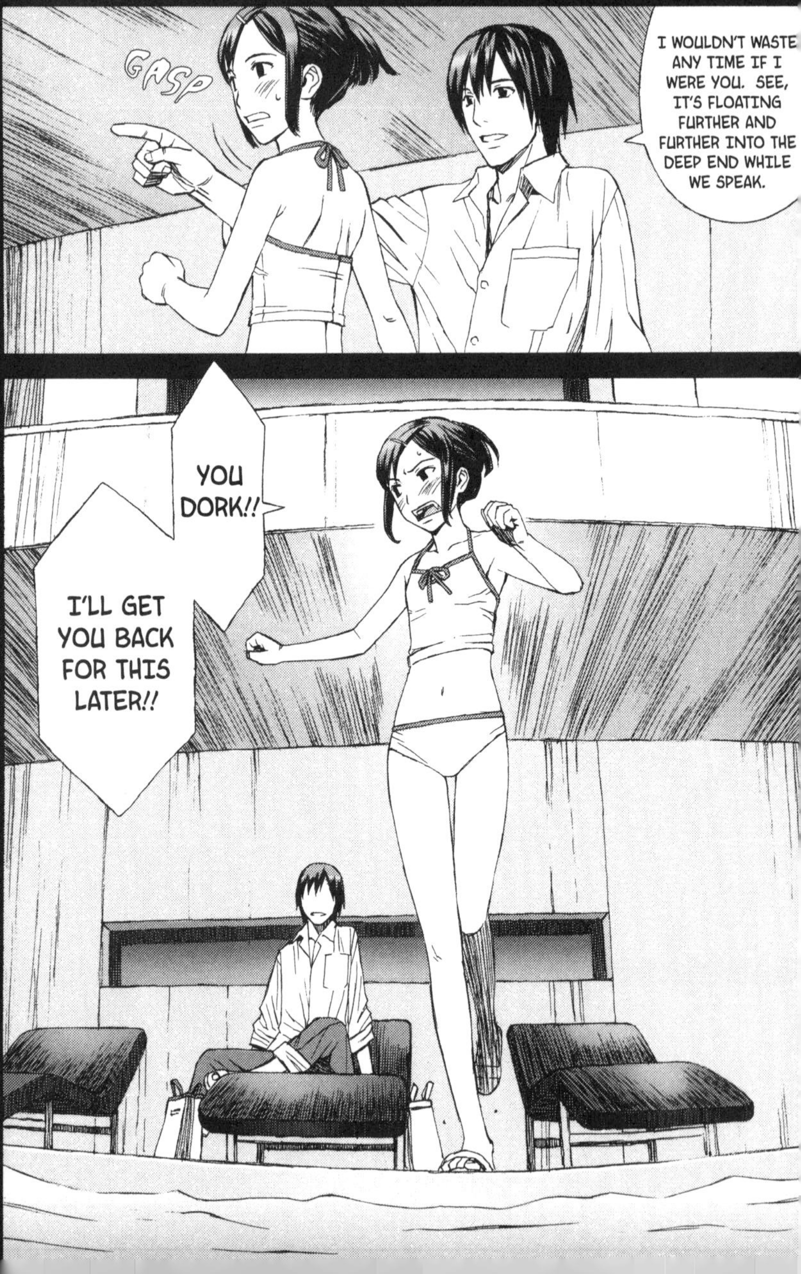
I WOULDN'T WASTE ANY TIME IF I WERE YOU. SEE, IT'S FLOATING FURTHER AND FURTHER INTO THE DEEP END WHILE WE SPEAK.
GASP
YOU DORK!!
I'LL GET YOU BACK FOR THIS LATER!!

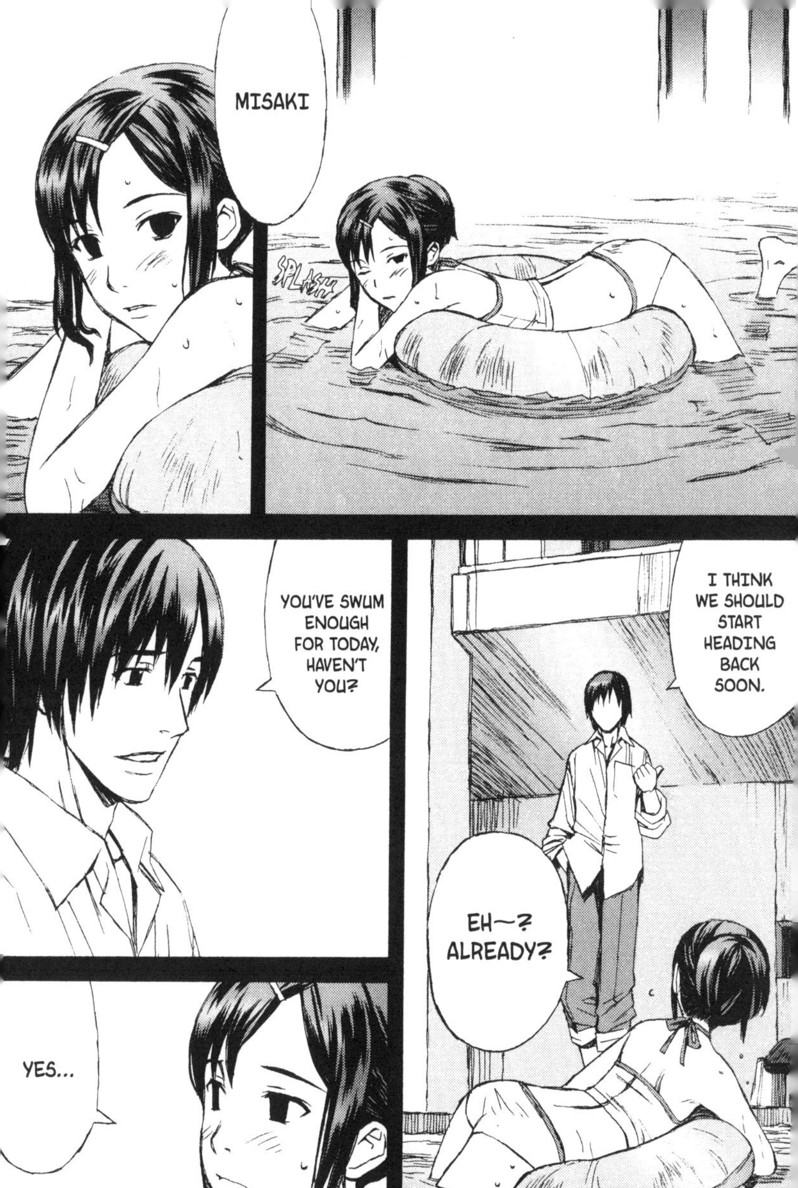
SPLASH
MISAKI
I THINK WE SHOULD START HEADING BACK SOON.
EH~? ALREADY?
YOU'VE SWUM ENOUGH FOR TODAY, HAVEN'T YOU?
YES...

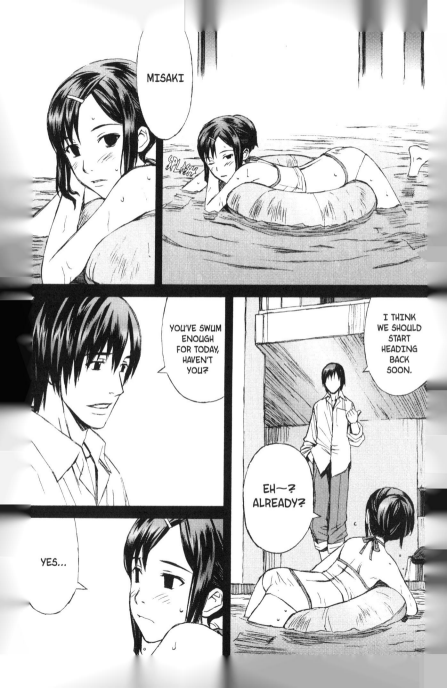

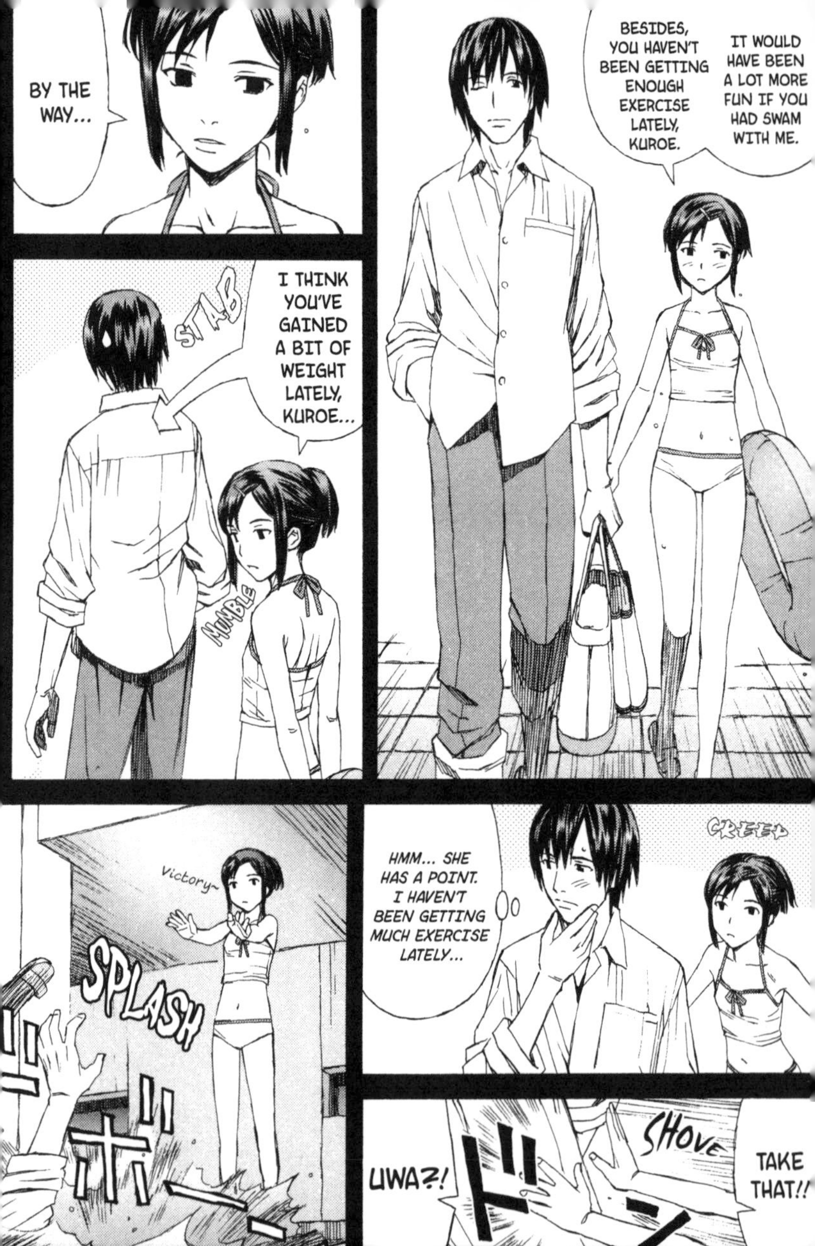
IT WOULD HAVE BEEN A LOT MORE FUN IF YOU HAD SWAM WITH ME.
BESIDES, YOU HAVEN'T BEEN GETTING ENOUGH EXERCISE LATELY, KUROE.
BY THE WAY...
I THINK YOU'VE GAINED A BIT OF WEIGHT LATELY, KUROE...
STAB
MUMBLE
CREEP
HMM... SHE HAS A POINT. I HAVEN'T BEEN GETTING MUCH EXERCISE LATELY...
TAKE THAT!!
SHOVE
UWA?!
Victory~
SPLASH

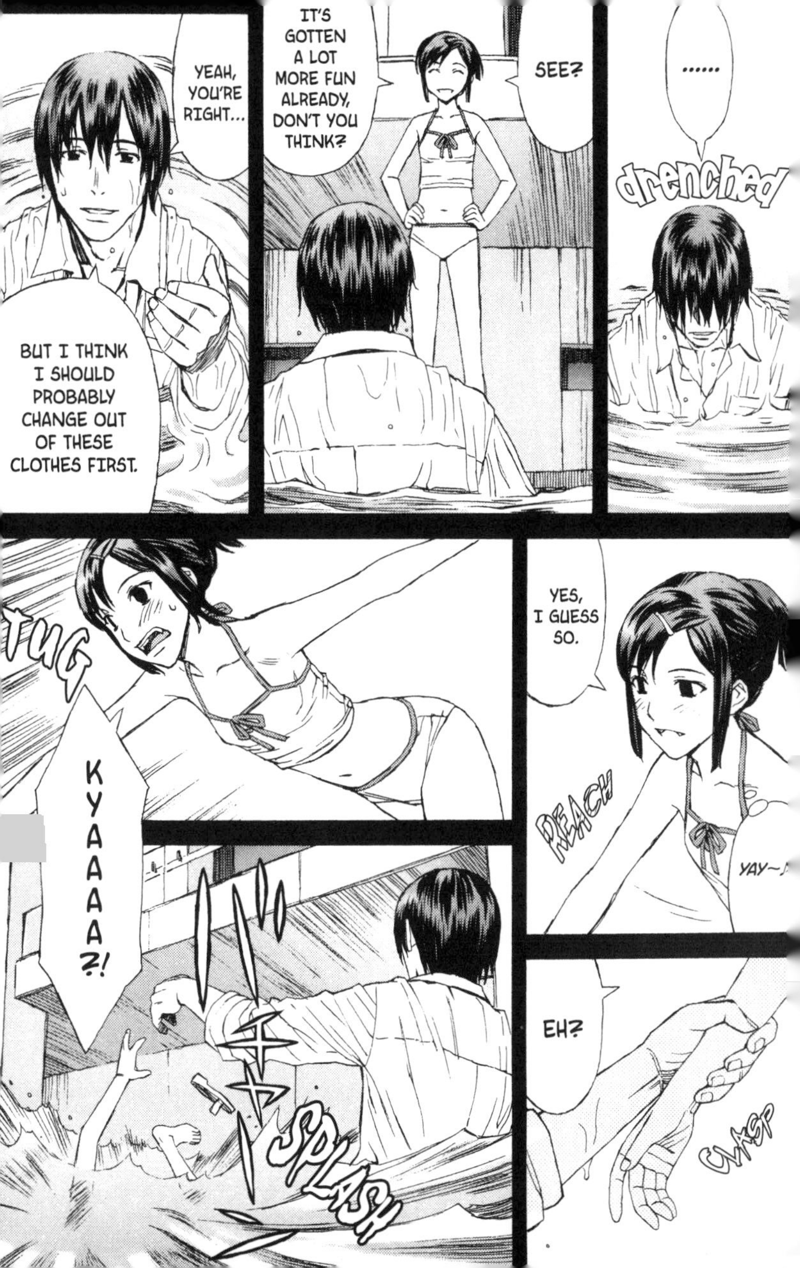
......
drenched
SEE?
IT'S GOTTEN A LOT MORE FUN ALREADY, DON'T YOU THINK?
YEAH, YOU'RE RIGHT...
BUT I THINK I SHOULD PROBABLY CHANGE OUT OF THESE CLOTHES FIRST.
YES, I GUESS SO.
YAY~♪
REACH
EH?
CLASP
TUG
KYAAAAA?!
SPLASH

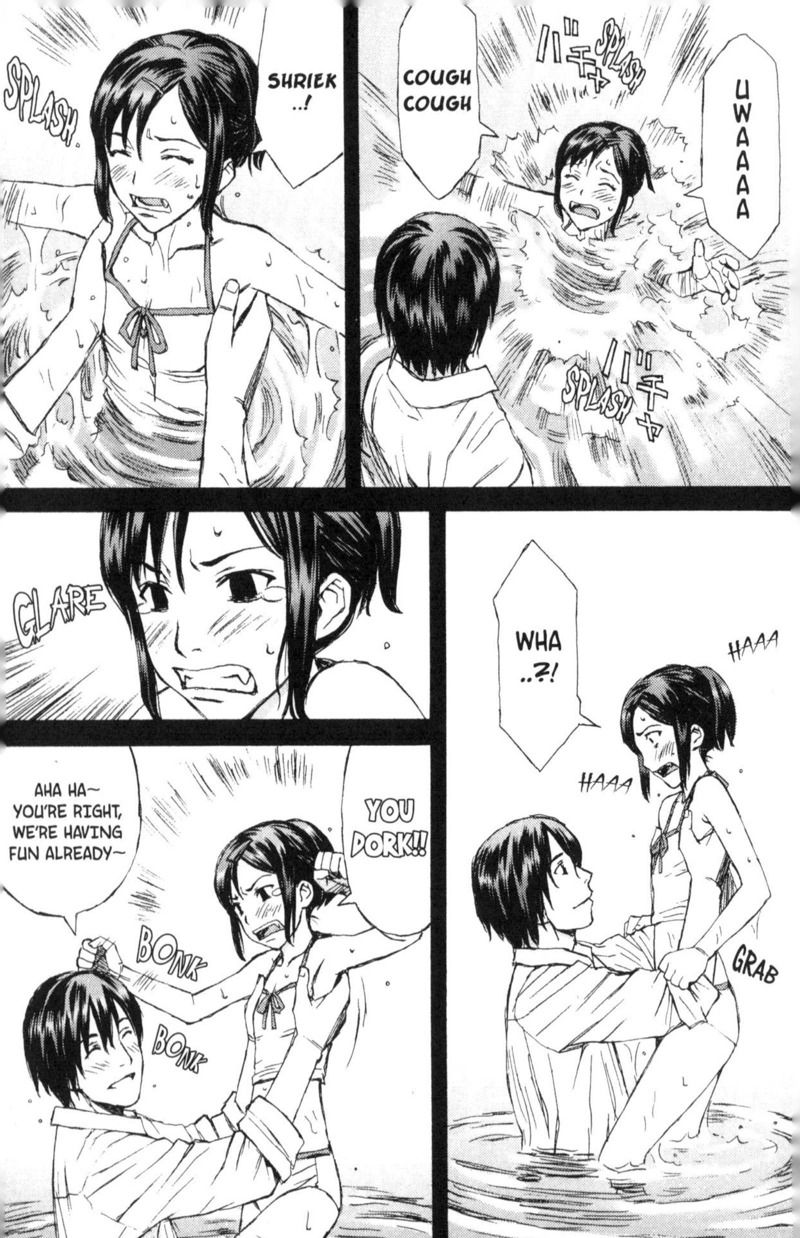
バチャ
SPLASH
UWAAAAA
COUGH COUGH
バチャ
SPLASH
SHRIEK ..!
SPLASH
WHA ..?!
HAAA
HAAA
GRAB
GLARE
YOU DORK!!
AHA HA~ YOU'RE RIGHT, WE'RE HAVING FUN ALREADY~
BONK
BONK

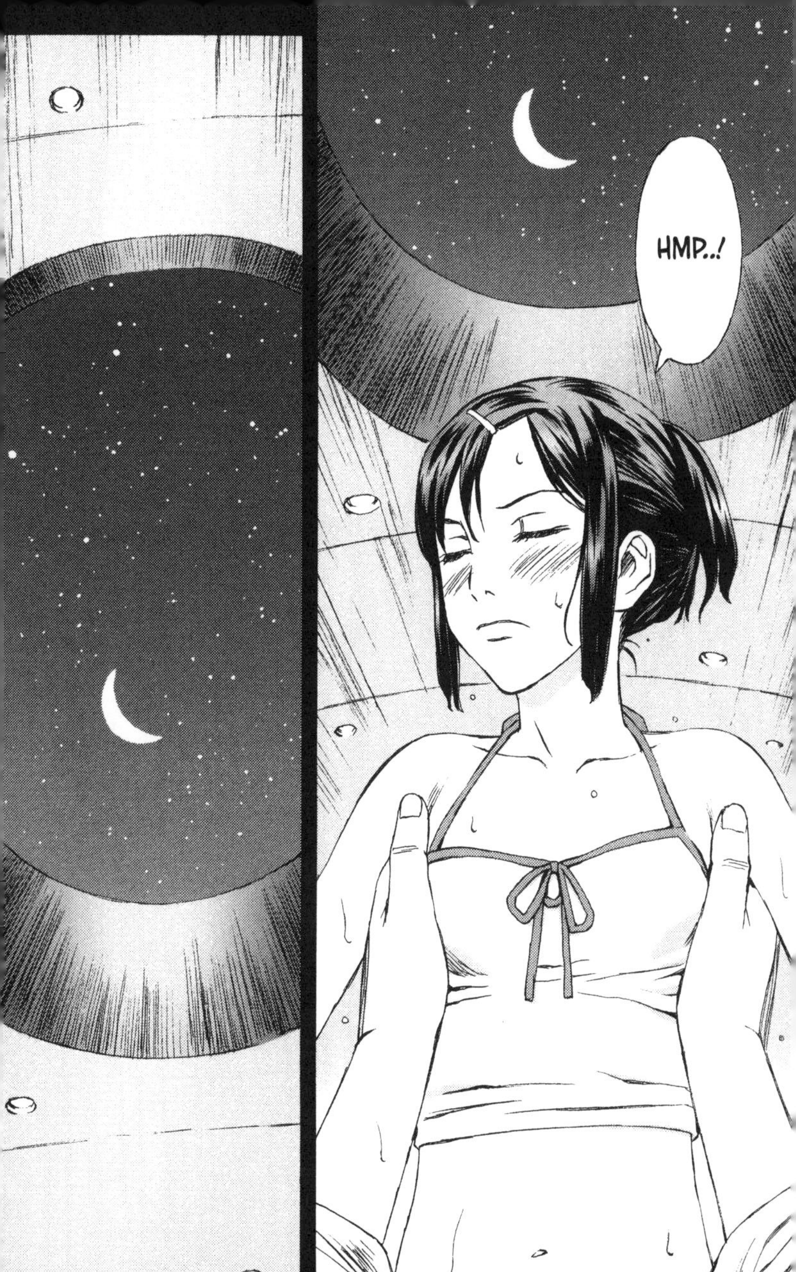
HMP..!

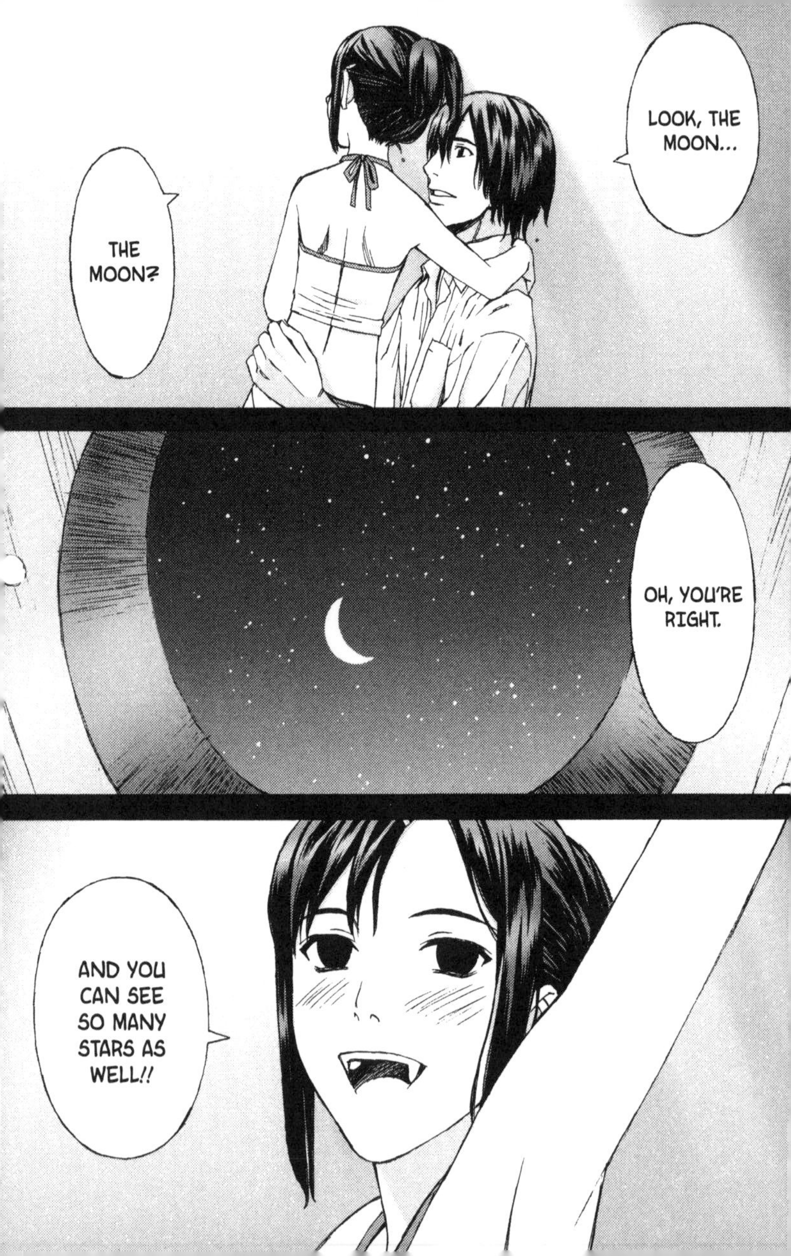
LOOK, THE MOON...
THE MOON?
OH, YOU'RE RIGHT.
AND YOU CAN SEE SO MANY STARS AS WELL!!

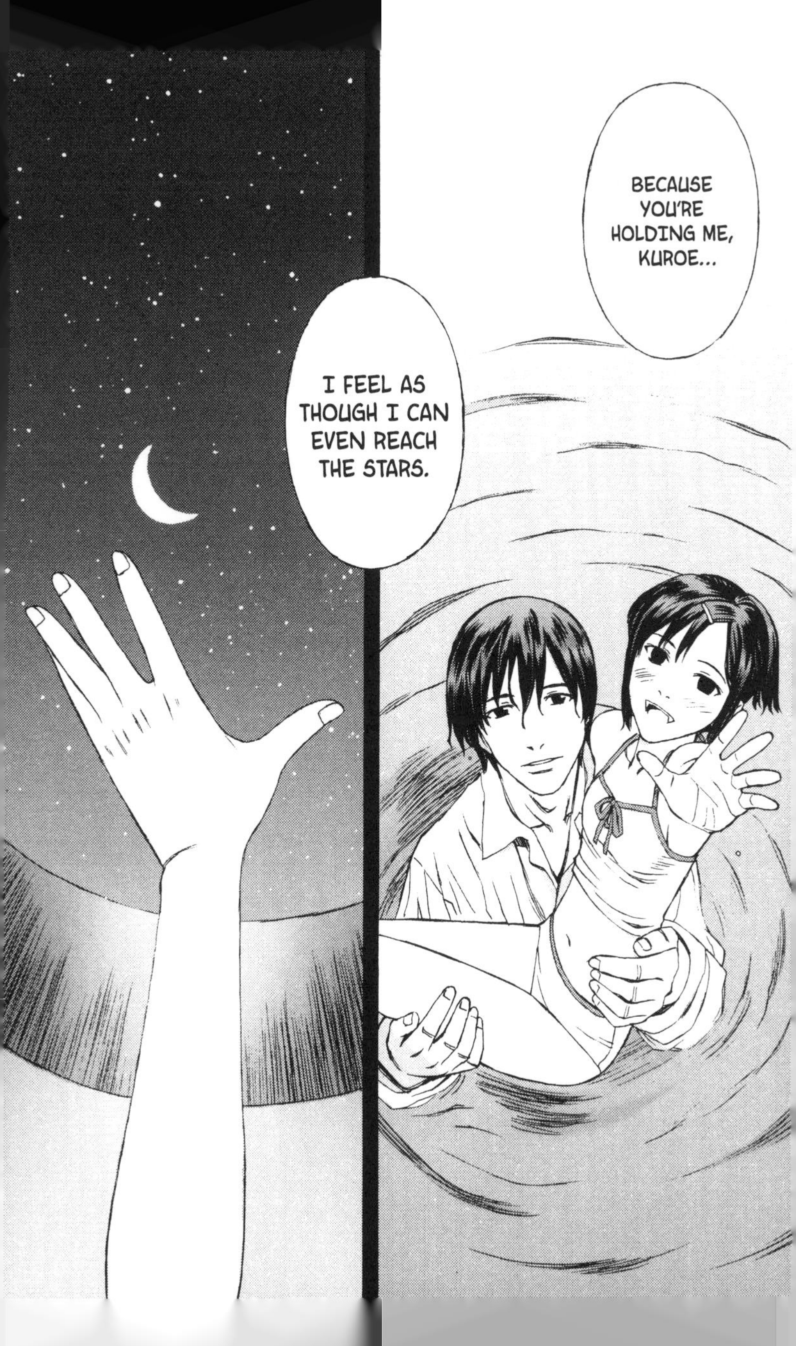
BECAUSE YOU'RE HOLDING ME, KUROE...
I FEEL AS THOUGH I CAN EVEN REACH THE STARS.

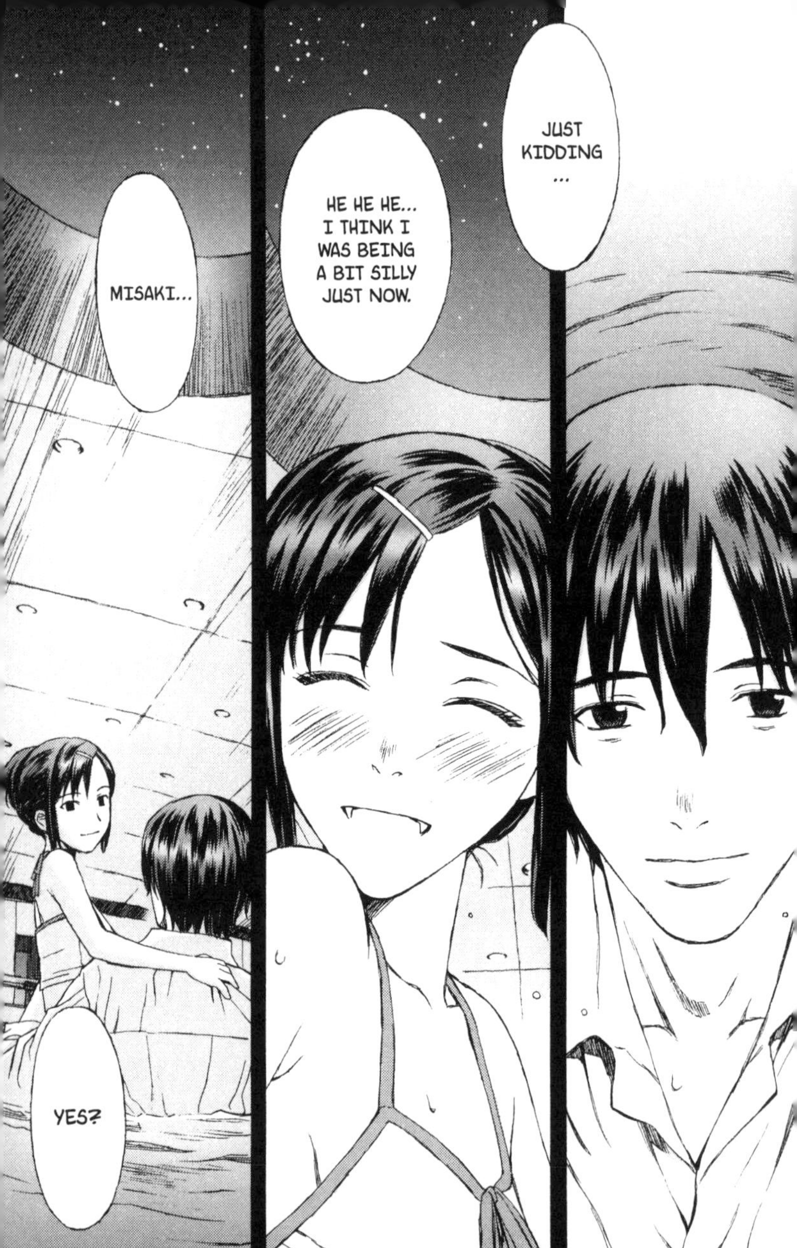
JUST KIDDING ...
HE HE HE... I THINK I WAS BEING A BIT SILLY JUST NOW.
MISAKI...
YES?

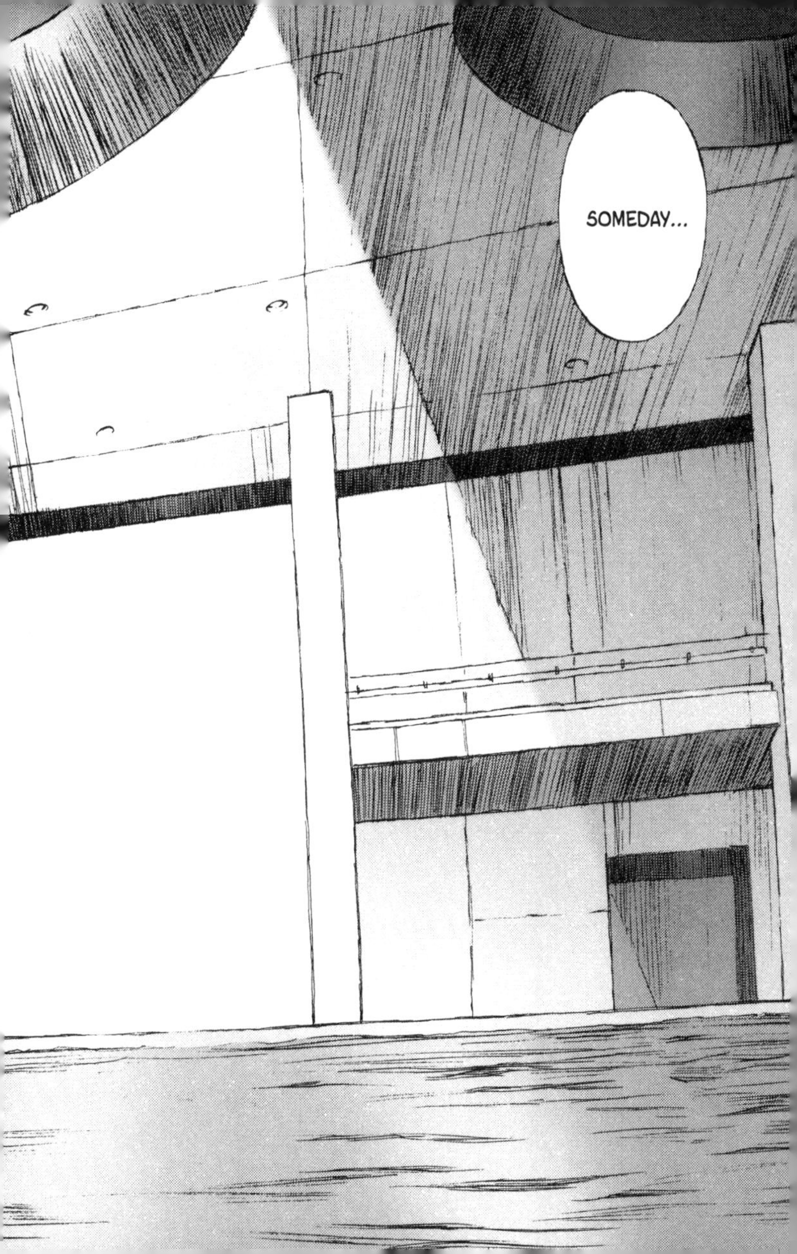
SOMEDAY...

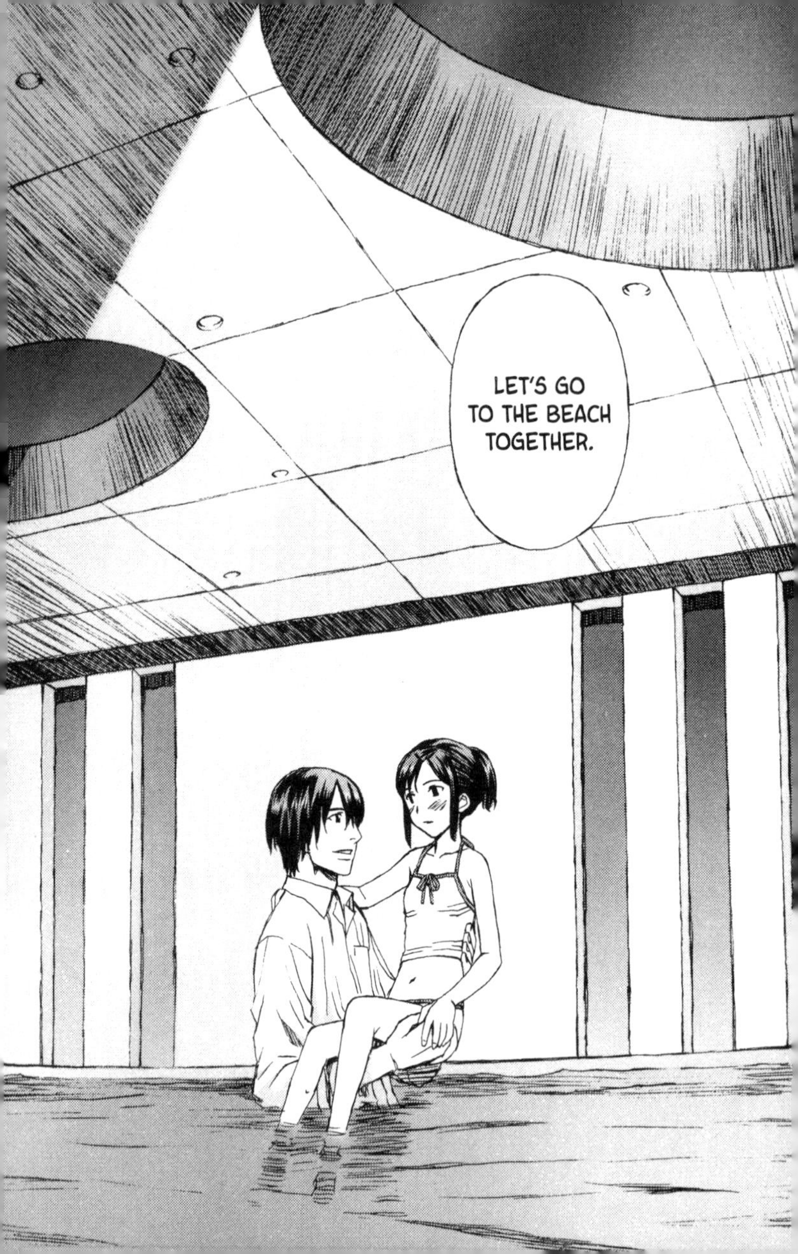
LET'S GO TO THE BEACH TOGETHER.

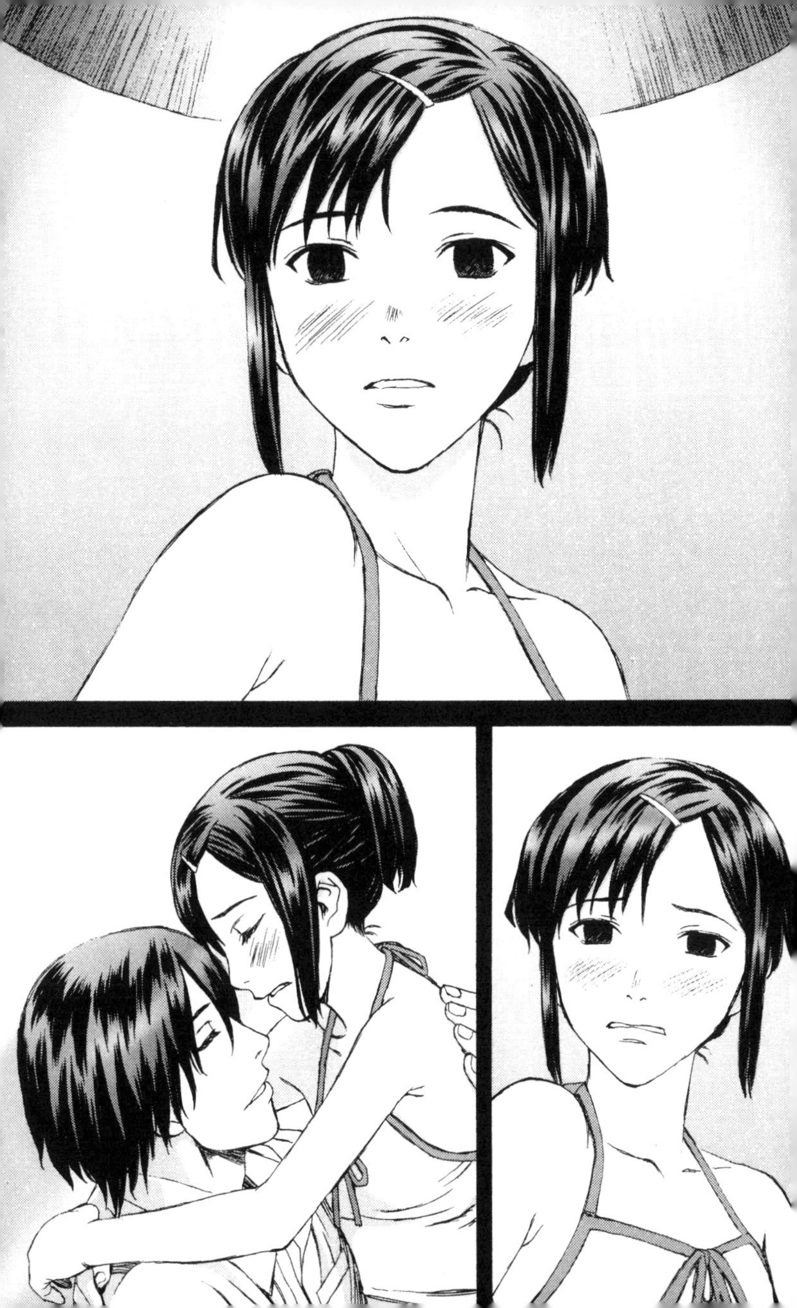

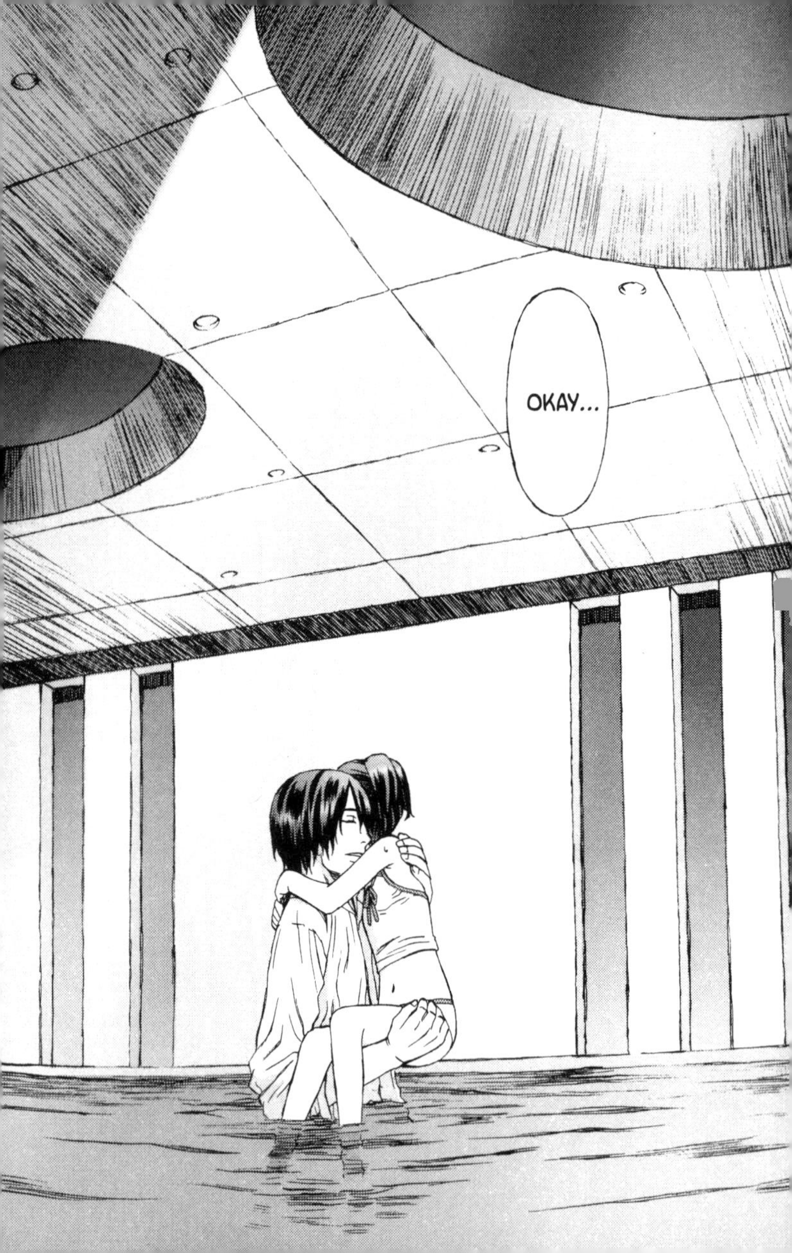
OKAY...

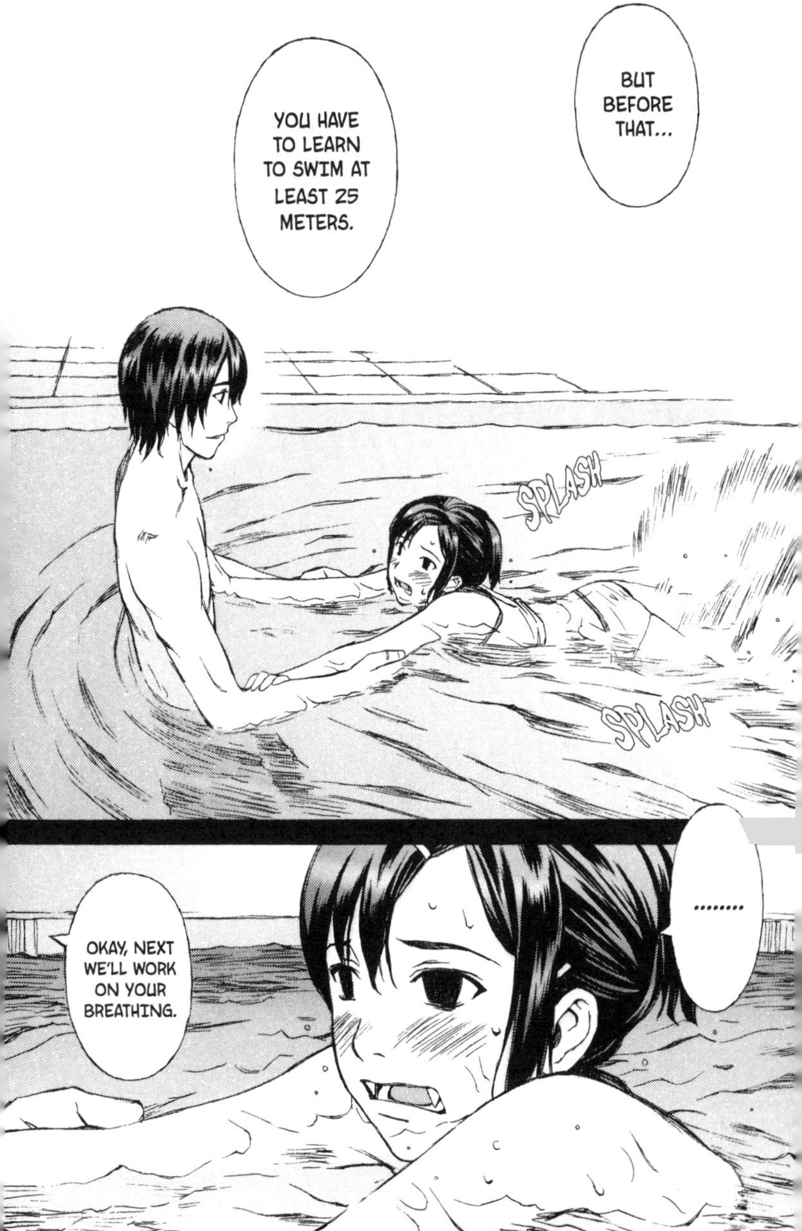
BUT BEFORE THAT...
YOU HAVE TO LEARN TO SWIM AT LEAST 25 METERS.
SPLASH
SPLASH
....
OKAY, NEXT WE'LL WORK ON YOUR BREATHING.

MIDNIGHT CRUISE

素顔の彼女 - Her True Face

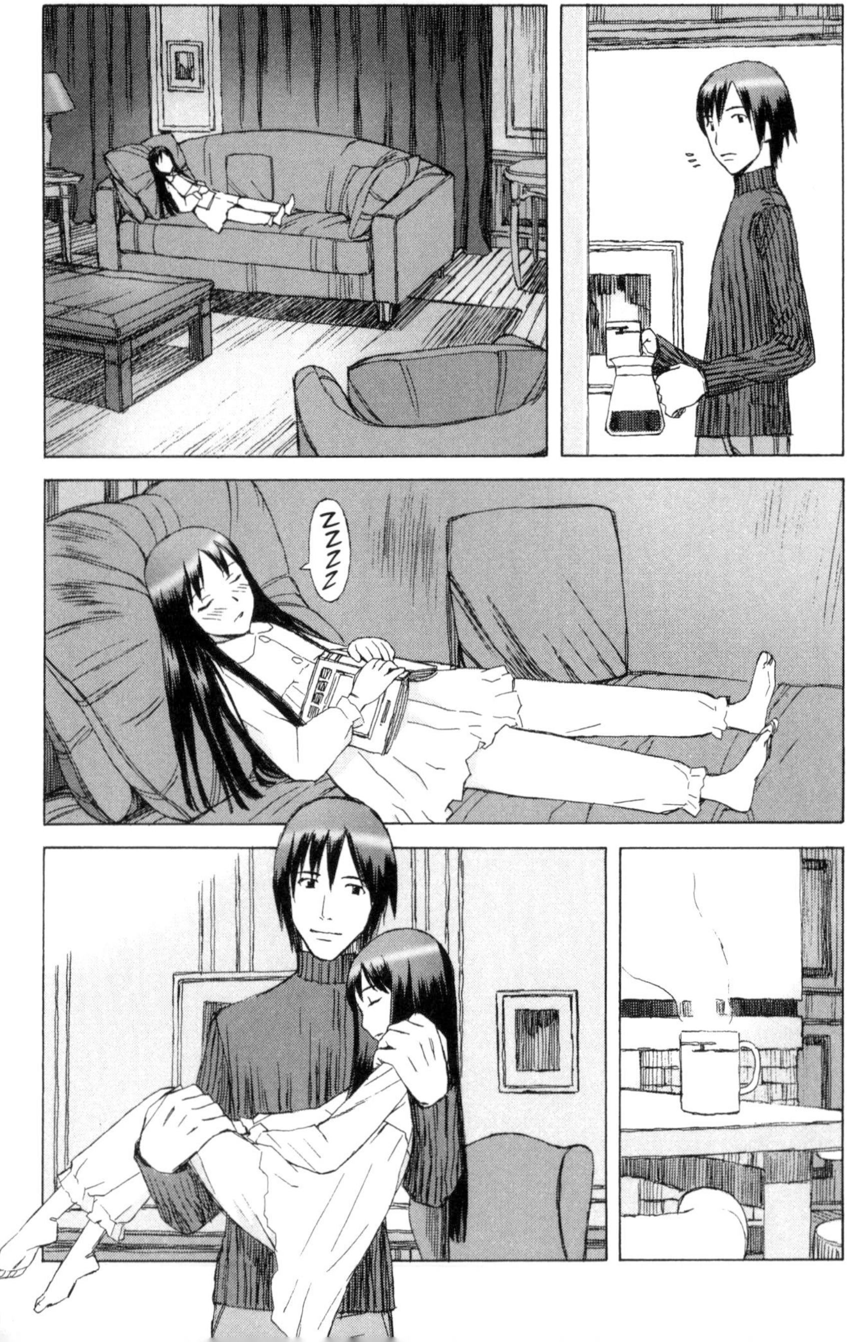
ZZZZ

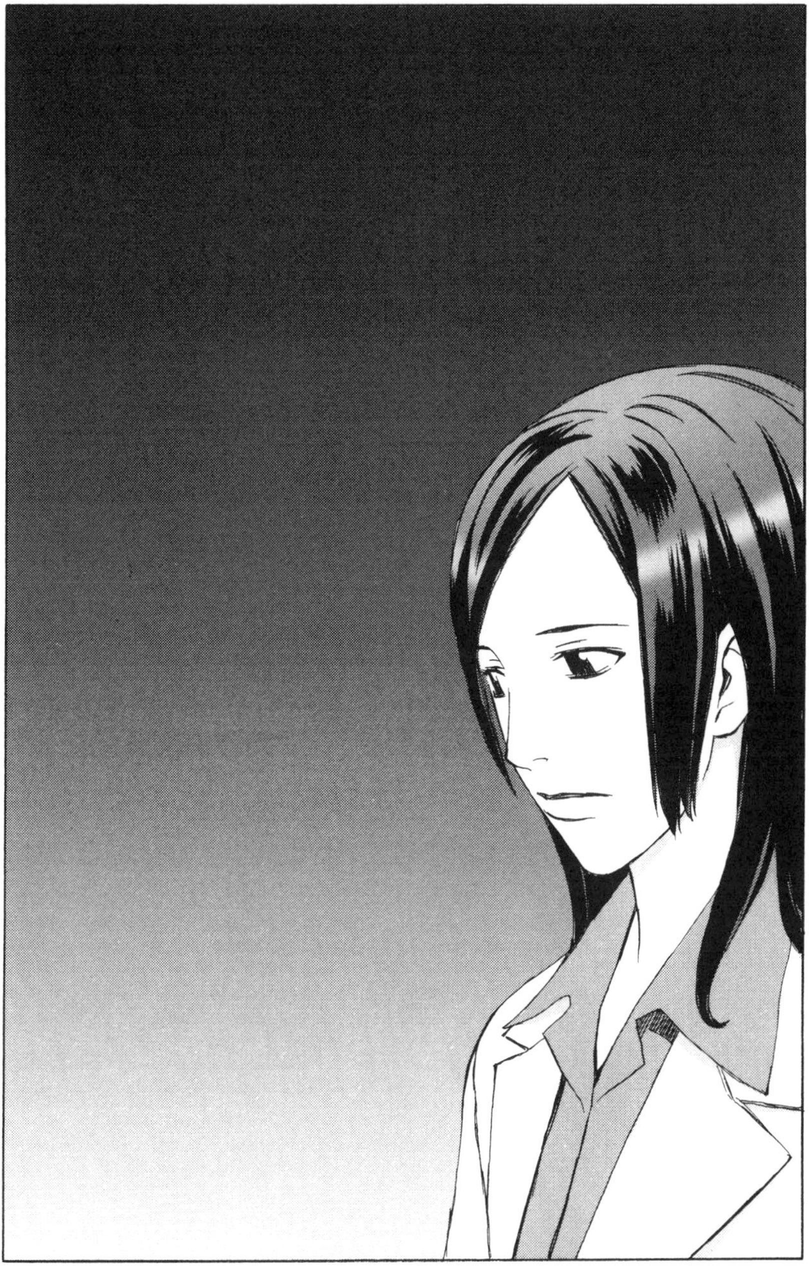

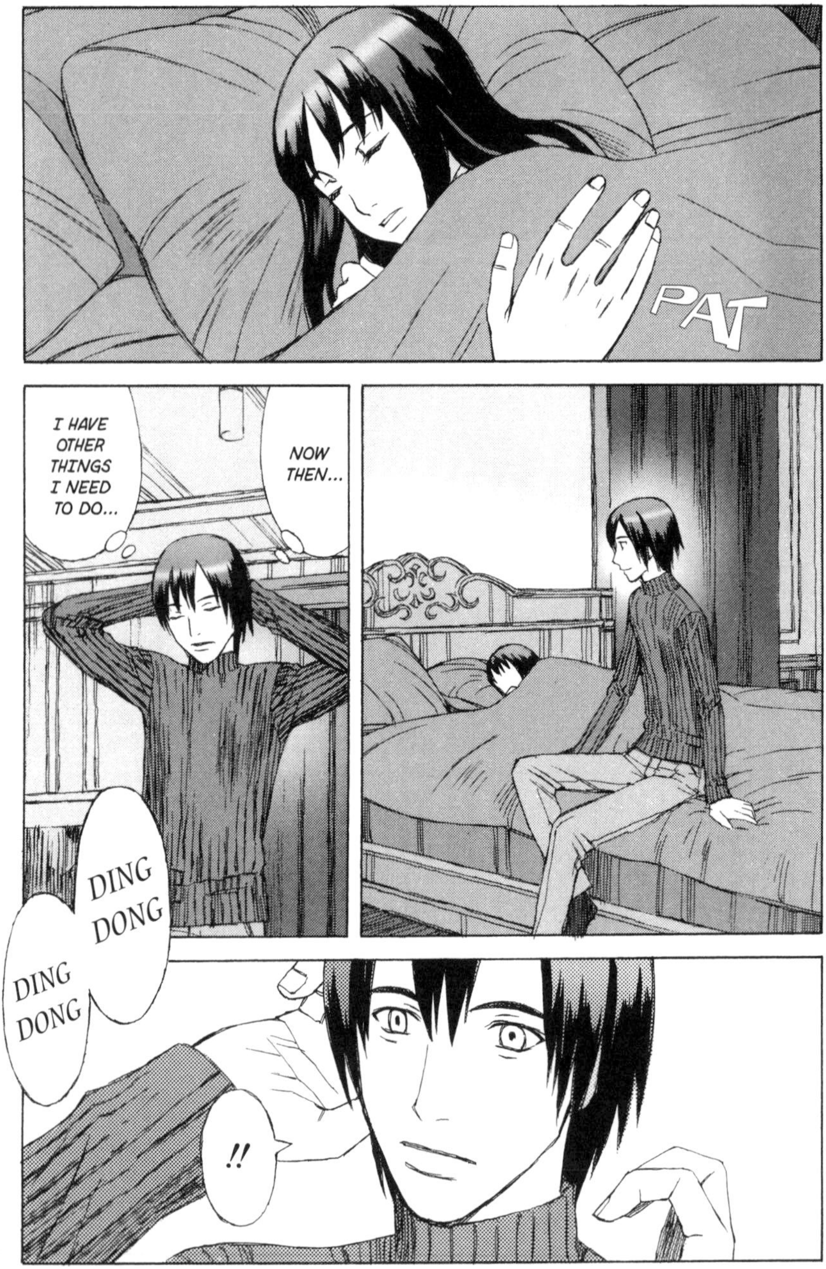
PAT
NOW THEN...
I HAVE OTHER THINGS I NEED TO DO...
DING DONG
DING DONG
!!

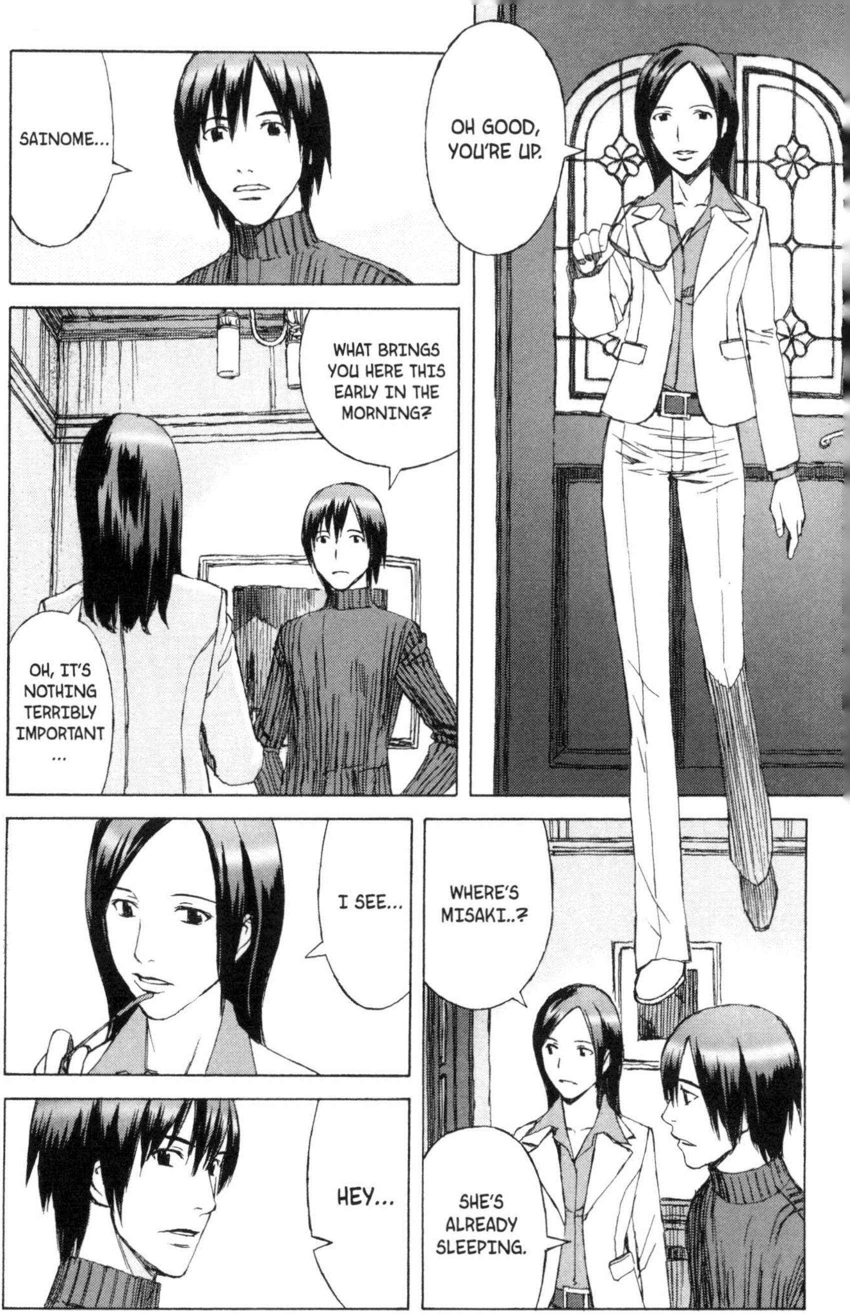
OH GOOD, YOU'RE UP.
SAINOME...
WHAT BRINGS YOU HERE THIS EARLY IN THE MORNING?
OH, IT'S NOTHING TERRIBLY IMPORTANT ...
WHERE'S MISAKI..?
SHE'S ALREADY SLEEPING.
I SEE...
HEY...

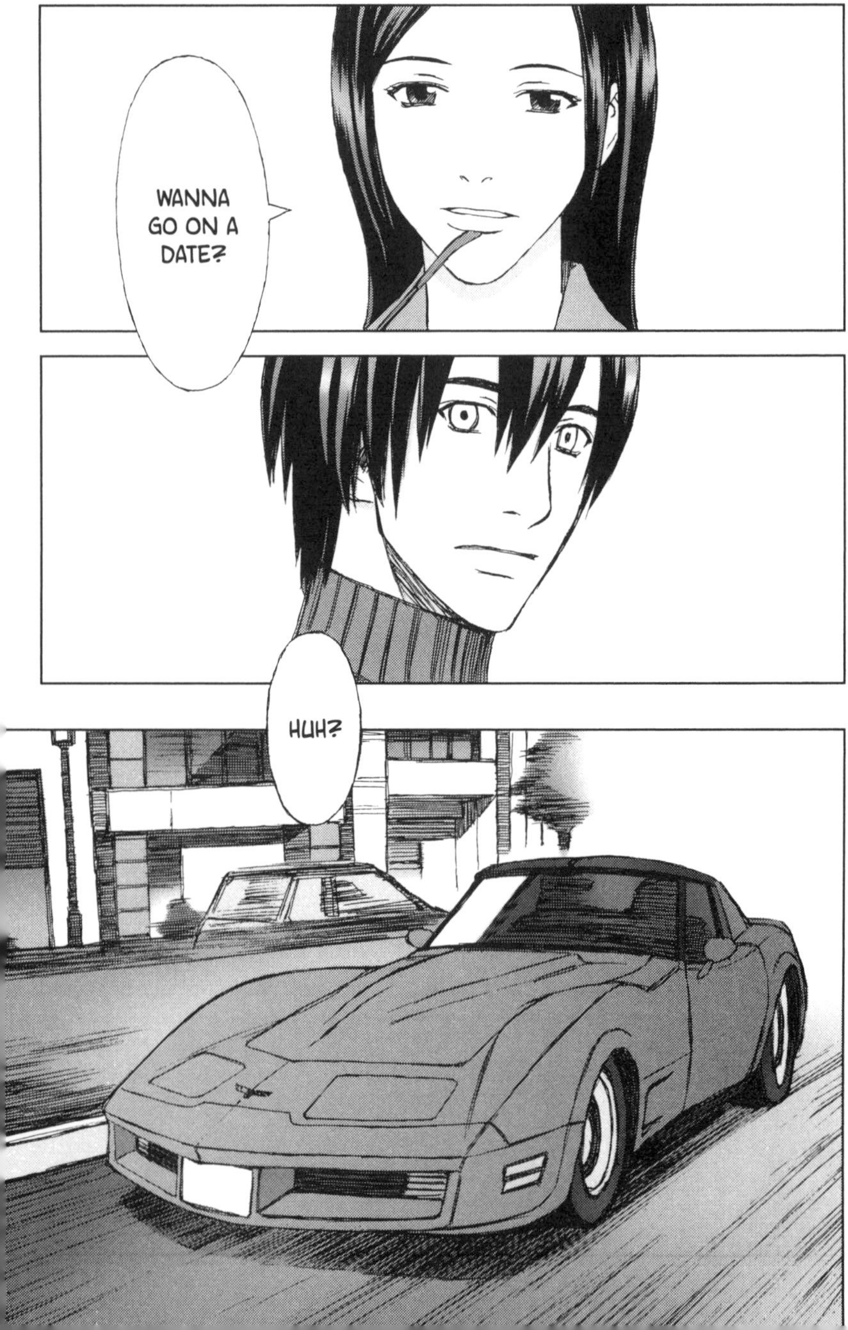
WANNA GO ON A DATE?
HUH?

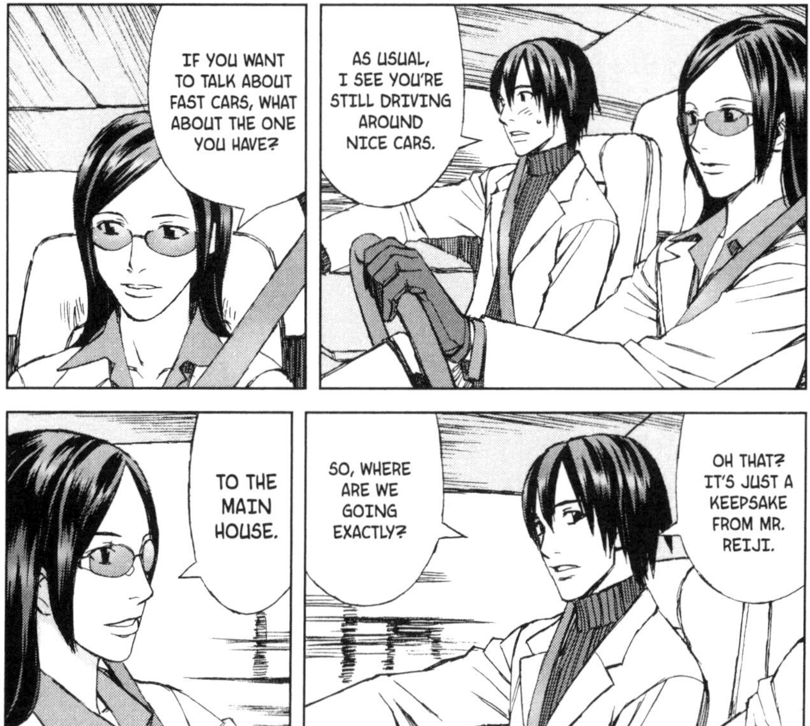
AS USUAL, I SEE YOU'RE STILL DRIVING AROUND NICE CARS.
IF YOU WANT TO TALK ABOUT FAST CARS, WHAT ABOUT THE ONE YOU HAVE?
OH THAT? IT'S JUST A KEEPSAKE FROM MR. REIJI.
SO, WHERE ARE WE GOING EXACTLY?
TO THE MAIN HOUSE.

Note : In Japan, the main house is where either the eldest family members live, or where a residence which has been passed down between generations is.

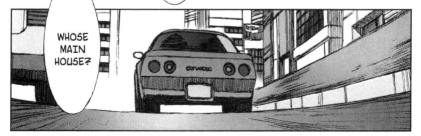

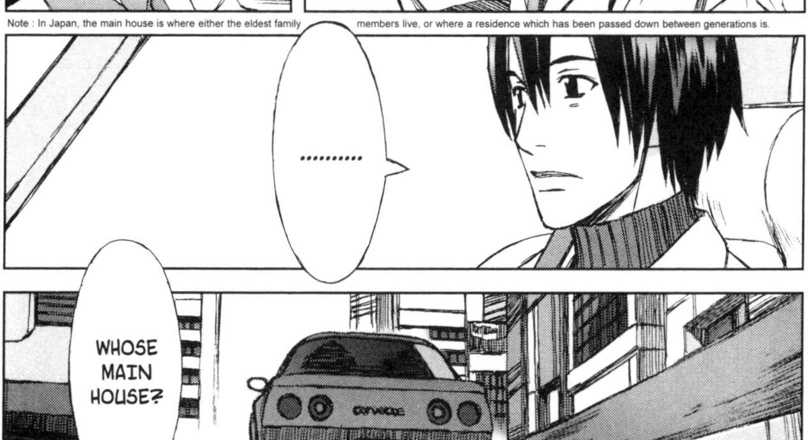
....
WHOSE MAIN HOUSE?

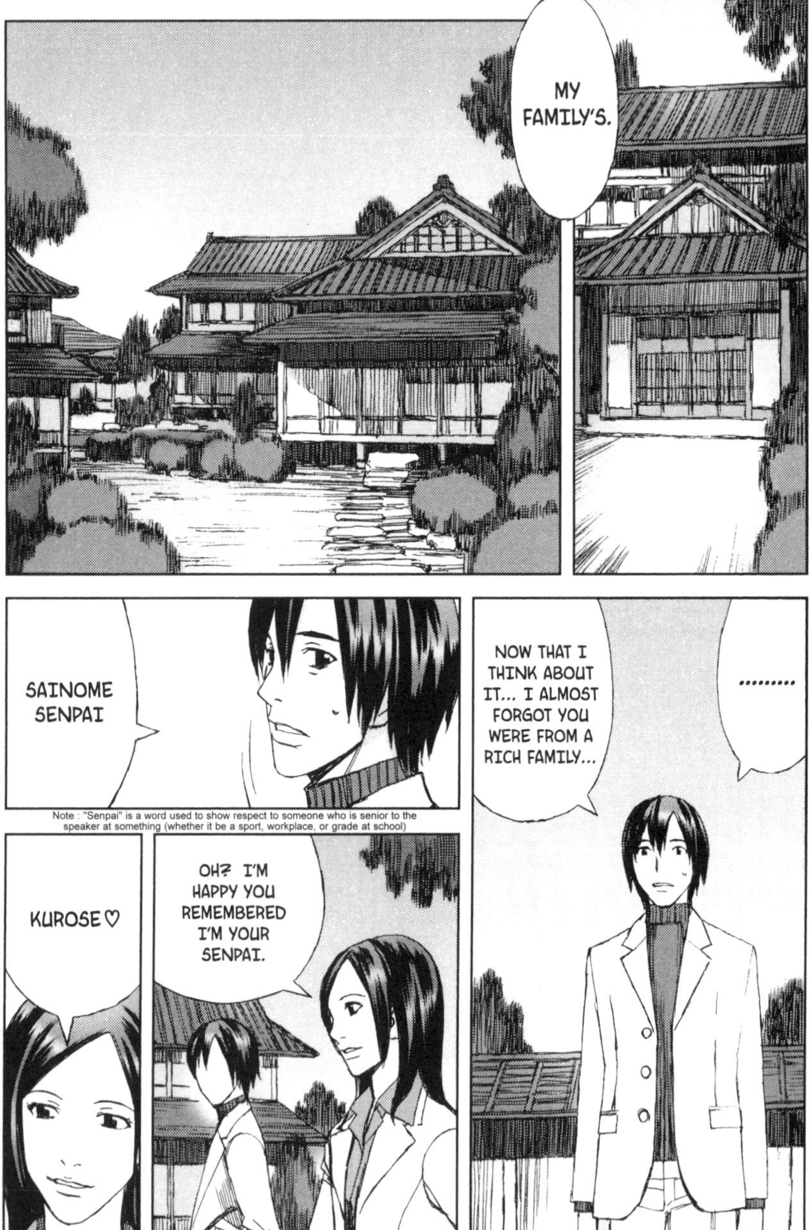
MY FAMILY'S.
....
NOW THAT I THINK ABOUT IT... I ALMOST FORGOT YOU WERE FROM A RICH FAMILY...
SAINOME SENPAI
Note : "Senpai" is a word used to show respect to someone who is senior to the speaker at something (whether it be a sport, workplace, or grade at school)
OH? I'M HAPPY YOU REMEMBERED I'M YOUR SENPAI.
KUROSE♡

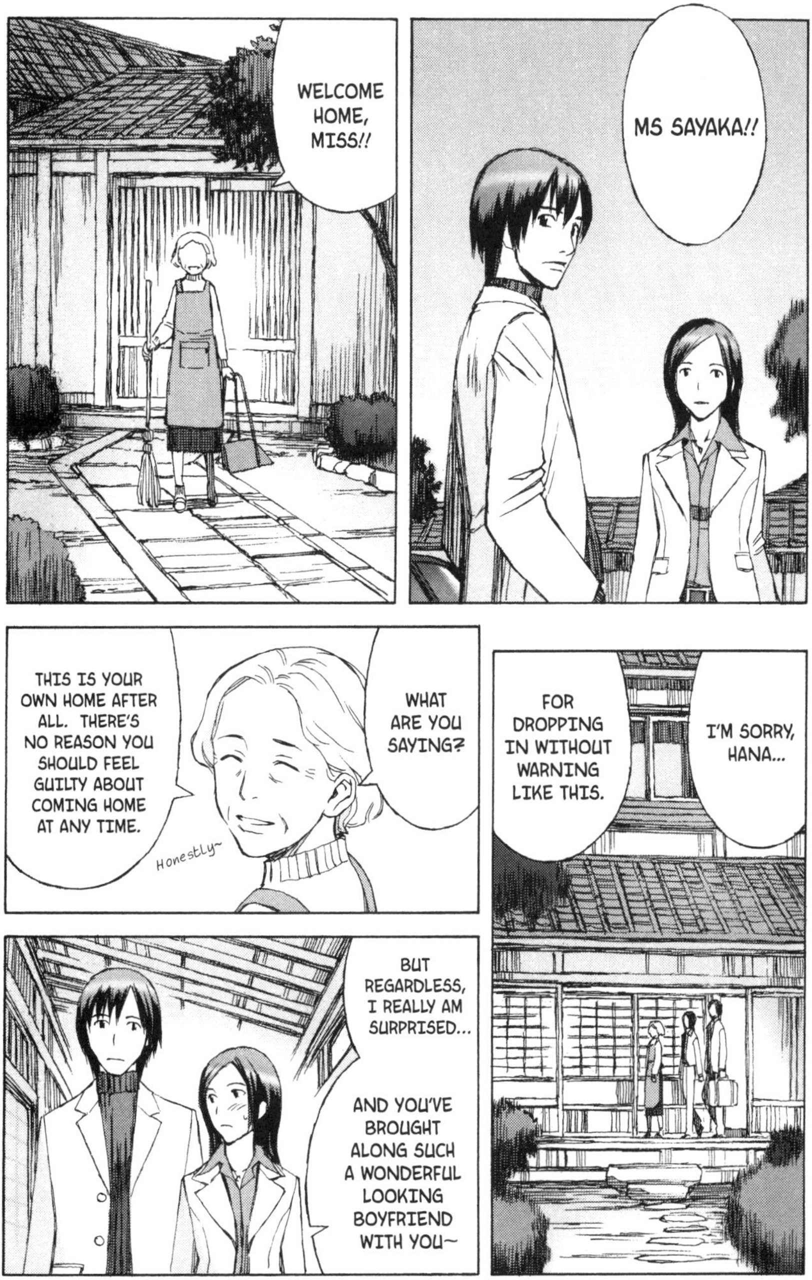
MS SAYAKA!!
WELCOME HOME, MISS!!
I'M SORRY, HANA...
FOR DROPPING IN WITHOUT WARNING LIKE THIS.
WHAT ARE YOU SAYING?
THIS IS YOUR OWN HOME AFTER ALL. THERE'S NO REASON YOU SHOULD FEEL GUILTY ABOUT COMING HOME AT ANY TIME.
Honestly~
BUT REGARDLESS, I REALLY AM SURPRISED...
AND YOU'VE BROUGHT ALONG SUCH A WONDERFUL LOOKING BOYFRIEND WITH YOU~

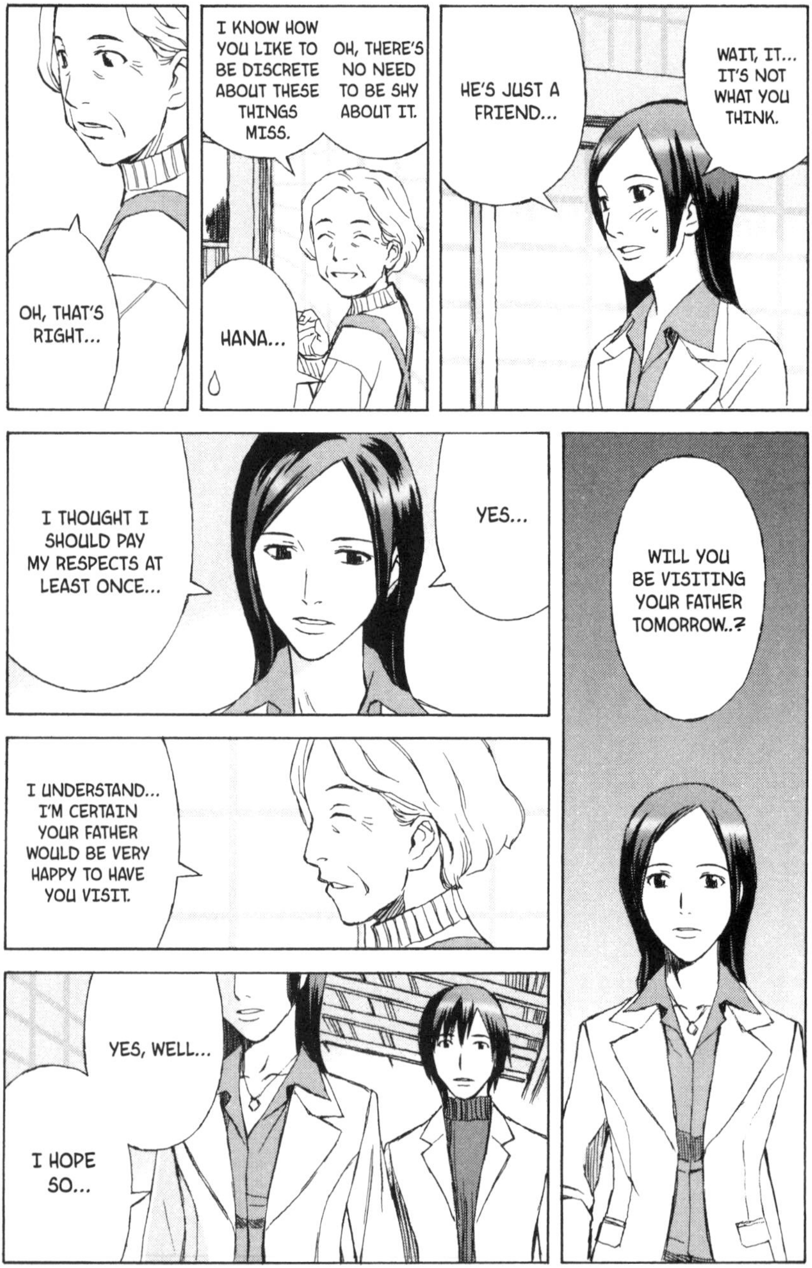
WAIT, IT... IT'S NOT WHAT YOU THINK.
HE'S JUST A FRIEND...
OH, THERE'S NO NEED TO BE SHY ABOUT IT.
I KNOW HOW YOU LIKE TO BE DISCRETE ABOUT THESE THINGS MISS.
HANA...
OH, THAT'S RIGHT...
WILL YOU BE VISITING YOUR FATHER TOMORROW..?
YES...
I THOUGHT I SHOULD PAY MY RESPECTS AT LEAST ONCE...
I UNDERSTAND... I'M CERTAIN YOUR FATHER WOULD BE VERY HAPPY TO HAVE YOU VISIT.
YES, WELL...
I HOPE SO...

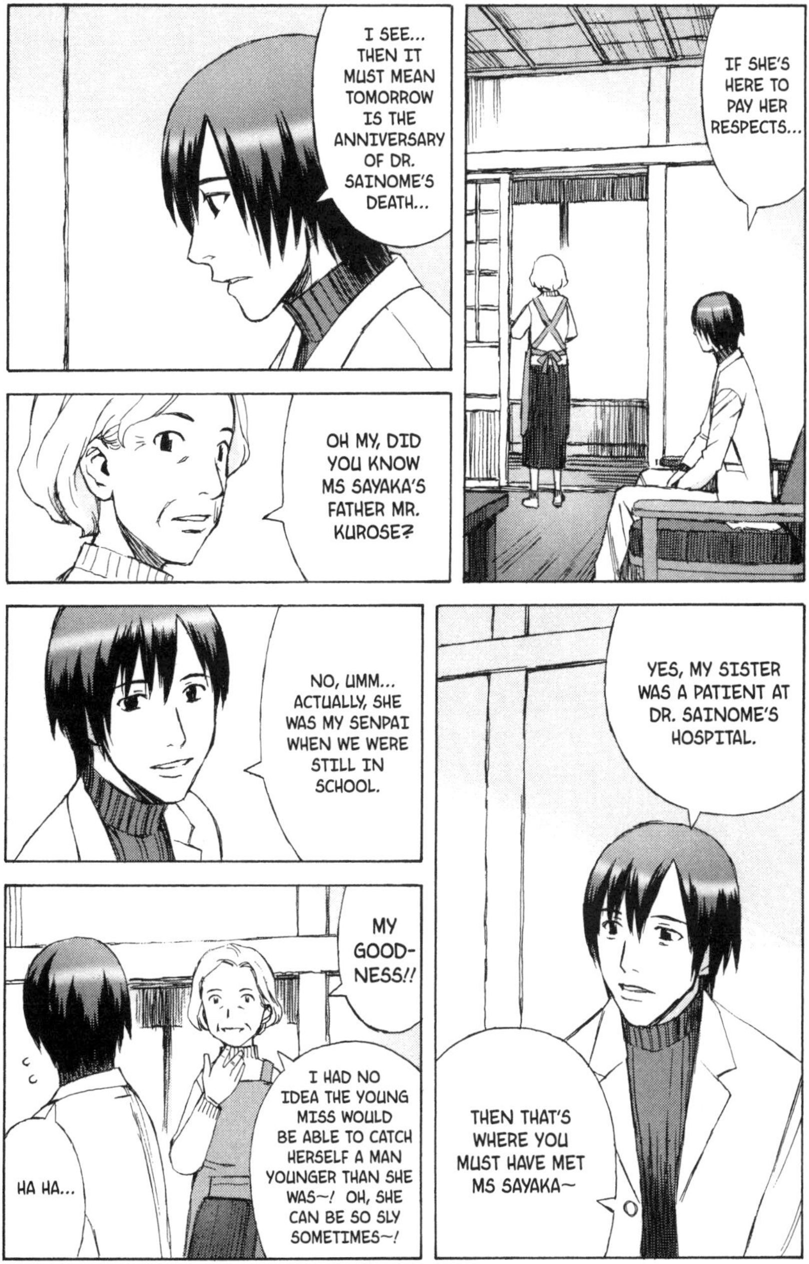
IF SHE'S HERE TO PAY HER RESPECTS...
I SEE... THEN IT MUST MEAN TOMORROW IS THE ANNIVERSARY OF DR. SAINOME'S DEATH...
OH MY, DID YOU KNOW MS SAYAKA'S FATHER MR. KUROSE?
YES, MY SISTER WAS A PATIENT AT DR. SAINOME'S HOSPITAL.
THEN THAT'S WHERE YOU MUST HAVE MET MS SAYAKA~
NO, UMM... ACTUALLY, SHE WAS MY SENPAI WHEN WE WERE STILL IN SCHOOL.
MY GOOD-NESS!!
I HAD NO IDEA THE YOUNG MISS WOULD BE ABLE TO CATCH HERSELF A MAN YOUNGER THAN SHE WAS~! OH, SHE CAN BE SO SLY SOMETIMES~!
HA HA...

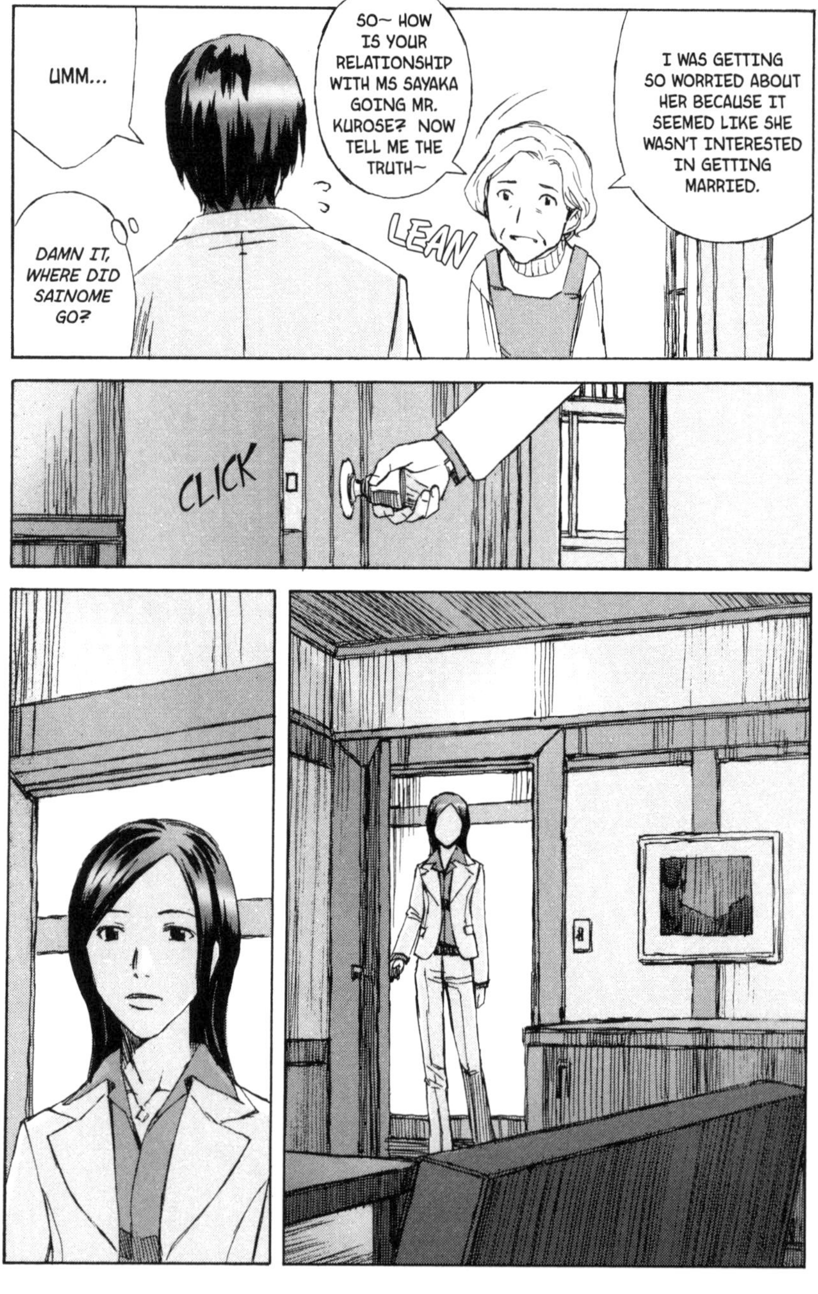
I WAS GETTING SO WORRIED ABOUT HER BECAUSE IT SEEMED LIKE SHE WASN'T INTERESTED IN GETTING MARRIED.
SO~ HOW IS YOUR RELATIONSHIP WITH MS SAYAKA GOING MR. KUROSE? NOW TELL ME THE TRUTH~
LEAN
UMM...
DAMN IT, WHERE DID SAINOME GO?
CLICK

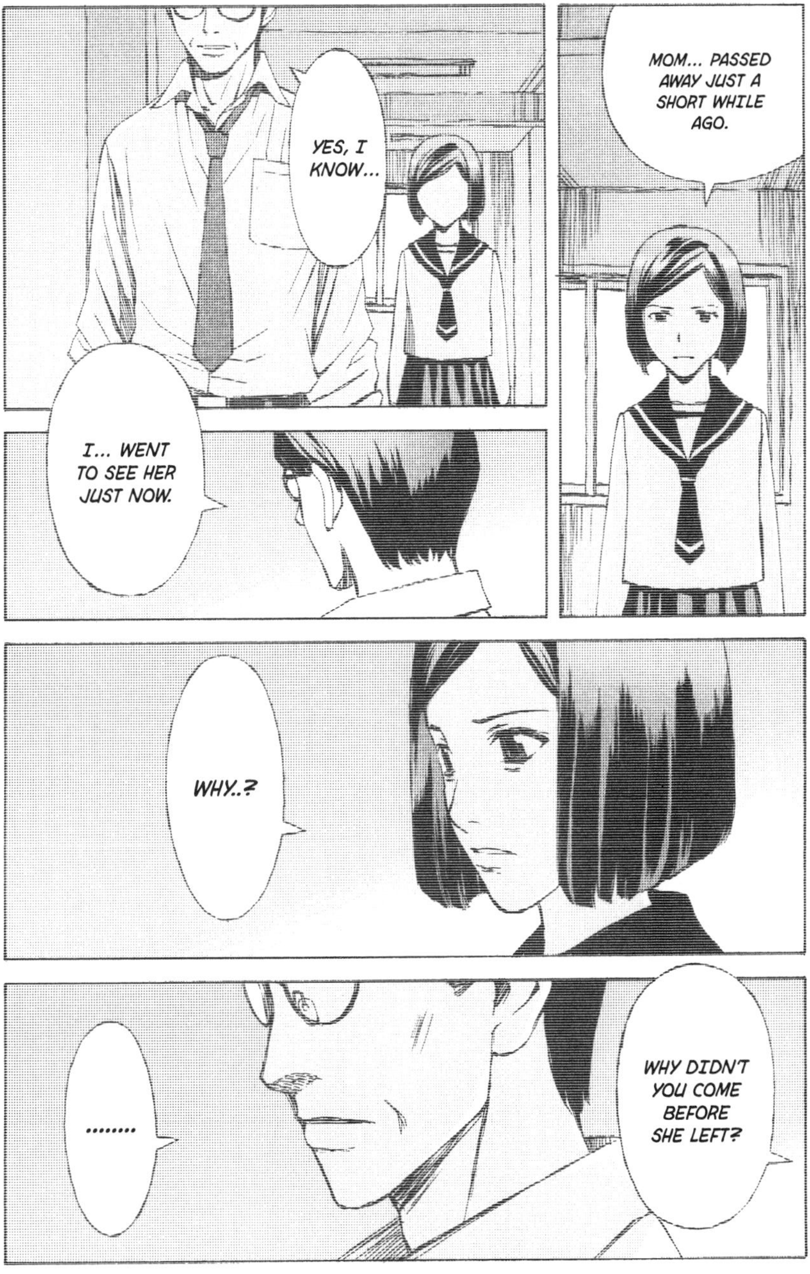
MOM... PASSED AWAY JUST A SHORT WHILE AGO.
YES, I KNOW...
I... WENT TO SEE HER JUST NOW.
WHY..?
WHY DIDN'T YOU COME BEFORE SHE LEFT?
....

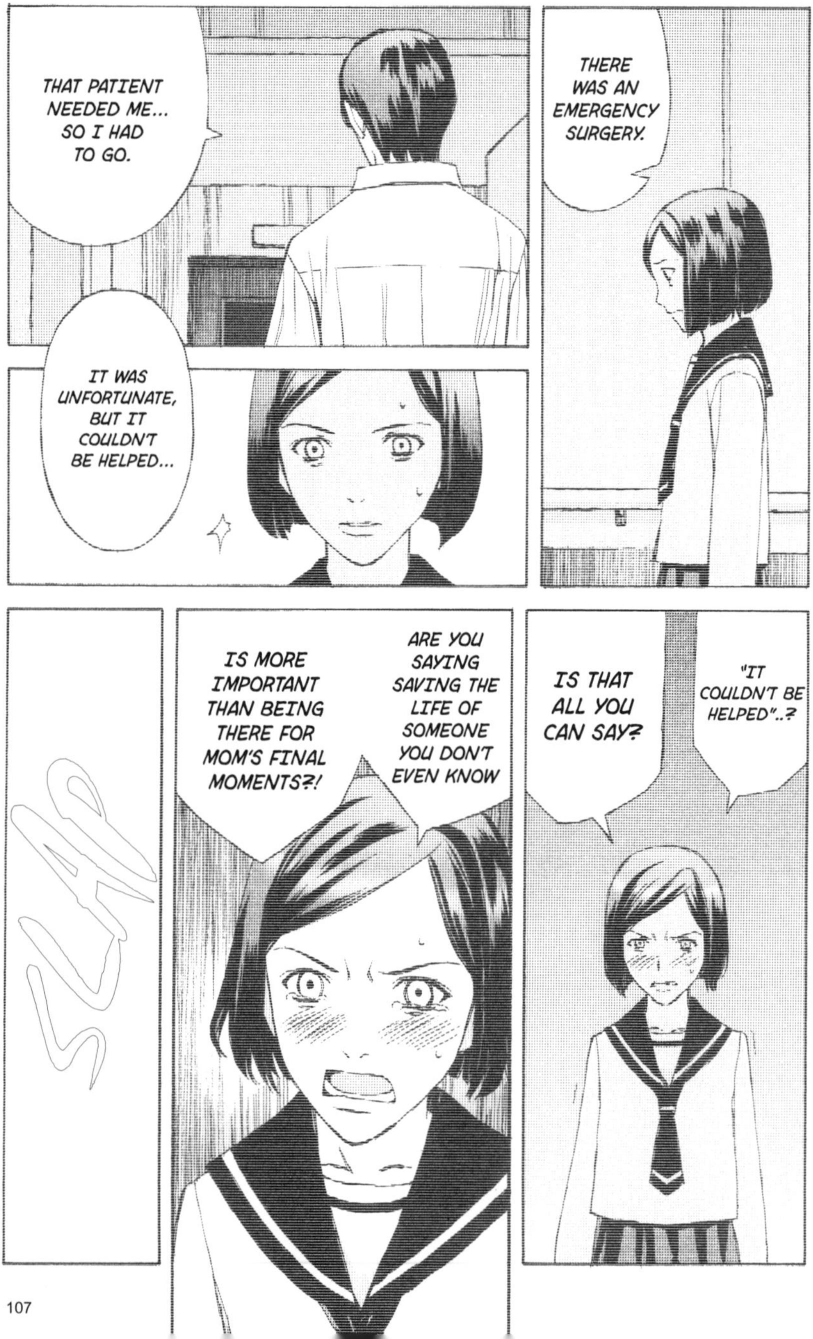
THERE WAS AN EMERGENCY SURGERY.
THAT PATIENT NEEDED ME... SO I HAD TO GO.
IT WAS UNFORTUNATE, BUT IT COULDN'T BE HELPED...
"IT COULDN'T BE HELPED"..?
IS THAT ALL YOU CAN SAY?
ARE YOU SAYING SAVING THE LIFE OF SOMEONE YOU DON'T EVEN KNOW
IS MORE IMPORTANT THAN BEING THERE FOR MOM'S FINAL MOMENTS?!
SLAP

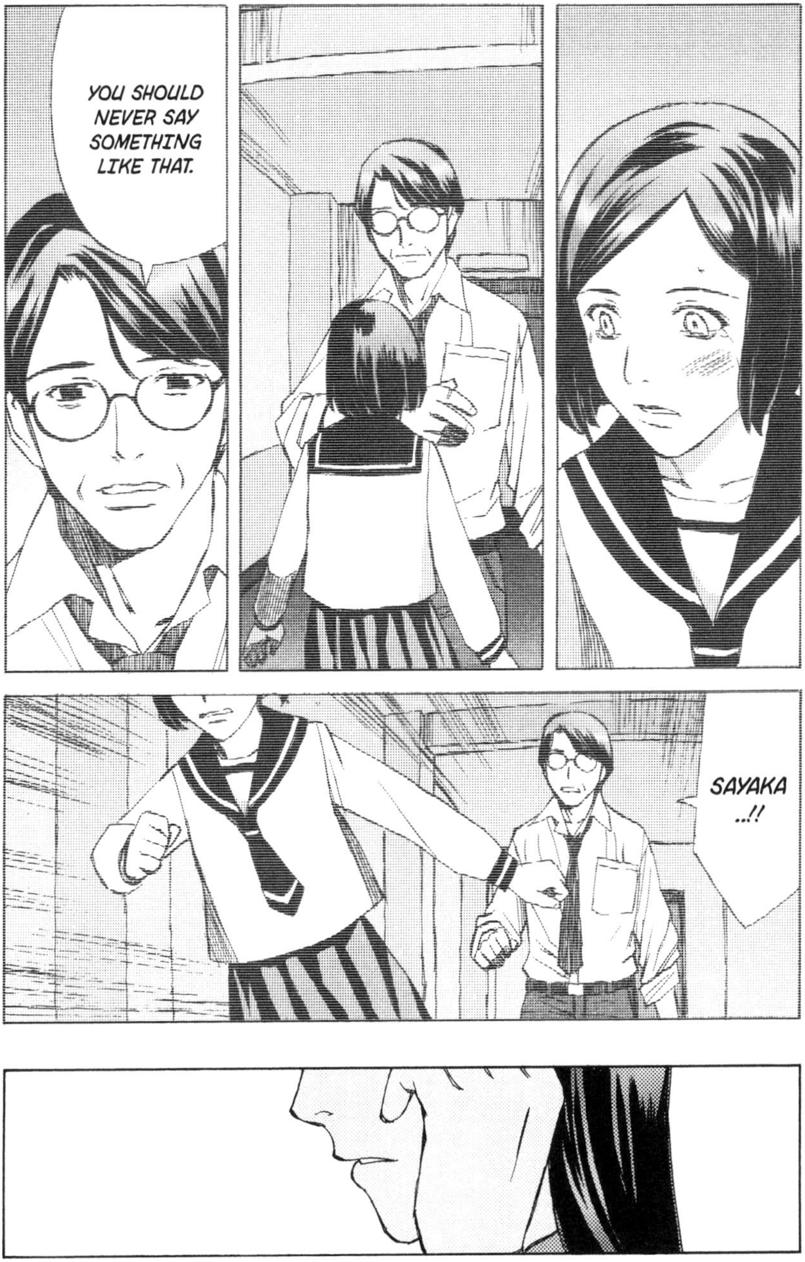
YOU SHOULD NEVER SAY SOMETHING LIKE THAT.
SAYAKA ..!!

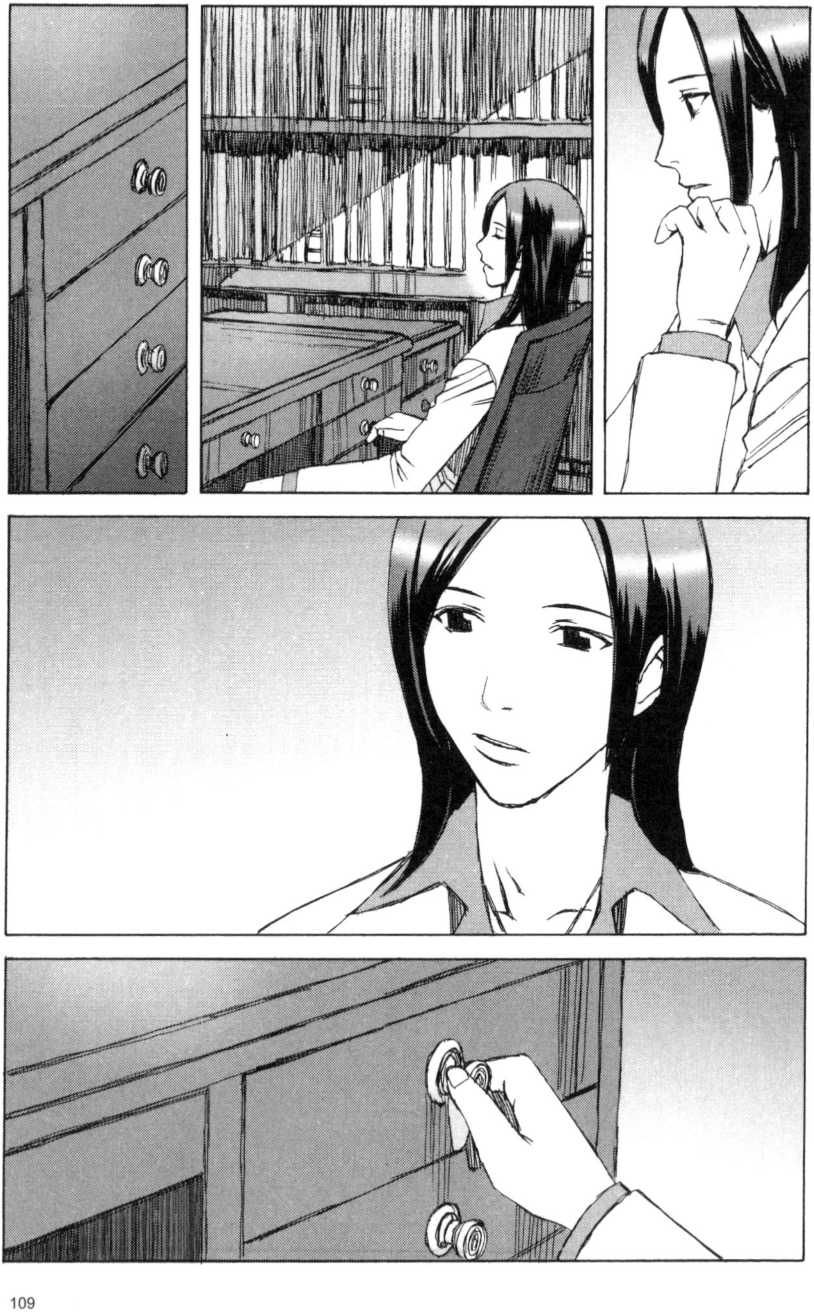

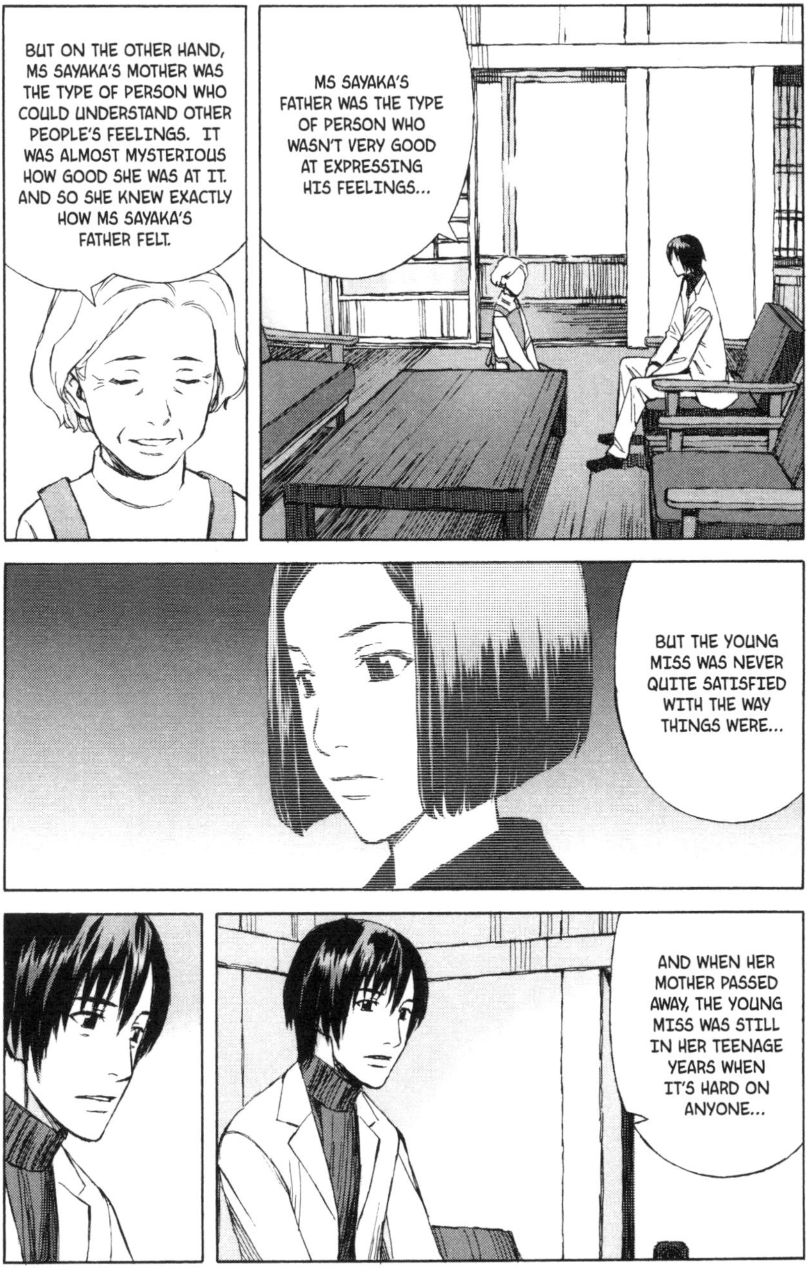
MS SAYAKA'S FATHER WAS THE TYPE OF PERSON WHO WASN'T VERY GOOD AT EXPRESSING HIS FEELINGS...
BUT ON THE OTHER HAND, MS SAYAKA'S MOTHER WAS THE TYPE OF PERSON WHO COULD UNDERSTAND OTHER PEOPLE'S FEELINGS. IT WAS ALMOST MYSTERIOUS HOW GOOD SHE WAS AT IT. AND SO SHE KNEW EXACTLY HOW MS SAYAKA'S FATHER FELT.
BUT THE YOUNG MISS WAS NEVER QUITE SATISFIED WITH THE WAY THINGS WERE...
AND WHEN HER MOTHER PASSED AWAY, THE YOUNG MISS WAS STILL IN HER TEENAGE YEARS WHEN IT'S HARD ON ANYONE...

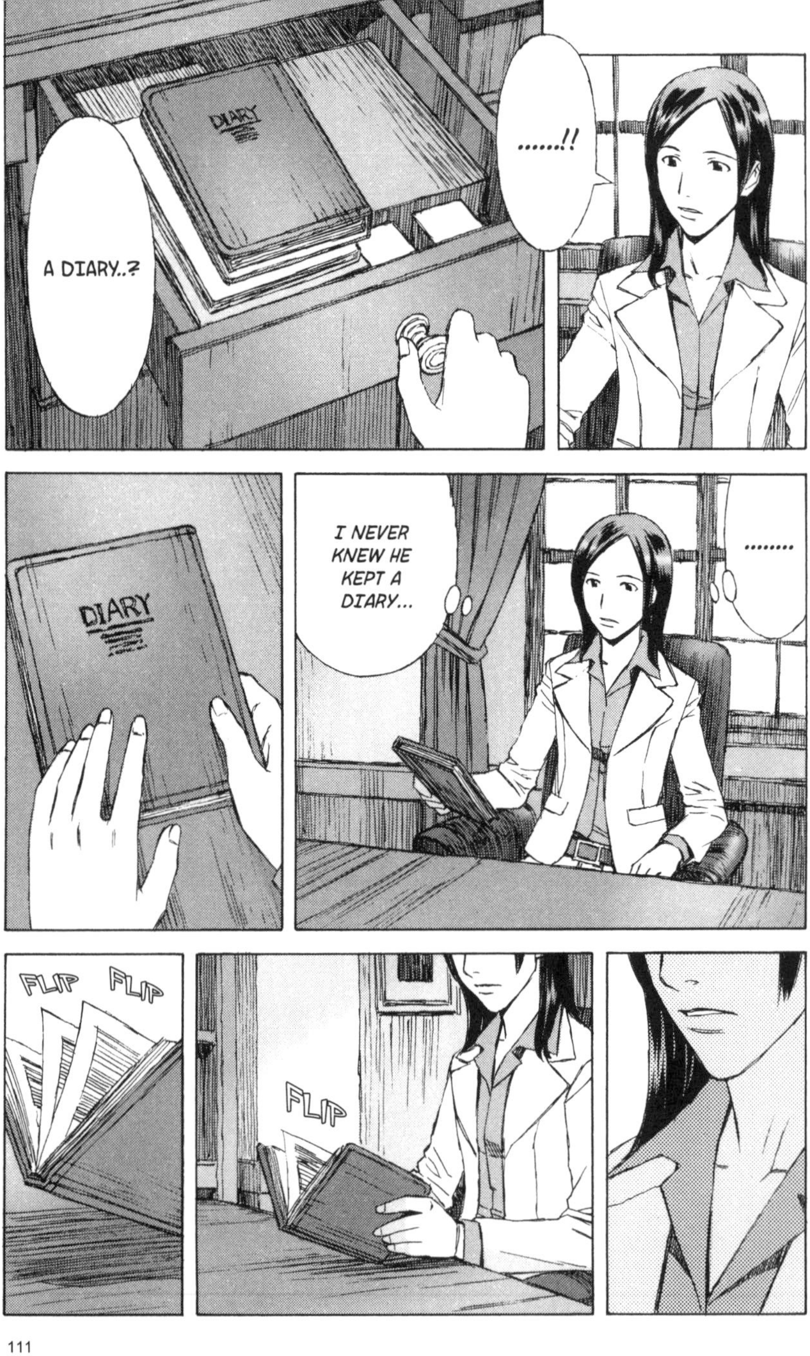
......!!
A DIARY..?
....
I NEVER KNEW HE KEPT A DIARY...
FLIP
FLIP
FLIP

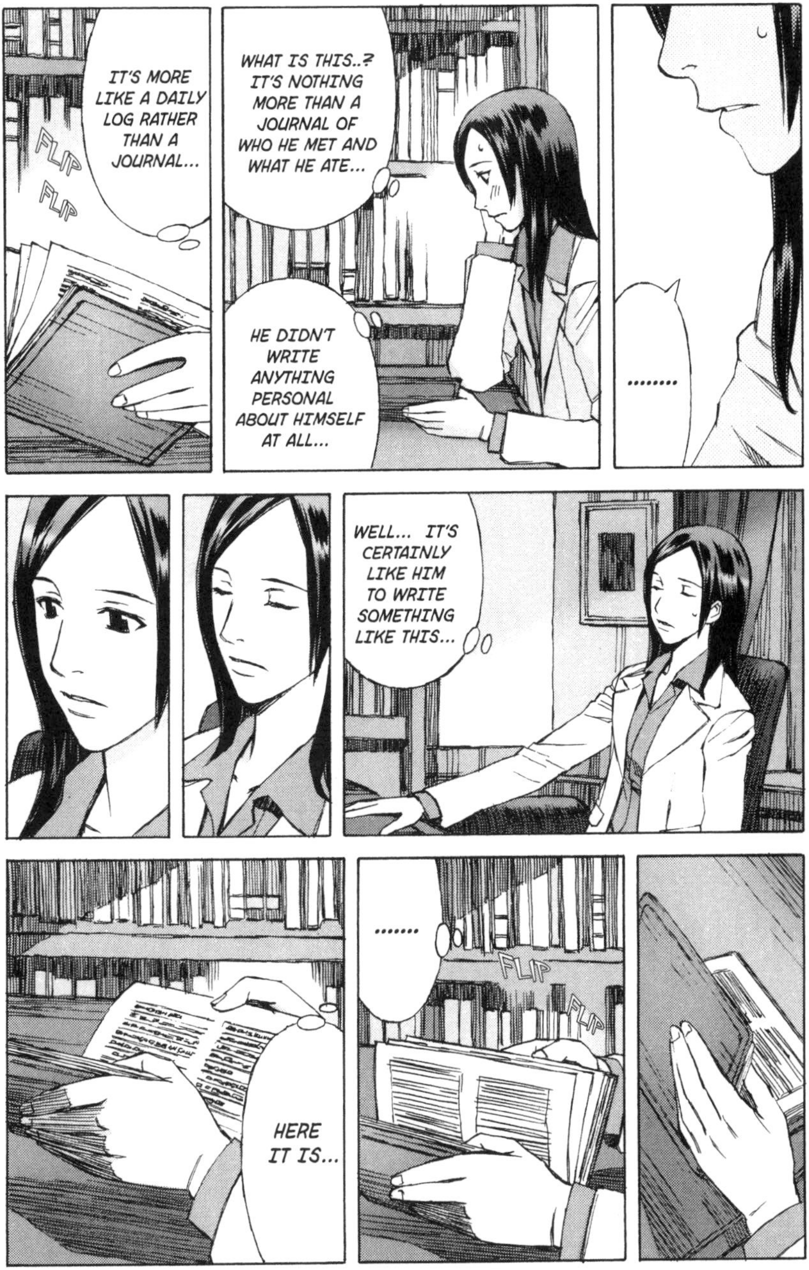
....
WHAT IS THIS..? IT'S NOTHING MORE THAN A JOURNAL OF WHO HE MET AND WHAT HE ATE...
HE DIDN'T WRITE ANYTHING PERSONAL ABOUT HIMSELF AT ALL...
IT'S MORE LIKE A DAILY LOG RATHER THAN A JOURNAL...
FLIP
FLIP
WELL... IT'S CERTAINLY LIKE HIM TO WRITE SOMETHING LIKE THIS...
....
FLIP
FLIP
HERE IT IS...

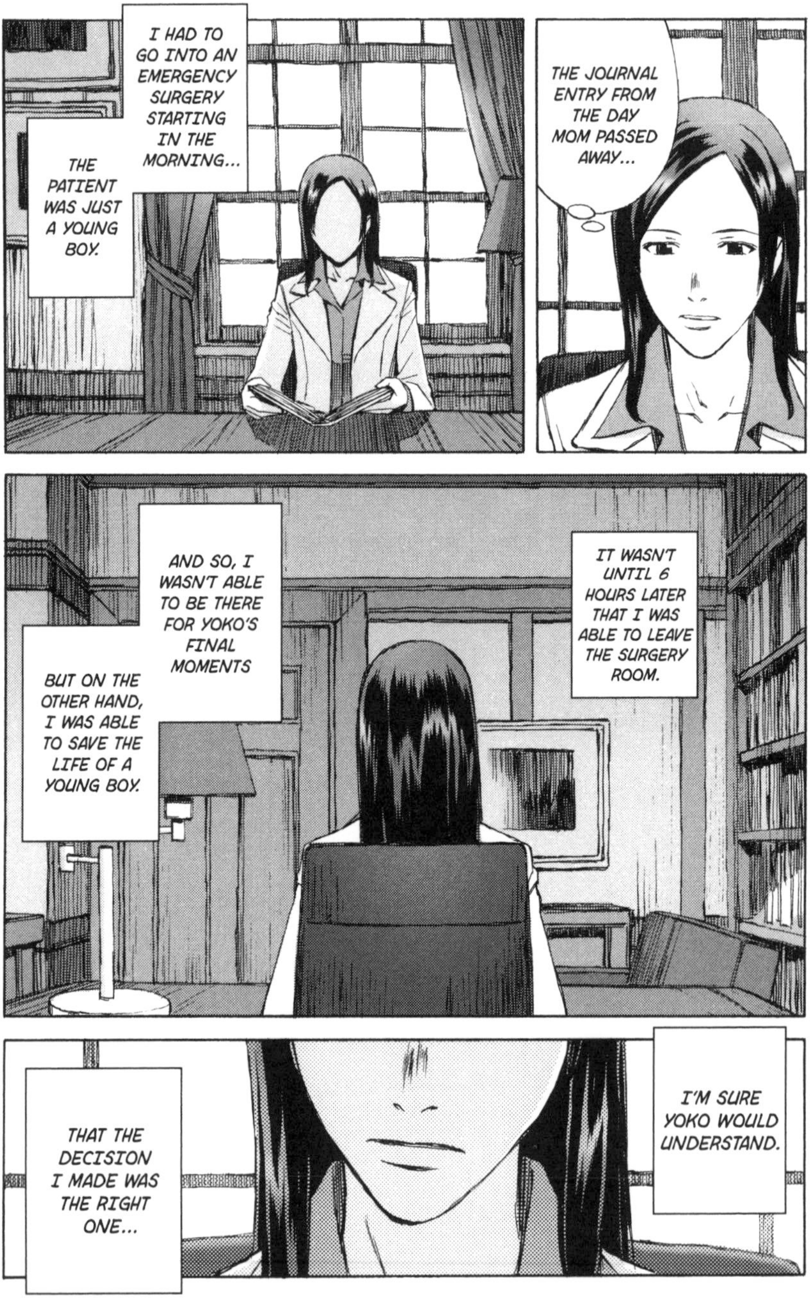
THE JOURNAL ENTRY FROM THE DAY MOM PASSED AWAY...
I HAD TO GO INTO AN EMERGENCY SURGERY STARTING IN THE MORNING...
THE PATIENT WAS JUST A YOUNG BOY.
IT WASN'T UNTIL 6 HOURS LATER THAT I WAS ABLE TO LEAVE THE SURGERY ROOM.
AND SO, I WASN'T ABLE TO BE THERE FOR YOKO'S FINAL MOMENTS
BUT ON THE OTHER HAND, I WAS ABLE TO SAVE THE LIFE OF A YOUNG BOY.
I'M SURE YOKO WOULD UNDERSTAND.
THAT THE DECISION I MADE WAS THE RIGHT ONE...

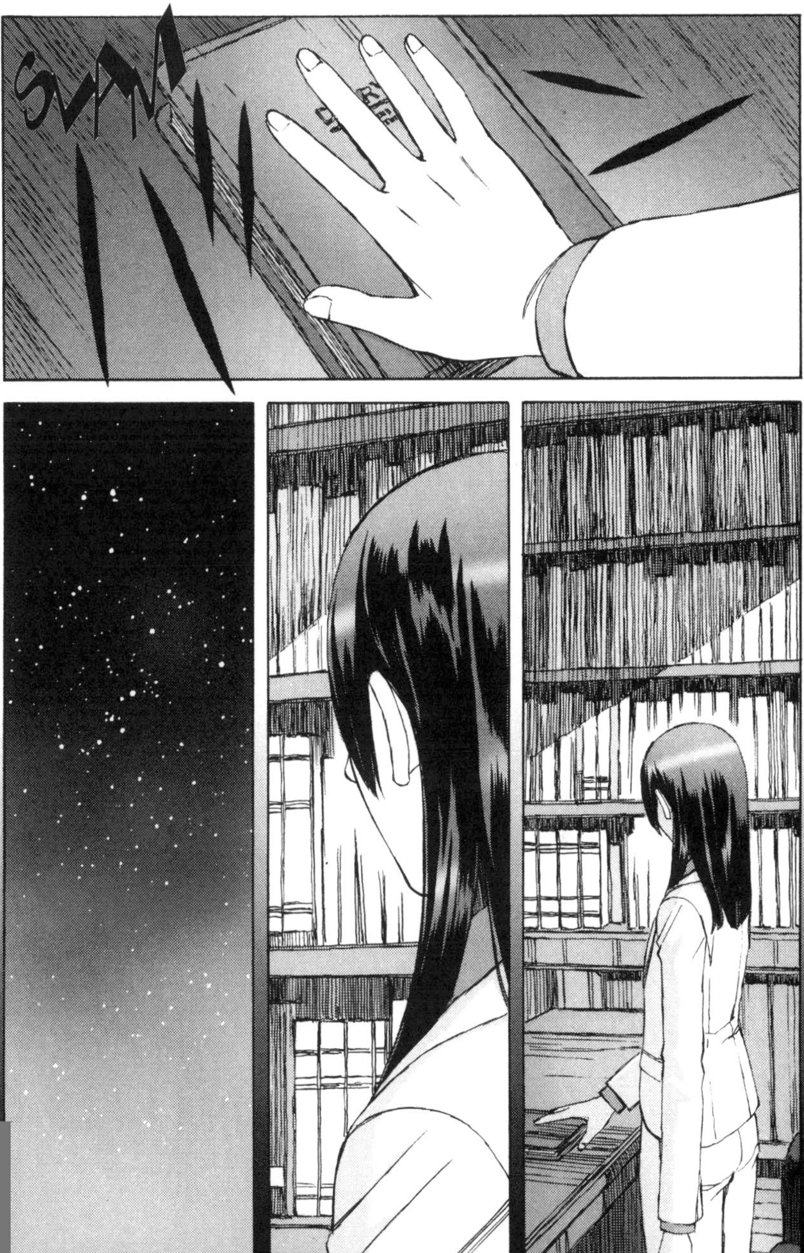
SLAM!

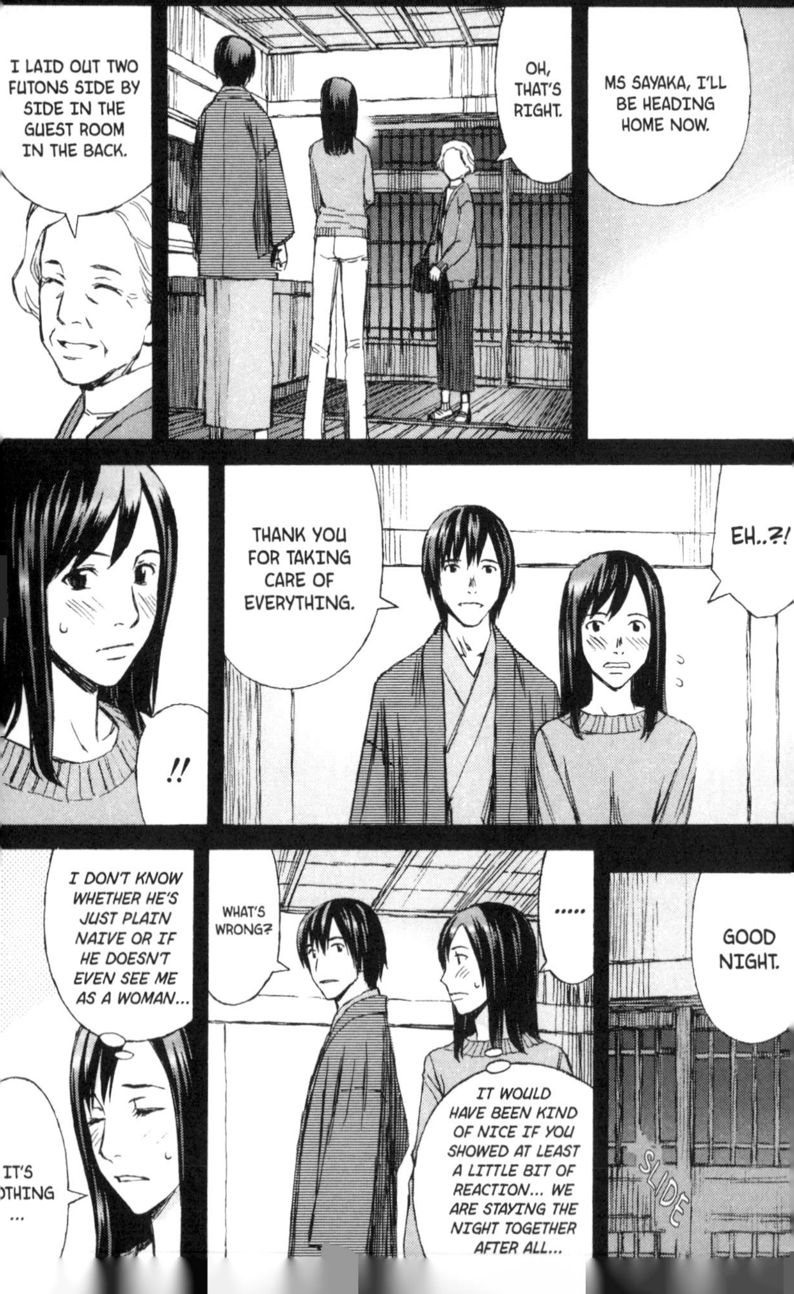
MS SAYAKA, I'LL BE HEADING HOME NOW.
OH, THAT'S RIGHT.
I LAID OUT TWO FUTONS SIDE BY SIDE IN THE GUEST ROOM IN THE BACK.
EH..?!
THANK YOU FOR TAKING CARE OF EVERYTHING.
!!
GOOD NIGHT.
SLIDE
.....
WHAT'S WRONG?
IT WOULD HAVE BEEN KIND OF NICE IF YOU SHOWED AT LEAST A LITTLE BIT OF REACTION... WE ARE STAYING THE NIGHT TOGETHER AFTER ALL...
I DON'T KNOW WHETHER HE'S JUST PLAIN NAIVE OR IF HE DOESN'T EVEN SEE ME AS A WOMAN...
IT'S OTHING ...

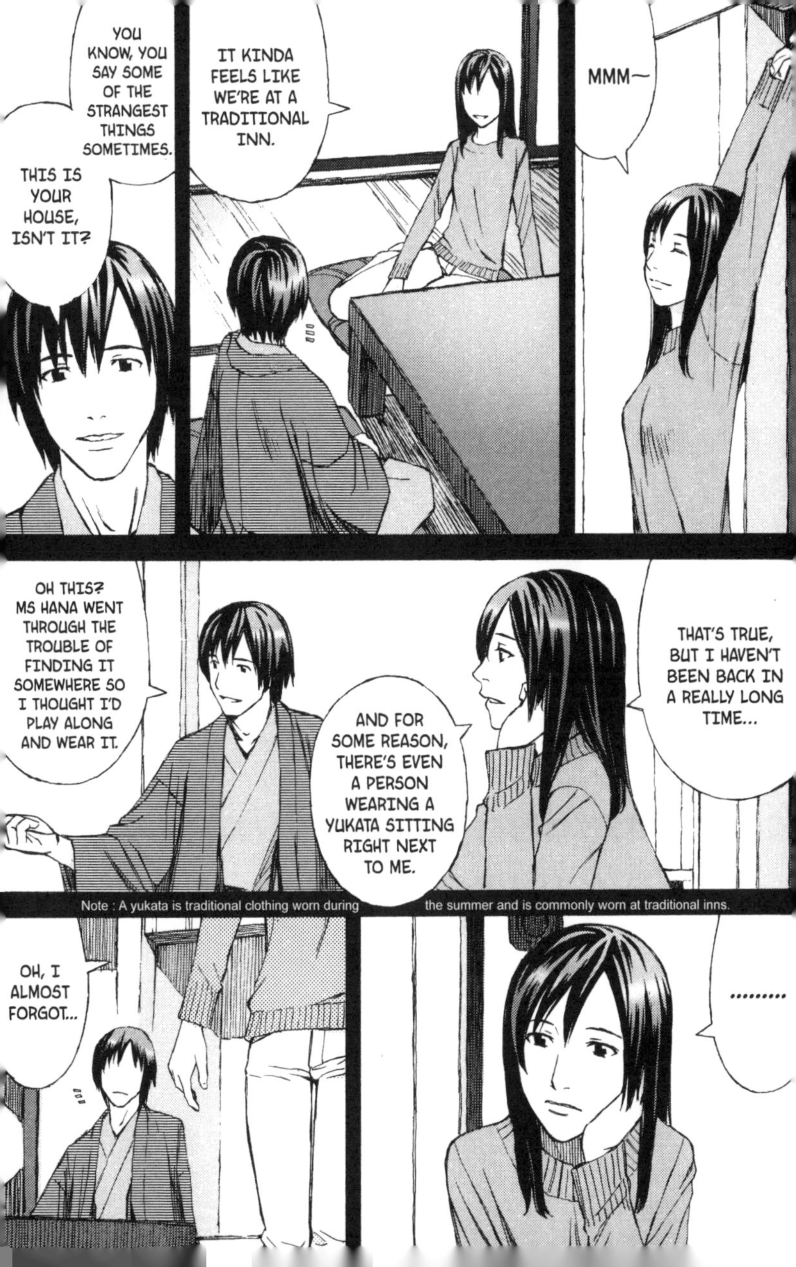
MMM~
IT KINDA FEELS LIKE WE'RE AT A TRADITIONAL INN.
YOU KNOW, YOU SAY SOME OF THE STRANGEST THINGS SOMETIMES.
THIS IS YOUR HOUSE, ISN'T IT?
THAT'S TRUE, BUT I HAVEN'T BEEN BACK IN A REALLY LONG TIME...
AND FOR SOME REASON, THERE'S EVEN A PERSON WEARING A YUKATA SITTING RIGHT NEXT TO ME.
OH THIS? MS HANA WENT THROUGH THE TROUBLE OF FINDING IT SOMEWHERE SO I THOUGHT I'D PLAY ALONG AND WEAR IT.
Note : A yukata is traditional clothing worn during the summer and is commonly worn at traditional inns.
....
OH, I ALMOST FORGOT...

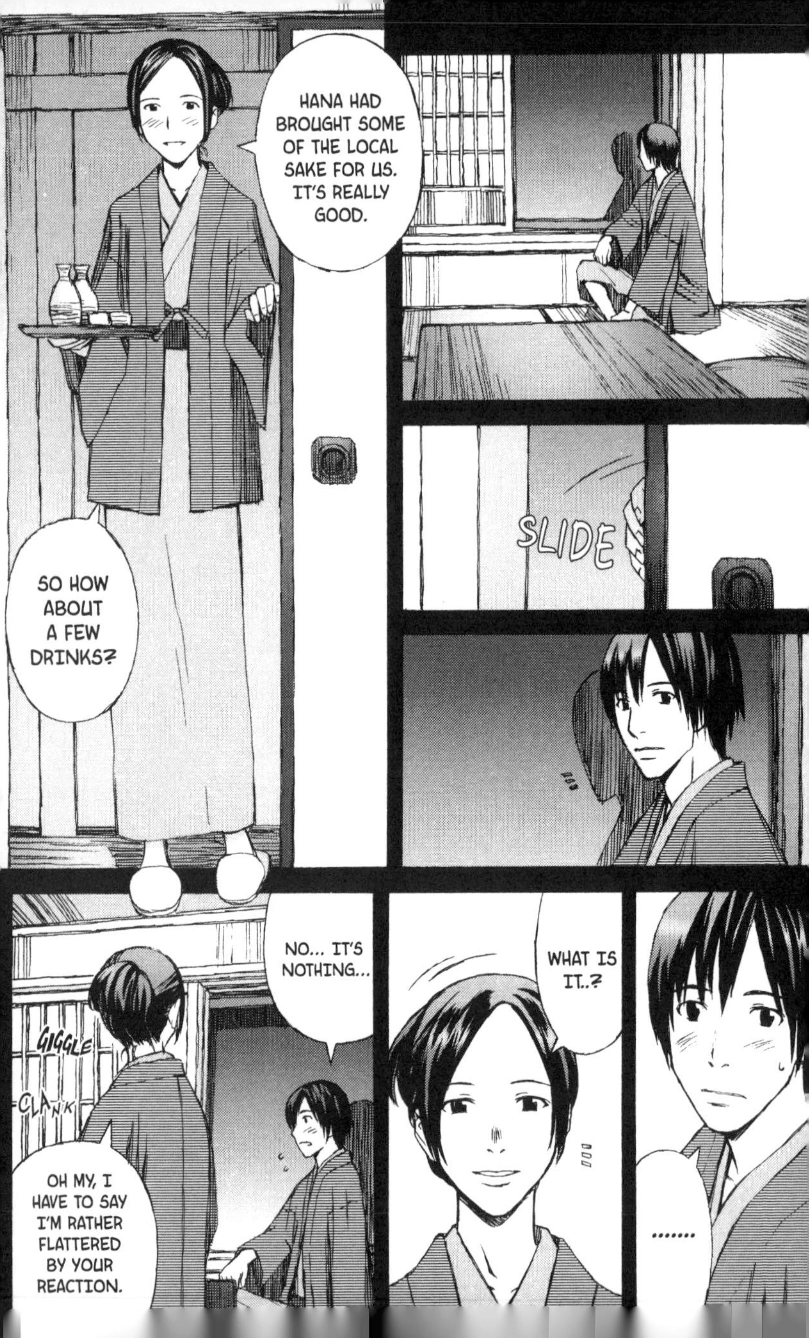
SLIDE
HANA HAD BROUGHT SOME OF THE LOCAL SAKE FOR US. IT'S REALLY GOOD.
SO HOW ABOUT A FEW DRINKS?
....
WHAT IS IT..?
NO... IT'S NOTHING...
GIGGLE
CLANK
OH MY, I HAVE TO SAY I'M RATHER FLATTERED BY YOUR REACTION.

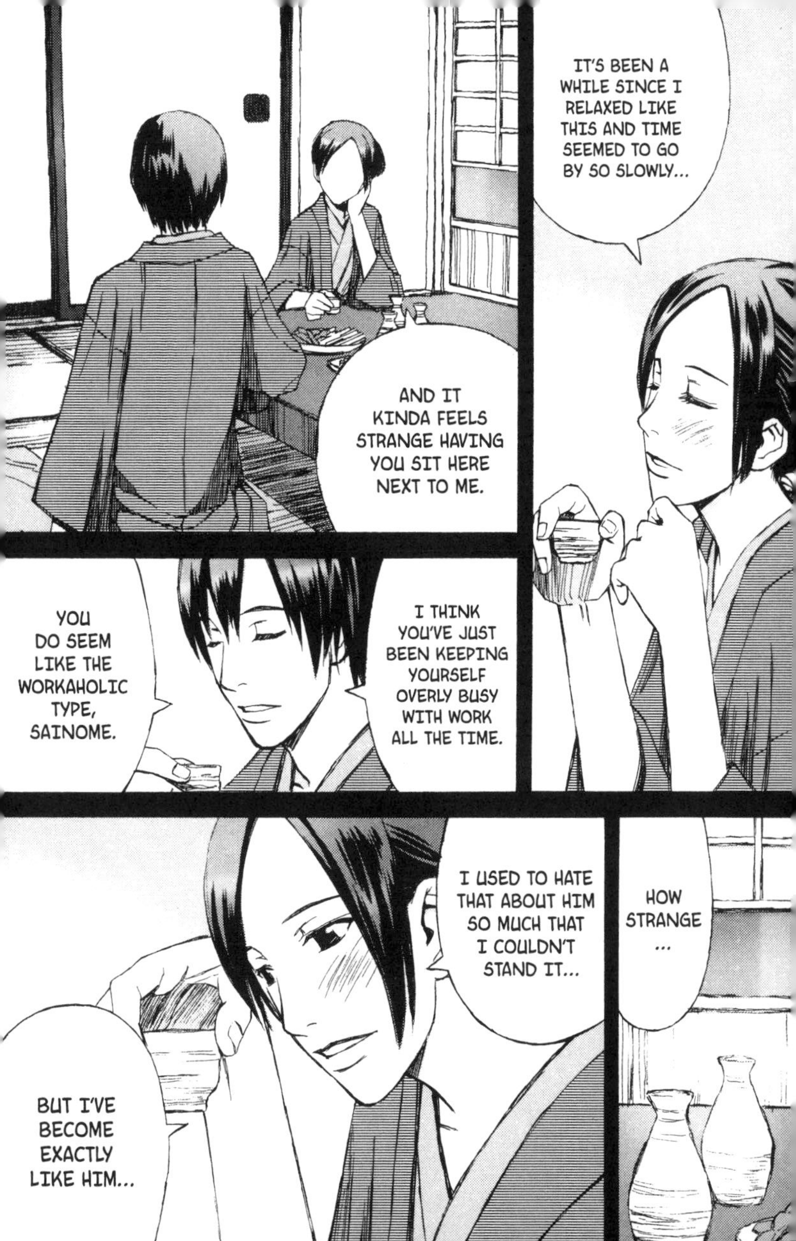
IT'S BEEN A WHILE SINCE I RELAXED LIKE THIS AND TIME SEEMED TO GO BY SO SLOWLY...
AND IT KINDA FEELS STRANGE HAVING YOU SIT HERE NEXT TO ME.
I THINK YOU'VE JUST BEEN KEEPING YOURSELF OVERLY BUSY WITH WORK ALL THE TIME.
YOU DO SEEM LIKE THE WORKAHOLIC TYPE, SAINOME.
HOW STRANGE ...
I USED TO HATE THAT ABOUT HIM SO MUCH THAT I COULDN'T STAND IT...
BUT I'VE BECOME EXACTLY LIKE HIM...

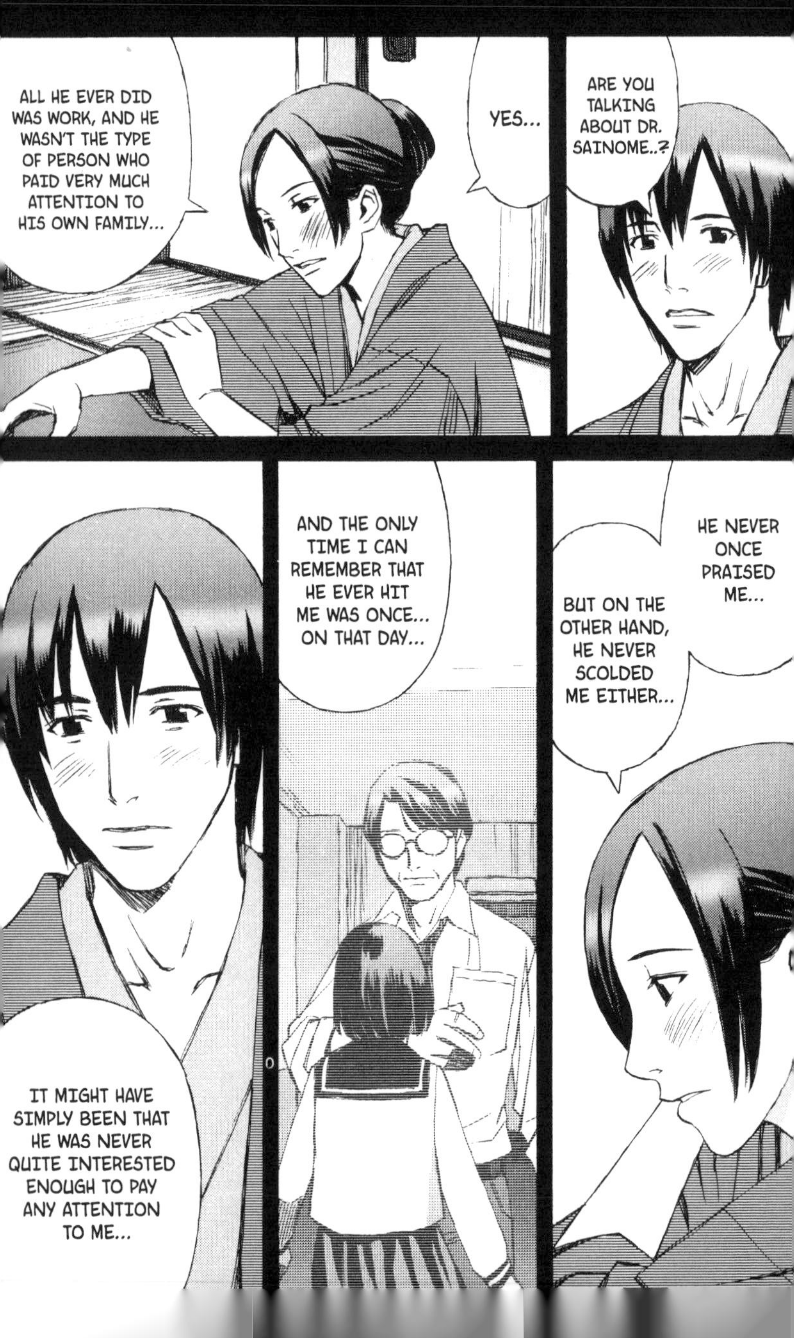
ARE YOU TALKING ABOUT DR. SAINOME..?
YES...
ALL HE EVER DID WAS WORK, AND HE WASN'T THE TYPE OF PERSON WHO PAID VERY MUCH ATTENTION TO HIS OWN FAMILY...
HE NEVER ONCE PRAISED ME...
BUT ON THE OTHER HAND, HE NEVER SCOLDED ME EITHER...
AND THE ONLY TIME I CAN REMEMBER THAT HE EVER HIT ME WAS ONCE... ON THAT DAY...
IT MIGHT HAVE SIMPLY BEEN THAT HE WAS NEVER QUITE INTERESTED ENOUGH TO PAY ANY ATTENTION TO ME...

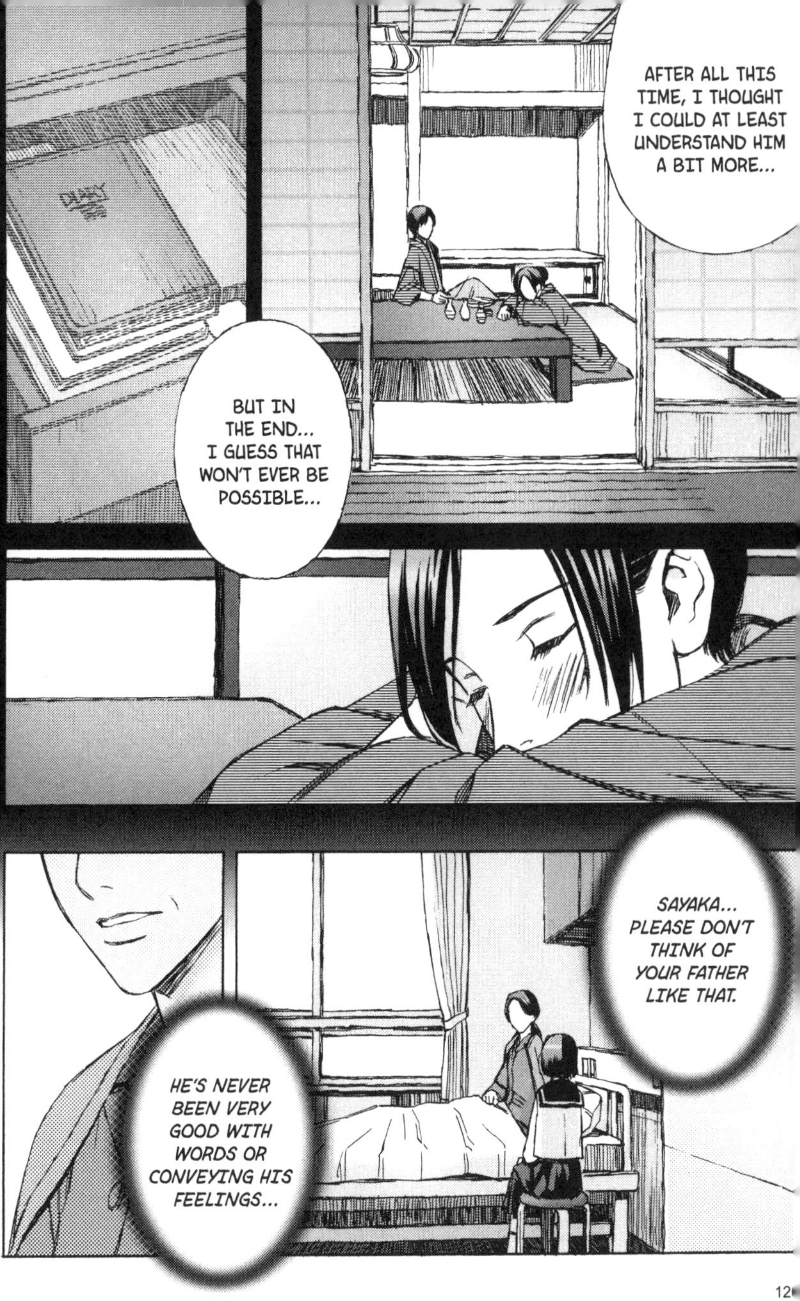
AFTER ALL THIS TIME, I THOUGHT I COULD AT LEAST UNDERSTAND HIM A BIT MORE...
BUT IN THE END... I GUESS THAT WON'T EVER BE POSSIBLE...
SAYAKA... PLEASE DON'T THINK OF YOUR FATHER LIKE THAT.
HE'S NEVER BEEN VERY GOOD WITH WORDS OR CONVEYING HIS FEELINGS...

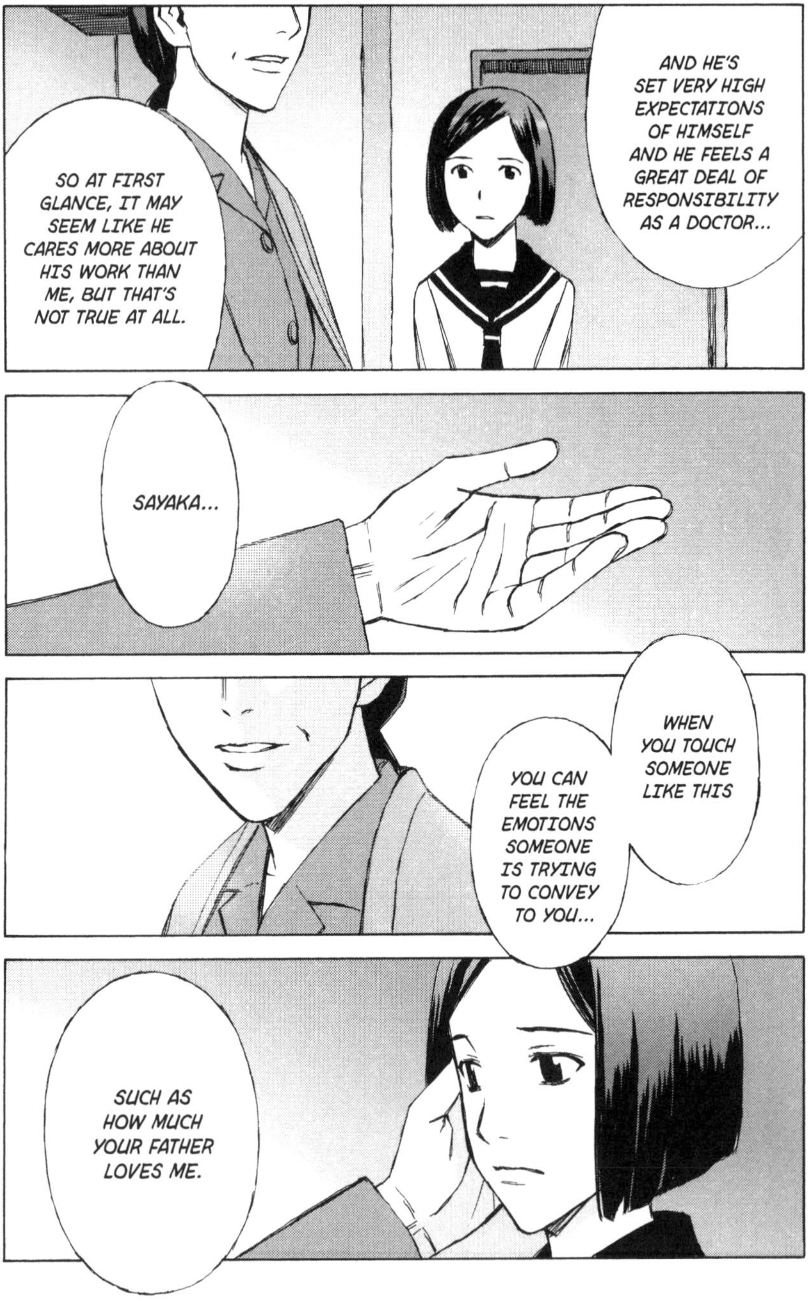
AND HE'S SET VERY HIGH EXPECTATIONS OF HIMSELF AND HE FEELS A GREAT DEAL OF RESPONSIBILITY AS A DOCTOR...
SO AT FIRST GLANCE, IT MAY SEEM LIKE HE CARES MORE ABOUT HIS WORK THAN ME, BUT THAT'S NOT TRUE AT ALL.
SAYAKA...
WHEN YOU TOUCH SOMEONE LIKE THIS
YOU CAN FEEL THE EMOTIONS SOMEONE IS TRYING TO CONVEY TO YOU...
SUCH AS HOW MUCH YOUR FATHER LOVES ME.

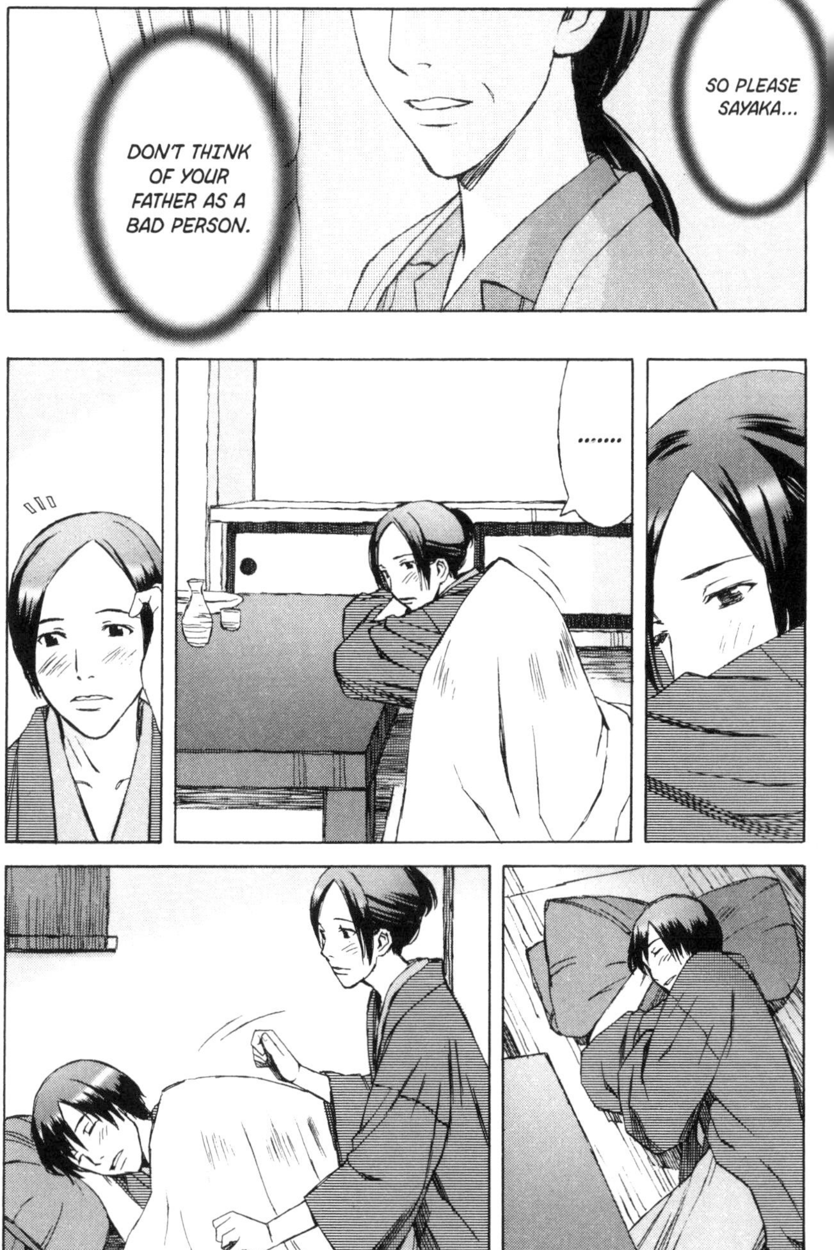
SO PLEASE SAYAKA...
DON'T THINK OF YOUR FATHER AS A BAD PERSON.
......

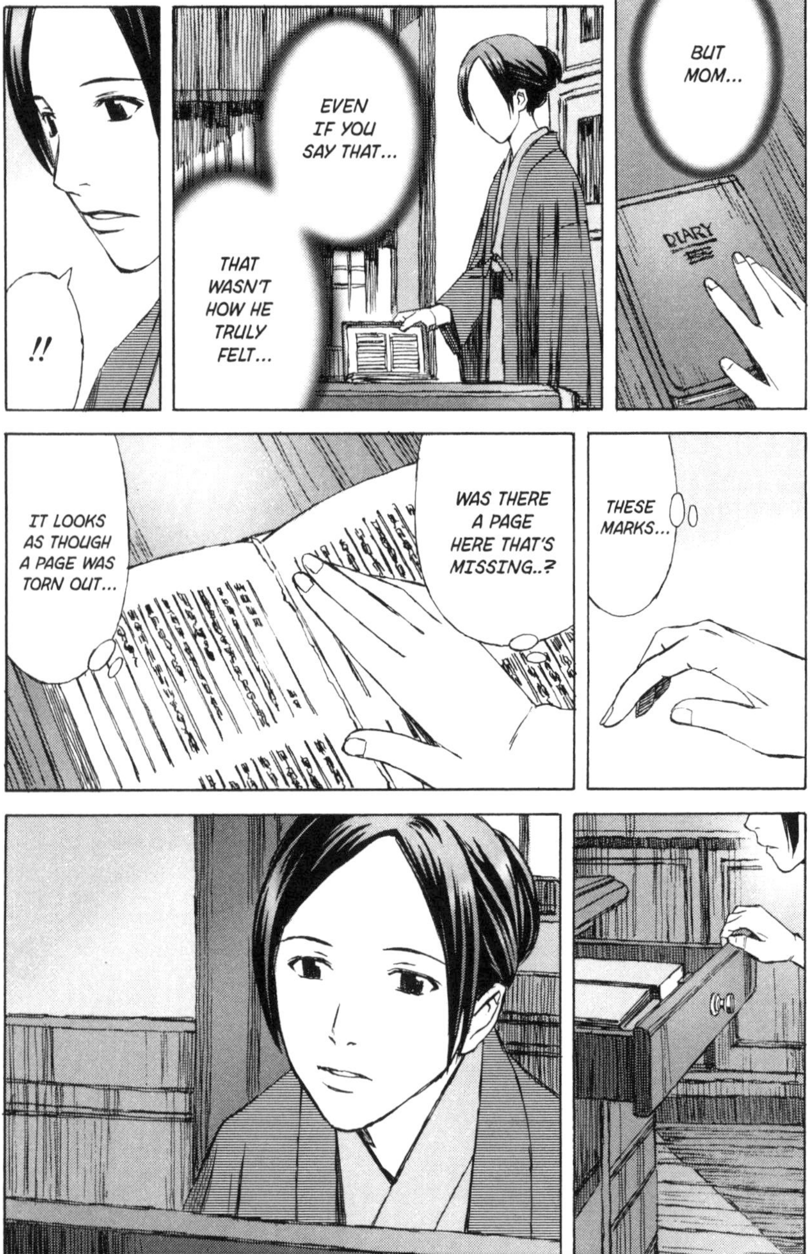
BUT MOM...
DIARY
EVEN IF YOU SAY THAT...
THAT WASN'T HOW HE TRULY FELT...
!!
THESE MARKS...
WAS THERE A PAGE HERE THAT'S MISSING..?
IT LOOKS AS THOUGH A PAGE WAS TORN OUT...

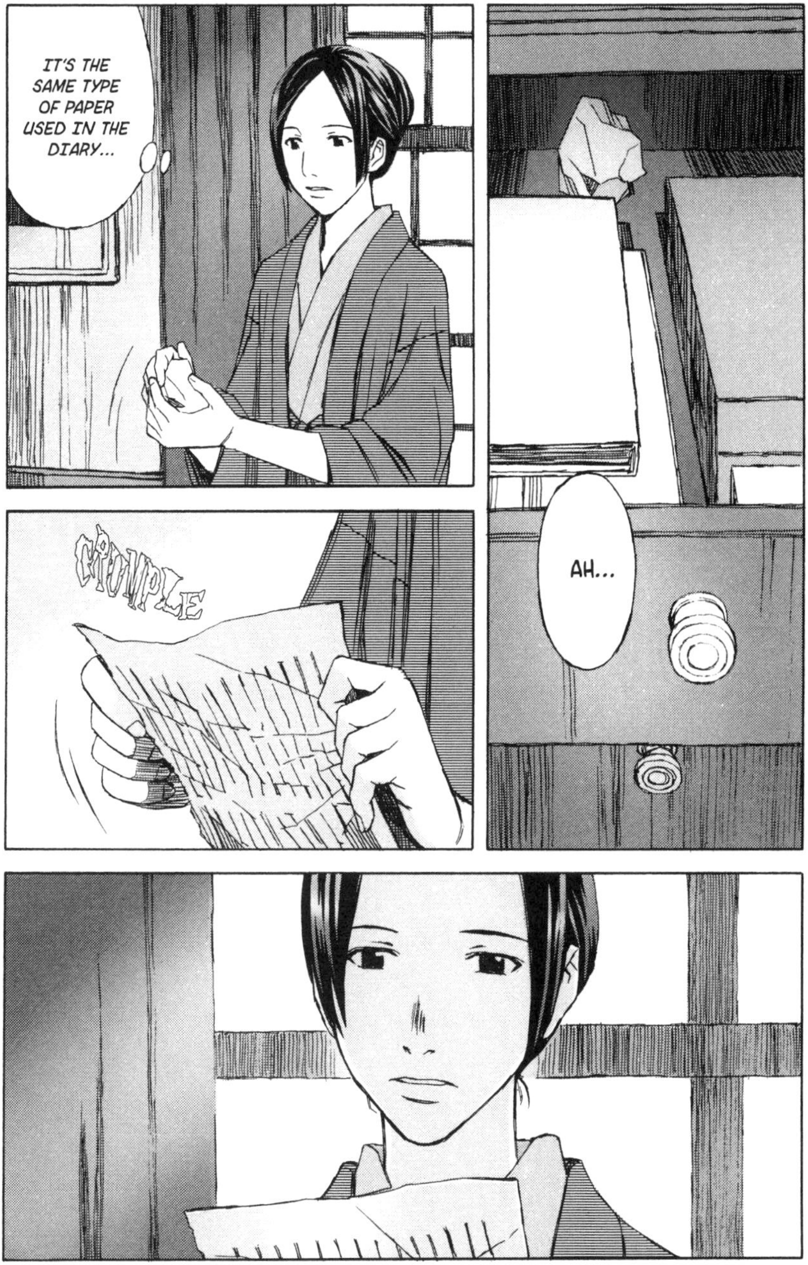
AH...
IT'S THE SAME TYPE OF PAPER USED IN THE DIARY...
CRUMPLE

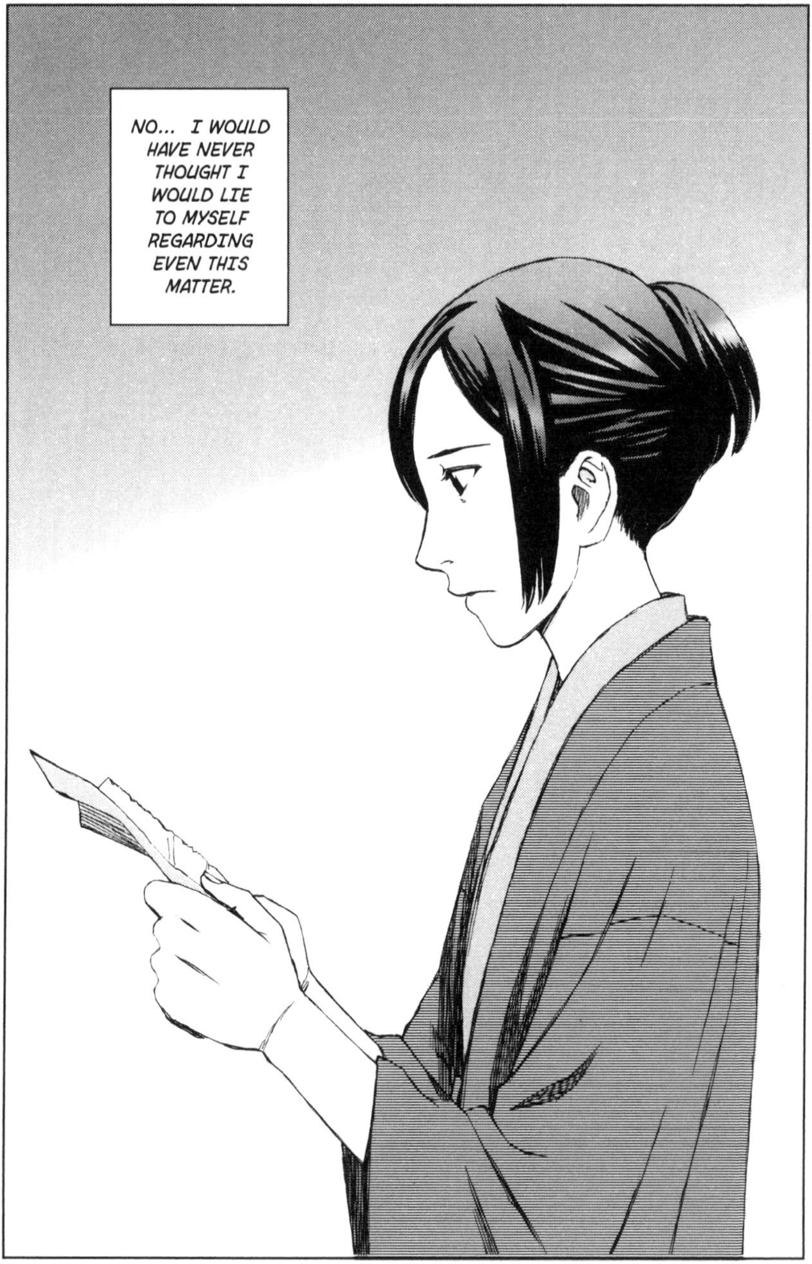
NO... I WOULD HAVE NEVER THOUGHT I WOULD LIE TO MYSELF REGARDING EVEN THIS MATTER.

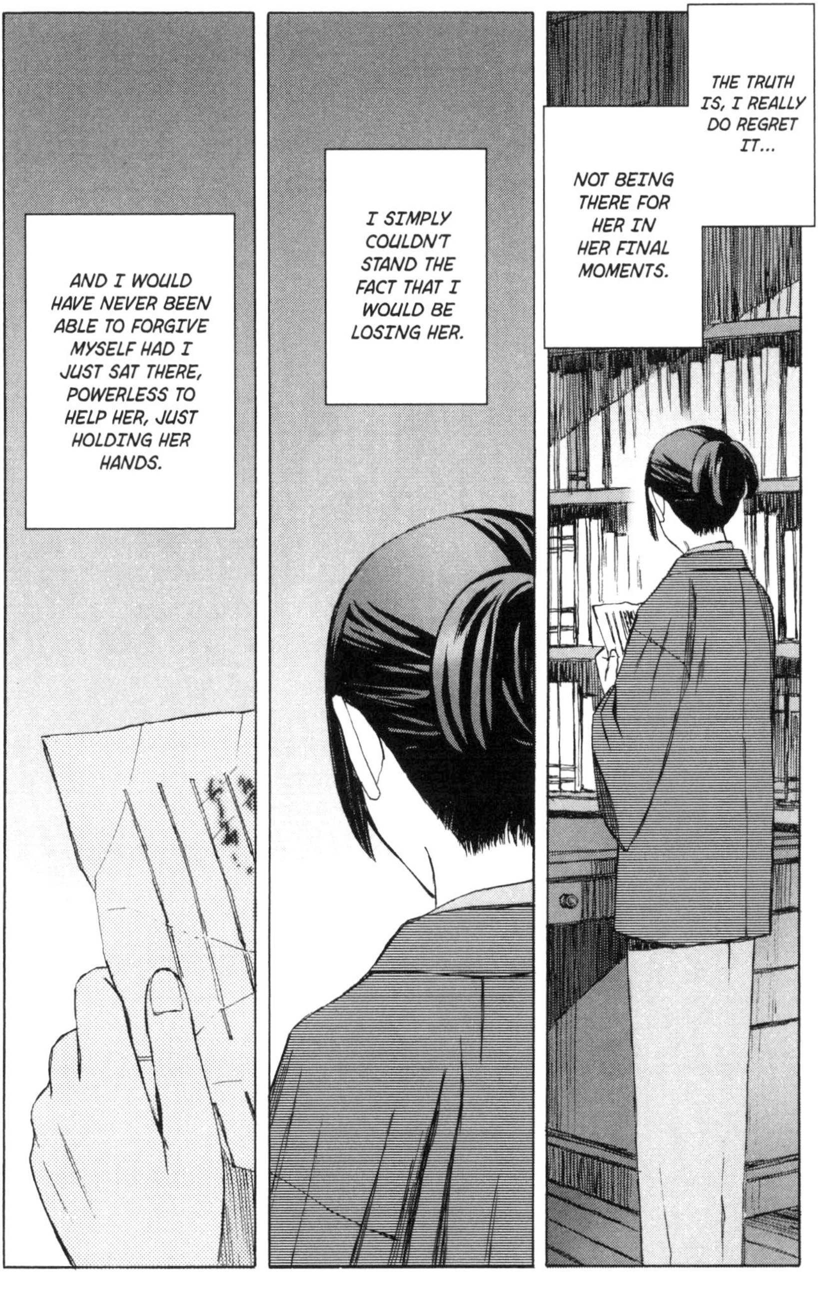
THE TRUTH IS, I REALLY DO REGRET IT...
NOT BEING THERE FOR HER IN HER FINAL MOMENTS.
I SIMPLY COULDN'T STAND THE FACT THAT I WOULD BE LOSING HER.
AND I WOULD HAVE NEVER BEEN ABLE TO FORGIVE MYSELF HAD I JUST SAT THERE, POWERLESS TO HELP HER, JUST HOLDING HER HANDS.

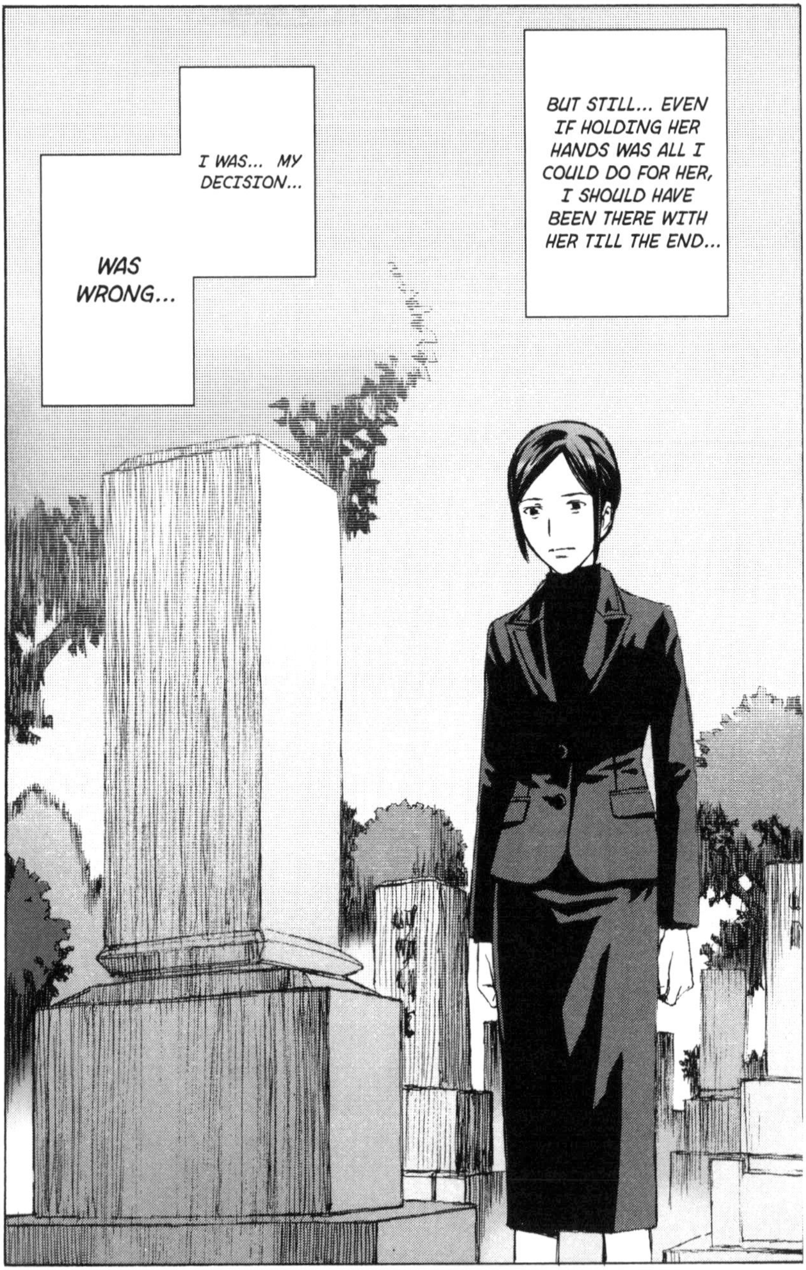
BUT STILL... EVEN IF HOLDING HER HANDS WAS ALL I COULD DO FOR HER, I SHOULD HAVE BEEN THERE WITH HER TILL THE END...
I WAS... MY DECISION...
WAS WRONG...

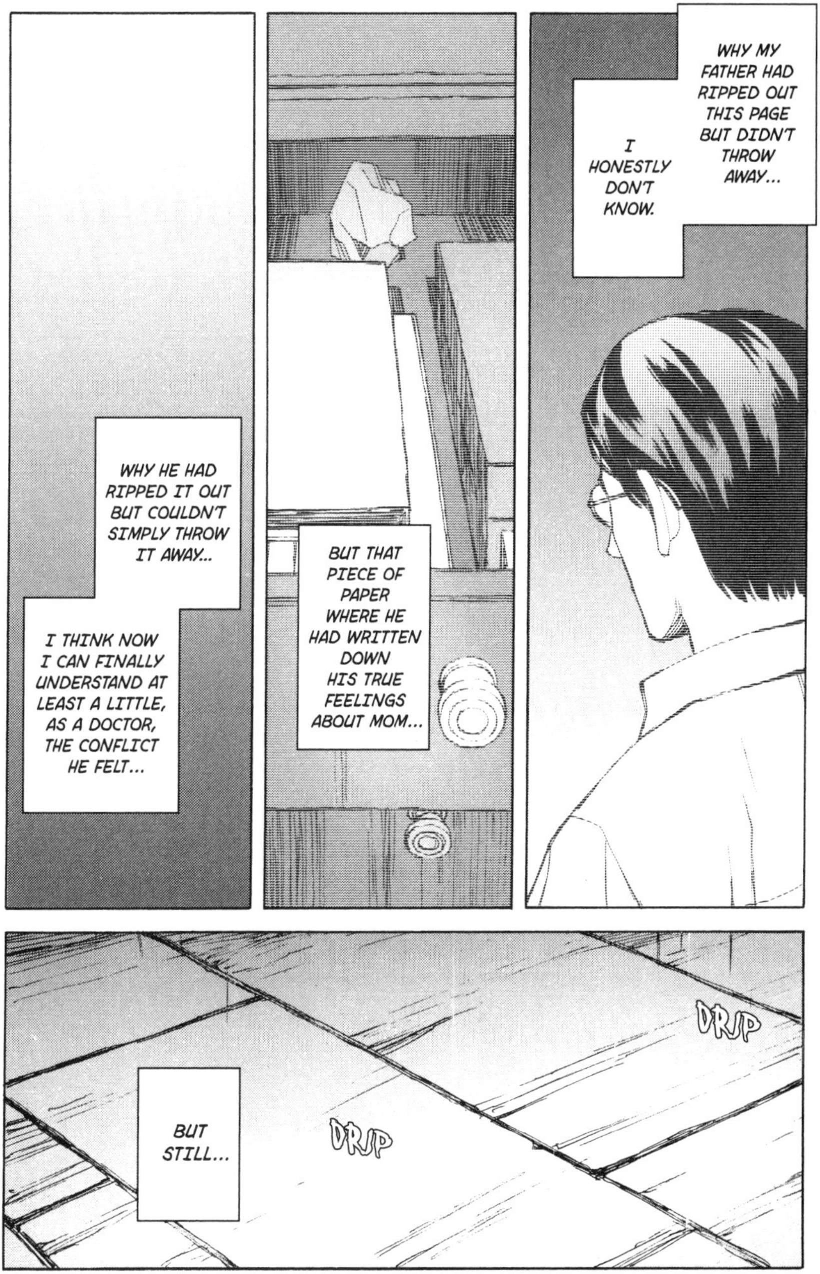
WHY MY FATHER HAD RIPPED OUT THIS PAGE BUT DIDN'T THROW AWAY...
I HONESTLY DON'T KNOW.
BUT THAT PIECE OF PAPER WHERE HE HAD WRITTEN DOWN HIS TRUE FEELINGS ABOUT MOM...
WHY HE HAD RIPPED IT OUT BUT COULDN'T SIMPLY THROW IT AWAY...
I THINK NOW I CAN FINALLY UNDERSTAND AT LEAST A LITTLE, AS A DOCTOR, THE CONFLICT HE FELT...
DRIP
DRIP
BUT STILL...

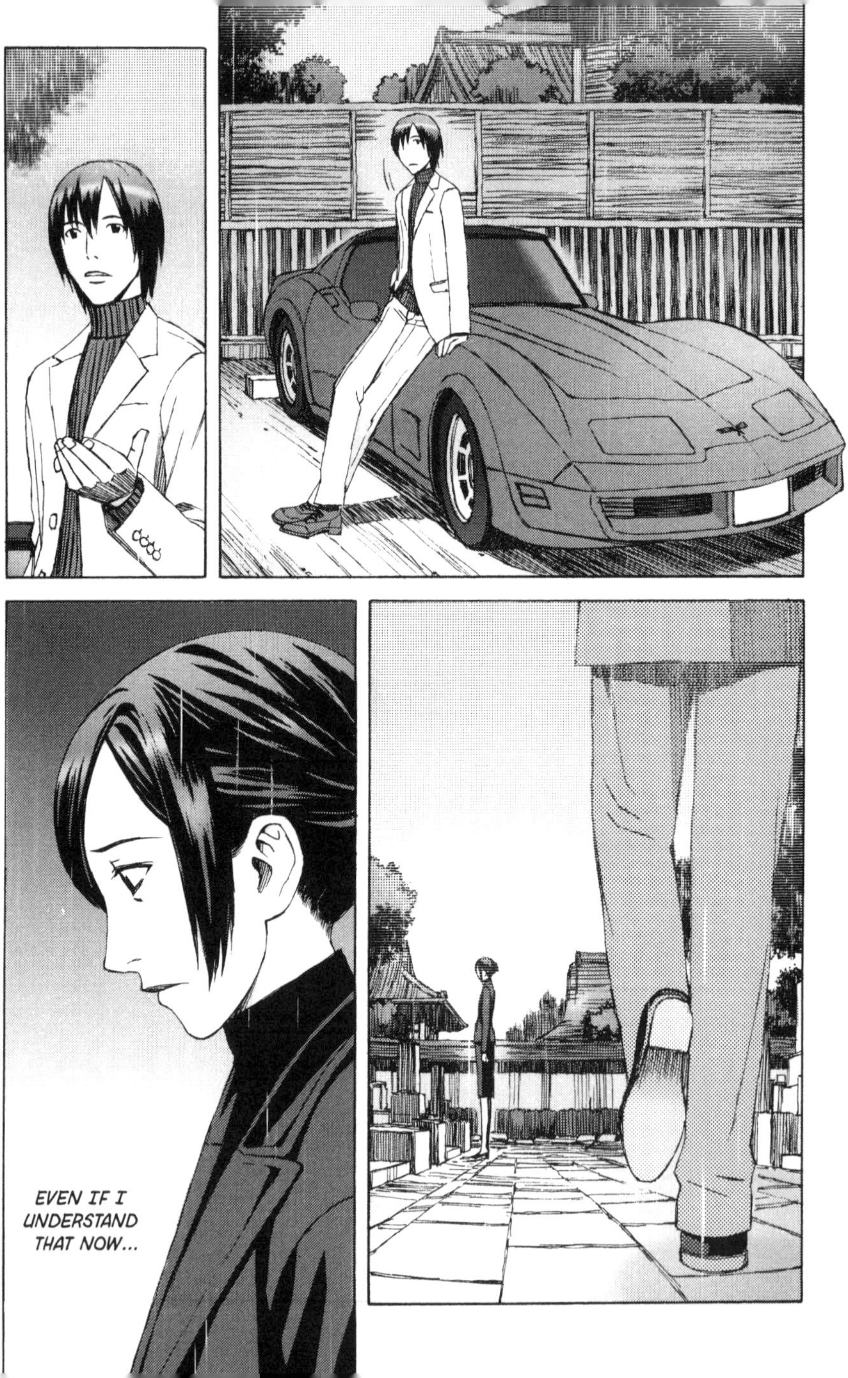
EVEN IF I UNDERSTAND THAT NOW...

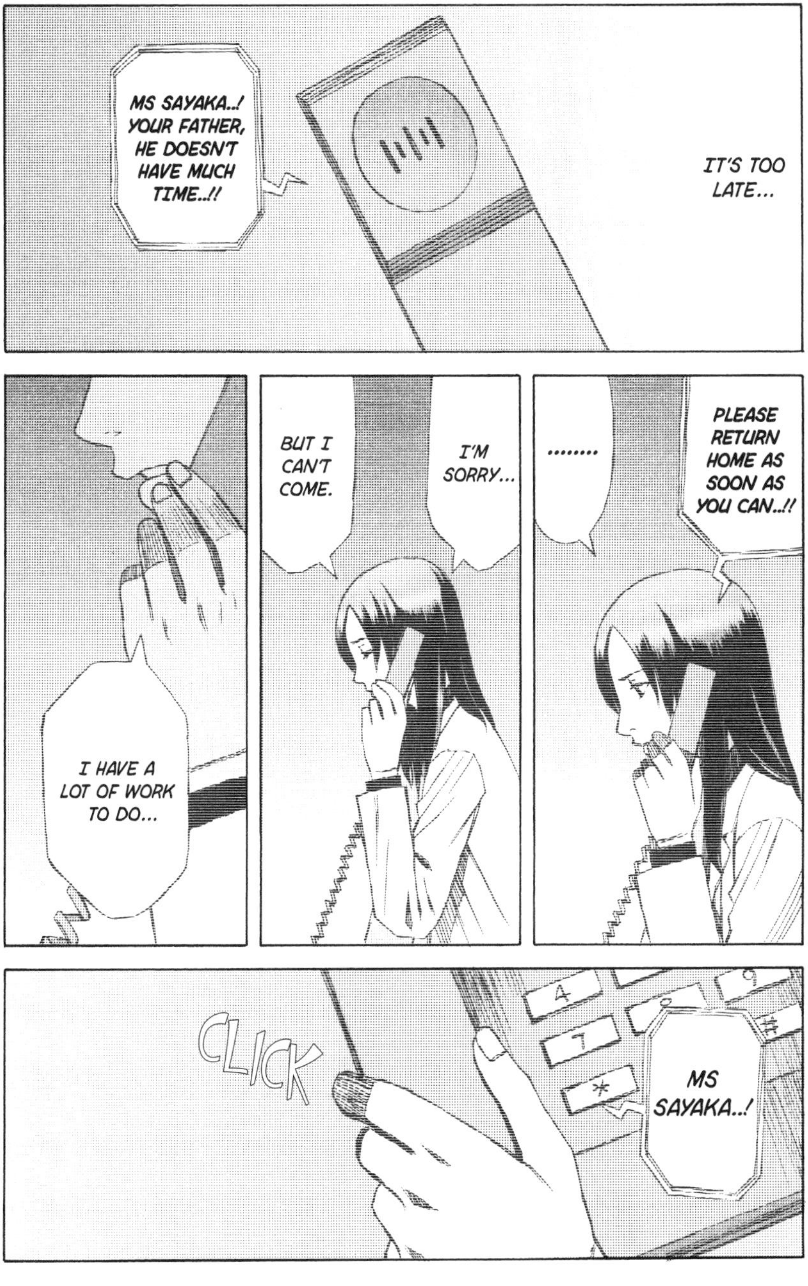
IT'S TOO LATE...
MS SAYAKA..! YOUR FATHER, HE DOESN'T HAVE MUCH TIME..!!
PLEASE RETURN HOME AS SOON AS YOU CAN..!!
....
I'M SORRY...
BUT I CAN'T COME.
I HAVE A LOT OF WORK TO DO...
MS SAYAKA..!
CLICK

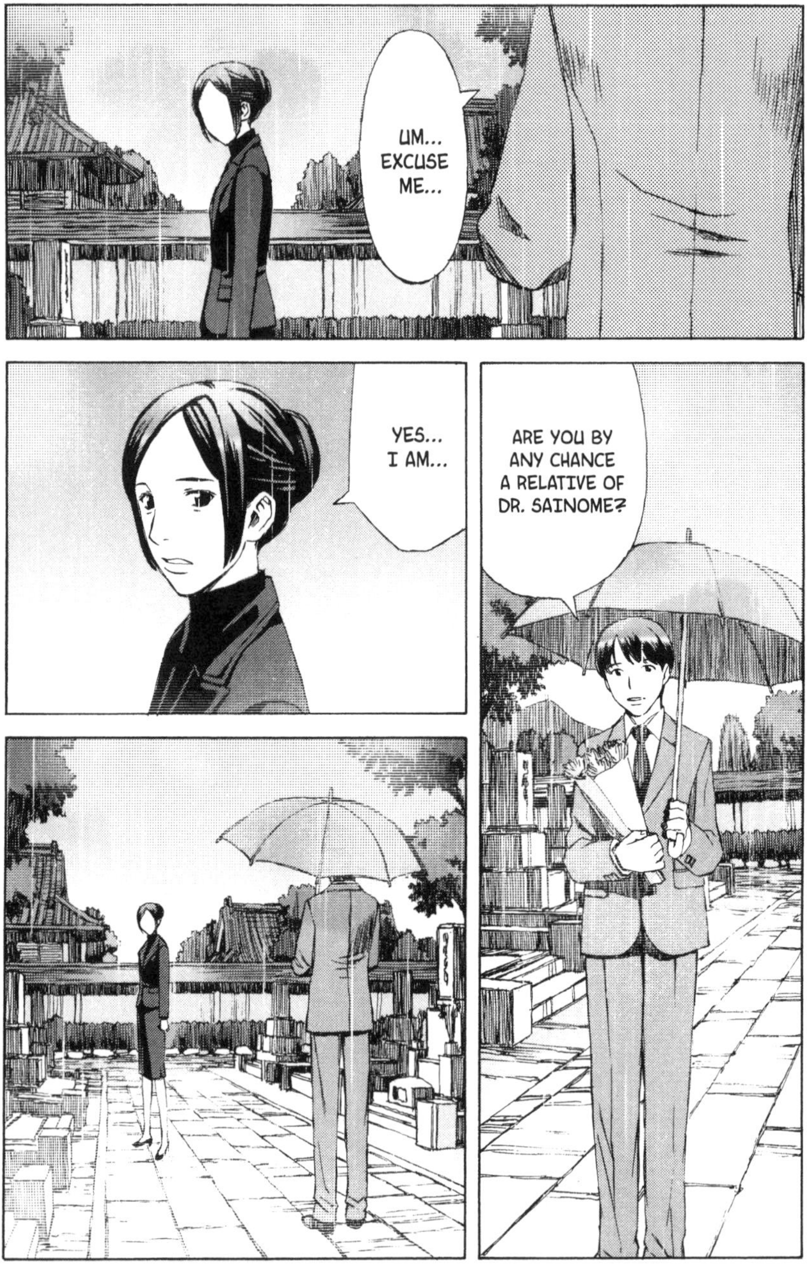
UM... EXCUSE ME...
ARE YOU BY ANY CHANCE A RELATIVE OF DR. SAINOME?
YES... I AM...

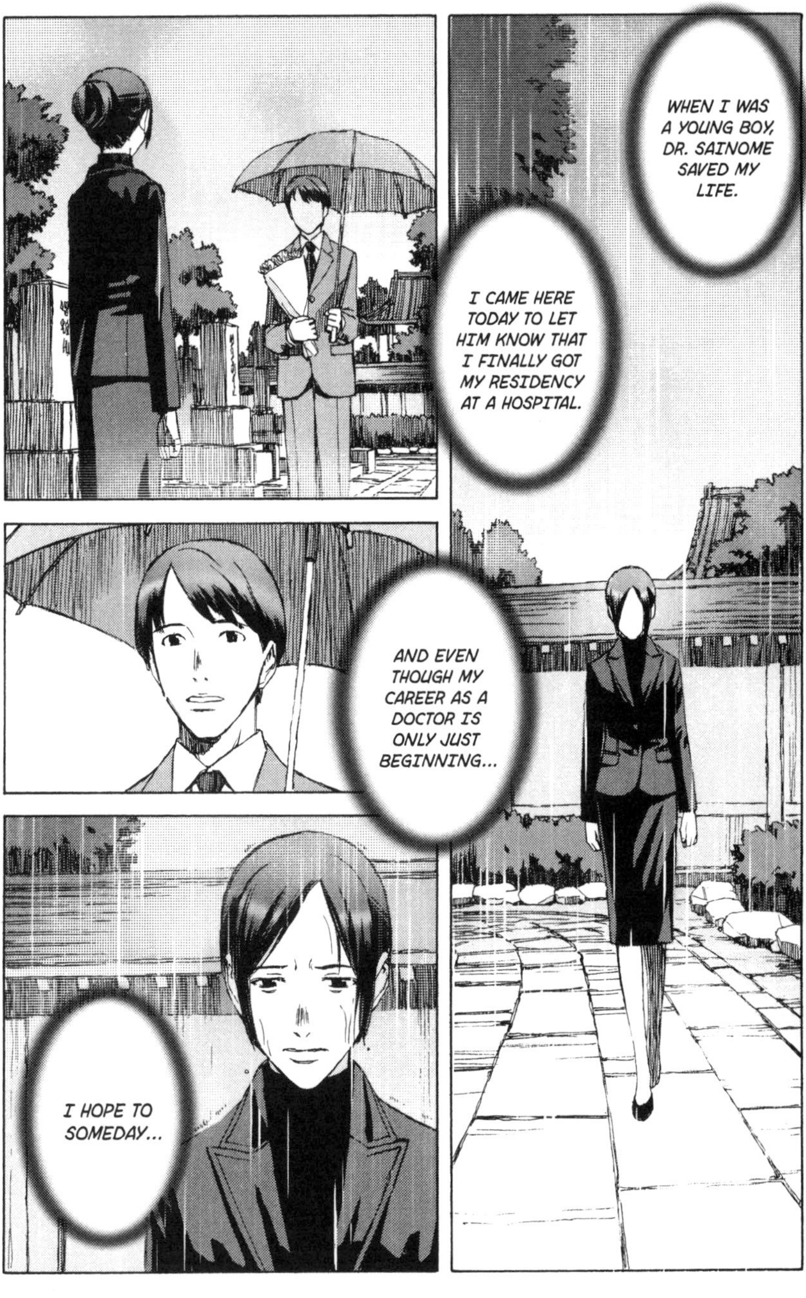
WHEN I WAS A YOUNG BOY, DR. SAINOME SAVED MY LIFE.
I CAME HERE TODAY TO LET HIM KNOW THAT I FINALLY GOT MY RESIDENCY AT A HOSPITAL.
AND EVEN THOUGH MY CAREER AS A DOCTOR IS ONLY JUST BEGINNING...
I HOPE TO SOMEDAY...

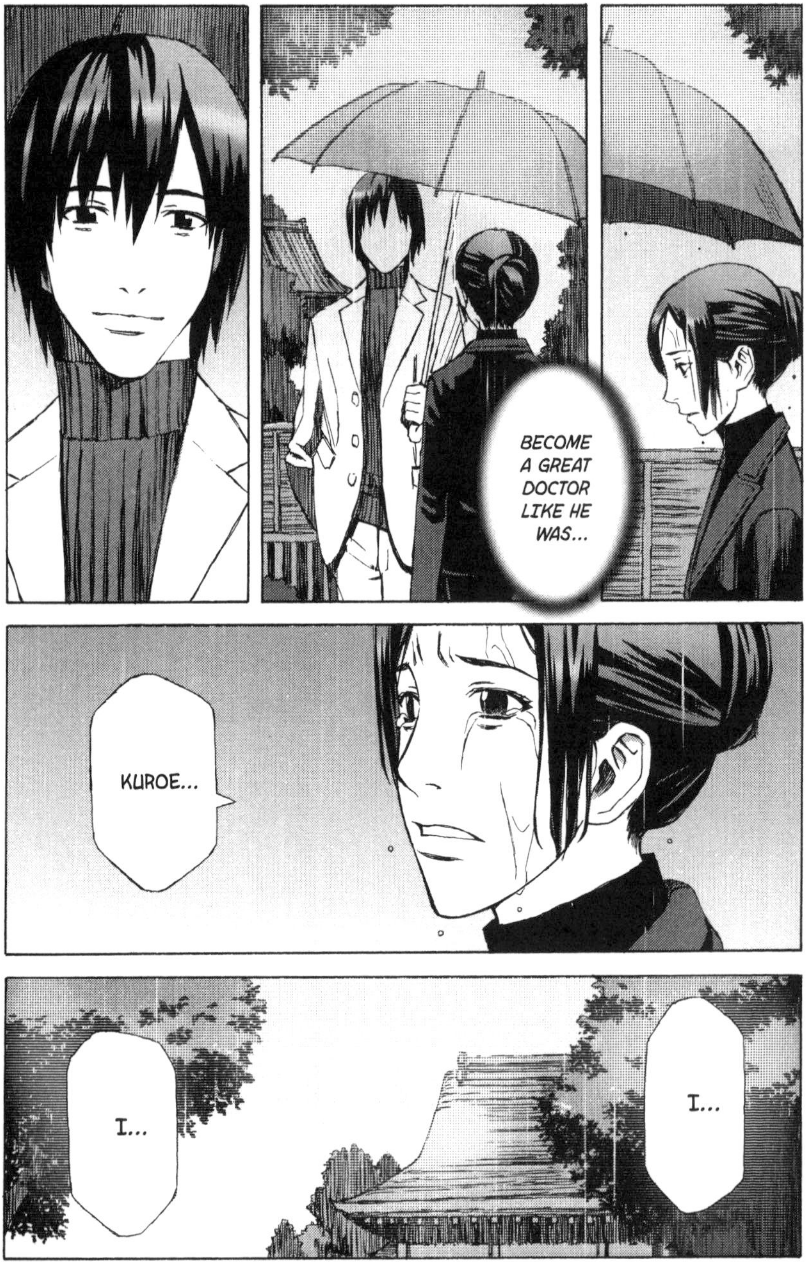
BECOME A GREAT DOCTOR LIKE HE WAS...
KUROE...
I...
I...

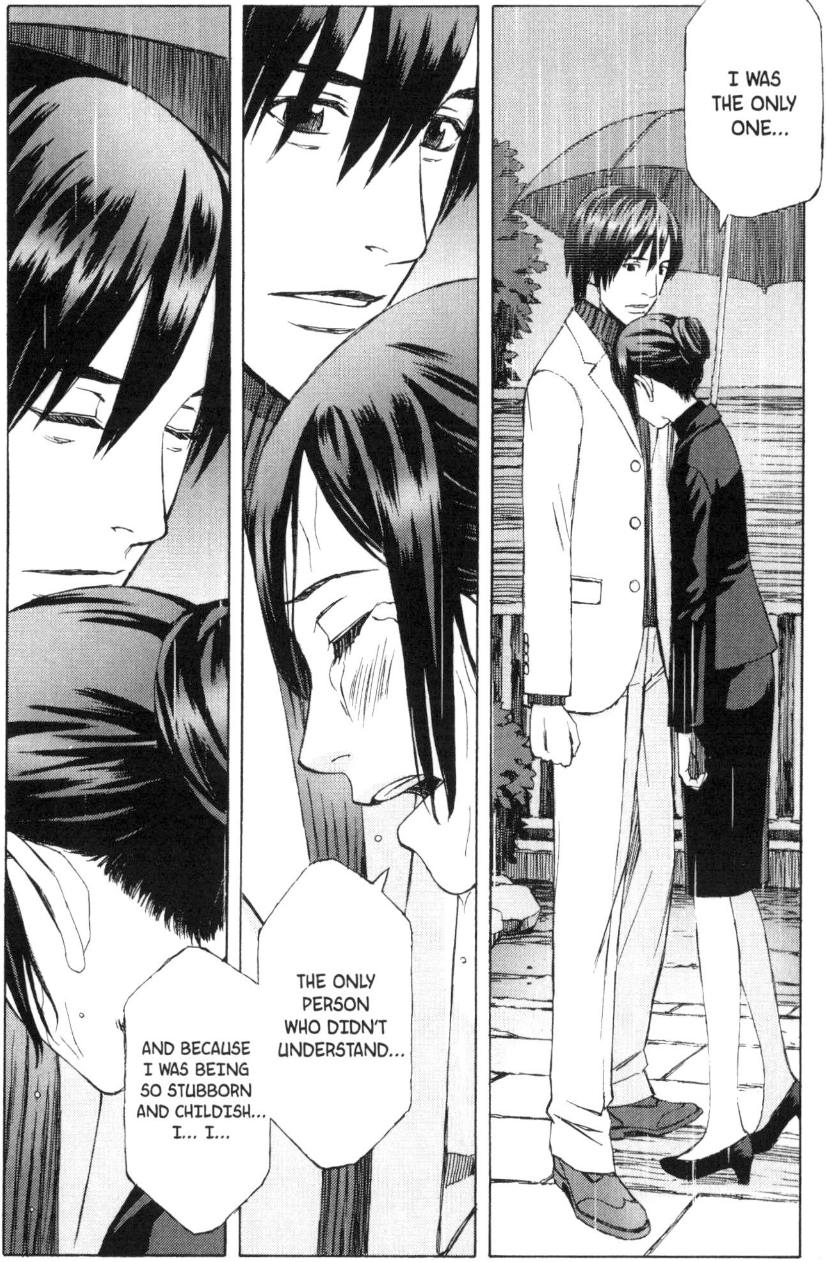
I WAS THE ONLY ONE...
THE ONLY PERSON WHO DIDN'T UNDERSTAND...
AND BECAUSE I WAS BEING SO STUBBORN AND CHILDISH... I... I...

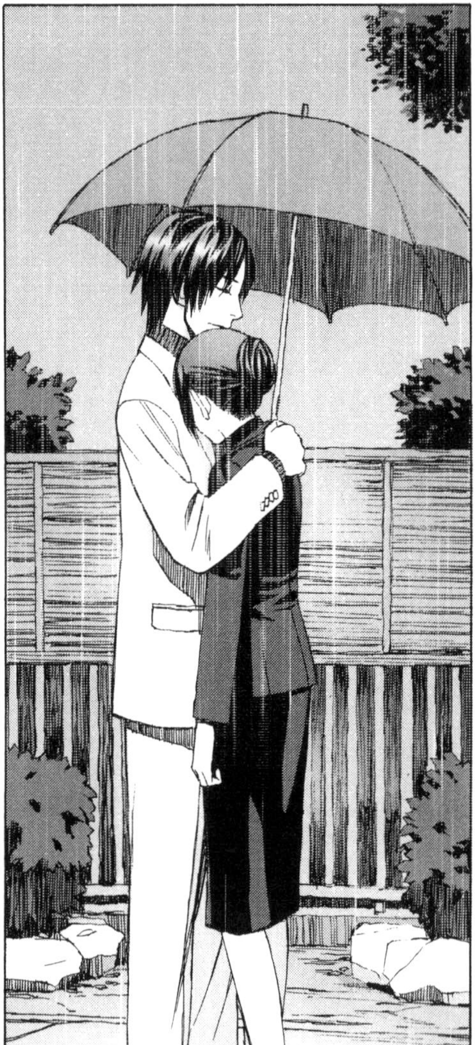
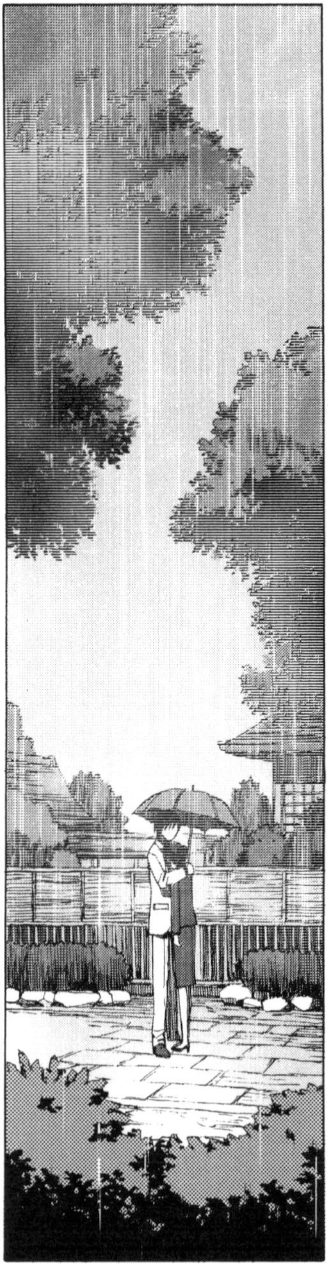

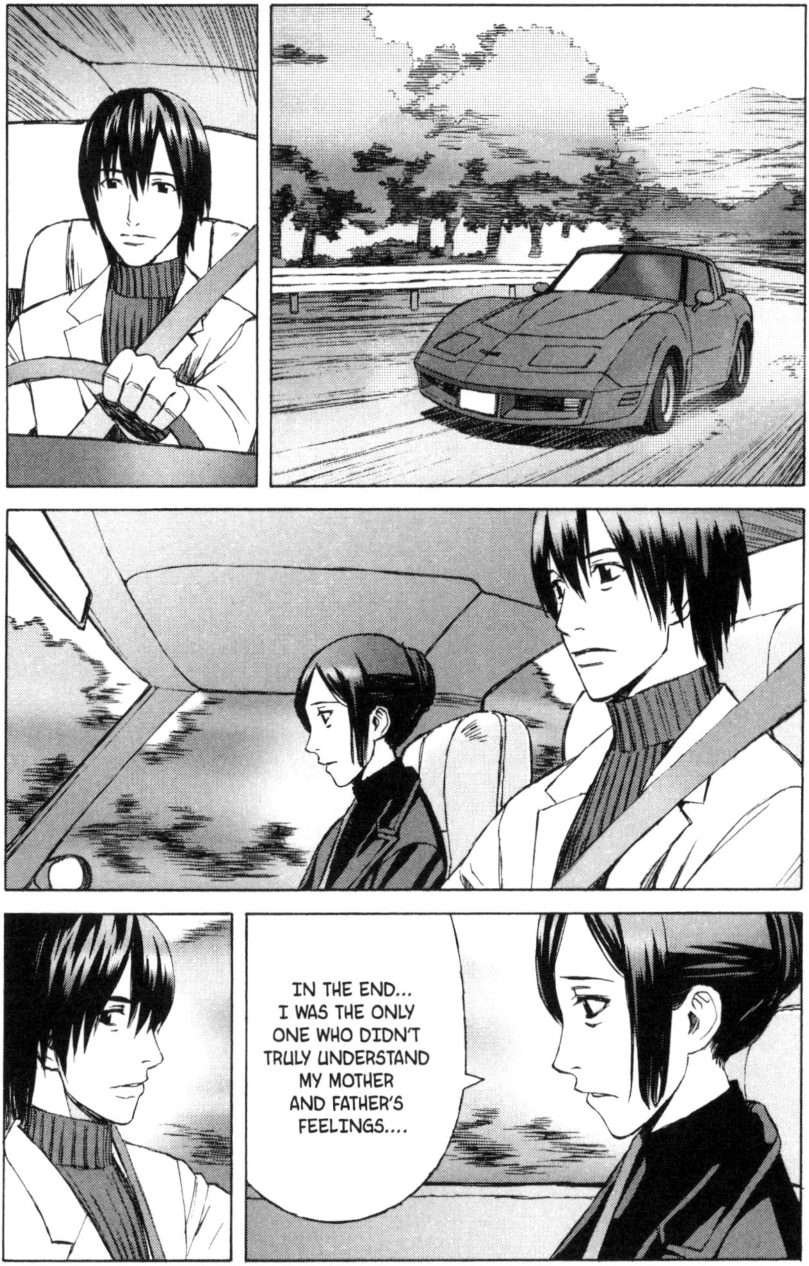
IN THE END... I WAS THE ONLY ONE WHO DIDN'T TRULY UNDERSTAND MY MOTHER AND FATHER'S FEELINGS....

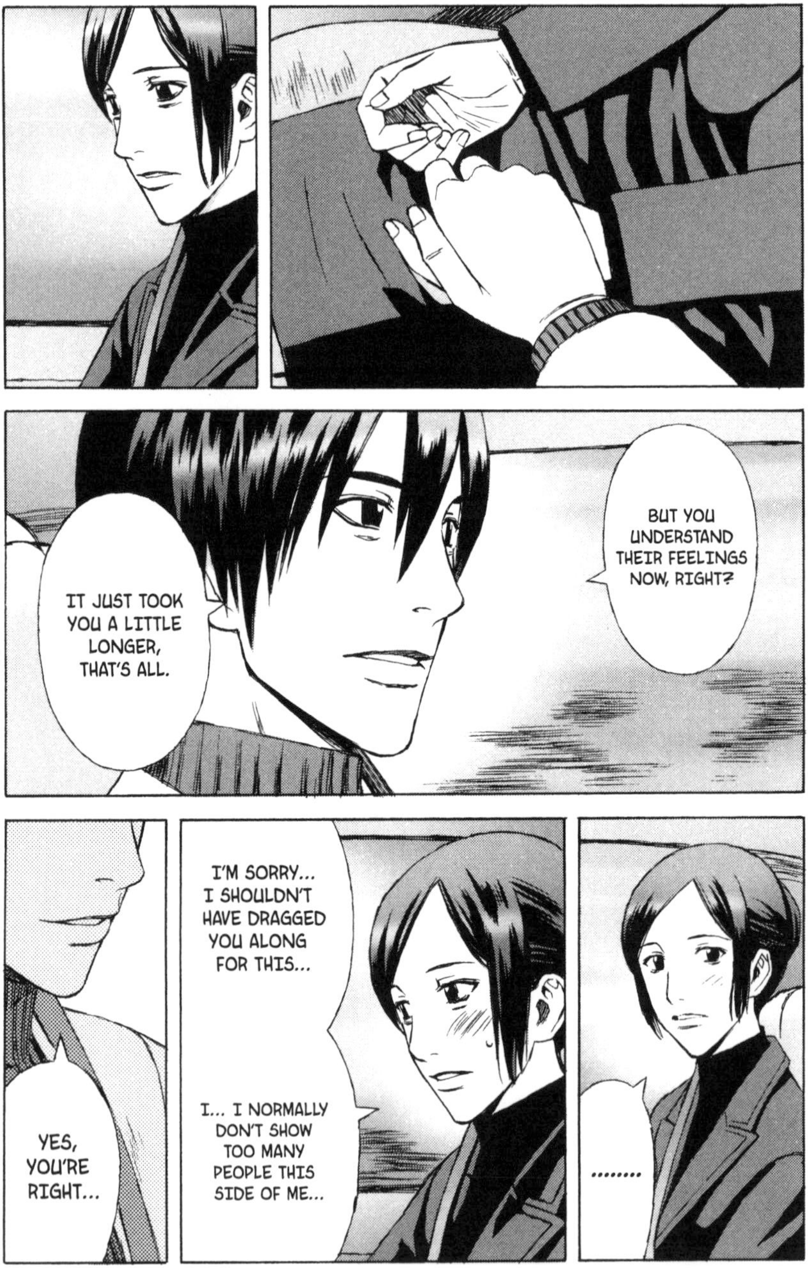
BUT YOU UNDERSTAND THEIR FEELINGS NOW, RIGHT?
IT JUST TOOK YOU A LITTLE LONGER, THAT'S ALL.
....
I'M SORRY... I SHOULDN'T HAVE DRAGGED YOU ALONG FOR THIS...
I... I NORMALLY DON'T SHOW TOO MANY PEOPLE THIS SIDE OF ME...
YES, YOU'RE RIGHT...

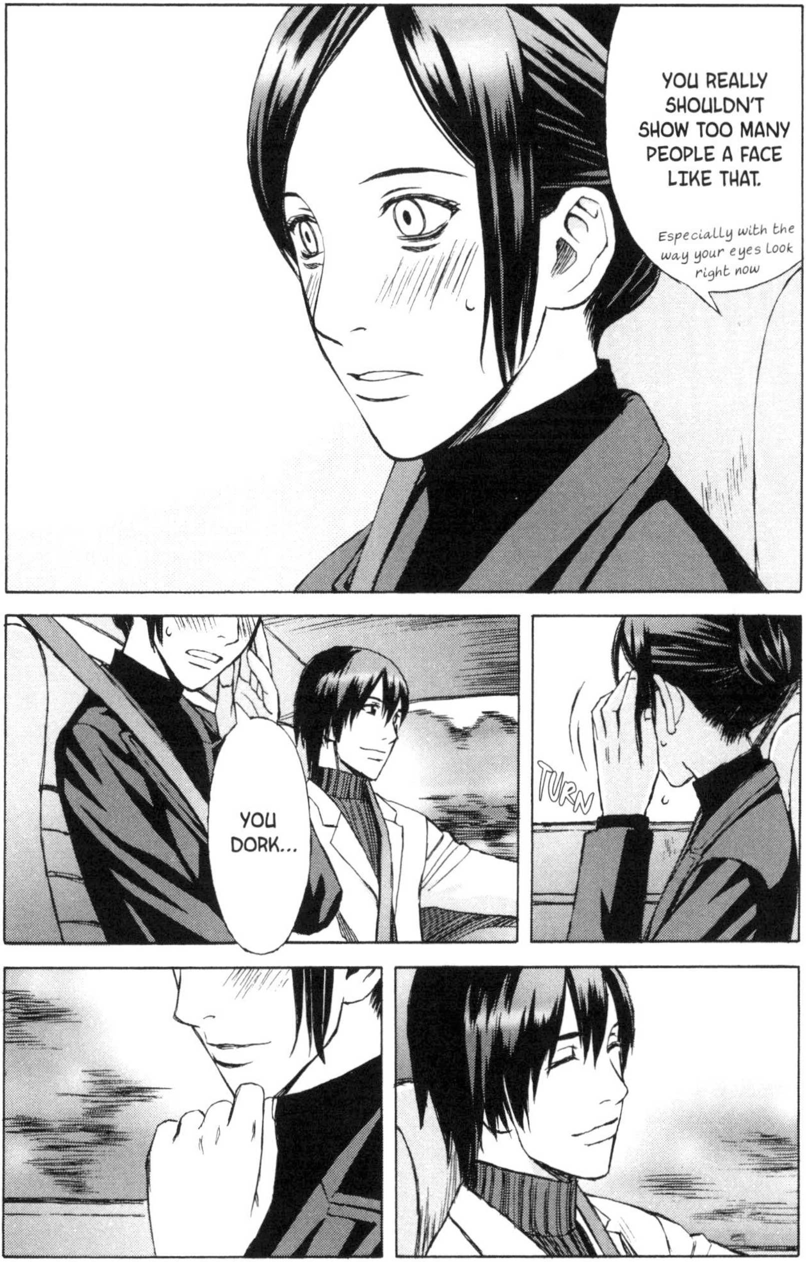
YOU REALLY SHOULDN'T SHOW TOO MANY PEOPLE A FACE LIKE THAT.
Especially with the way your eyes look right now
TURN
YOU DORK...

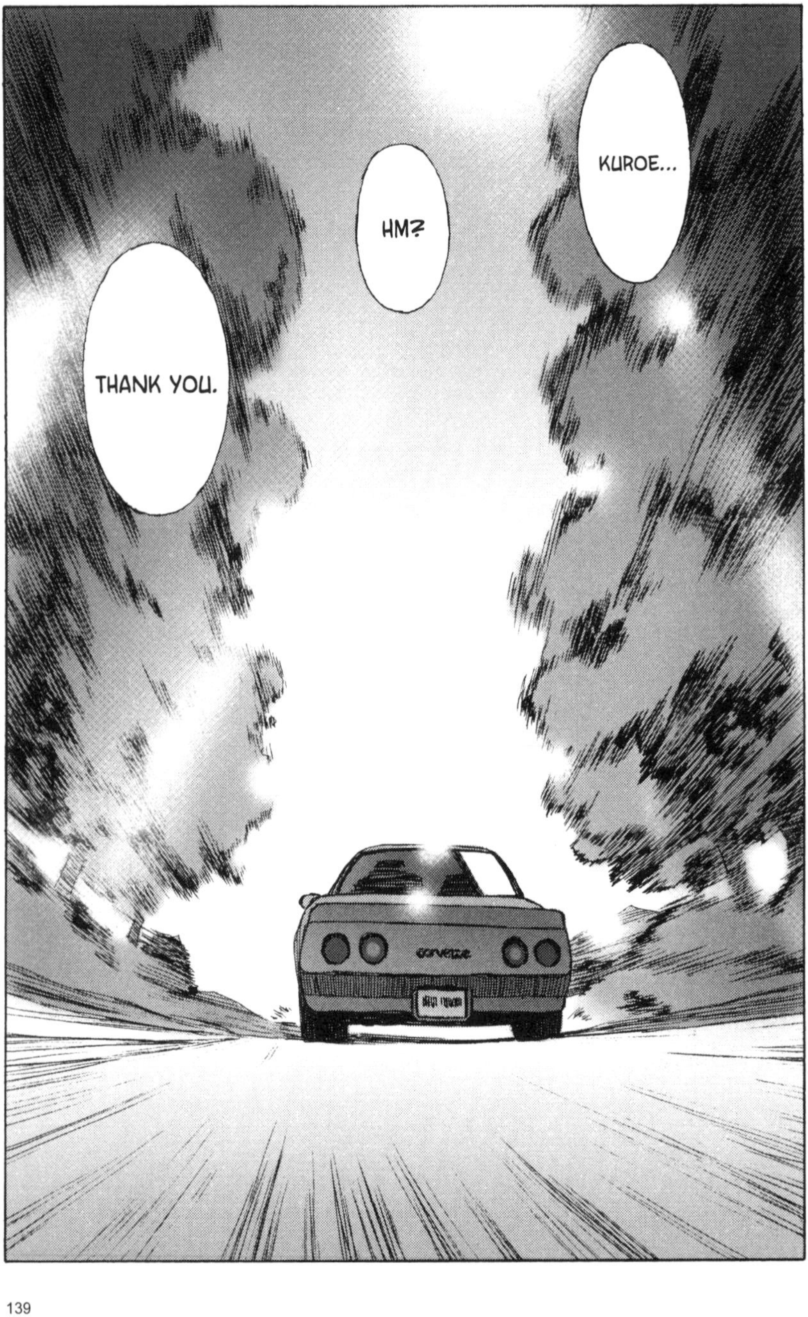
KUROE...
HM?
THANK YOU.

Episode 19
HOME ALONE
あなたのいない部屋 – The Room Without You There

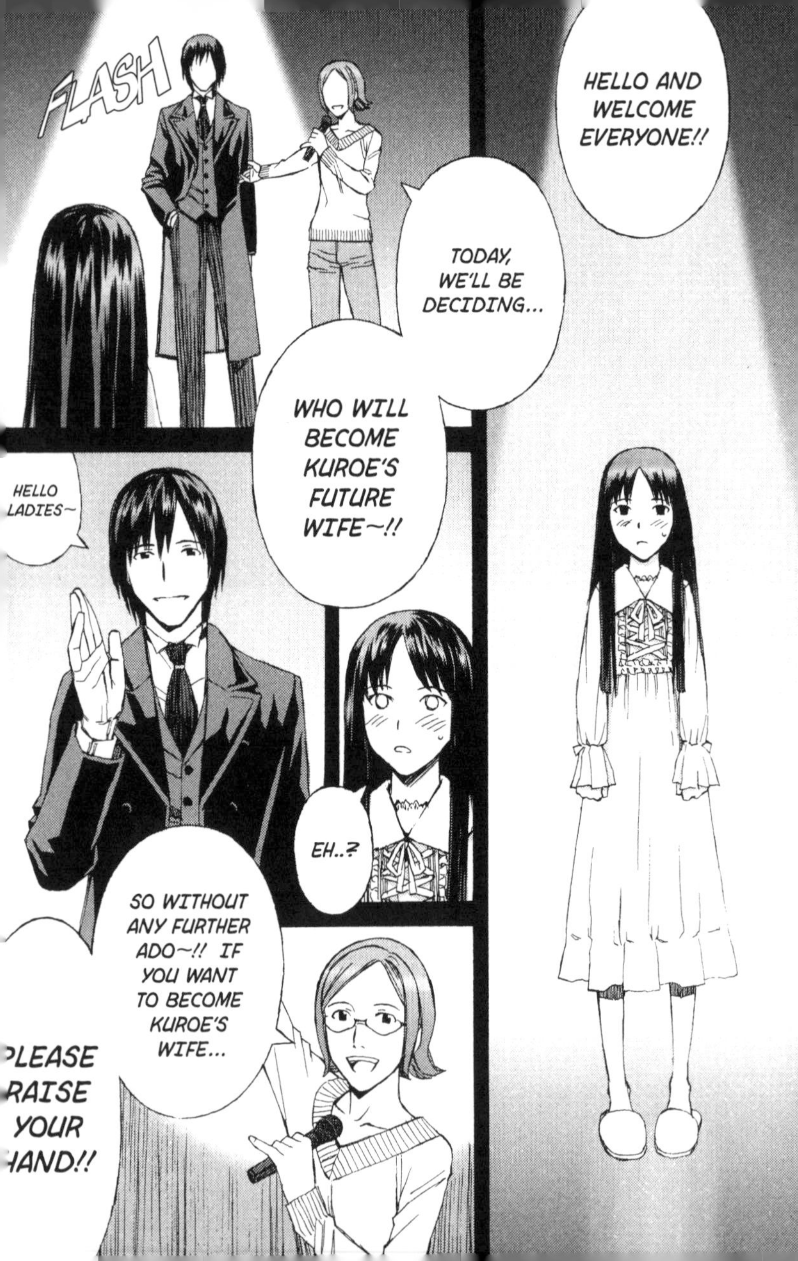
HELLO AND WELCOME EVERYONE!!
TODAY, WE'LL BE DECIDING...
FLASH
WHO WILL BECOME KUROE'S FUTURE WIFE~!!
EH..?
HELLO LADIES~
SO WITHOUT ANY FURTHER ADO~!! IF YOU WANT TO BECOME KUROE'S WIFE...
PLEASE RAISE YOUR HAND!!

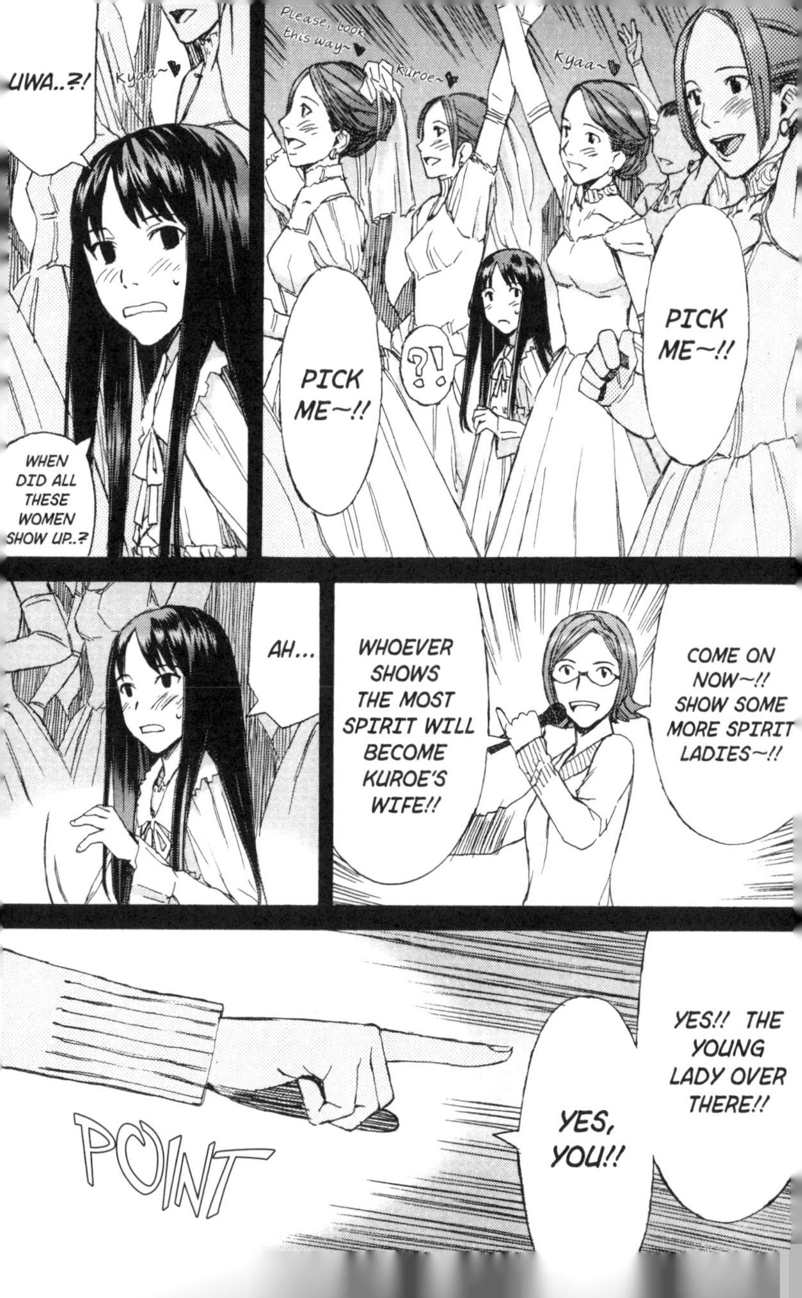
Kyaa~♥
Kuroe~♥
Please, look this way~♥
PICK ME~!!
?!
PICK ME~!!
UWA..?!
Kyaa~♥
WHEN DID ALL THESE WOMEN SHOW UP..?
COME ON NOW~!! SHOW SOME MORE SPIRIT LADIES~!!
WHOEVER SHOWS THE MOST SPIRIT WILL BECOME KUROE'S WIFE!!
AH...
YES!! THE YOUNG LADY OVER THERE!!
YES, YOU!!
POINT

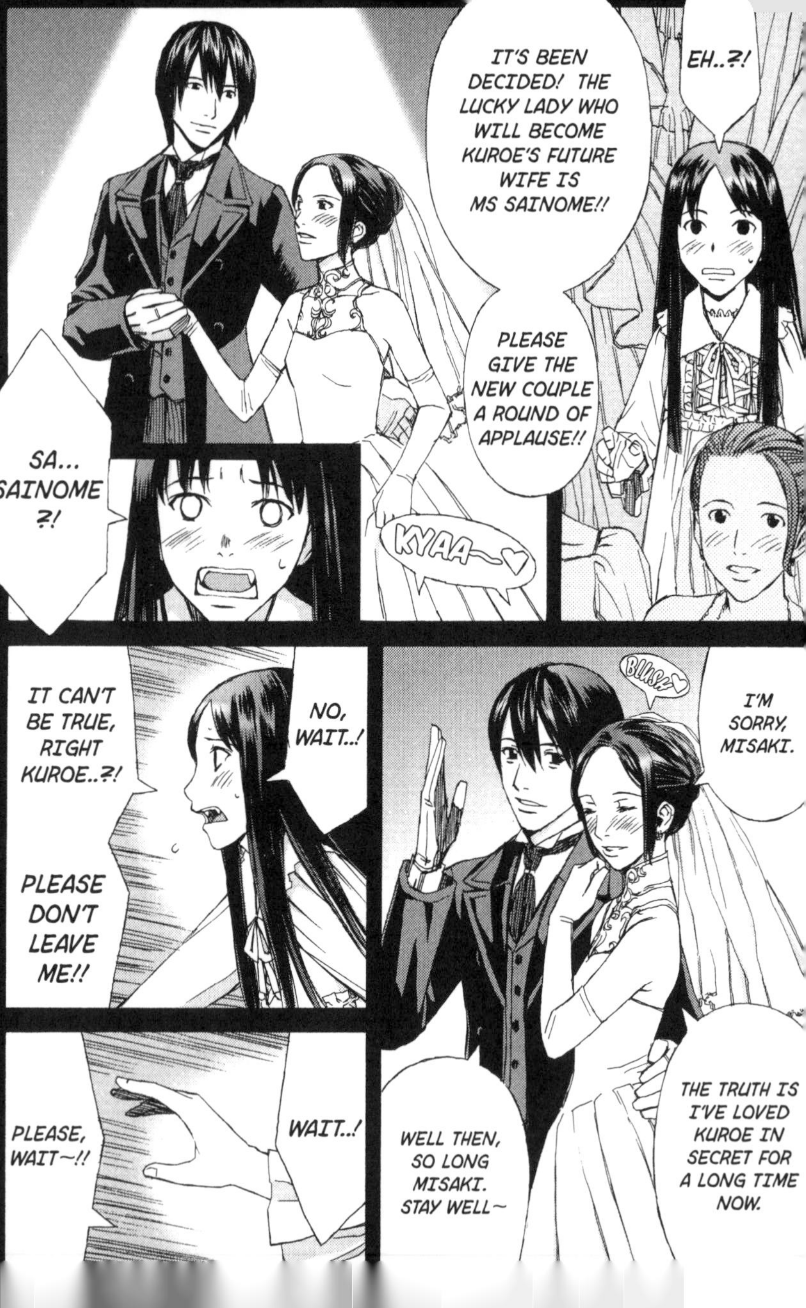
IT'S BEEN DECIDED! THE LUCKY LADY WHO WILL BECOME KUROE'S FUTURE WIFE IS MS SAINOME!!
EH..?!
PLEASE GIVE THE NEW COUPLE A ROUND OF APPLAUSE!!
KYAA~♥
SA... SAINOME ?!
BLUSH♥
I'M SORRY, MISAKI.
THE TRUTH IS I'VE LOVED KUROE IN SECRET FOR A LONG TIME NOW.
WELL THEN, SO LONG MISAKI. STAY WELL~
NO, WAIT..!
IT CAN'T BE TRUE, RIGHT KUROE..?!
PLEASE DON'T LEAVE ME!!
WAIT..!
PLEASE, WAIT~!!

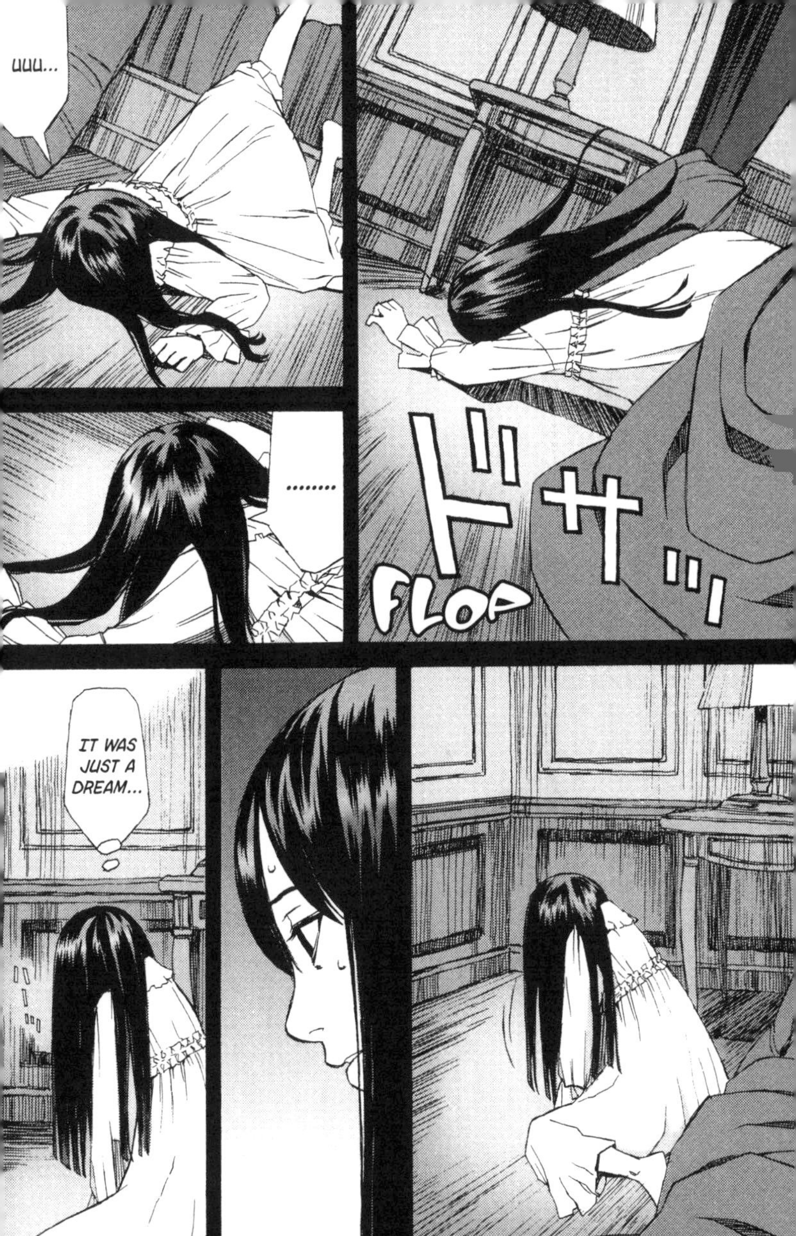
ドサッ
FLOP
uuu...
....
IT WAS JUST A DREAM...

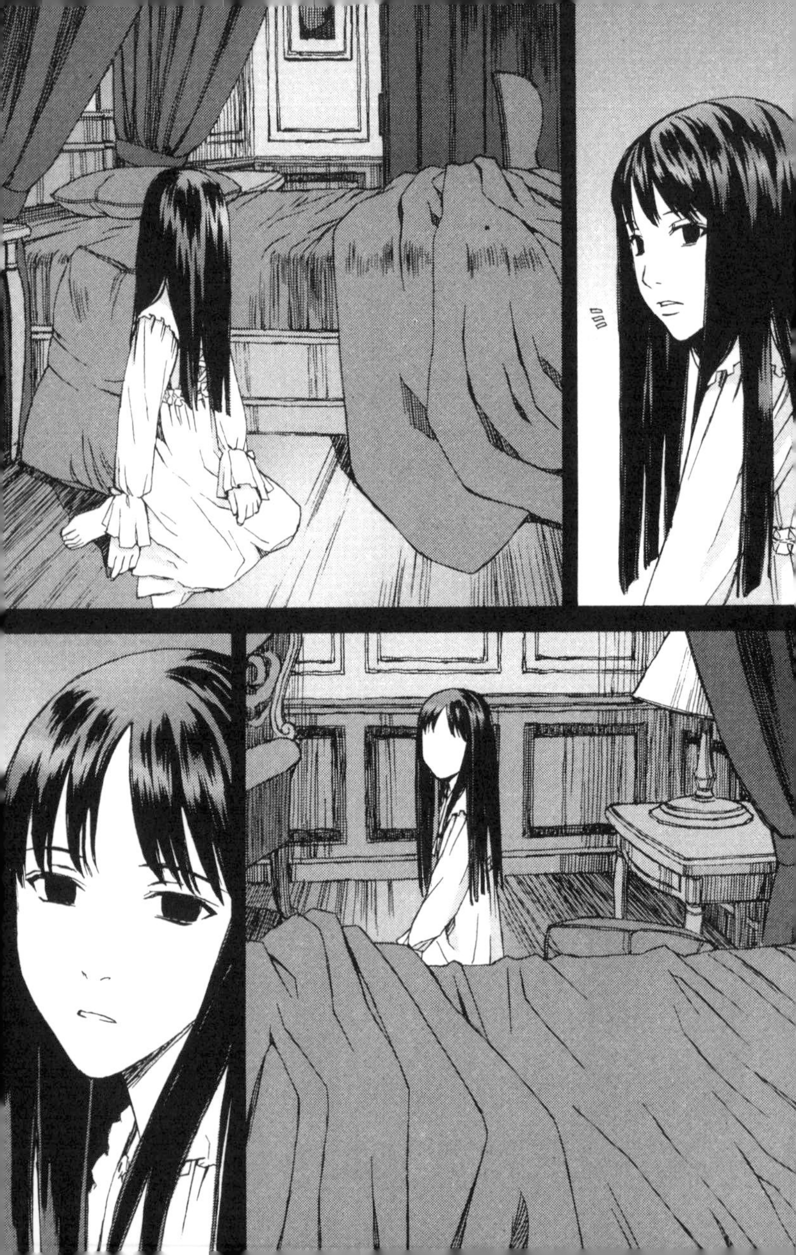

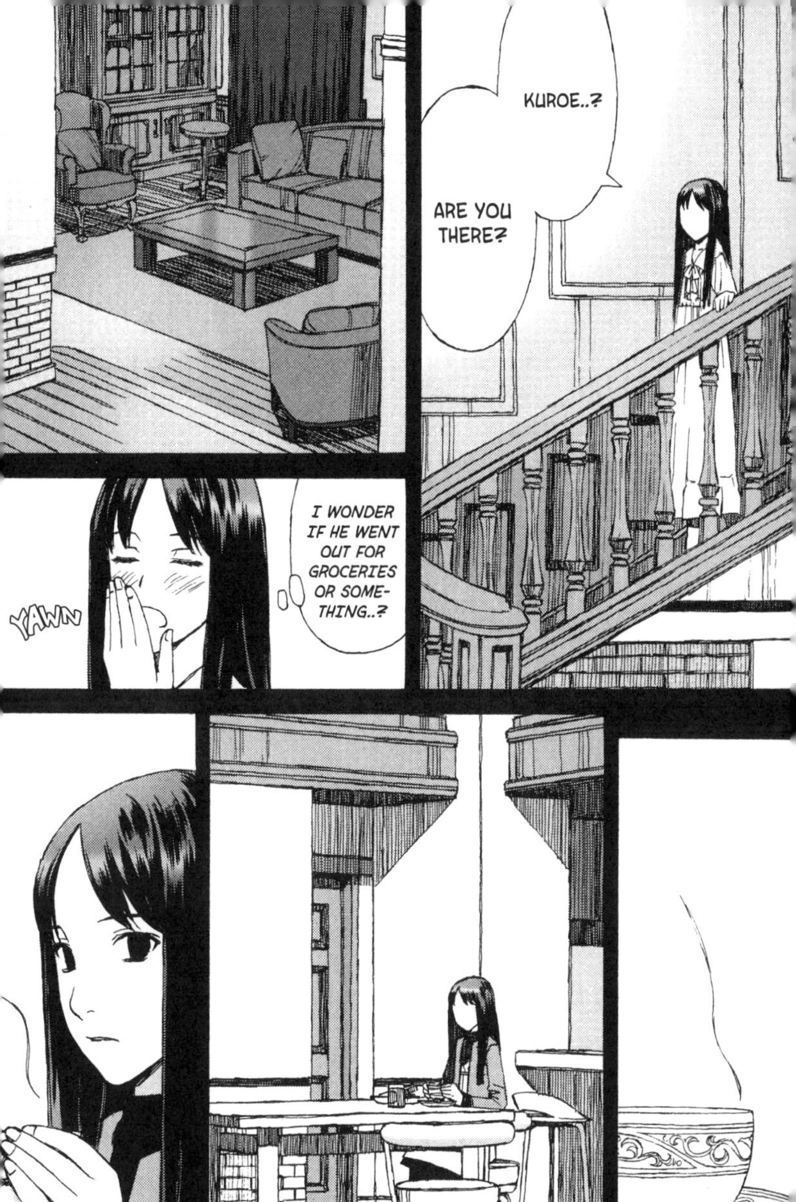
KUROE..?
ARE YOU THERE?
I WONDER IF HE WENT OUT FOR GROCERIES OR SOMETHING..?
YAWN

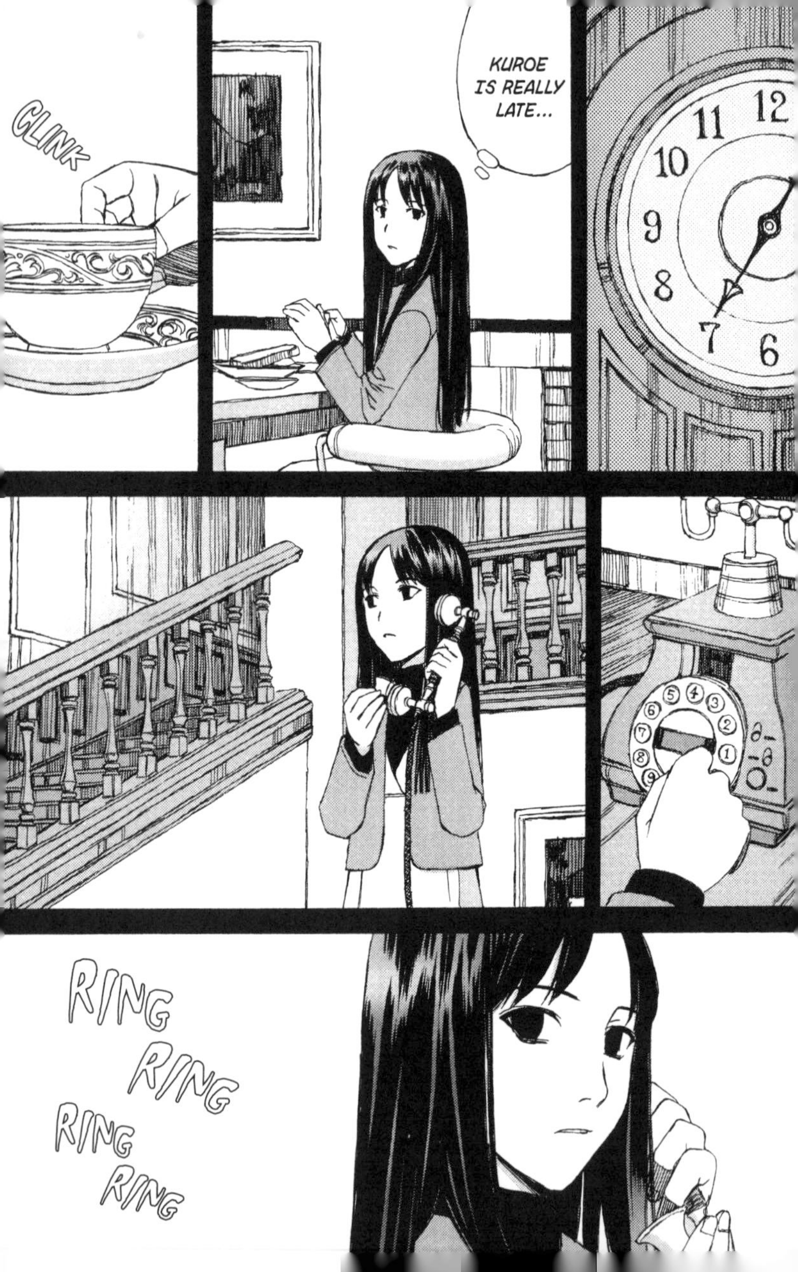
KUROE IS REALLY LATE...
CLINK
RING
RING
RING
RING

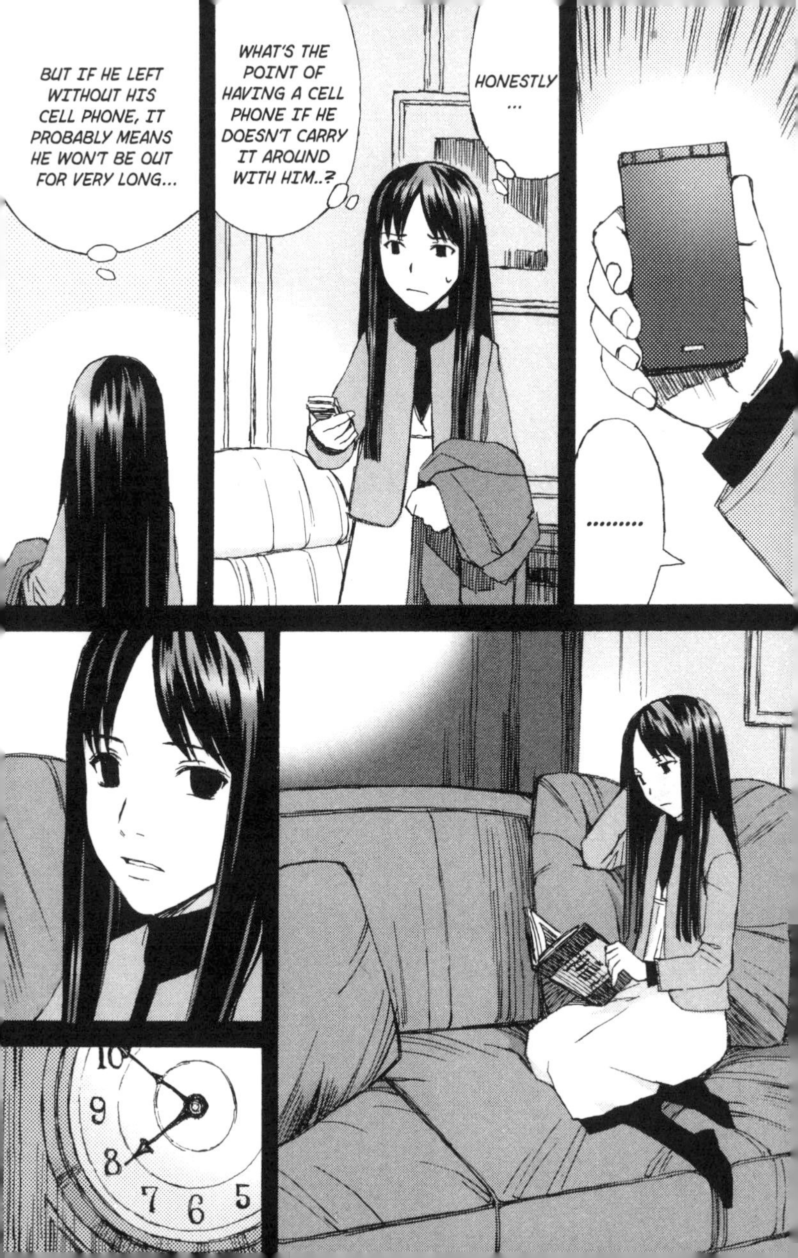
....
HONESTLY ...
WHAT'S THE POINT OF HAVING A CELL PHONE IF HE DOESN'T CARRY IT AROUND WITH HIM..?
BUT IF HE LEFT WITHOUT HIS CELL PHONE, IT PROBABLY MEANS HE WON'T BE OUT FOR VERY LONG...

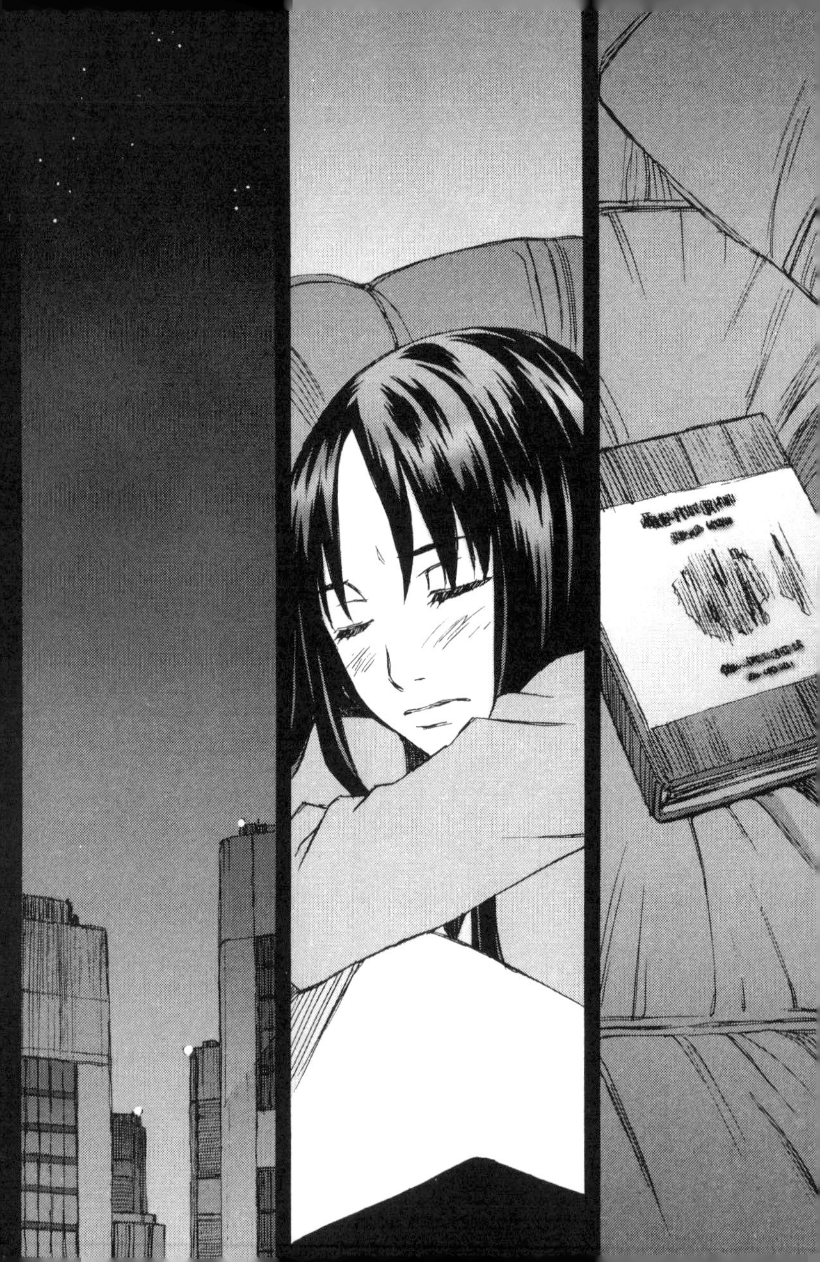

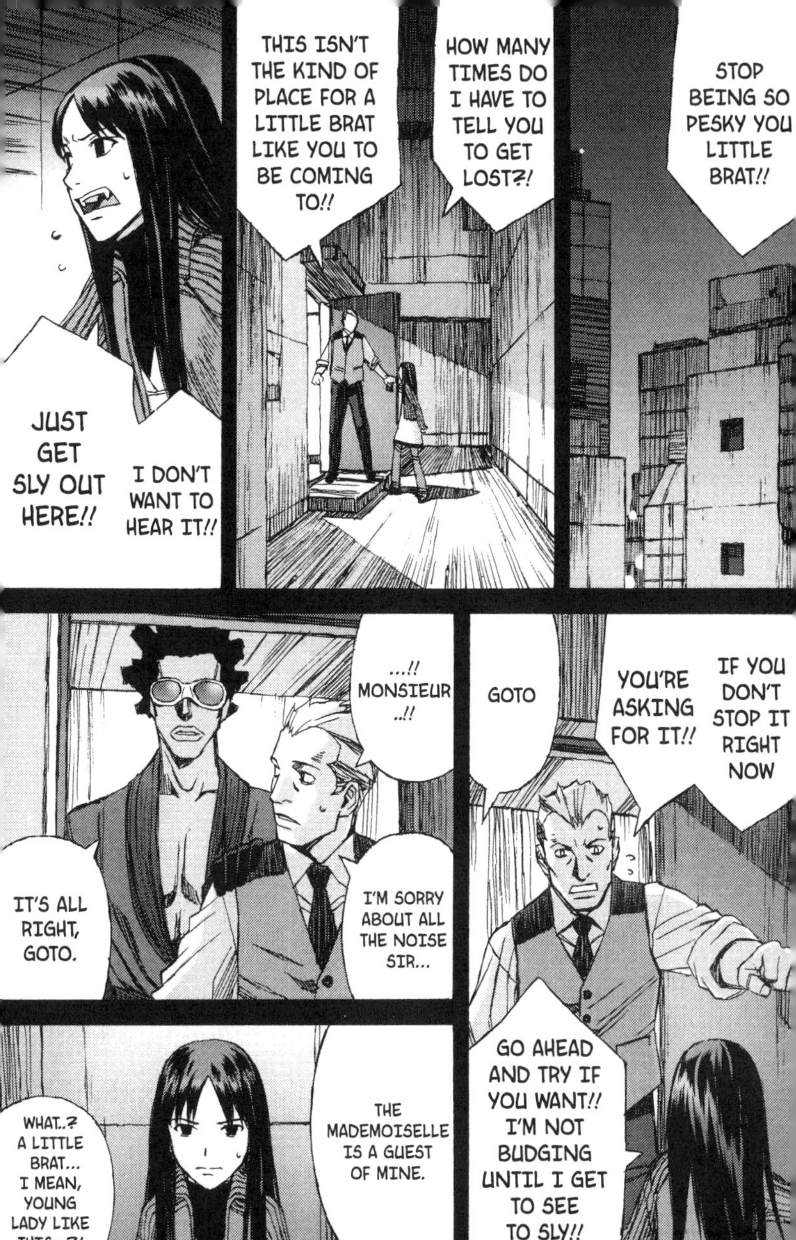
STOP BEING SO PESKY YOU LITTLE BRAT!!
HOW MANY TIMES DO I HAVE TO TELL YOU TO GET LOST?!
THIS ISN'T THE KIND OF PLACE FOR A LITTLE BRAT LIKE YOU TO BE COMING TO!!
I DON'T WANT TO HEAR IT!!
JUST GET SLY OUT HERE!!
IF YOU DON'T STOP IT RIGHT NOW
YOU'RE ASKING FOR IT!!
GOTO
GO AHEAD AND TRY IF YOU WANT!! I'M NOT BUDGING UNTIL I GET TO SEE TO SLY!!
...!! MONSIEUR ..!!
I'M SORRY ABOUT ALL THE NOISE SIR...
IT'S ALL RIGHT, GOTO.
THE MADEMOISELLE IS A GUEST OF MINE.
WHAT..?! A LITTLE BRAT... I MEAN, YOUNG LADY LIKE THIS~?!

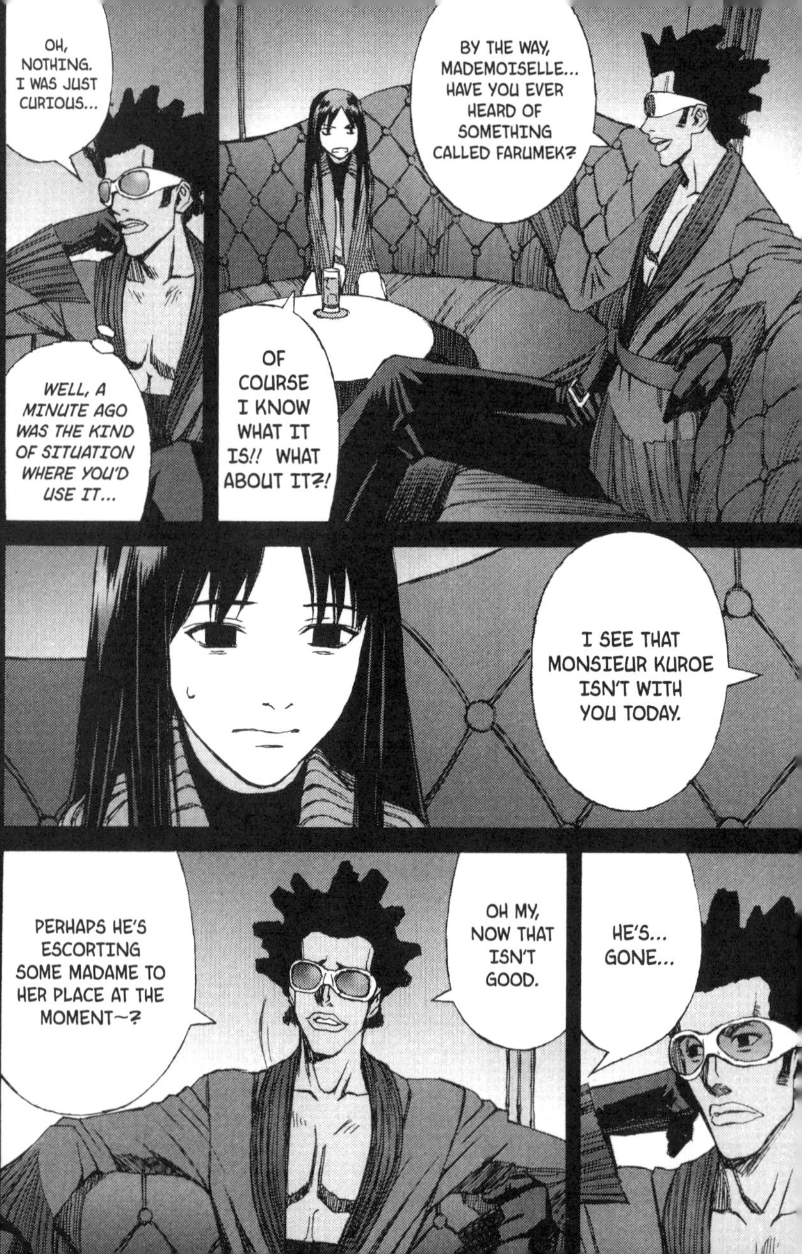
BY THE WAY, MADEMOISELLE... HAVE YOU EVER HEARD OF SOMETHING CALLED FARUMEK?
OF COURSE I KNOW WHAT IT IS!! WHAT ABOUT IT?!
OH, NOTHING. I WAS JUST CURIOUS...
WELL, A MINUTE AGO WAS THE KIND OF SITUATION WHERE YOU'D USE IT...
I SEE THAT MONSIEUR KUROE ISN'T WITH YOU TODAY.
HE'S... GONE...
OH MY, NOW THAT ISN'T GOOD.
PERHAPS HE'S ESCORTING SOME MADAME TO HER PLACE AT THE MOMENT~?

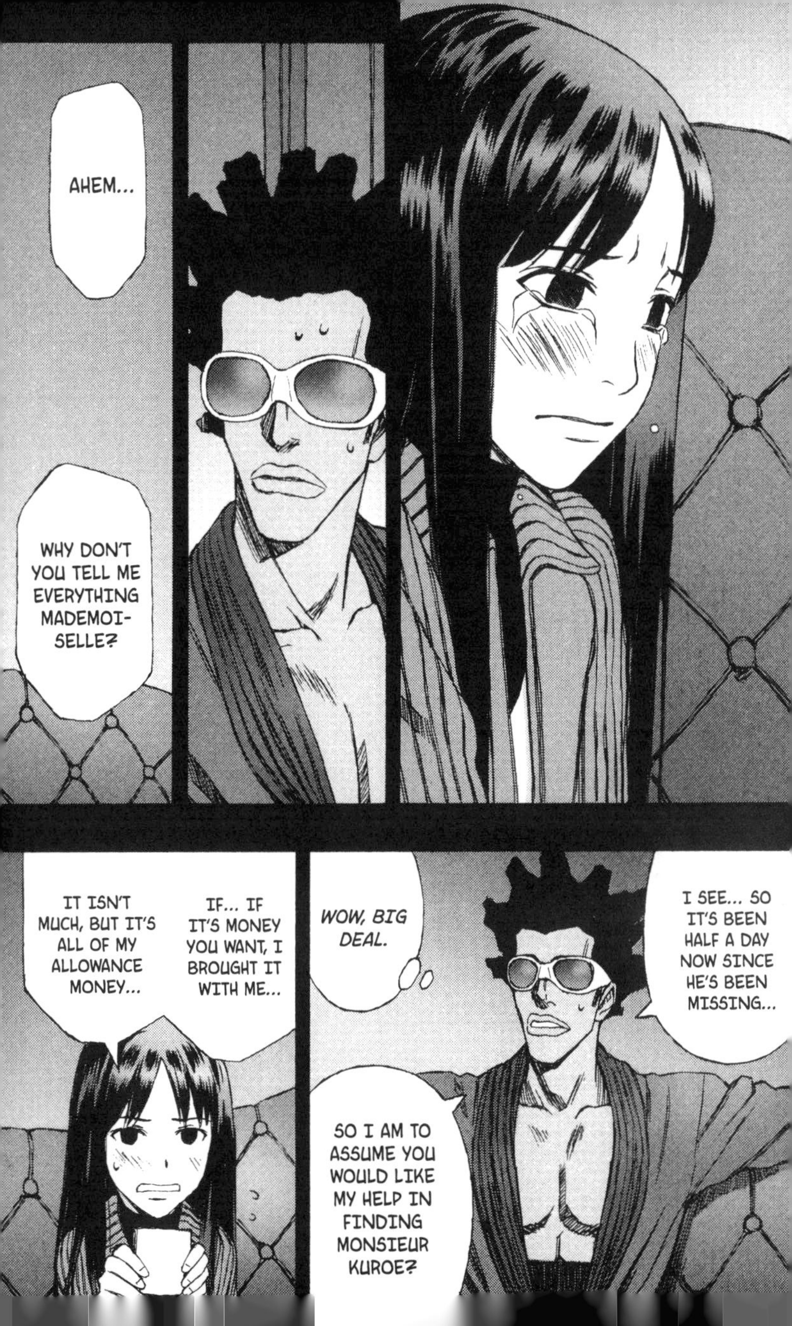
AHEM...
WHY DON'T YOU TELL ME EVERYTHING MADEMOI-SELLE?
I SEE... SO IT'S BEEN HALF A DAY NOW SINCE HE'S BEEN MISSING...
WOW, BIG DEAL.
SO I AM TO ASSUME YOU WOULD LIKE MY HELP IN FINDING MONSIEUR KUROE?
IF... IF IT'S MONEY YOU WANT, I BROUGHT IT WITH ME...
IT ISN'T MUCH, BUT IT'S ALL OF MY ALLOWANCE MONEY...

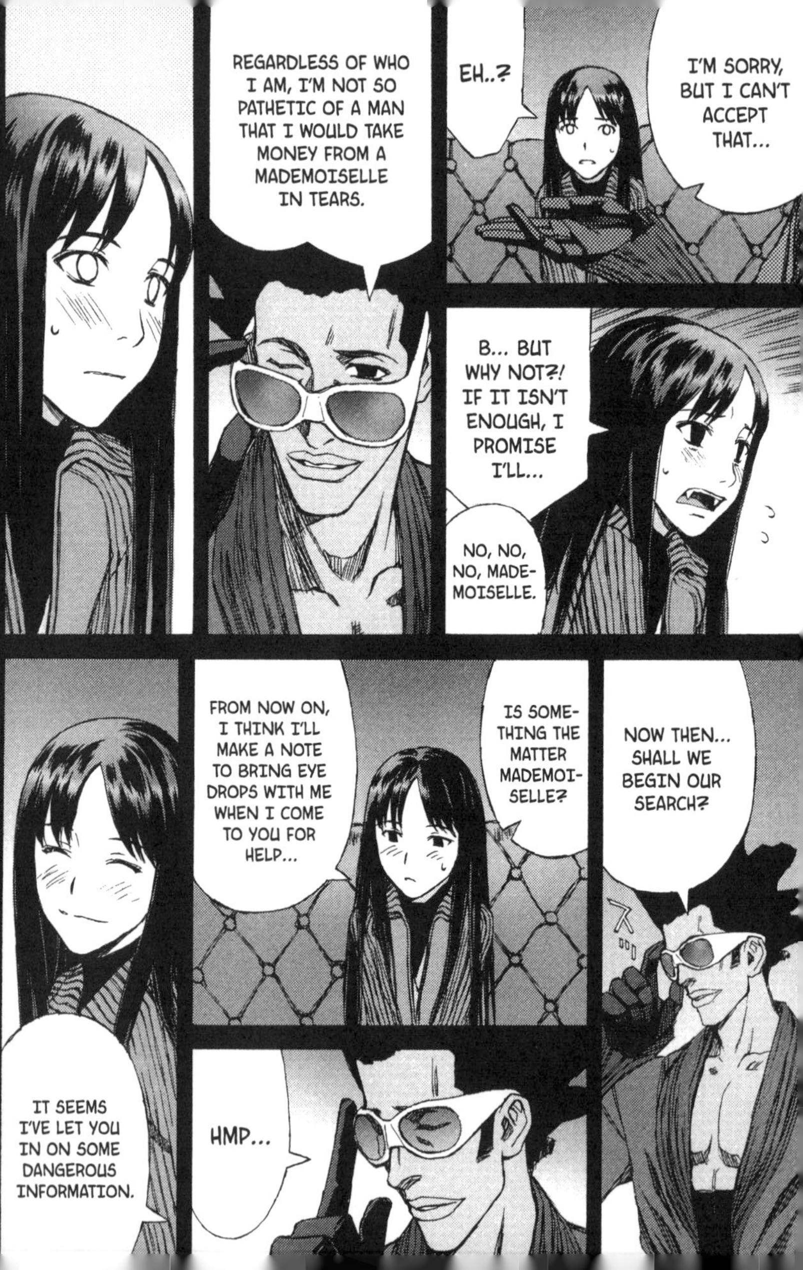
I'M SORRY, BUT I CAN'T ACCEPT THAT...
EH..?
B... BUT WHY NOT?! IF IT ISN'T ENOUGH, I PROMISE I'LL...
NO, NO, NO, MADE-MOISELLE.
REGARDLESS OF WHO I AM, I'M NOT SO PATHETIC OF A MAN THAT I WOULD TAKE MONEY FROM A MADEMOISELLE IN TEARS.
NOW THEN... SHALL WE BEGIN OUR SEARCH?
IS SOME-THING THE MATTER MADEMOI-SELLE?
FROM NOW ON, I THINK I'LL MAKE A NOTE TO BRING EYE DROPS WITH ME WHEN I COME TO YOU FOR HELP...
HMP...
IT SEEMS I'VE LET YOU IN ON SOME DANGEROUS INFORMATION.

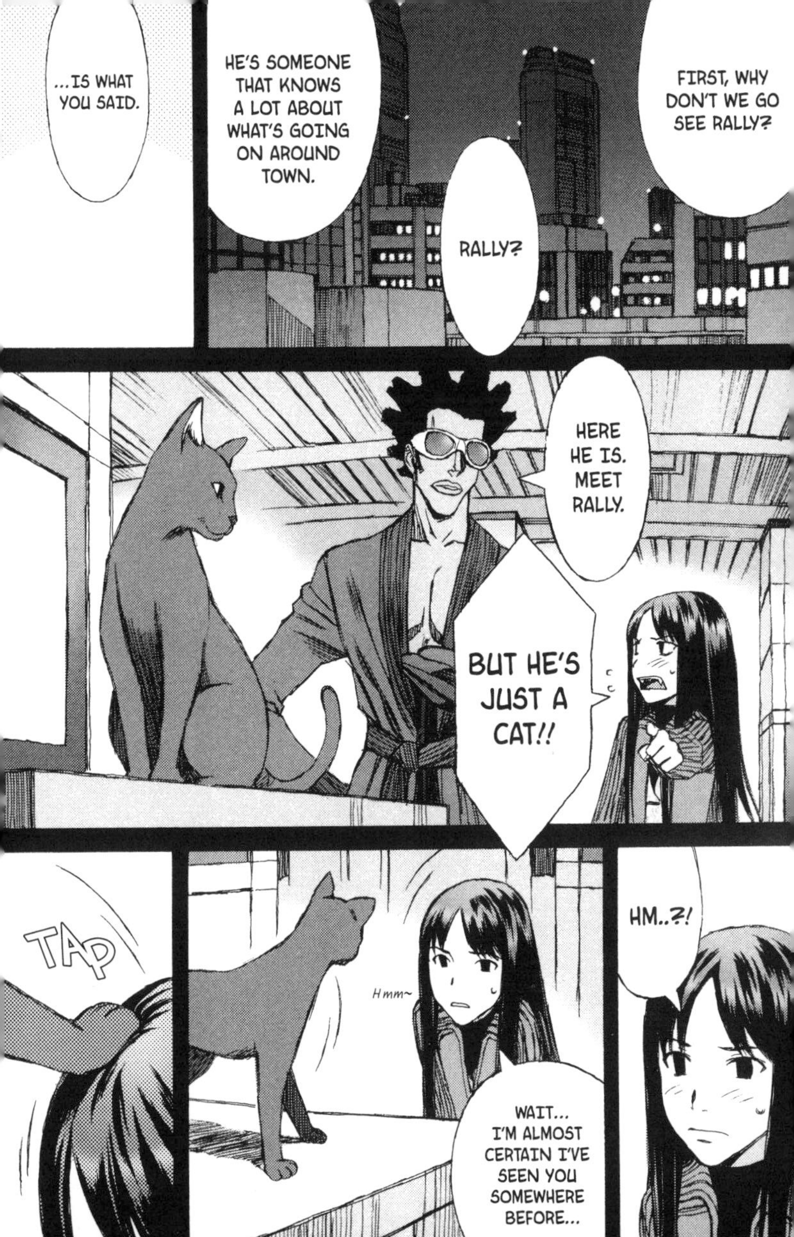
FIRST, WHY DON'T WE GO SEE RALLY?
RALLY?
HE'S SOMEONE THAT KNOWS A LOT ABOUT WHAT'S GOING ON AROUND TOWN.
...IS WHAT YOU SAID.
HERE HE IS. MEET RALLY.
BUT HE'S JUST A CAT!!
HM..?!
Hmm~
WAIT... I'M ALMOST CERTAIN I'VE SEEN YOU SOMEWHERE BEFORE...
TAP

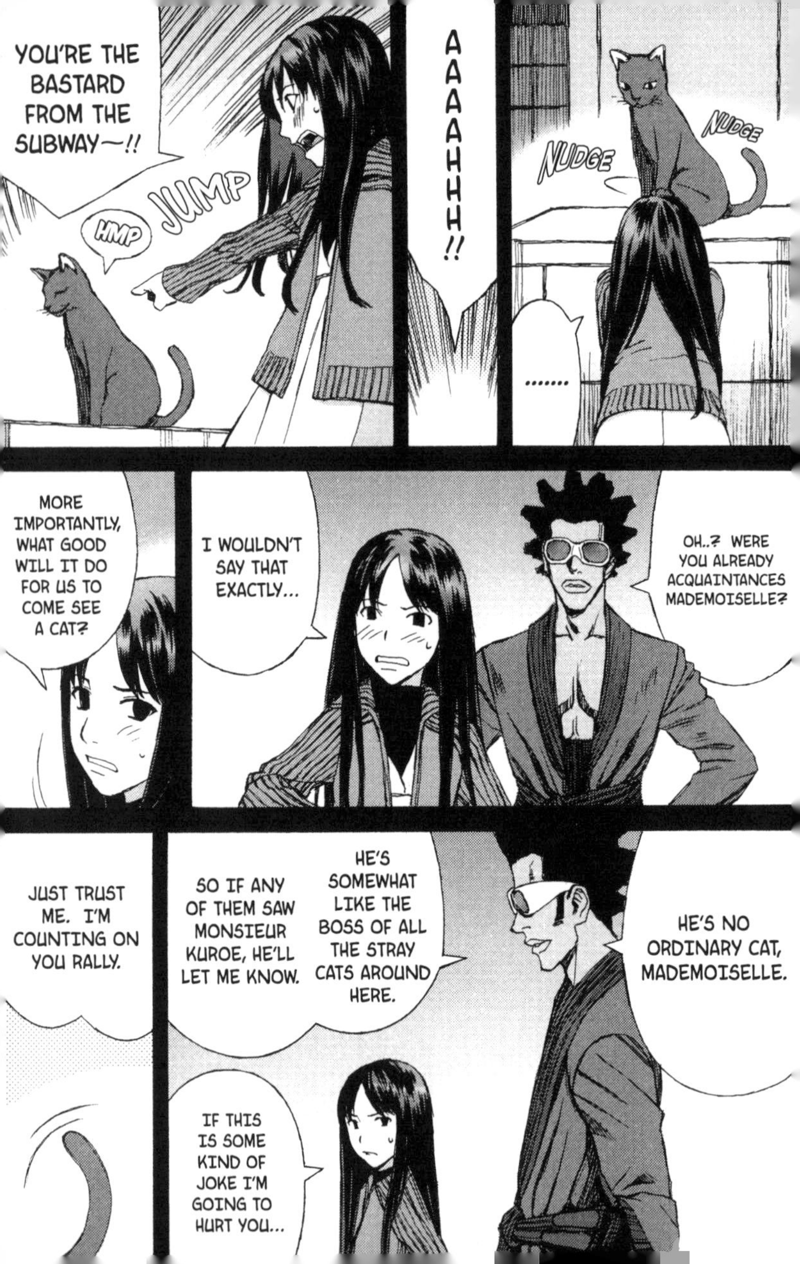
NUDGE
NUDGE
......
AAAAHHH!!
YOU'RE THE BASTARD FROM THE SUBWAY~!!
JUMP
HMP
OH..? WERE YOU ALREADY ACQUAINTANCES MADEMOISELLE?
I WOULDN'T SAY THAT EXACTLY...
MORE IMPORTANTLY, WHAT GOOD WILL IT DO FOR US TO COME SEE A CAT?
HE'S NO ORDINARY CAT, MADEMOISELLE.
HE'S SOMEWHAT LIKE THE BOSS OF ALL THE STRAY CATS AROUND HERE.
SO IF ANY OF THEM SAW MONSIEUR KUROE, HE'LL LET ME KNOW.
IF THIS IS SOME KIND OF JOKE I'M GOING TO HURT YOU...
JUST TRUST ME. I'M COUNTING ON YOU RALLY.

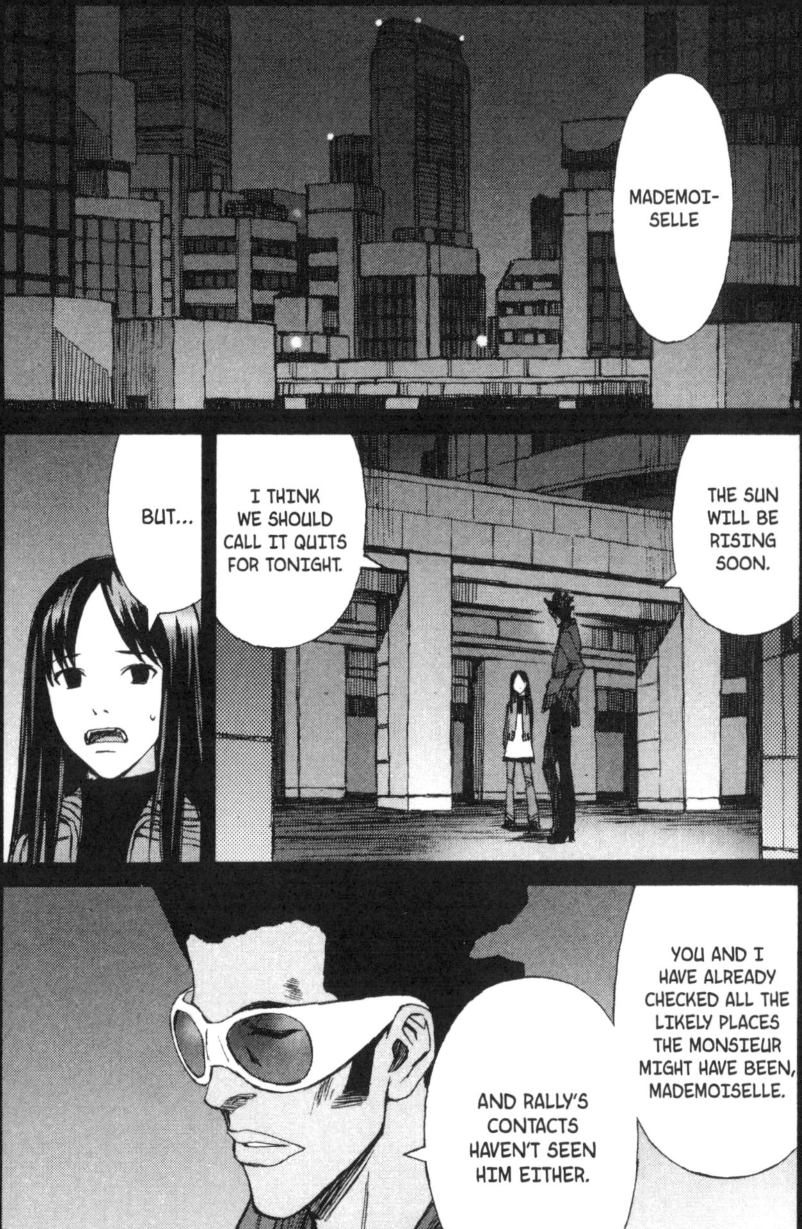
MADEMOI-SELLE
THE SUN WILL BE RISING SOON.
I THINK WE SHOULD CALL IT QUITS FOR TONIGHT.
BUT...
YOU AND I HAVE ALREADY CHECKED ALL THE LIKELY PLACES THE MONSIEUR MIGHT HAVE BEEN, MADEMOISELLE.
AND RALLY'S CONTACTS HAVEN'T SEEN HIM EITHER.

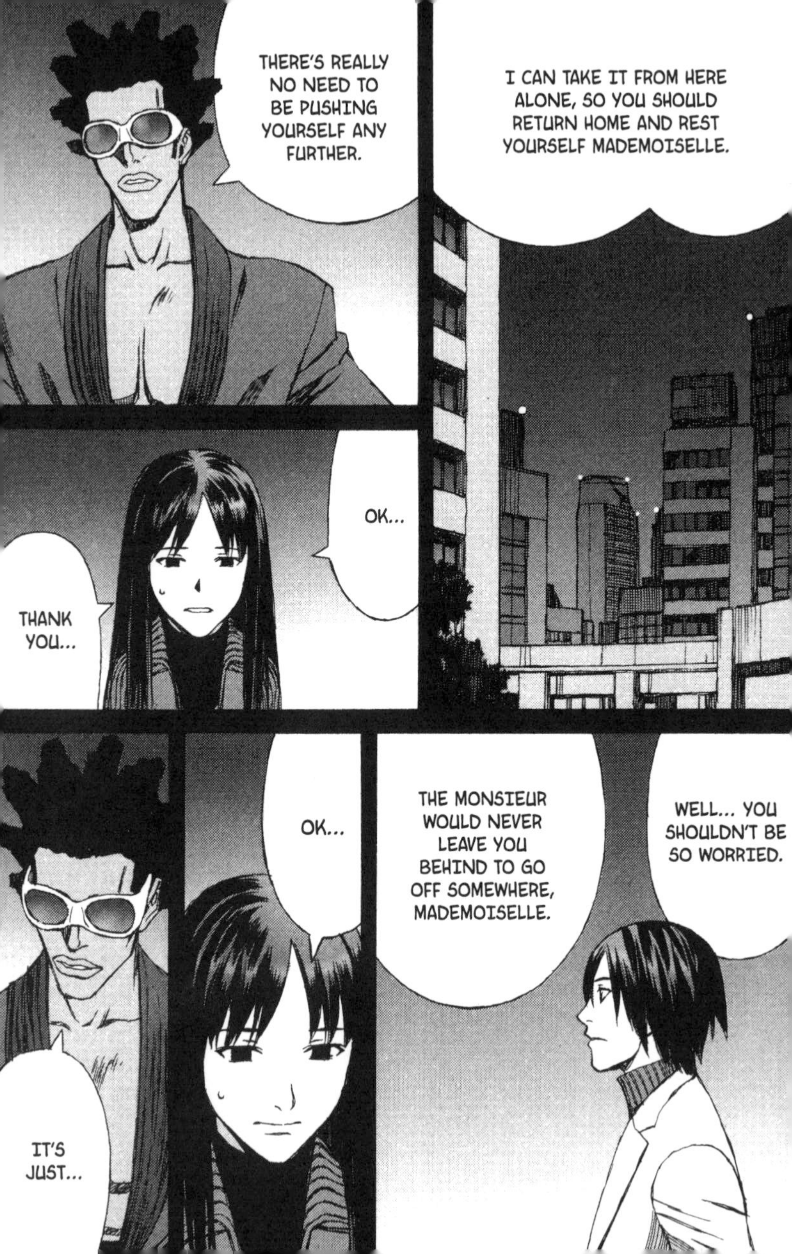
I CAN TAKE IT FROM HERE ALONE, SO YOU SHOULD RETURN HOME AND REST YOURSELF MADEMOISELLE.
THERE'S REALLY NO NEED TO BE PUSHING YOURSELF ANY FURTHER.
OK...
THANK YOU...
WELL... YOU SHOULDN'T BE SO WORRIED.
THE MONSIEUR WOULD NEVER LEAVE YOU BEHIND TO GO OFF SOMEWHERE, MADEMOISELLE.
OK...
IT'S JUST...

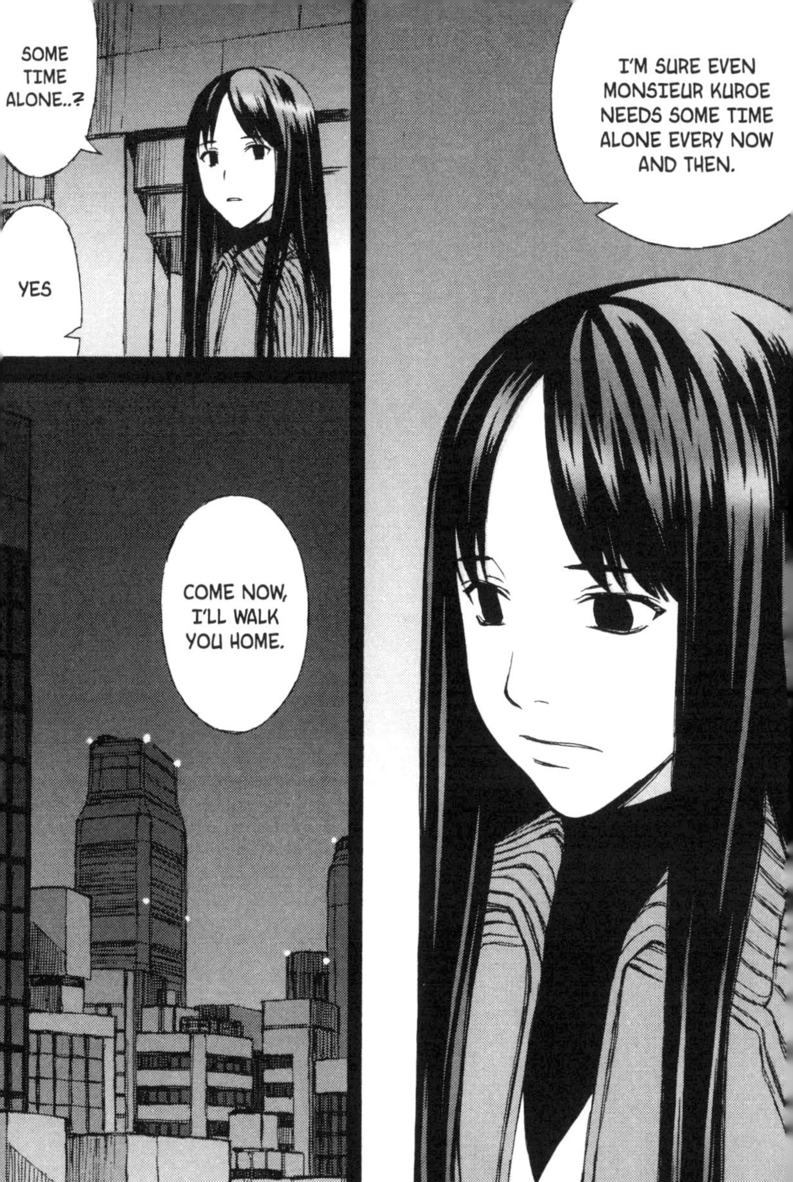
I'M SURE EVEN MONSIEUR KUROE NEEDS SOME TIME ALONE EVERY NOW AND THEN.
SOME TIME ALONE..?
YES
COME NOW, I'LL WALK YOU HOME.

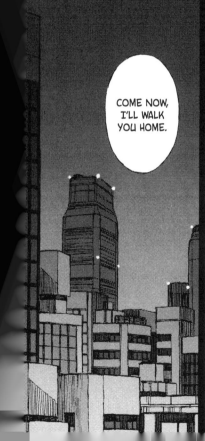

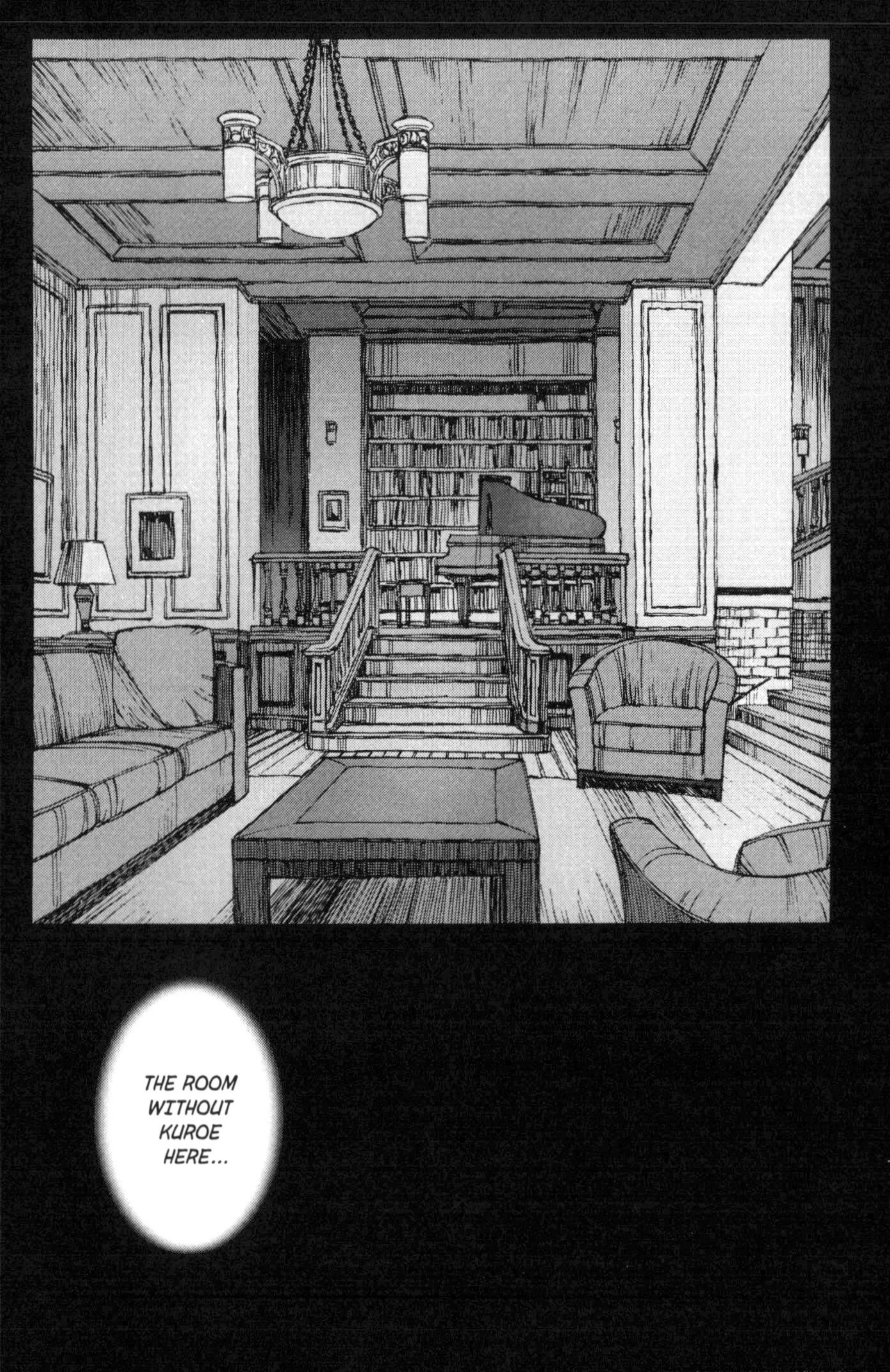
THE ROOM WITHOUT KUROE HERE...

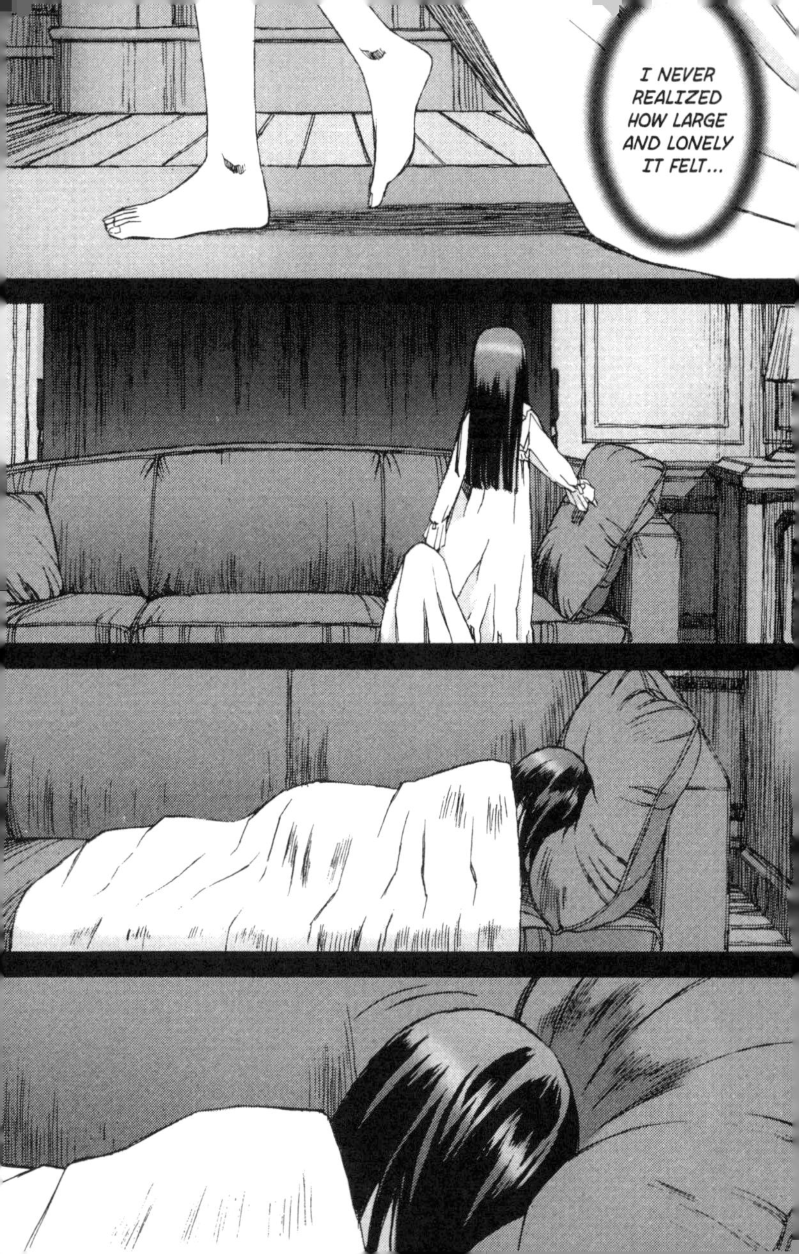
I NEVER REALIZED HOW LARGE AND LONELY IT FELT...

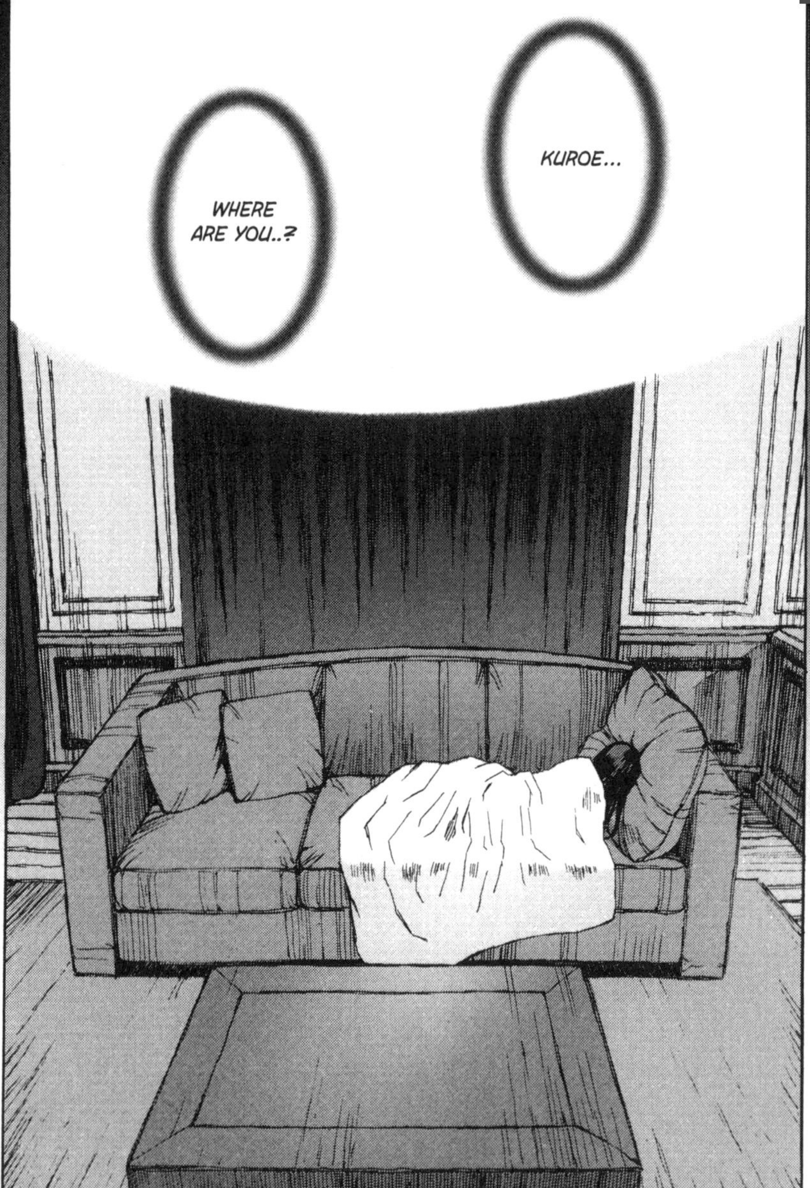
KUROE...
WHERE ARE YOU..?

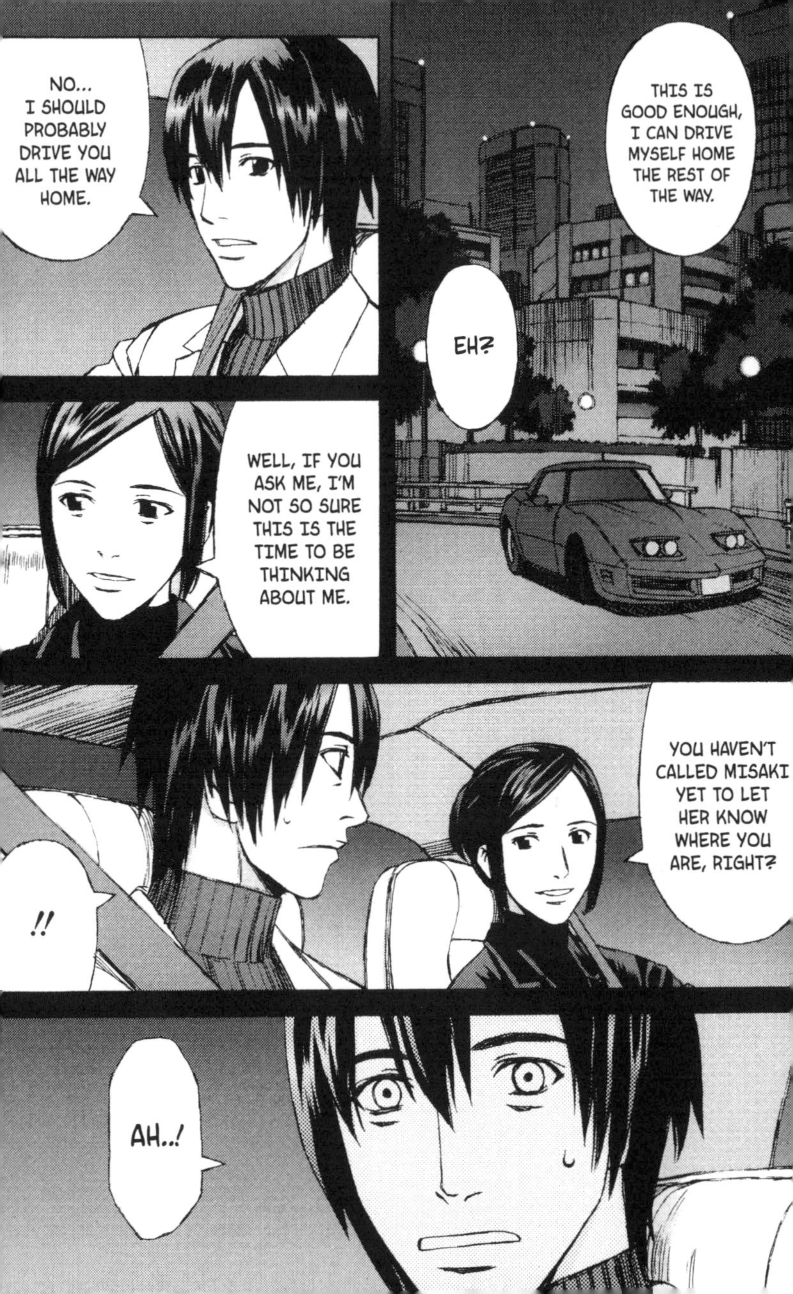
THIS IS GOOD ENOUGH, I CAN DRIVE MYSELF HOME THE REST OF THE WAY.
EH?
NO... I SHOULD PROBABLY DRIVE YOU ALL THE WAY HOME.
WELL, IF YOU ASK ME, I'M NOT SO SURE THIS IS THE TIME TO BE THINKING ABOUT ME.
YOU HAVEN'T CALLED MISAKI YET TO LET HER KNOW WHERE YOU ARE, RIGHT?
!!
AH..!

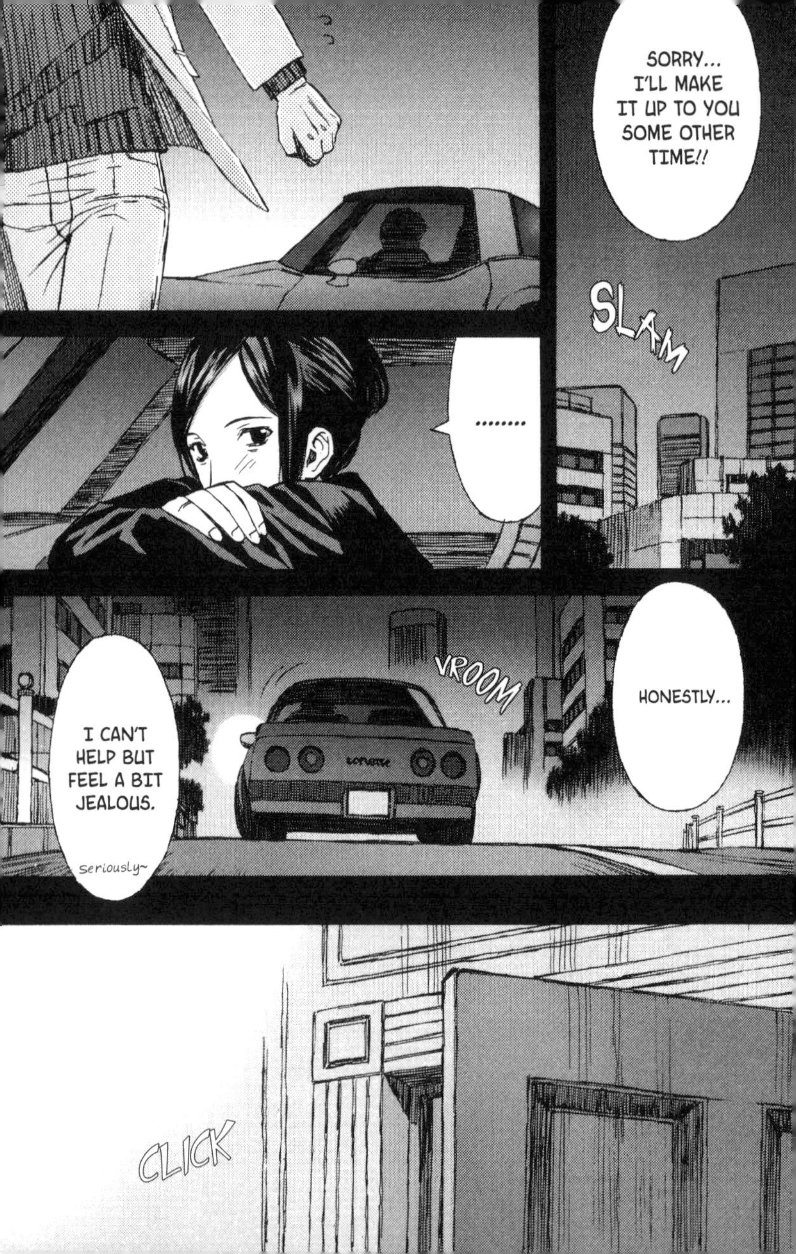
SORRY... I'LL MAKE IT UP TO YOU SOME OTHER TIME!!
SLAM
....
HONESTLY...
VROOM
I CAN'T HELP BUT FEEL A BIT JEALOUS.
seriously~
CLICK

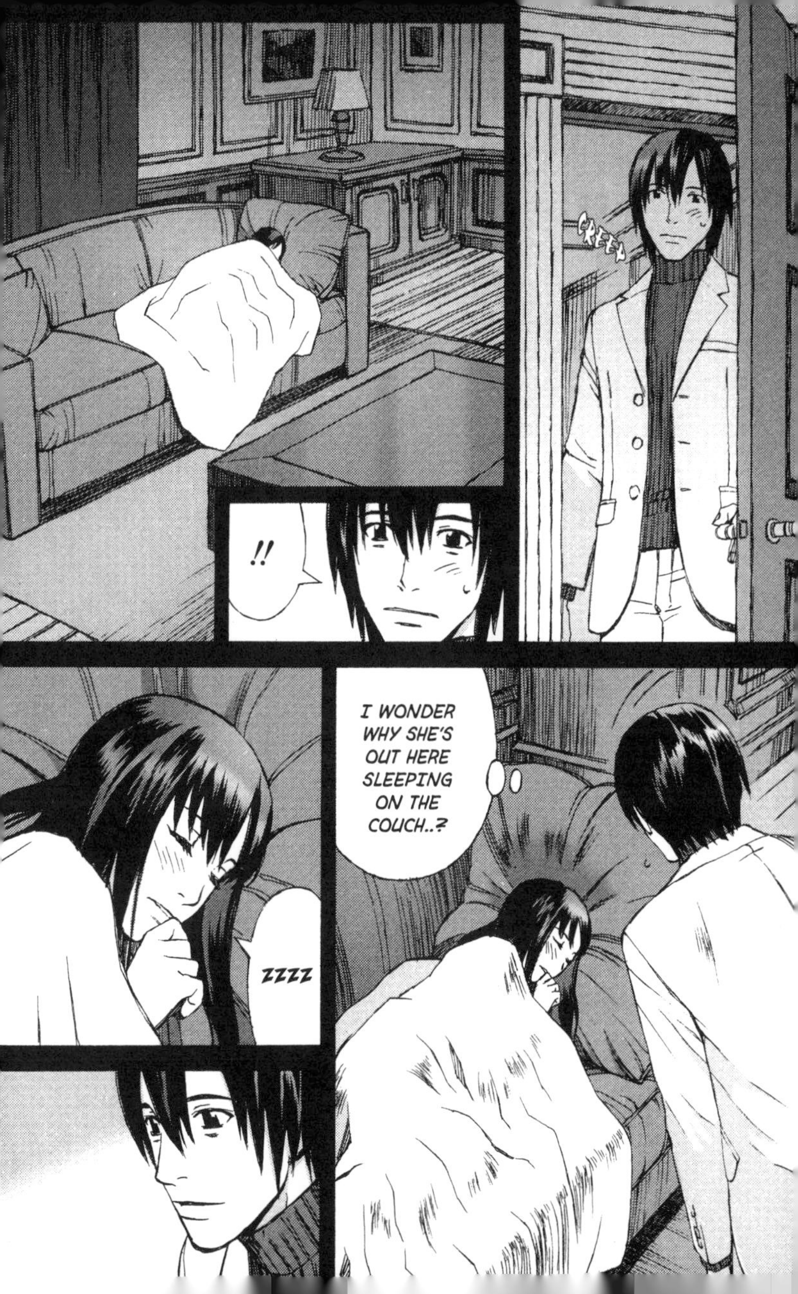
CREEP
!!
I WONDER WHY SHE'S OUT HERE SLEEPING ON THE COUCH..?
ZZZZ

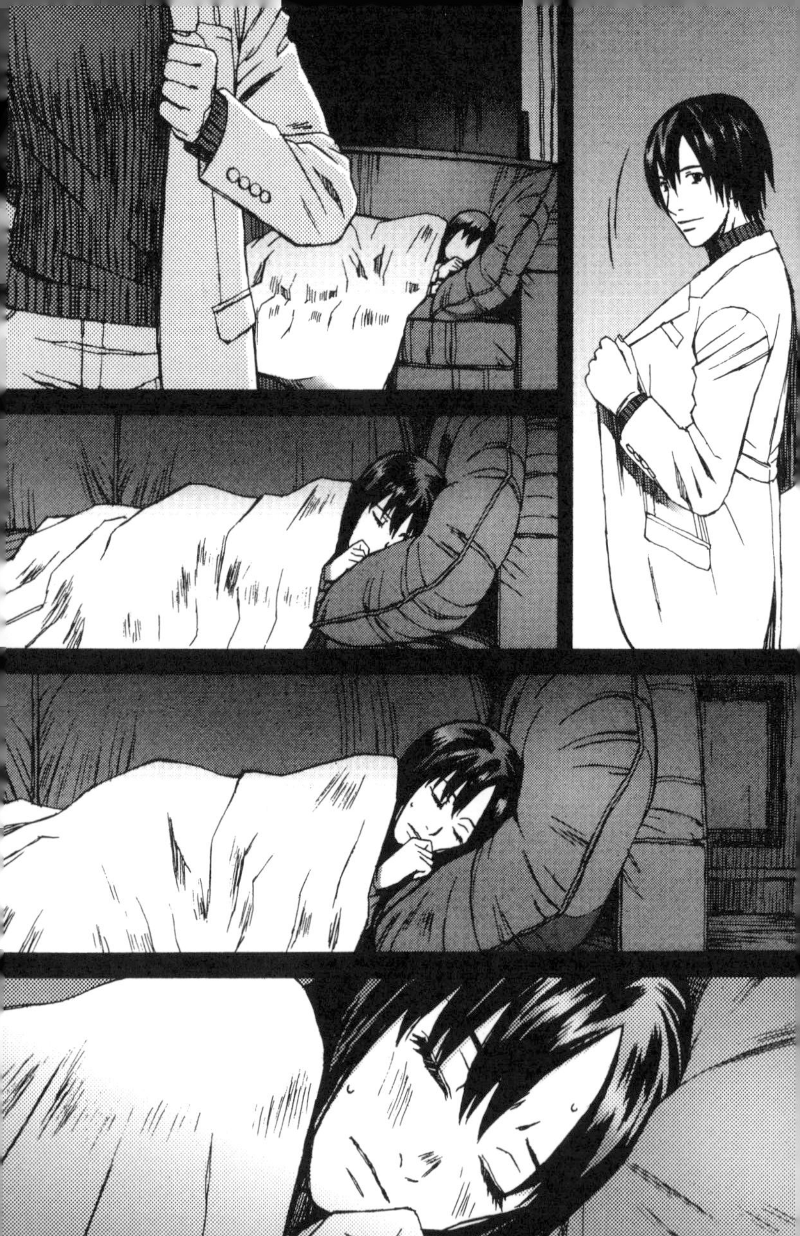

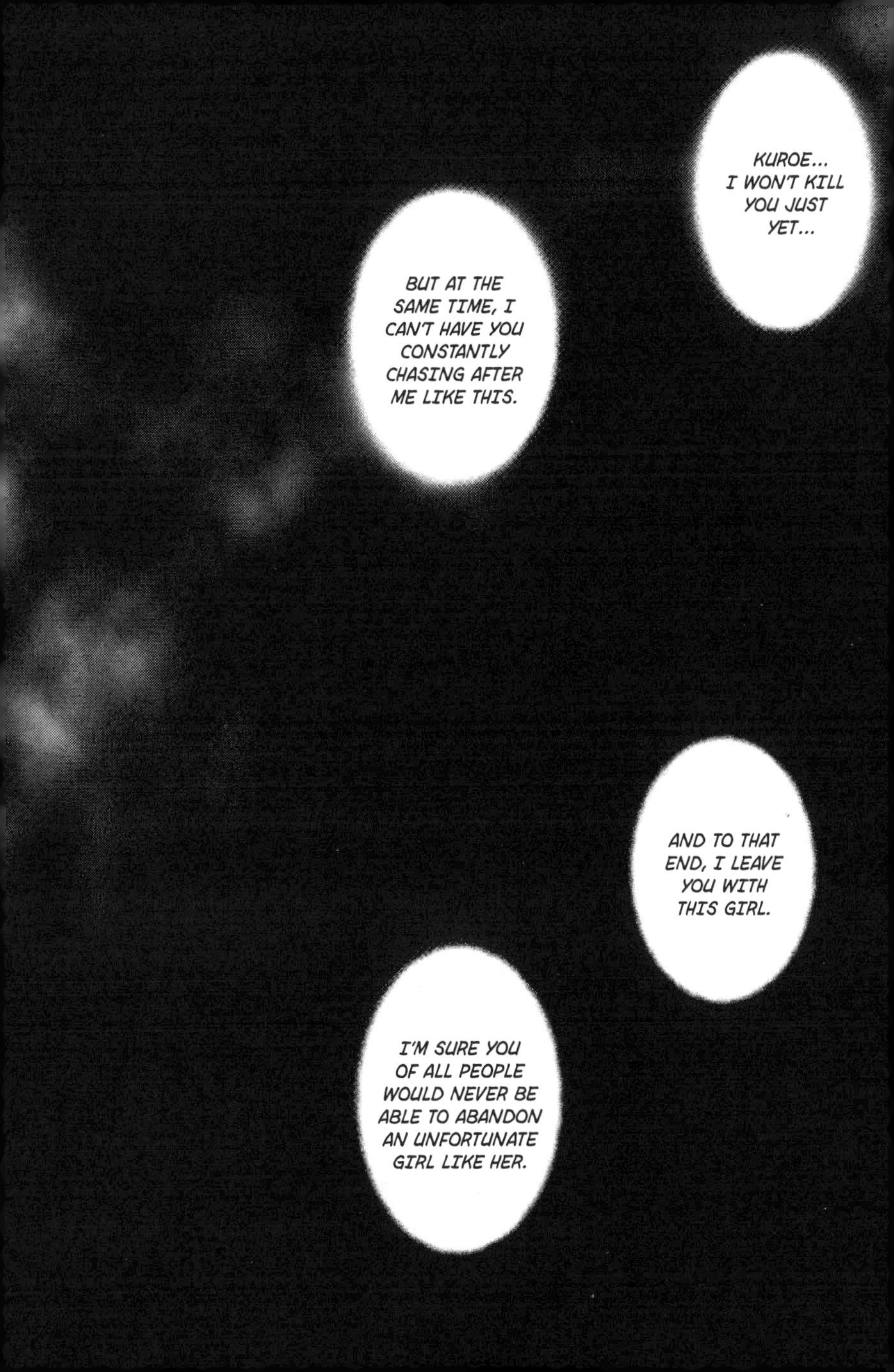
KUROE... I WON'T KILL YOU JUST YET...
BUT AT THE SAME TIME, I CAN'T HAVE YOU CONSTANTLY CHASING AFTER ME LIKE THIS.
AND TO THAT END, I LEAVE YOU WITH THIS GIRL.
I'M SURE YOU OF ALL PEOPLE WOULD NEVER BE ABLE TO ABANDON AN UNFORTUNATE GIRL LIKE HER.

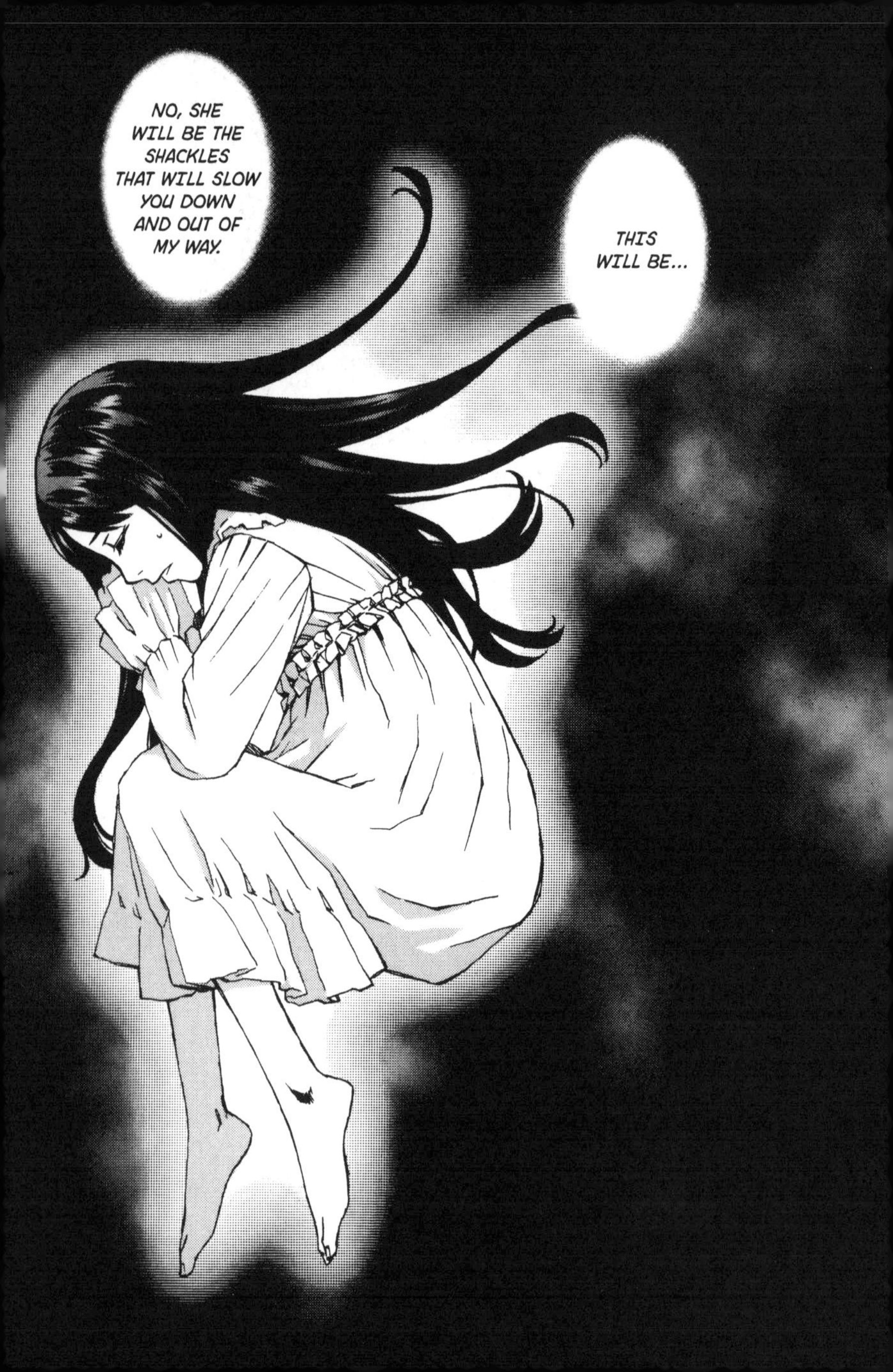
THIS WILL BE...
NO, SHE WILL BE THE SHACKLES THAT WILL SLOW YOU DOWN AND OUT OF MY WAY.

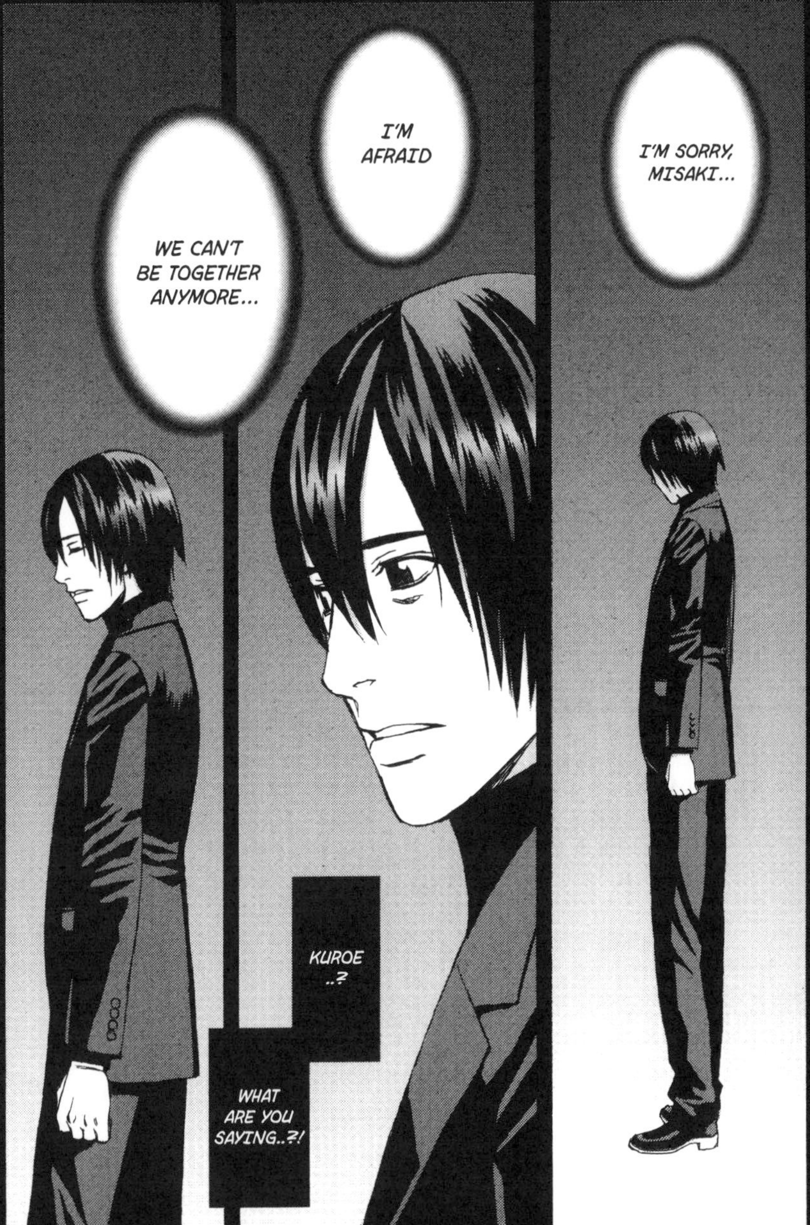
I'M SORRY, MISAKI...
I'M AFRAID
WE CAN'T BE TOGETHER ANYMORE...
KUROE ..?
WHAT ARE YOU SAYING..?!

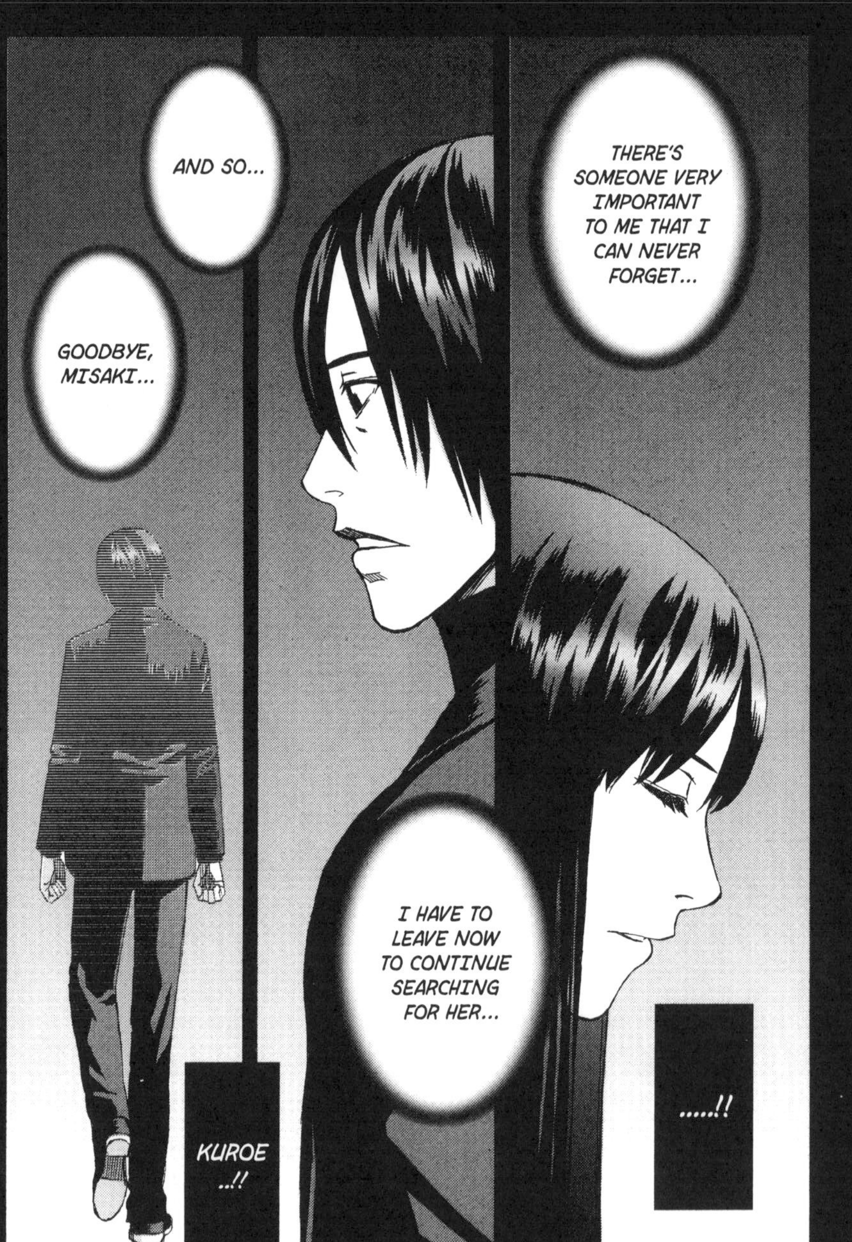
THERE'S SOMEONE VERY IMPORTANT TO ME THAT I CAN NEVER FORGET...
I HAVE TO LEAVE NOW TO CONTINUE SEARCHING FOR HER...
......!!
AND SO...
GOODBYE, MISAKI...
KUROE ..!!

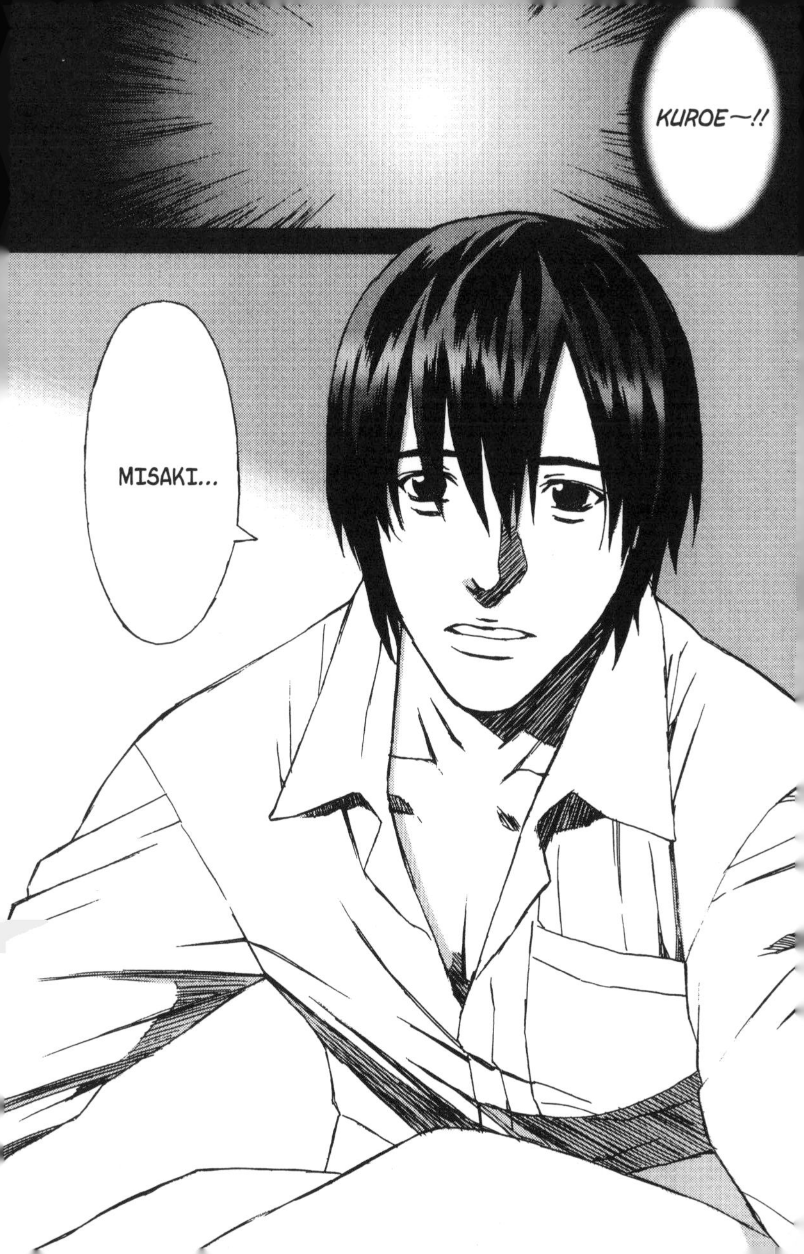
KUROE~!!
MISAKI...

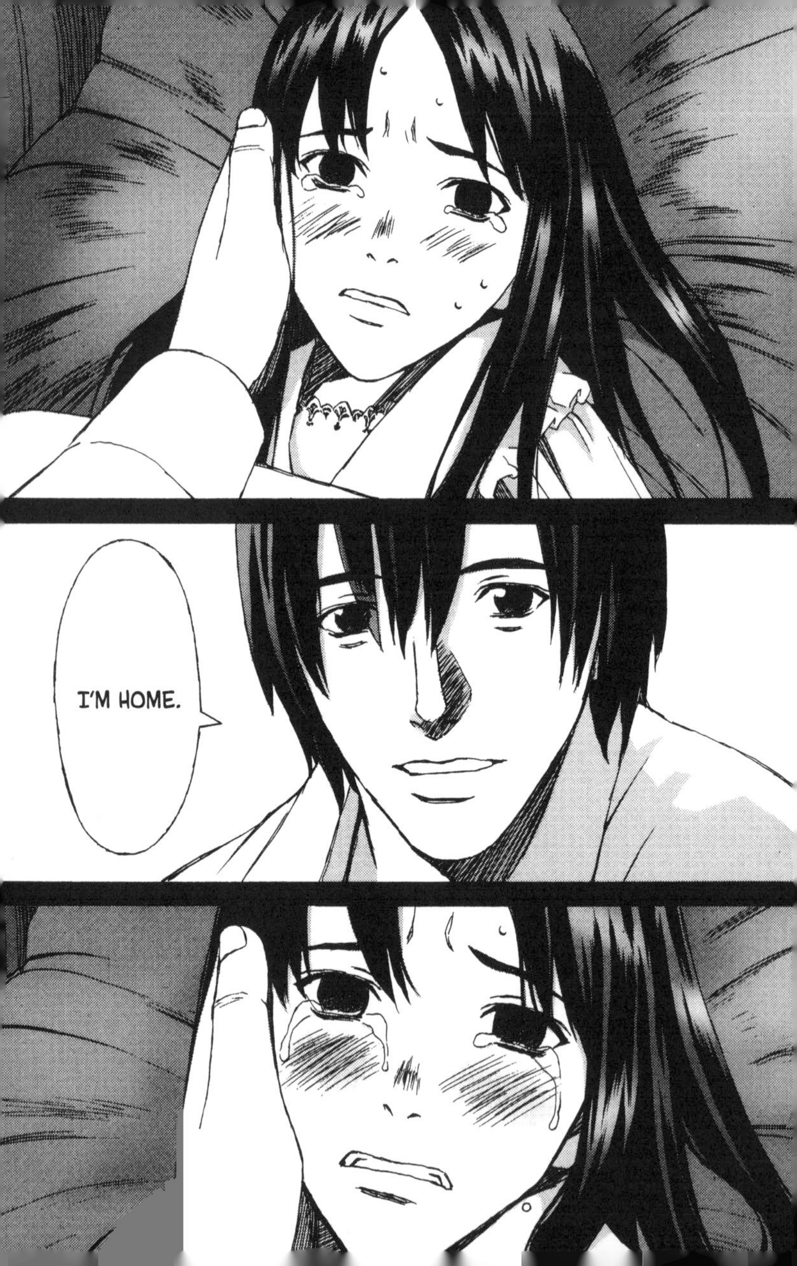
I'M HOME.

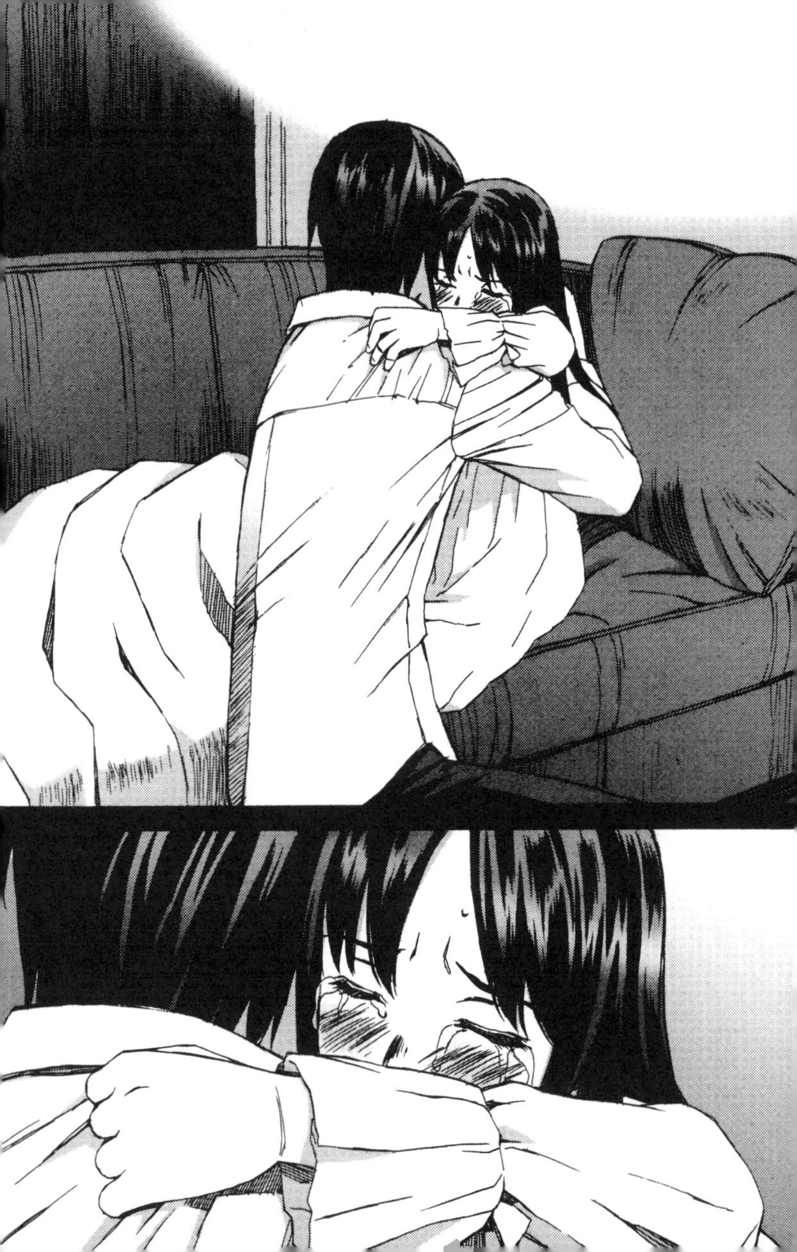

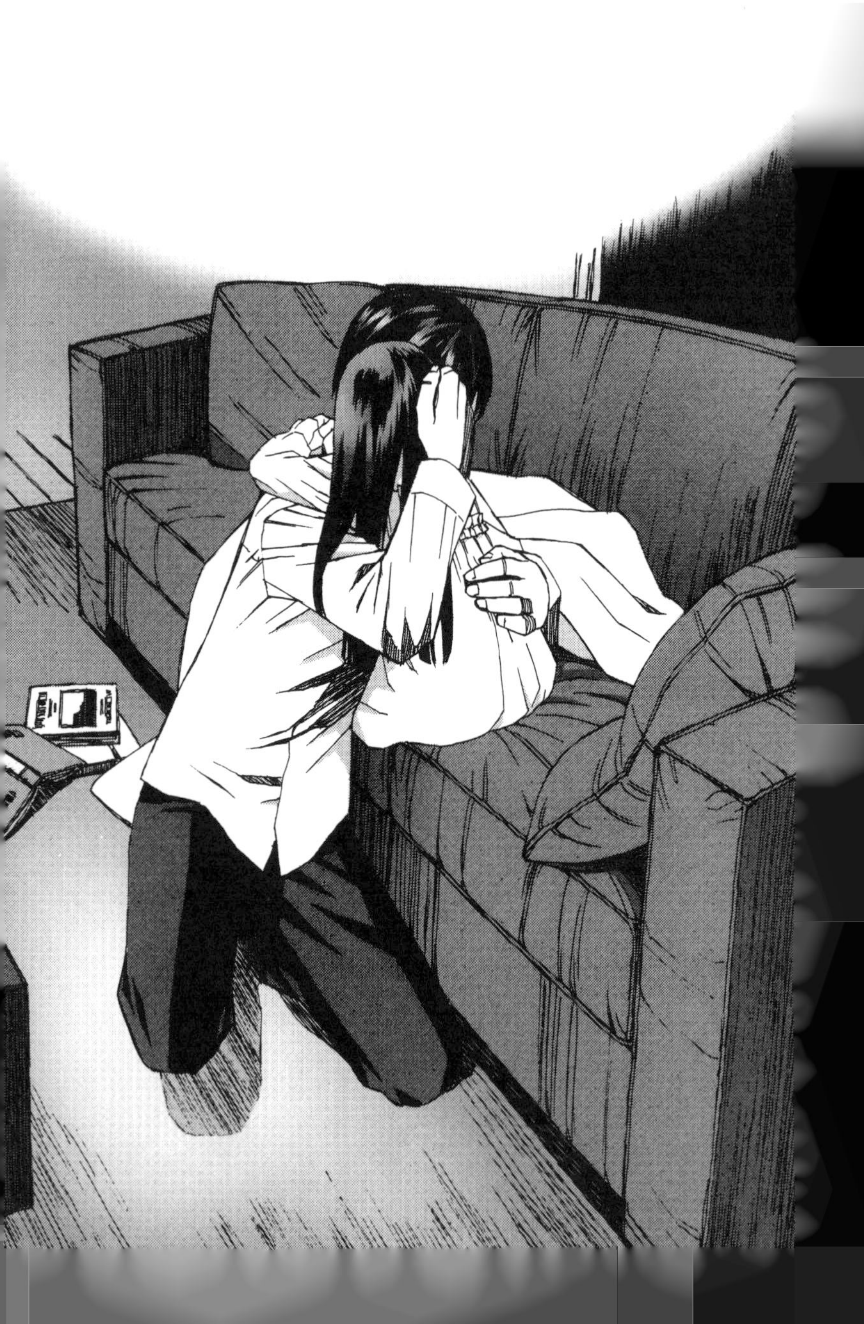

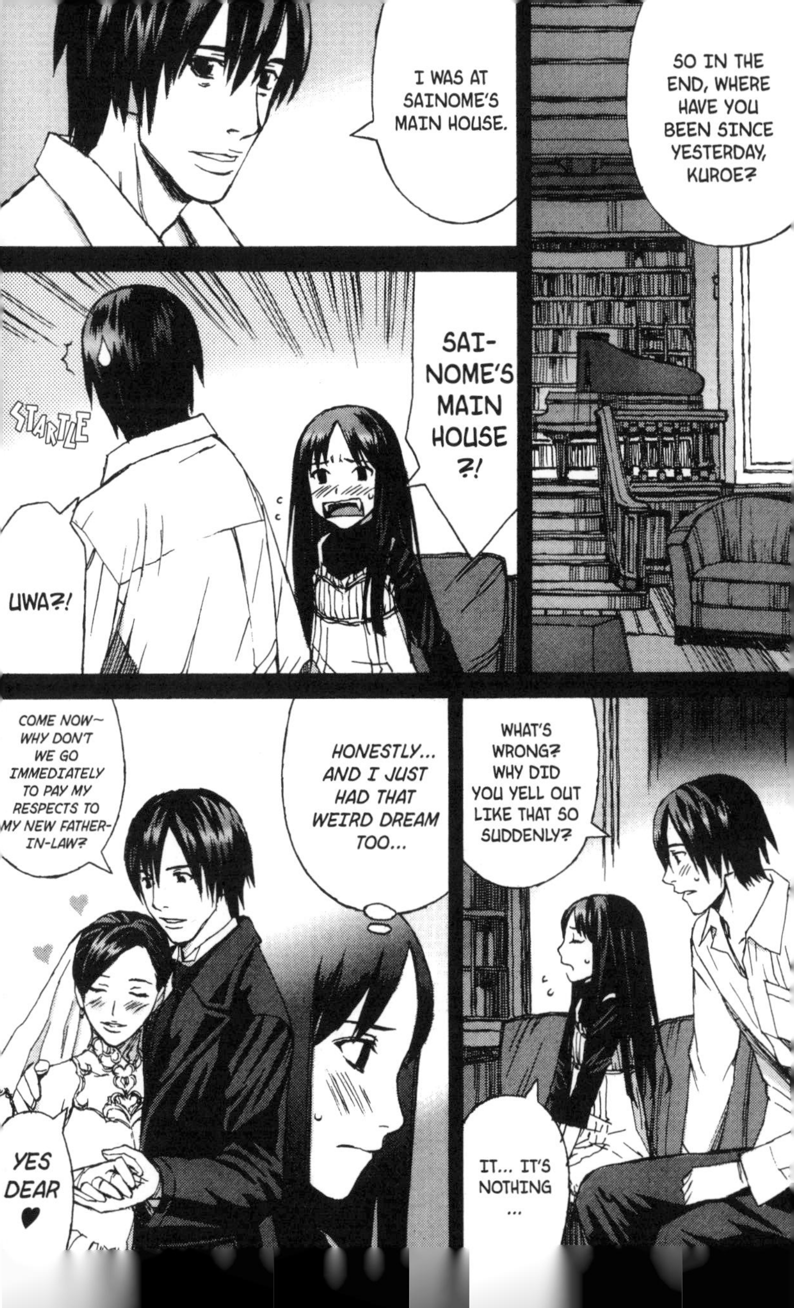
SO IN THE END, WHERE HAVE YOU BEEN SINCE YESTERDAY, KUROE?
I WAS AT SAINOME'S MAIN HOUSE.
SAI-NOME'S MAIN HOUSE ?!
STARTLE
UWA?!
WHAT'S WRONG? WHY DID YOU YELL OUT LIKE THAT SO SUDDENLY?
IT... IT'S NOTHING ...
HONESTLY... AND I JUST HAD THAT WEIRD DREAM TOO...
COME NOW~ WHY DON'T WE GO IMMEDIATELY TO PAY MY RESPECTS TO MY NEW FATHER-IN-LAW?
YES DEAR ♥

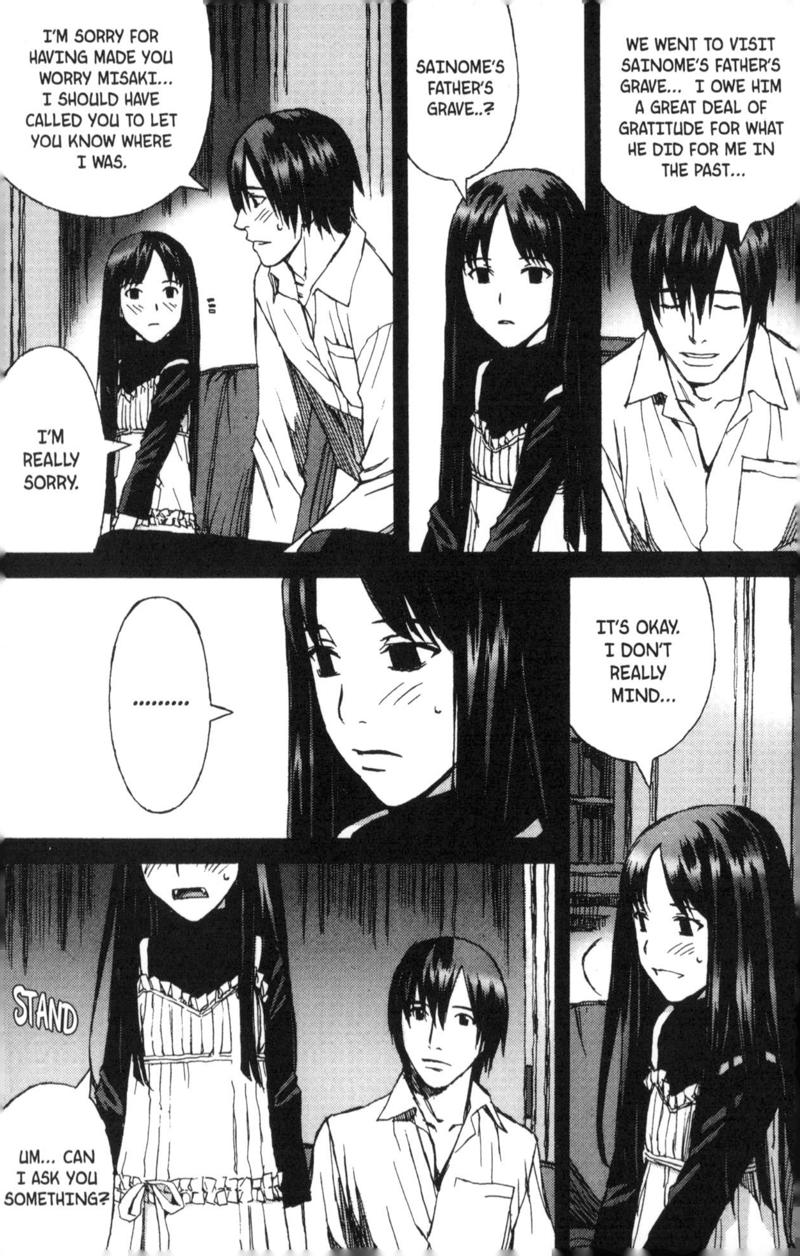
WE WENT TO VISIT SAINOME'S FATHER'S GRAVE... I OWE HIM A GREAT DEAL OF GRATITUDE FOR WHAT HE DID FOR ME IN THE PAST...
SAINOME'S FATHER'S GRAVE..?
I'M SORRY FOR HAVING MADE YOU WORRY MISAKI... I SHOULD HAVE CALLED YOU TO LET YOU KNOW WHERE I WAS.
I'M REALLY SORRY.
IT'S OKAY. I DON'T REALLY MIND...
....
STAND
UM... CAN I ASK YOU SOMETHING?

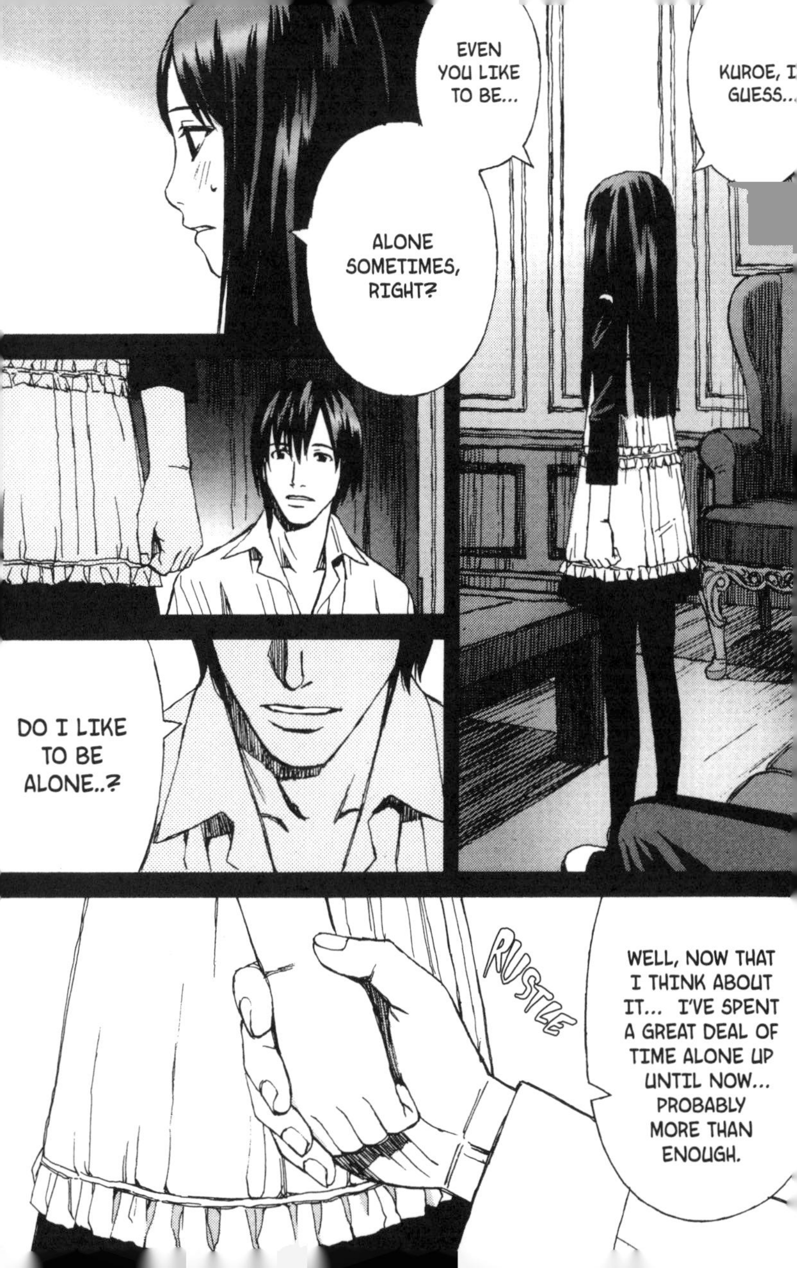

KUROE, I GUESS...
EVEN YOU LIKE TO BE...
ALONE SOMETIMES, RIGHT?
DO I LIKE TO BE ALONE..?
RUSTLE
WELL, NOW THAT I THINK ABOUT IT... I'VE SPENT A GREAT DEAL OF TIME ALONE UP UNTIL NOW... PROBABLY MORE THAN ENOUGH.

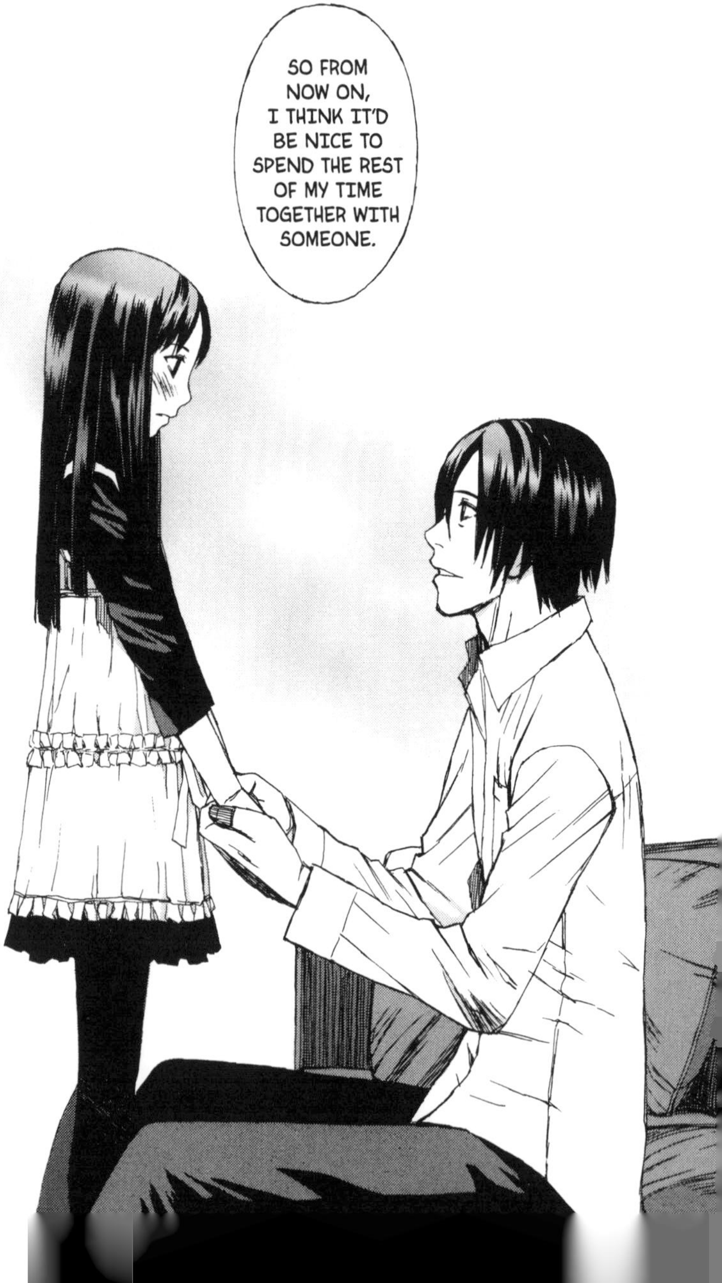
SO FROM NOW ON, I THINK IT'D BE NICE TO SPEND THE REST OF MY TIME TOGETHER WITH SOMEONE.

Episode 16

AFTER THE DANCE

その後のサイノメ

Sainome Later that Night

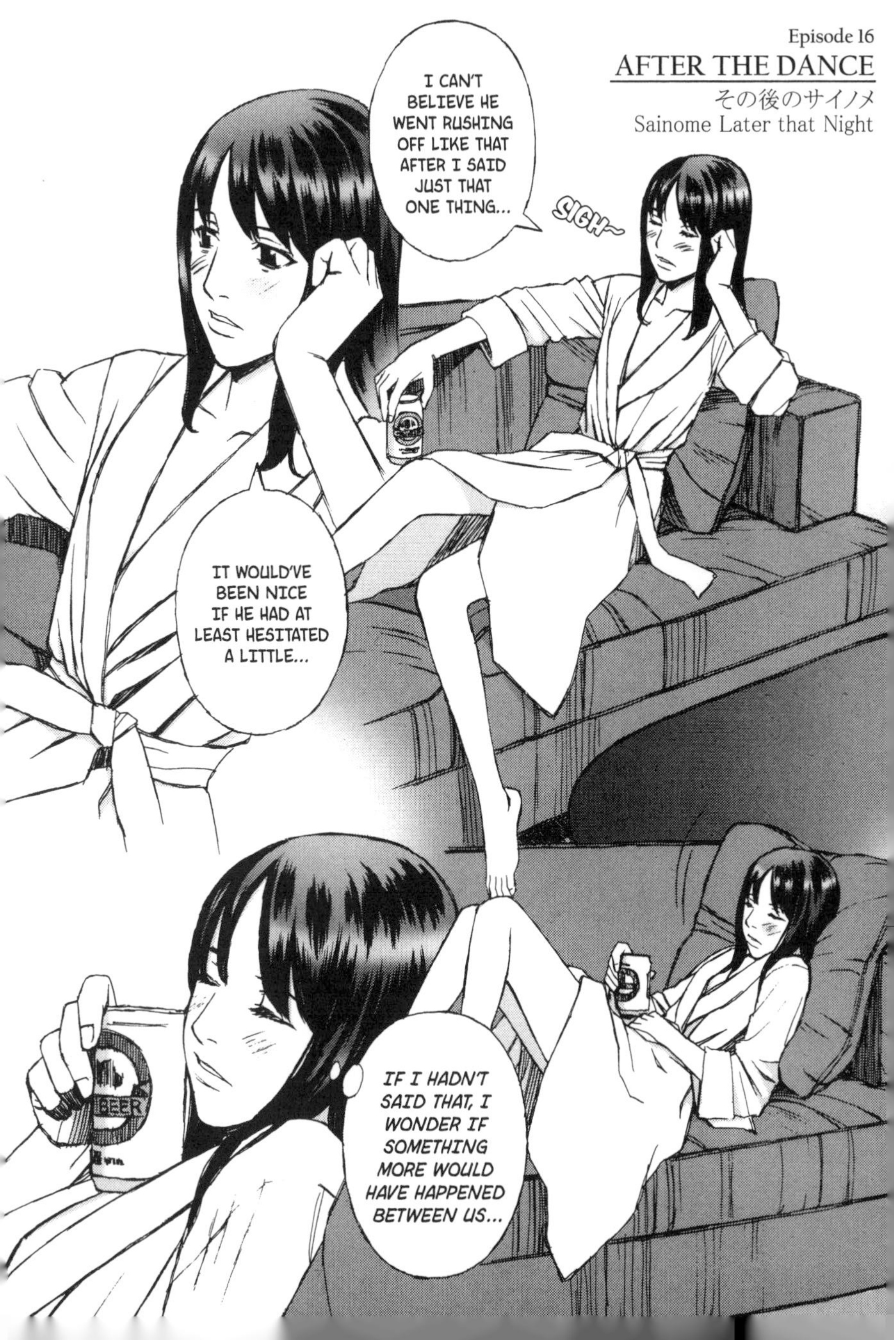
SIGH~
I CAN'T BELIEVE HE WENT RUSHING OFF LIKE THAT AFTER I SAID JUST THAT ONE THING...
IT WOULD'VE BEEN NICE IF HE HAD AT LEAST HESITATED A LITTLE...
IF I HADN'T SAID THAT, I WONDER IF SOMETHING MORE WOULD HAVE HAPPENED BETWEEN US...

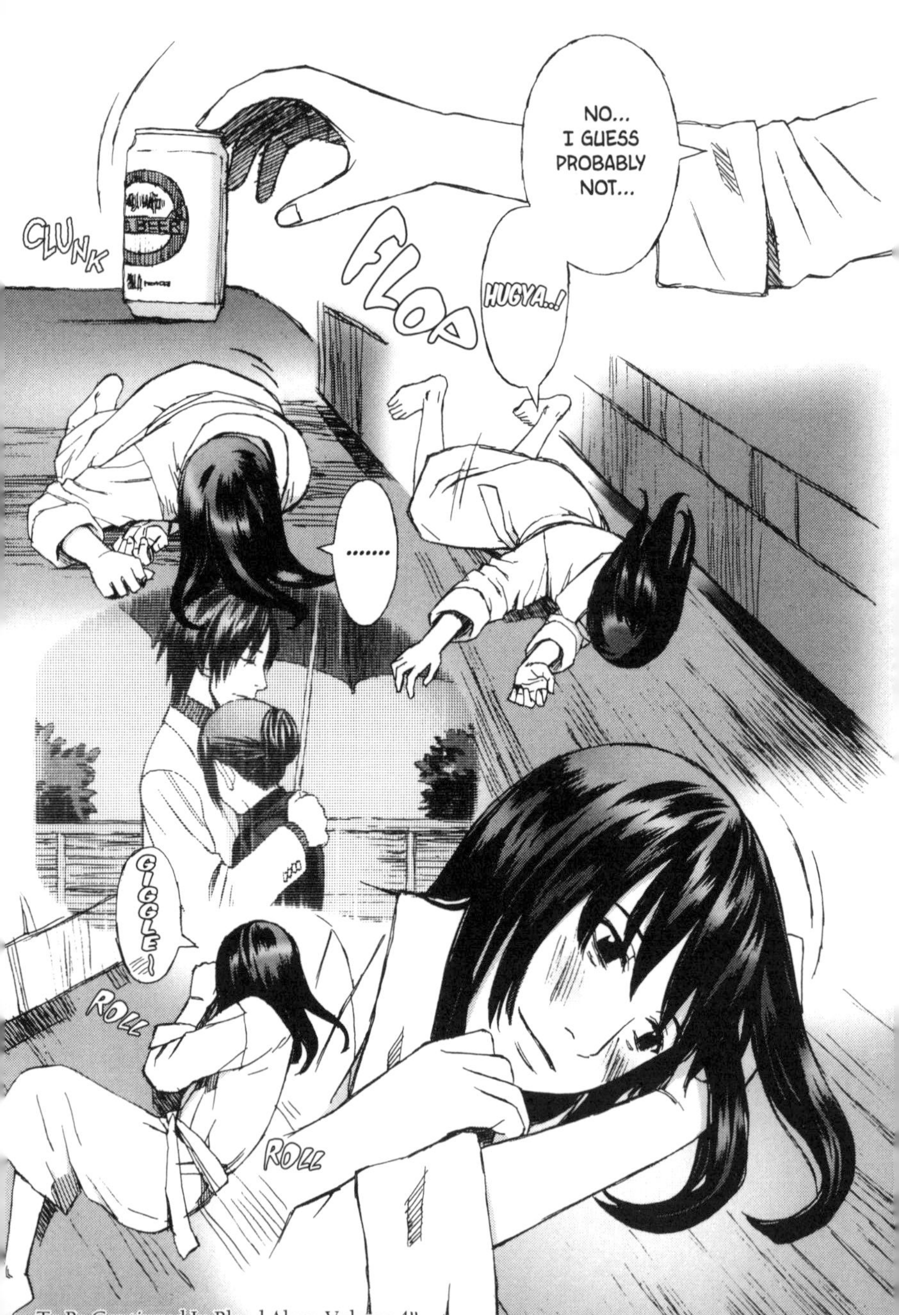
NO... I GUESS PROBABLY NOT...
HUGYA..!
FLOP
CLUNK
....
GIGGLE~
ROLL
ROLL

To Be Continued In Blood Alone Volume 4!!

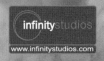

www.infinitystudios.com

Volume 4 Available
Fall 2007

Infinity Studios Presents
Masayuki Takano's

BLOOD ALONE

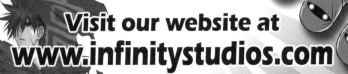

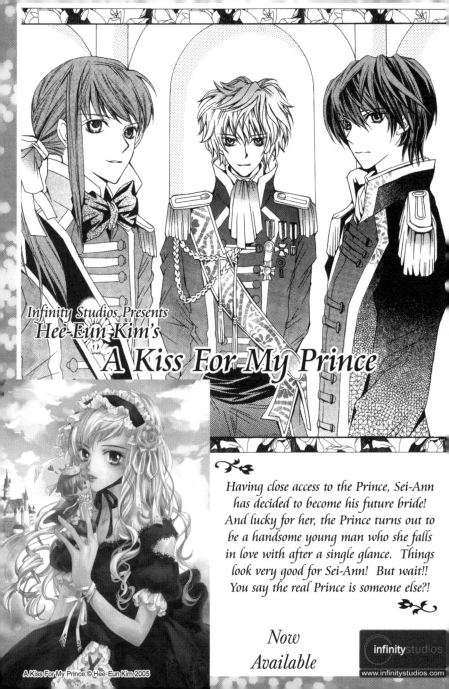

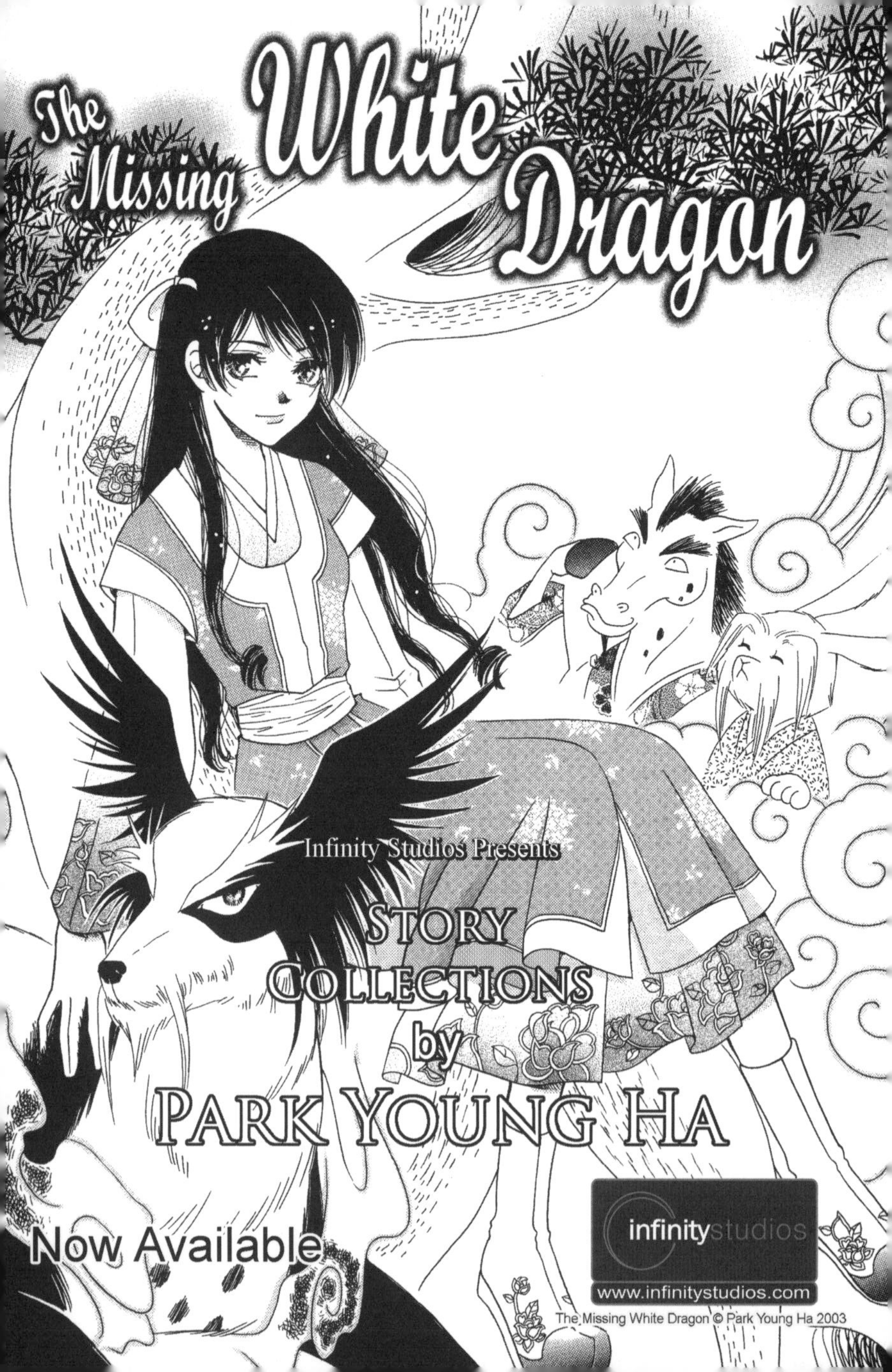
The Missing White Dragon
Infinity Studios Presents
STORY COLLECTIONS by
PARK YOUNG HA
Now Available
infinitystudios
www.infinitystudios.com
The Missing White Dragon © Park Young Ha 2003

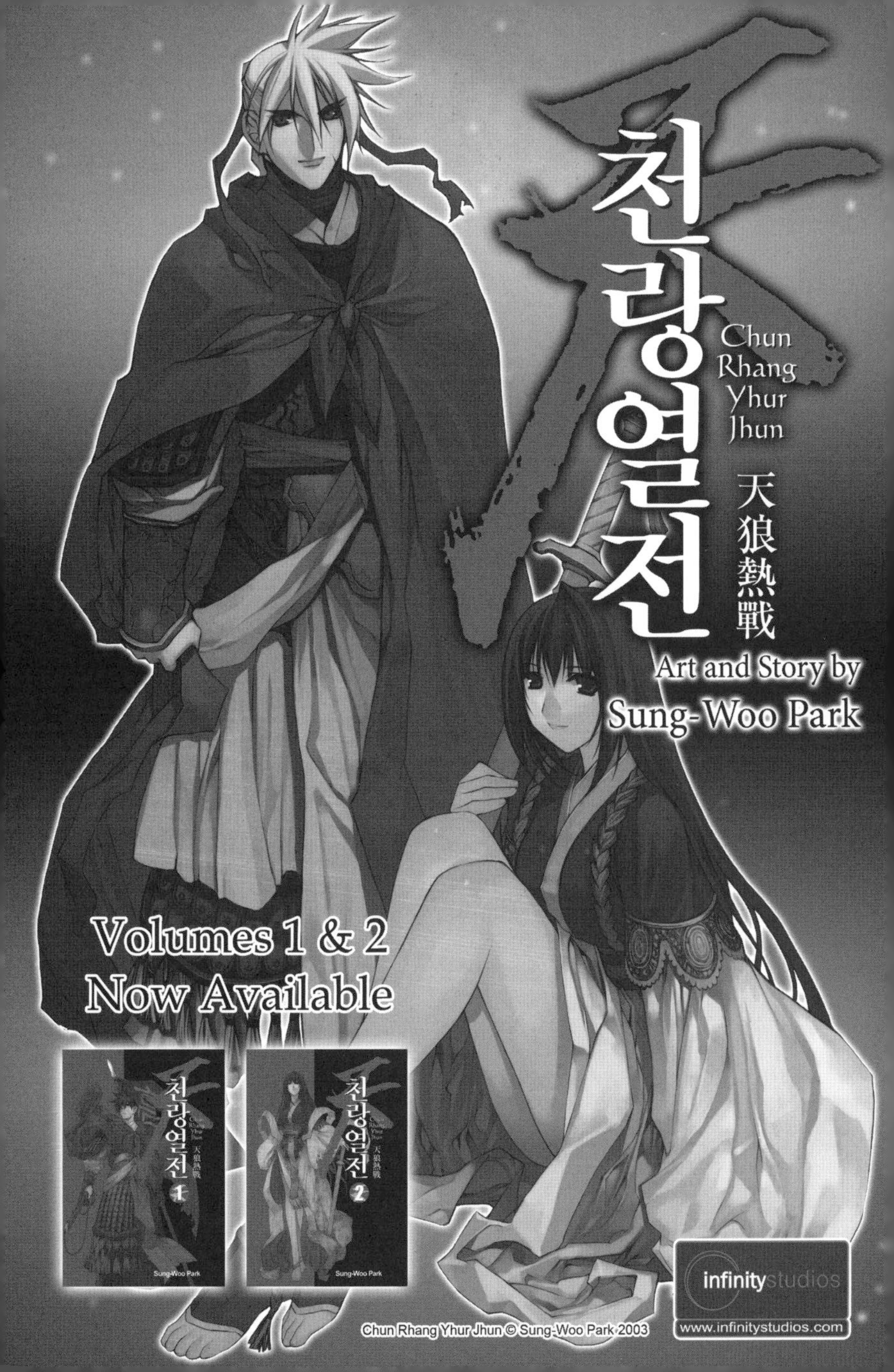
천랑열전
Chun Rhang Yhur Jhun
天狼熱戰
Art and Story by
Sung-Woo Park
Volumes 1 & 2
Now Available
천랑열전
Chun Rhang Yhur Jhun
天狼熱戰
1
Sung-Woo Park
천랑열전
Chun Rhang Yhur Jhun
天狼熱戰
2
Sung-Woo Park
infinitystudios
www.infinitystudios.com
Chun Rhang Yhur Jhun © Sung-Woo Park 2003

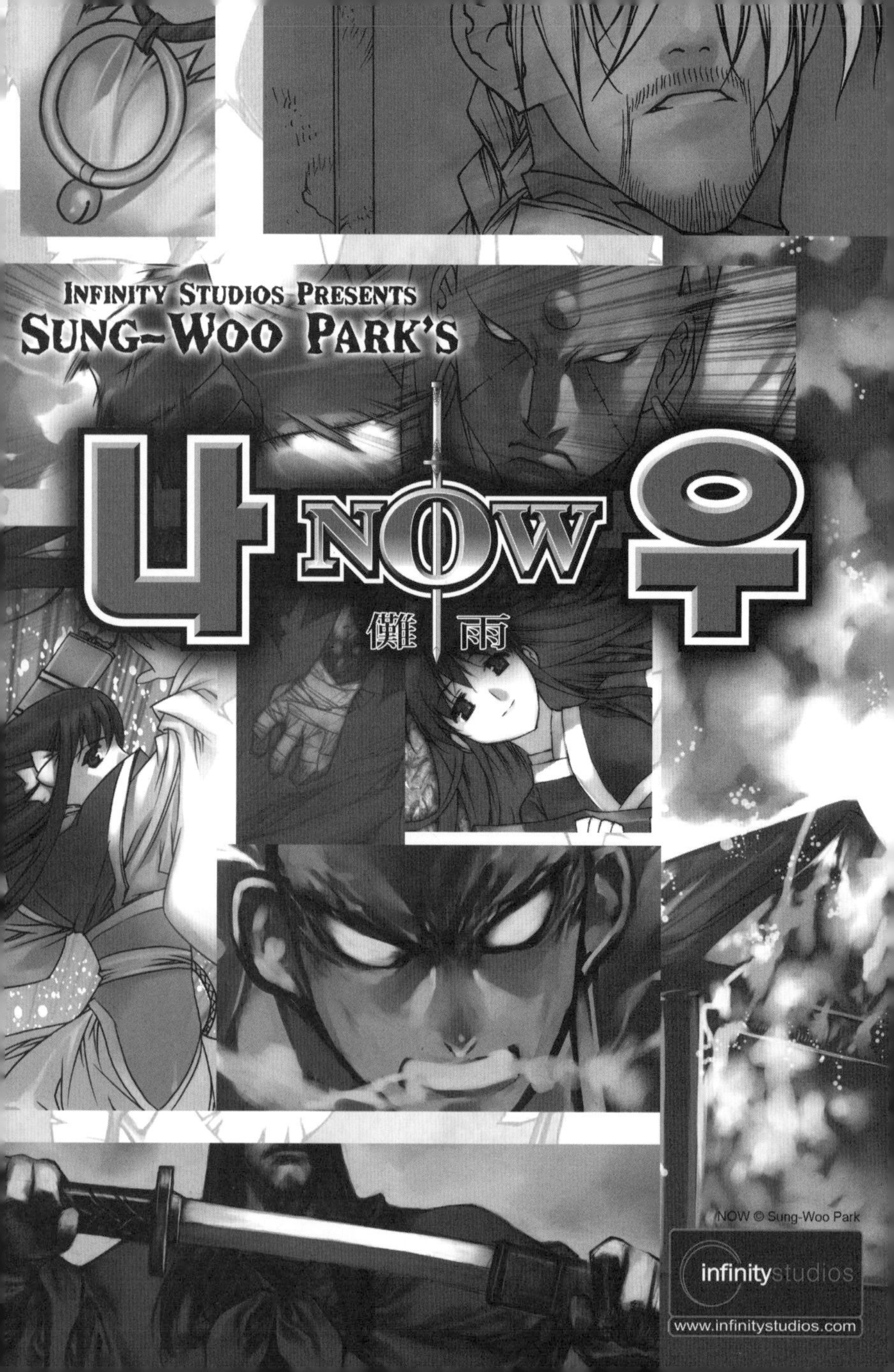
INFINITY STUDIOS PRESENTS
SUNG-WOO PARK'S
나 NOW 우
儺 雨
NOW © Sung-Woo Park
infinitystudios
www.infinitystudios.com

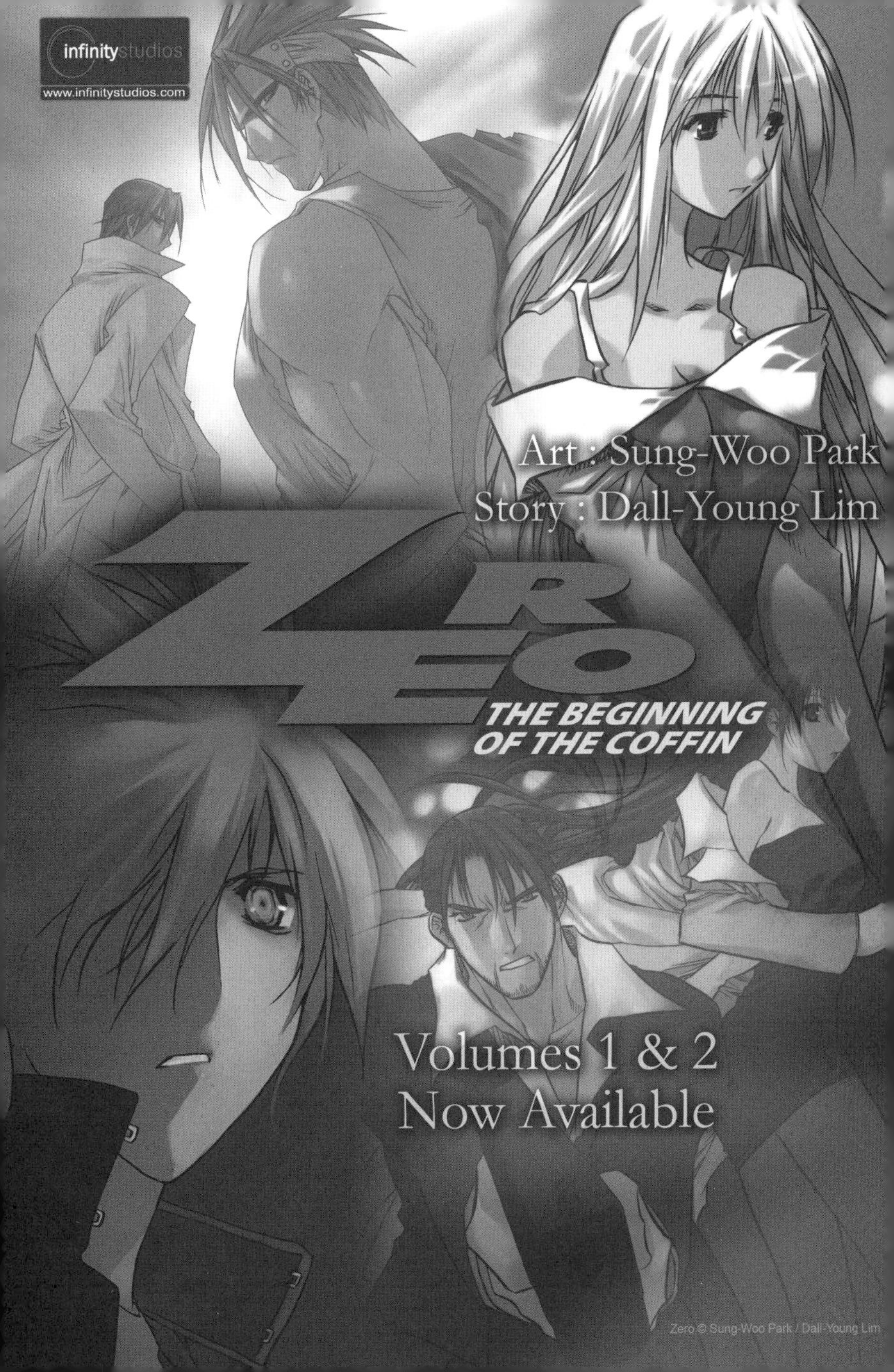
infinitystudios
www.infinitystudios.com
Art : Sung-Woo Park
Story : Dall-Young Lim
ZERO
THE BEGINNING OF THE COFFIN
Volumes 1 & 2
Now Available
Zero © Sung-Woo Park / Dall-Young Lim

Infinity Studios Presents
Ryoichi Koga's

ニニンがシノブ伝

NININ GA SHINOBUDEN

infinitystudios

www.infinitystudios.com

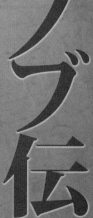

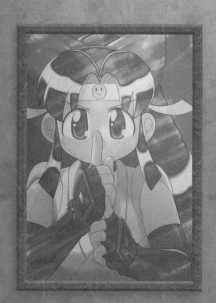

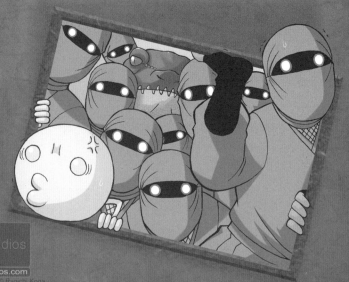

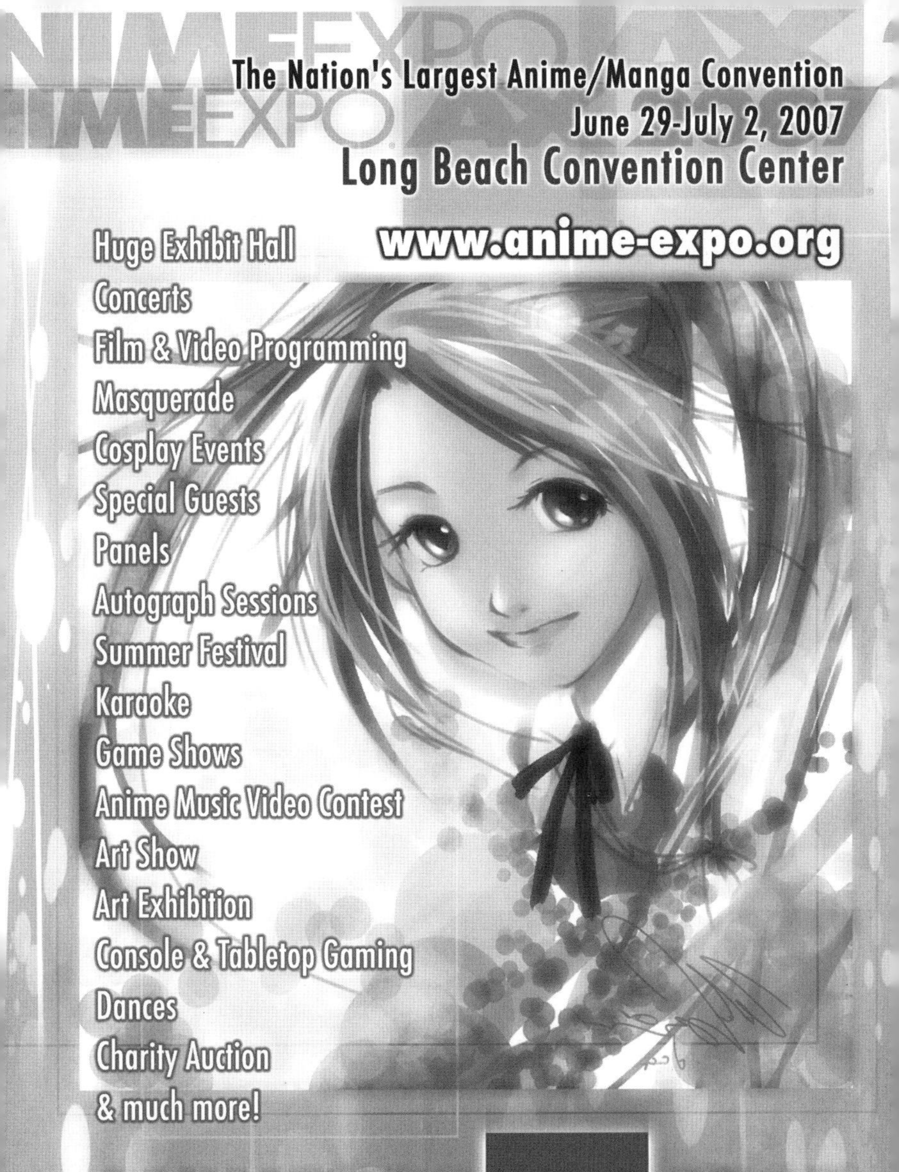
The Nation's Largest Anime/Manga Convention
June 29-July 2, 2007
Long Beach Convention Center
www.anime-expo.org
Huge Exhibit Hall
Concerts
Film & Video Programming
Masquerade
Cosplay Events
Special Guests
Panels
Autograph Sessions
Summer Festival
Karaoke
Game Shows
Anime Music Video Contest
Art Show
Art Exhibition
Console & Tabletop Gaming
Dances
Charity Auction
& much more!
ANIME EXPO AX 2007

illustrated by Zelda C. Wang